FORM AND MEANING
IN DRAMA

A Study of Six Greek Plays and of *Hamlet*

H. D. F. KITTO

METHUEN & CO LTD
11 *New Fetter Lane, London EC*4

First published by Methuen & Co Ltd 5 July 1956
Second edition 1964
S.B.N. 416 58180 3

First published as a University Paperback 1960
Reprinted three times
Reprinted 1971
S.B.N. 416 67520 4

Printed in Great Britain by
T. & A. Constable Ltd.
Edinburgh 7

Distributed in the U.S.A.
by Barnes & Noble Inc.

Preface

IT HAS not been easy to choose a legitimate title for this book, which discusses, in detail, three plays by Aeschylus, three by Sophocles, and one of Shakespeare's. The reason for the choice of the six Greek plays is that I wished to expand, amend or destroy what I had written about them before. The reason why my earlier criticism seemed unsatisfactory was always the same: it did not honestly or completely account for the form and style in which the dramatist had cast the play. I have come to believe more firmly, and I hope to follow more consistently, as a principle of criticism, the idea that in a great work of art, whether a play, a picture, or a piece of music, the connexion between the form and the content is so vital that the two may be said to be ultimately identical.

If this is true, it follows that it is quite meaningless to consider one of them without constant reference to the other. It seems that when a critic approaches a play in the grand manner, as a philosopher, a historian of ideas, or of literature, he can say almost anything about it, according to his own sympathies and prepossessions. But there is a simple control: we can look at the structure of the play, in all its details. If the interpretation that we advance implies that the play is imperfectly designed, then either the dramatist has not done his job very well, or the critic has failed in his. The presumption with Aeschylus, Sophocles and Shakespeare when he wrote *Hamlet*, is that the dramatist was competent. If the dramatist had something to say, and if he was a competent artist, the presumption is that he has said it, and that we, by looking at the form which he created, can find out what it is.

At this point two important questions arise: what does a dramatist 'say'? and how does he say it?

The art of drama does not consist simply of language; language is only one—though the most important—of its means of saying things. Others, obviously, are the dramatic juxtaposition of situations and persons, the 'timing' of events, gesture, tone, visual effects, many other such things. In a highly integrated work of dramatic art, these are not adventitious ornaments; they are among the means which the dramatist uses for saying what he means. Some of them, evidently, can be realised only in performance, where they are conjecturally restored by the producer and the actors—who may be wrong. Nevertheless, some of the most important—those which may be classed as belonging to structure and style— are available to the reasonably sensitive critic, and if he does not use them, but conscientiously 'sticks to the text', he is neglecting part of his evidence, and that is not scientific or scholarly procedure. In the plays under discussion there are several instances where the dramatist 'says' things of the utmost importance without using a single word. After all, if he could not do this he would not be much of a dramatist.

Secondly, what does a dramatist 'say'? It is one theory—and I think that it commands respect—that a work of art means only itself; that if for example we are asked what the *Antigone* means, the only answer is that it means the *Antigone*. Nevertheless, if a musician should declare that one difference between Beethoven and Cherubini is that Beethoven had something to say, and Cherubini hadn't, we should understand what he meant, even though it is only in a general and tentative way that we can distinguish what a composer 'says' from the sounds and patterns that he creates. In this respect drama is different from music, as *Paradise Lost* is different from a breath-taking lyric; especially is classical drama different. There are some kinds of drama—impressionistic drama, light comedy, farce—which, like music, do not 'say' anything that we can translate into prose; they exist for their own sake, and are none the worse for that. But classical drama, especially tragedy, deals seriously and consciously with serious things, so that it is possible, up to a point, to state in logical terms what the dramatist 'means', and to do it in some detail. It was not out of childlike naïveté that the Greeks asserted that the artist was a teacher. They might equally have said that the teacher was an artist; the reason why they did not was that up to the fifth century they had had no teachers who were not artists: the fact was too obvious to need pointing out. In our own times Aeschylus, for example, has always, and rightly, been regarded as a profound and serious thinker; and I am bold enough to say that the only reason why the profundity of Sophocles' thought has not always been appreciated is that his art has not always been properly appreciated either. But it remains true that drama, like music, is an art; that its real 'meaning' is the total impact which it makes on the senses and the spirit and the mind of the audience; and that when we reduce it to the logical formulae of prose, as the critic must, we are gravely attenuating it. We are making a kind of translation; and translations can be poor ones.

But they need not be entirely misconceived. It may be asked: If the 'meaning' is the total impact of the play on the audience, how is it possible to say what it is, since audiences vary from age to age? The answer is: If you will trust the dramatist, if you will consider the form of his play, patiently and with some imagination, as being probably the best possible expression of what he meant, then you will be giving yourself the best chance of appreciating what impact he was hoping to make on the audience for which he was writing. What knowledge we may acquire, extraneously, about the mental habits of the dramatist's own period will of course help—provided that we keep it in its place: the *Antigone*, after all, was written by Sophocles, not by the Periclean Age, and *Hamlet* not by the Elizabethan Age, but by Shakespeare.

Close preoccupation with Greek drama does not preclude one from occasionally seeing and reading Shakespeare, and from asking oneself why the general form of the Greek and the English classical drama differ so widely. In the matter of English drama, I am conscious of being very much of an amateur—though there is the consoling thought that few people can claim professional status in both. I hope that students of Shakespeare will be reasonably indulgent to this chapter, and that what I have found to say on the topic will be of some interest to them. The short study of *Hamlet*, with which the book ends, will perhaps need more indulgence. My reasons for embarking on it are given hereinafter: briefly, that the study of the style and structure of the six Greek plays led to the notion which I have tried to formulate as Religious Drama, a kind of drama which implies its own critical principles; and that *Hamlet* seemed to be of this kind too. (Professor Peter Alexander's book on this interesting play has appeared too recently for me to have been able to make any use of it.)

I have several obligations to acknowledge with gratitude. First to the University of London, which some years ago honoured me with an invitation to deliver a series of Special Lectures. It was the Senate's courteous hope, rather than an express condition, that the lectures should be published; the hope is now fulfilled, as the substance of the lectures, altered and amplified, now appears in the following chapters on the *Oresteia*. I also offer my thanks for careful and salutary criticism of sundry parts of the book given to me by my colleagues Professor L. C. Knights and Mr D. E. Eichholz, and by Professor Hubert Heffner, of the University of Indiana, and Professors Friedrich Solmsen and Gordon Kirkwood, of Cornell University. Finally, my colleague in the Department of Drama, Dr Glynne Wickham, has not only saved me from making one or two specific errors, but also has taught me, about drama in general, much more than he is aware of.

UNIVERSITY OF BRISTOL   H.D.F.K.

Contents

CHAPTER ONE

Agamemnon

WHAT is the significance of the omen, the adverse winds, and the sacrifice of Iphigenia? Why did Aeschylus contrive that very odd scene which Housman parodied so amusingly and yet so closely?

> *But if it be that you are deaf and dumb*
> *And cannot understand a word I say,*
> *Then wave your hand to signify as much.*

Why does he make the chorus so elaborately impotent when Agamemnon is being murdered? Why does he so arrange the *Agamemnon* that the events earliest in time, namely Atreus' feud with Thyestes, come at the end of the play? The closing scenes of the play suggest that Agamemnon is the victim of the Curse in the house of Atreus: the first part suggests that he is the victim of his own crimes at Troy, particularly his sacrifice of Iphigenia: which does Aeschylus mean? or if he means both, is there any connexion between them? Why, in the *Choephori* and *Eumenides* are Agamemnon's sins entirely forgotten, even by his adversaries? Why, in the *Eumenides*, does Apollo use that curious argument about parentage, and why does Athena give so frivolous a reason for voting as she does?

These are some of the questions which the trilogy suggests: others will arise as we proceed. They are really parts of one question, namely, why did Aeschylus give his work this particular form and treatment? If Aeschylus was a competent artist, the answers ought all to be the same, namely, 'Because this is what he *meant*'. And Aeschylus' meaning is what we would like to find.

Our first question concerns the omen, the winds and the sacrifice. What did Aeschylus mean by this? It is an accepted interpretation of the omen that 'the hare is Troy, destined to fall in the tenth year, just as the hare was to have been delivered in the tenth month',[1] and we are commonly told that Artemis demanded the sacrifice because Agamemnon was guilty of hybris. This interpretation of the omen is impossible, because of a simple biological fact known to everyone who has kept rabbits, and surely not unknown to Aeschylus, that the period of gestation of the hare is not ten months nor even ten weeks. The omen therefore has no reference to the duration of the war; we must look for some other significance. Nor is it very clear that Artemis demands the sacrifice because of anything in the character of Agamemnon, for Agamemnon's character does not come into the picture until this demand has been made. What Artemis is objecting to is not so much Agamemnon as Zeus. This becomes clear as soon as we look at the text, and put from our minds the idea that the only deities who can quarrel with Aeschylus' Zeus are 'rebels' like Prometheus and benighted creatures like the Furies.

In the first ode, including its anapaestic prelude, the Trojan expedition is presented in what we may call its theological aspect. The presentation is perfectly clear. This is what the anapaests tell us: It is ten years since the Atreidae, claimants for justice, kings by divine grace, left for Troy, crying havoc, like two eagles robbed of their young, who cry to the gods, and are heard; for the gods send an Erinys, a Fury, soon or late, to bring vengeance upon the transgressors. So does Zeus Xenios, god of hosts and guests, send the Atreidae against Paris, for a wanton woman. Zeus will bring hard conflict and death to Greeks and Trojans alike. No supplication can bend the stubborn temper of the gods (vv. 40-71).

There is no ambiguity here. Great wrong has been done, and this is the plan decreed by Zeus for the righting of the wrong. 'The Kings who launched this expedition are ministers of justice, servants of the will of Zeus.'[2] Nothing could be plainer.

The next thing that we hear about it is that another deity, Artemis, does her best to thwart this plan by sending adverse winds to hold up the ships; but before considering this, we may note that in another part of the play we have the expedition

---

[1] Thomson, *Oresteia* 1, p. 19.

[2] J. T. Sheppard, *Aeschylus the Prophet of Greek Freedom*, p. 11.

presented in another aspect, the human. When Agamemnon returns, the chorus says to him (799 ff) 'When you were starting out on this expedition—I will not conceal it from you—I set you down in no flattering colours. I saw no good judgment in your seeking to bring back a willing wanton at the cost of men's lives. But now, since you are victorious—all's well that ends well.' To the same effect, the chorus has told us earlier (445 ff) how the Argives had muttered angrily against the Atreidae, 'champions of Justice', for leading warriors to their death for another man's wife.

Surely a remarkable situation? On the theological plane we see Zeus decreeing this war, with all its misery for Greek and Trojan alike; on the human plane, although the φιλόμαχοι βραβῆς, 'lords eager for war', were bent on it, the mature judgment of the Argive Elders condemned it before it began, and the Greeks in general cursed its promoters before it ended. Moreover, in order that we should not miss the point, Aeschylus uses each time a phrase which contains the essence of the matter. Zeus 'sends the sons of Atreus against Paris πολυάνορος ἀμφὶ γυναικός, in the cause of a promiscuous woman'; the Greeks mourn those who died ἀλλοτρίας διαὶ γυναικός, 'for another man's wife'; the Elders condemned a war for a θάρσος ἑκούσιον, 'a willing wanton'.[1]

But this is anticipation. For the moment we see the action on the divine plane only. The anapaests make it quite clear that this is a war instigated by Zeus for the sake of Justice, and that the natural consequences of the war are foreseen by Zeus. Now comes the omen. The eagles are the Atreidae, the ministers of justice; the hare can be nothing but Troy; and the young within the hare can be nothing but the innocent population of Troy, now threatened with destruction by the expedition of Zeus Xenios and his eagle-kings. We are told explicitly what all this means: the merciful Artemis hates 'the winged hounds of her Father'; she loathes 'the eagles' lawless feast'. Therefore she sends adverse winds to prevent this outrage. At least, they will prevent it, unless Agamemnon will pay the price which Artemis demands—and assuredly it is a price which a man of courage and sense would refuse to pay.

[1] Vv. 62, 448, 803. (The text of 803-804 is doubtful, but the general sense is clear enough.)

Certainly Agamemnon's choice is no easy one, but it is a complete mistake, I think, to say (as more than one critic has said) that he can only choose between two evil deeds. He can go forward, through blood, or he can take the warning, and give up the expedition. Fraenkel, arguing that the latter would be wrong too, cites Agamemnon's use of the word λιπόναυς (212), 'deserting the fleet', and says, correctly of course, that it has associations with the crime of λιποταξία, 'desertion'. But this is beside the point. Aeschylus uses the word only to show how the choice presented itself to Agamemnon's mind; it does not in the least follow that Aeschylus thought, and wanted us to think, the same. Aeschylus does not wish us to abdicate our common-sense, and to regard this 'war for a wanton woman' as a just one. If we must have specific proof of this, vv. 799 ff (cited above) provide it.

The reason why Artemis holds up the fleet is given quite clearly, and it is not the traditional one. This was that Aga-memnon had angered her by boastfully killing one of her stags. Why does Aeschylus, in this respect, alter the myth?

Art differs from life in this important respect: in life we cannot safely deduce the purpose of an action from its results, but in art we can. The result of this alteration in the traditional story is that the cause of Artemis' anger is not something that Agamemnon has already done, but something that he is going to do; Artemis, in this play, has no quarrel with Agamemnon, except that he is contemplating a war. Such is the effect of the abolition of the stag; we can be quite sure then that this is the reason why Aeschylus abolished it. Artemis is angry at the lawless feast of the eagles; no other cause for anger is admitted.

But why does she demand this particular price for the lifting of her ban? There are two reasons. The first is indeed not stated, but it is clear enough, once we are accustomed to the idea that Aeschylus, like Pindar, Sophocles, Shakespeare and sundry other poets, sometimes uses sharp juxtaposition rather than words to express his thought: the lawless bloodshed of which Agamemnon will be guilty if he kills his daughter is exactly parallel to the lawless bloodshed of which he will be guilty if he goes on with this war 'for a wanton woman'. He is nearly committed to this war which will destroy countless innocent lives; very well: if he must do this, let him first destroy an innocent of his own—and take the consequences. Let him brand himself as a man of blood; let it be manifest what he has been doing. This is the first reason; the second is stated. Artemis is 'bent on a second sacrifice, lawless and monstrous' (150). He who does such a thing as this, to wage a war and to kill his daughter in order to do it, shall be destroyed in return, through the wrath that his action will create.

Here we have the explanation of what is always implied later in the play, that Clytemnestra avenges on Agamemnon not only the outrage that he has done on her, but also the wrong that he has done to Greece and to Troy, in slaughtering so many of their sons. In a crucial passage we are told 'The gods are not regardless of men of blood' (461 ff): τῶν πολυκτόνων γὰρ οὐκ ἄσκοποι θεοί. The gods will bring upon Agamemnon retribution for all his bloodshed and violence, and Clytemnestra will be their instrument. Her motive is simply vengeance for her daughter, suddenly reinforced, at the last moment, by Agamemnon's last insult to her in bringing home Cassandra; but because the sacrifice of Iphigenia is paradeigmatic or symbolic of all the bloodshed that the war involves, she is in effect avenging this too.

But what about Artemis? At this moment she seems to be in complete revolt against Zeus and his eagles, but later it is either 'the gods' or Zeus who punish Agamemnon; Artemis disappears, and we hear no more of her revolt. The question raises itself here; we will add it to our original list, and hope to answer it later.

We have, then, on the one level, a minister of Justice or Dikê, appointed by Zeus to avenge a crime, like an Erinys, while another deity, intervening, ordains that he shall not do this except in a way that shall make his guilt manifest and his punishment certain. But on another level we find that Agamemnon is quite unconscious of having any divine mission. Zeus has given him no direct command such as Apollo gives to Orestes in the next play; when he is presented with his hard choice it does not occur to him to plead that unless he kills his daughter he cannot carry out the mission on which Zeus is sending him. What he does say is that he cannot desert his ships and abandon his alliance; and what Aeschylus says next is not that he determined to do the will of Zeus, but that he was filled with 'an accursed unholy spirit . . . a cruel base-contriving frenzy' (219-223). This it is that sweeps him over the brink.

Since this situation becomes the very foundation, moral and dramatic, of the whole play, we must be quite clear that this indeed is the situation. It is emphatically not the case that Artemis objects to Agamemnon's expedition because Agamemnon was wicked, if by that we mean that in some way—through hybris—Agamemnon exceeded the commission that Zeus gave him, or that he turned a just war into an unjust one. Professor Thomson rightly observes[1] that the oppressed, that is, the robbed eagles, have turned into oppressors, and have to pay the price; but it is necessary to observe also that there was no other way in which Agamemnon could carry out the mission of Zeus as it is described in the anapaestic prelude. As Zeus ordained, so Agamemnon acted, and for acting so, his punishment is ensured. Those who, on theological grounds, deny that Aeschylus wrote the *Prometheus* must either prove that this is not the situation here, or conclude that Aeschylus did not write the *Agamemnon* either. For what sort of a god is it who sends a man on a mission of justice, like eagles lawlessly devouring a pregnant hare, a mission condemned even by men as folly or worse, and one that must involve him in punishment—and that too not by death in battle, but at the hands of an adulterous wife? Yet it is made quite clear that this is precisely what Zeus is doing; and Agamemnon's character is relevant only to this extent, that if Agamemnon proves to be not the sort of man to kill his daughter, the mission will perforce be abandoned by him, and justice will not be done on Paris.

It seems clear that if we would answer the simple question 'What is the *Oresteia* about?' we must above all try to understand what Aeschylus' conception of Zeus is. This, in fact, is the moment which Aeschylus chooses to tell us; for as soon as the chorus has expounded the situation described above, it sings what we may well call a Hymn to Zeus:

When I contemplate all things, I can form no image except of Zeus, if a man would truly cast from his mind its vain burden.

God is the answer to the moral problem, and Him it is agreed to call Zeus.

[1] *Oresteia*, 1, 19.

This is a stanza which even Plato might have refrained from damning—but not the next one, for in this Aeschylus deliberately brings to our minds the old cycle of cosmogonical myth which makes Zeus a new-comer among gods, all of whom conquered by violence. I say 'deliberately' because it is surely inconceivable that Aeschylus wrote anything without deliberation, and because I think the distinction is a false one which has been made between his 'religious thought' and his 'mythology'. If the mythology that he uses is not a vehicle for his religious thinking, what is the essential difference between mythology in Aeschylus and in Ovid? In fact, his mythology crystallises his thought in the same way that his images and metaphors do.

When we read this second stanza we may reflect that the great difference between Greek theology (before Plato) and Hebrew and Christian theology is that in the latter God created Heaven and Earth, while in the Greek, Heaven and Earth created the gods. The Greek gods may be everlasting, but they are not eternal—and in the *Prometheus* Aeschylus contemplates contingently the overthrow even of Zeus.[1] To the Greek, the eternal things are not the gods, for they once were born. The eternal things are the Law—Anankê, Dikê and the like. In the *Prometheus* we are confronted with a Zeus who is young and imperfect. His adversary, wrong though he may be in some respects, nevertheless stands for something which in the end is accepted by Zeus, when the reconciliation comes which leaves Zeus the unquestioned lord of the universe, but one who has learned mercy, and has accepted the existence of humanity. The second stanza of this Hymn takes us into the same circle of ideas: Zeus is the Conqueror. It remains to be seen if he has yet consolidated his power. The *Eumenides* will show us that he has not. There, as in the *Prometheus*, older deities are in revolt against him, there too championing a principle which Zeus comes to accept.

But in the *Oresteia* it is the wisdom rather than the absolute power of Zeus that is set before us. It is Zeus who has set man on the road that leads to wisdom, though it is a hard road, for knowledge comes only out of suffering, and the blessings of Heaven come only by violence. So with the commander of the

---

[1] *P.V.* 907-912. The curse which Cronos laid on him will be fulfilled, unless . . .

Achaean ships—and we may notice here how Aeschylus uses his dance to illustrate his thought; for the first of the stanzas in which Agamemnon's dilemma is presented is couched in the trochaic rhythm of the Hymn, dovetailing the particular case into the exposition of the general law.

Therefore, if we are dismayed or puzzled that Zeus, for the sake of Dikê, should appoint an avenger who must inevitably be destroyed for doing what Zeus ordains that he shall do, we can reflect that the road which leads to wisdom is a long one, and that at this stage we may be only at the beginning of it.

We may now survey the three or four scenes that follow. In them this original situation is amplified.

Clytemnestra appears and delivers her splendid beacon-speech. What is the point of it?—for it is surely not enough to say that it is splendid poetry. Aeschylus is hardly the man to write splendid poetry unless it is a logical part of his design. The speech continues, from the Watchman, the symbol of light coming out of darkness. This is one of the images which pervade the trilogy; it finds its fulfilment in the last scene, the procession with torches. But why is the relay of beacons treated as such a marvel? Aeschylus makes much of this; he returns to the point three times. At the end of the second ode he makes the chorus very sceptical of the whole story. Presently, when the Herald is seen coming, the chorus says: 'This man will *talk* —not merely light us a row of beacon-fires.' Finally, Clytemnestra says: 'When the beacon-message came they called me a fool to put my trust in bonfires. "How like a woman!" they said. Still, I went on with my sacrifices—and now, what need for *you* to tell me more?'

The dramatic effect of this, properly handled, is to raise Clytemnestra to a level higher than that on which the chorus moves; and this, not merely for the sake of character-drawing, which to Aeschylus was a matter of secondary importance. It is perfectly true that all this shows, in action, her ἀνδρόβουλον κέαρ, her 'mind that counsels like a man's'. What is more important than her character is her stature; we realise that this woman who triumphs so contemptuously over the chorus will be equal to her task, a sure instrument of vengeance.

It is important to realise what the dramatic stature of Clytemnestra is. Later in the play she cries:

μή μ' ἐπιλεχθῇς
'Αγαμεμνονίαν εἶναί μ' ἄλοχον —

*Call me not Agamemnon's wife! I am the ancient cruel Curse
of Atreus in the shape of this man's wife* (1478 ff).

Already we have been told (155) that there is a 'terrible treacherous unforgetting Wrath dwelling in the house to avenge a child', a Wrath called into existence by Artemis to avenge the hare lawlessly slain by the eagles of Zeus.

In fact, she is an agent in a divine drama, as well as in her own; an instrument of the gods, just as Agamemnon is. He is being used to punish Paris, and she will be used to punish Agamemnon; and she will triumph over him as completely as she triumphs over the chorus here. This present triumph gives us her measure.

Another small point is related to this. The chorus asks 'How is it possible for you to know so soon? Are you relying on a dream? What messenger could come so fast?' She gives her answer at once: Hephaestus—and we should not be tempted to see in this name nothing but a poetic alternative to the word 'fire'. Aeschylus had nothing to do with these literary elegancies. When he meant 'fire' he said 'fire', and when he said 'Hephaestus' he meant 'Hephaestus'. The beacon-system was in fact no more than a competent bit of organisation; Aeschylus makes the Fire-god the messenger, and clothes the whole thing in magnificent poetry, raising it to the verge of the miraculous —like the storm later—in order to make us feel that something elemental is at work here. What Clytemnestra will do is no mere domestic murder.

It is this stature of Clytemnestra, as the appointed instrument of vengeance, that explains her second speech too. She gives, out of her imagination, a description of the terror that has fallen on Troy, and she gives a warning, or expresses the hope, that the Greeks will not commit sacrilege, for they still need a safe homecoming. Things of this kind, imaginative pictures and moral reflections, are normally entrusted to the chorus, for obvious reasons. Why does Aeschylus give both of them here to Clytemnestra? The description for one reason, the warning for two. The additional reason for entrusting the warning to Clytemnestra is the grim point that she is anxious for Agamemnon to come home safely, in order that she herself may deal with him. The other reason, and the reason why she is also made to describe the scenes of plunder and death in Troy, is that it is more impressive, and makes for tighter construction, that we should hear of these things from the lips of her who is going, however unconsciously, to punish them. The first part of the speech is the counterpart of the omen: the eagles are ripping the body of the hare. The sacrilege, foreshadowed in the second part, is the same spirit of Hybris displaying itself in a different way. It is right that we should hear of these things not from the chorus but from the Wrath who will, thanks to Artemis, punish them.

We come to the second ode, the one that begins with the destruction of Paris, and ends with the image of Ares, the money-changer of Death, and with apprehension about Agamemnon. As it happens, this ode offers an interesting example of the way in which one age can easily misinterpret the art of a different age; also of the way in which we can, sometimes, control our own natural misconceptions by taking the form into consideration.

A great ode follows, which reflects the changing moods of Argos in the time between the Queen's announcement and the King's return—first, relief from strain, the joy and thankfulness; then the cold fit, the counting of the cost, the obstinate questioning. Was the war really just? Has not the leader innocent blood on his hands? In their first flood of joy the Elders have no doubts.

In these words a sensitive modern interpreter of Aeschylus describes what is surely the natural, even inevitable, dramatic development: these loyal Elders have been awaiting news, good or bad, for years; at last news has come—and it is Victory. Of course they rejoice.

But it will not do. This inevitable development is not inevitable at all—not for Aeschylus. There is no flood of joy. The proof is quite simple. This ode was, of course, danced and sung. We have lost both the dance and the music, but their rhythms are left—in the poetry, and that is enough.[1] Aeschylus was

[1] I have discussed these rhythms in detail in an article on 'The Tragic Dance', *Journal of Hellenic Studies*, LXXV (1955).

quite competent in choral composition. It could not have escaped him that a mood of joy and a mood of fear need contrasting rhythms; but this long ode (except for the recurring short refrains, and a dramatic and intelligible interruption at 448-451, 467-470) is composed in the same rhythm throughout, a four or six foot iambic rhythm varied only by the incidence of prolonged syllables: dotted crotchets, so to speak, standing for a crotchet and a quaver. Aeschylus is trying to express not a contrast of mood, but uniformity. And we can go further, for this rhythm is the same one that predominates in the last part of the first ode (from v. 192), when the chorus is contemplating the bloody deed at Aulis, and is fearful of its outcome. To give only one illustration: v. 209, said of Agamemnon,

μιαίνων παρθενοσφάγοισιν

is in exactly the same metre as the first verse of the second ode:

Διὸς πλαγὰν ἔχουσιν εἰπεῖν.[1]

Not only this; for the same rhythm recurs in the last four stanzas of the third ode, when the chorus is reflecting how doom befell the Trojans because of the coming of Helen, and how disaster inevitably comes from sin. Here, v. 754 for example exactly repeats the particular syllabic form already cited:

τεκνοῦσθαι μηδ' ἄπαιδα θνῄσκειν
It dies not childless; nay, it breedeth.

In short, out of twenty-five consecutive stanzas, twenty-one are based either wholly or in part on this one rhythm.

If we make the not very extravagant hypothesis that some idea lies behind this, it would be that the remarkable persistence of this verse-rhythm was expressed also in the music and the dance. What form these took we cannot possibly tell. We can however notice that the same rhythm, and therefore presumably the same type of music and dance-figure, is used always in association with the ideas of sin and retribution. We can notice too that when the chorus begins to sing and dance about the destruction of Paris at the opening of the second ode, what we see with our eyes and hear with our ears is already familiar:

---

[1] I append Thomson's isometric renderings: 'With unclean hands before the altar'; 'By Zeus struck down. 'Tis truly spoken.'

we heard and saw it as we heard about Aulis and the frenzy that swept Agamemnon into sin.

So that we must think differently about this ode. Its form enforces on us quite a different interpretation from the one that seemed so natural and so dramatic; and we find what I hope we shall find elsewhere, that the new interpretation to which the form forces us is a finer one than the other.

As in the first ode, there is an important prelude, in anapaests. The former anapaestic passage told us what the plan of Zeus was; this one tells us that it has been fulfilled. Zeus Xenios, god of hosts and guests, after holding for a long time his arrow pointed at Paris, has let it fly; he has cast over Troy a net such that neither young nor old could escape. The hunter's net, we observe, was thrown by Zeus, though his agent has been Agamemnon. The quarry has been utterly destroyed. It recalls the hunting eagles who destroyed the hare, and the anger of Artemis; and later in the play we shall hear of another net, also 'too high to leap over' (1376). This is the one thrown over Agamemnon by Clytemnestra.

The blow has come from Zeus because Paris, led by temptation, 'trod underfoot the beauty of holy things'—as Agamemnon will do later in the play, not metaphorically but in fact. Justice has found both Paris and the city which he involved in his own sin. Helen's crime has brought ruin to Troy as her dowry. She left a gathering war behind her, and mourning in the house of Menelaus; mourning too in every home in Greece, as the ashes of dead men came back, in place of the living men who had gone forth. Resentment is fierce in Argos against the Atreidae, those ministers of Dikê, for leading men to death in a war for another man's wife; and resentment like this amounts to a public curse. The gods are not regardless of men of blood. May I never be a sacker of cities!

Such is the substance of the ode. The unchanging rhythm, dance and music compel us to think of Paris, Helen, Troy and Agamemnon all together, and Aulis is bound up with it. We might say that the reason why the rhythm does not change is that the course of Dikê does not change. The ode gives us, as it were, a proportion sum:

Paris' crime : his destruction :: Agamemnon's crime : ?

It is important to observe that Agamemnon is not accused of exceeding the commission given him by Zeus Xenios. There is no mention, in this ode, of any uncovenanted crime. He is πολυκτόνος, a 'man of blood', and for this he is under a curse:

τῶν πολυκτόνων γὰρ οὐκ ἄσκοποι θεοί —

The gods are not regardless of men of blood.

But without being this he could not have been the 'Minister of Justice'. He is πτολιπόρθης, a 'sacker of cities'; and to be such is perilous. But this was inherent in the mission on which Zeus sent him. Zeus sent him 'like some Fury', in the cause of a wanton woman, against Paris; and Zeus was bringing death to Greeks and Trojans alike (59-67). Zeus has used him for the ends of Justice, and now we see that this same Justice must destroy him for what he has done. We take note of the problem and pass on.

The Herald-scene occupies nearly two hundred verses. Why does Aeschylus need so much space for it? Not simply to tell us 'The King is coming'. In his first speech the Herald thanks the gods for his safe return, those gods who were so murderous to the Greeks before Troy. But the great king has overthrown and utterly blotted out Troy τοῦ δικηφόρου Διὸς μακέλλῃ, 'with the crowbar of Zeus who brings Dikê',[1] and Paris has paid his debt twice over. The second speech describes the sufferings of the Greek army, and then, like the first, ends on a note of triumph. Abruptly, Clytemnestra appears, to taunt the chorus with its scepticism, and to send her false message of welcome to Agamemnon. Finally, the Herald describes the storm.

Now, Aeschylus is no talkative or confidential dramatist. He composes architecturally, and he does not lecture his audience in the Euripidean manner. Rather, he reveals his thought by his use of poetic symbols and by his imaginative juxtapositions. If we bear this in mind, and if we realise too that Aeschylus was not an eager primitive, doing all he could to be a suitable forerunner of Sophocles, the long Herald-scene makes both sense and drama. It contains five important themes.

In his first speech, the Herald appears to us, like the Watchman at the beginning of the play, as one who has 'escaped from toil'. It has often been pointed out that the whole trilogy is

[1] Vv. 525 ff.

suffused with images like ἀπαλλαγὴ πόνων, 'release from toil', healing and light coming out of darkness. Two of them, Healing and Light, figure in the first speech, and 'toils' are the burden of both this speech and the next. The Justice of Zeus, as outlined in the first anapaests, has brought these sufferings upon the Greeks, by sea and by land. This is the first theme.

The second is contained in the Herald's repeated note of triumph; in his assumption that all trouble is now at an end. 'Agamemnon is victorious. Welcome him! Dedicate the spoils in the temples, and give thanks to the gods!' The Herald more amply says what the Watchman said—though without his undercurrent of apprehension—'Begin the dance! This is the triple-six for me!' Moreover, the thought is re-echoed by the chorus, Agamemnon, and Clytemnestra; it is like the receding horizon. 'All's well that ends well', says the chorus to Agamemnon (805 f). 'May Victory, who has attended me so far, ever remain with me', says Agamemnon (854). 'May the Daemon in the house of Pleisthenes now be content, and visit some other house', says Clytemnestra (1568 ff): and at the end (1673) she says to Aegisthus 'You and I will rule, and we will order all things well.' It is the cry for Finality, summed up in Clytemnestra's prayer (993 f):

> Ζεῦ Ζεῦ Τέλειε, τὰς ἐμὰς εὐχὰς τέλει,
> μέλοι δέ τοι σοὶ τῶνπερ ἂν μέλλῃς τελεῖν —

which goes better into French than into English:

> Zeus, Zeus, par qui tout s'achève, achève mes souhaits, et songe
> bien à l'oeuvre que tu dois achever.[1]

All these characters in turn think, or hope, that Finality has come, but all are deceived, for with the present conception of Justice no finality is possible; something always remains to be paid for.

The next theme perhaps hints at the reason for this. Another image that is restated in this scene is that of the law-suit: 'Priam and his city have lost their case, and have paid twice over. He has forfeited all that he stole, and his city has been blotted out' (532-537). But is this Dikê, 'justice', or is it what the Greek instinctively feared, πλεονεξία, 'getting too much'? Professor Fraenkel points out, in his note on the passage, that Attic law

---

[1] Mazon.

regularly prescribed a double penalty: full restitution, *plus* a fine. That is true; but the 'fine' here is total ruin, the wanton destruction about which Agamemnon uses such ominous language when he speaks (818-820) of the clouds of rich smoke that are even yet rising from the conquered city. What the Herald says, I think, is meant to suggest the thought that Agamemnon's 'justice' is in fact no justice at all.

For he has just said something of even greater significance. I translate the passage in full, because it involves a textual point of the first importance.

Give him a great welcome, for he has earned it, he who has utterly cast down Troy with the crowbar of Zeus the bringer of Dikê, and with it has devastated the land; and the altars and temples of the gods are no more, and the seed of the whole country is destroyed.

Some editors delete the fourth of these five verses: βωμοὶ δ' ἄιστοι καὶ θεῶν ἱδρύματα: 'the altars and the temples of the gods are no more.' The credit for first removing it from the text goes to Saltzmann; among recent editors, Headlam, Thomson and Fraenkel follow him. Three chief reasons are given for removing this blot on the landscape. (1) It occurs in the *Persae*, at v. 811, with the insignificant difference that καὶ θεῶν here is δαιμόνων there. This at once creates the presumption that it is an interpolation here. (2) It is inconceivable that Aeschylus should have put 'this proud boast in the mouth of this religious Herald'. So Headlam, seconded by Thomson and Fraenkel. (3) The verse interrupts the logical sequence of ideas, for without it the Herald moves smoothly from the city which has been destroyed to the countryside which has been devastated and rendered sterile. The mention of the temples and altars takes us from the country back to the city, from which we go again to the country.

As for (1), the argument would be conclusive if it were incredible that Aeschylus should have so nearly repeated, in 458 B.C. a verse which he had used in 472. I cannot find it at all incredible. As for (2), this might be an argument if we knew for certain that Aeschylus was incapable of any approach to tragic irony. The Herald is certainly pious; let us by all means go further and call him religious, provided we realise how very small is Aeschylus' interest in his character, and how unimportant it is in the structure of the play. But since when has piety been a guarantee of understanding? For Headlam's comment I would substitute something like this: 'By a fine stroke of irony Aeschylus makes the simple and pious Herald mention, almost incidentally, a detail which makes the audience shiver with dread.' (3) There is more than one way of finding a logical sequence of ideas here. Keeping the verse, we have an emphatic repetition: the city is laid in ruins and the land devastated; the temples are overthrown and the very seed in the fields destroyed. Of the four statements, the third and fourth repeat the first and second, but in a more absolute form.

The case against the deletion is that it obliterates one of the finest and most eloquent things in the whole play, a brilliant example of the way in which the real dramatist can talk without using much language. Clytemnestra has said:

> If they are respecting the guardian gods of the captured city, and the shrines of the gods, then their victory may not turn into disaster. May no frenzy come upon them and drive them to pillage where they should not; they still need a safe return home.

She had just described, out of her imagination, the wild scenes of carnage and tumult inside the captured city, and if our minds are not firmly fixed on irrelevant things, such as Clytemnestra's personal motives for saying this, we cannot fail to think of the body of the hare which the eagles ripped open, and of the anger of Artemis.

Now comes the Herald, innocently exulting in the victory and thanking the gods for it: Troy is ruined, lifeless; the shrines and temples, the very seed in the soil, are no more. As Murray briefly observes, in his Oxford text: Id quod maxime timendum erat factum est; that has been done which was most to be feared.

But this is only part of the story. The Herald-scene continues. Presently he is telling us at some length how the army suffered before Troy. Some, he says, found the peace of death; for the others, all is over now. Glory has come to Argos and its commanders! Give thanks to Zeus who has brought this to pass.

Now the doors of the Palace open,[1] and the Avenger stands before us, the Wrath incarnate. First she speaks to, or at, the

---

[1] Though it is possible that she has been visible since v. 82.

chorus: 'They called me a fool; they said "How like a woman, to be so excited!" But I went on with my sacrifices.'

What does Aeschylus mean by this? He is very deliberate about it, for he wrote an epode to the second ode in order to lead up to it. This contemptuous triumph of hers over the chorus increases our sense of her stature; she, the Avenger, is equal to her part. In the same way she will triumph over Agamemnon. Then she will come out to triumph over Cassandra—and this time she will not succeed.

Then, turning abruptly to the Herald, she bids him take to Agamemnon a message, which tells us clearly enough of her hatred for him, and of her treachery; and the doors close behind her. She has come and gone, like a black shadow cast across the Herald's tale of triumph.[1]

Now, reluctantly, the Herald passes on to his last theme, which is in fact the fulfilment of his previous one. Again, he does not understand the inner meaning of what he is saying, but *we* can. There has been a storm at sea. 'Those ancient enemies, Fire and Water, made a compact to destroy the Greek fleet.' This is not simply poetic diction; it is very plain language to an audience brought up on religious drama. Only the King's ship has reached land (so far as the Herald knows), and it was no human helmsman who saved it from the storm, but some god held the rudder.

'Let them respect the altars; they still need a safe homecoming.' They destroyed the altars—unless we frustrate Aeschylus by deleting the verse. They have not found a safe return: Fire and Water, ancient enemies, joined together for once. The gods have struck at the Greeks, swiftly and terribly. Only Agamemnon has survived, saved by a god, brought home —to Clytemnestra.

Drama of this order is worth any amount of subtle character-drawing, and is incompatible with it. What Aeschylus has done, in the Herald-scene, is to add another term to our proportion-sum. Paris sinned, and Zeus struck him down; the Greek host sinned, and the gods have struck them; Agamemnon sinned . . . and we have been shown the Avenger, waiting.

The third ode begins with Helen. The second ode also had

---

[1] This scene is further discussed below, pp. 201 ff.

something to say about Helen: about the mourning which she brought upon Greece. This time we are to hear about the ruin she brought to Troy. Another point of comparison between these two odes is their metres. As we have seen, the second, but for the refrains, is in the same metre throughout, and this is uncommon; the third uses a variety of metres—and they are significant. Aeschylus begins with the slow trochaic measure which he often uses to convey a mood of serious reflection or anxious thought.[1] This metre, which we must try to imagine as married to the appropriate dance-figure, conveys, in the strophe, the feeling which the chorus has of the strange fitness of Helen's name; in the antistrophe, the thought that she was driven to Ilium by an avenging Μῆνις, a Wrath. The solemn trochaics give way to the lilting anacreontic with its fascinating side-step, a rhythm often (though not always) associated with love, wine and gaiety. To this metre the lovely Helen steals

> From the silk veils of her chamber, sailing seaward
> With the Zephyr's breath behind her.[2]

To the same metre

> The armed legions of men sent out to hunt her
> On the path that leaves no imprint:

and in the antistrophe Troy 'learns another music', and cries of despair are heard—still in the anacreontics which celebrated Helen's coming. We have lost the dance, but we need not doubt that it made this grim irony even grimmer.[3]

The next two stanzas, in easily-moving glyconics, give us the parable of the lion-cub. The parable generalises: it indicates that what we are considering belongs to the very nature of things; that the ruin that came on Troy was inevitable, an ἄτη (735). Then:

> Πάραντα δ' ἐλθεῖν ἐς Ἰλίου πόλιν —

Yet another rhythm, but a familiar one: it comes to us from the last part of the first ode and from the second, heavily charged now with its acquired associations with blind infatua-

[1] Compare *Persae* 115 ff, *Agamemnon* 160 ff, *Choephori* 585 ff, 782 ff, *Eumenides* 490 ff.
[2] Professor Thomson's brilliant 'isometric' translation.
[3] See 'The Tragic Dance', *J.H.S.*, LXXV.

tion sweeping a man to ruin, and of sin inevitably ending in destruction.

> And so it seemed once there came to Ilium
> A sweet-smiling calm, without cloud, serene, beguiling,
> A rare gem set in crown of riches,
> Shaft of a softly-glancing eye . . .

But it 'swerved aside'—as the metre too does at this point—and what came to Ilium, guided by Zeus Xenios, was an Erinys. The final stanzas bring this oppressive rhythm to its conclusion[1]: 'One act of hybris begets another, until the day of reckoning comes. But Justice, hating the wicked whose hands are unclean (σὺν πίνῳ χερῶν), honours the pure; and she brings all to the end appointed.'—*Enter* Agamemnon, royally, in a chariot. This is the tremendous climax to which the long-sustained dance and music have been leading us.

But at the very moment of making this climax, Aeschylus doubles its force by adding something else, for Agamemnon does not enter alone: beside him in his chariot is a woman, the Trojan princess and prophetess Cassandra, another victim of his blindness, another witness to his folly, a last and deadly insult to Clytemnestra. For a long time Cassandra is silent: Aeschylus well understood that the dramatist can often say things best by not saying them at all. His reasons for keeping her silent we shall discuss later[2]; meanwhile, there she is, before our eyes, and as we read the text we must not forget her.

The chorus addresses the King at some length. We must look carefully at what they say; it is important, and neither the text nor the interpretation of it is beyond dispute. I translate the whole passage:

Hail, King, sacker of Troy, son of Atreus! How am I to address you? How can I honour you without going too far or falling short in my joy and gratitude? And (or 'but', though not 'for') many men prefer the semblance of truth when they have transgressed justice, and everyone is ready to sigh with the unfortunate, but there is no pang of grief in their hearts. They make show too of rejoicing with the happy, forcing smiles upon an unsmiling face . . . but the good judge of his flock no man's eye can deceive, those

---

[1] Though it is heard later in the play, and with obvious significance: vv. 1485-1497 and 1530-1536.
[2] P. 29.

eyes which seem (?) out of a loyal heart to fawn upon him with a watered love.

You, when you led out your expedition for Helen—I will not conceal it from you—were set down by me in no flattering colours; I thought it no act of prudence to try to bring back a willing wanton at the cost of men's lives. But now, in love and sincerity—All's well that ends well. You will find out in time, as you make enquiry, who has been guarding the city honestly and who dishonestly.

That something has been lost after 794 ('an unsmiling face') is agreed. Not all agree with Headlam that something has been lost after 805 too, but it seems likely, though the loss is not serious. But can we seriously maintain that the first part makes sense? What is the logical connexion between the second sentence and the first? The conjunction δέ implies continuation, but whatever this sentence continues it can hardly be the first. And what does it mean? The chorus goes on to speak of insincerity. The insincere man does indeed prefer 'the semblance of truth', τὸ δοκεῖν εἶναι; but if this is the point, why say that the insincere do this 'when they have transgressed justice'? For they do it habitually. The words cannot mean that they do it 'unjustly', for in the first place you cannot 'prefer the semblance of truth' otherwise than 'unjustly', so that the qualification is meaningless; and in the second place the participle is aorist and not present. The sense might be that the wrongdoer is forced into insincerity to cover his wrong, but this would give no satisfactory connexion with the sentence that precedes or with the one that follows. There seems good reason to suppose that the text is seriously defective here.

But apart from this particular difficulty, what is the chorus driving at in the passage as a whole? It is commonly supposed that it is trying to warn Agamemnon against Clytemnestra, and that Agamemnon's reply shows how completely he misses their point. I cannot believe this. It is true that some of their language suits her well enough, notably 'forcing a smile upon an unsmiling face'; but the first part of the sentence conspicuously does not suit her, for she has very keenly felt the δῆγμα λύπης, the 'pang of grief' in her heart. What would be the substance of their warning? Not that she may be planning murder: the fourth ode and the way in which they receive Cassandra's

warning show that they have no idea that she is planning anything of the sort. If they are trying to warn him of her, it can
only be of her adultery and faithlessness. To be sure, it is a
matter of some delicacy and even of danger to tell a King that
his Queen is false; a certain obscurity would be natural. But
does the chorus here succeed even in being obscure about it?

The second part of the passage is as clear as it is surprising: 'I
condemned you then, but now I am reconciled to it.' This,
introduced by a simple δέ, not by any strong transitional formula, is surely part of one whole argument, especially as the
passage ends on the thought with which (apparently) it began;
the distinction between the true friend and the false. That is,
the chorus is saying: 'I am quite straightforward. I was against
the expedition, and I do not deny it, but now I am your sincere
supporter: you have succeeded.'[1]

In this second half, the chorus is obviously thinking of itself,
protesting its own sincerity—in contrast with whom? Not
Clytemnestra, or not her in particular, but other citizens—τὸν
ἀκαίρως πόλιν οἰκουροῦντα πολιτῶν.[2] We have heard of those who
muttered angrily against the Atreidae, and of the fear that
something may be done under cover of night. 'There are those
in Argos who will, like us, welcome you, but not sincerely. We
are sincere': this is what the chorus must be saying here. It is
afraid—but not of Clytemnestra.

We have noticed already, and shall discuss later, the remarkable fact that the chorus, in this passage, says that it condemned
what was (as we have been told) the plan of Zeus. If this is
nothing but an oversight on the part of the dramatist, it is a
very surprising one.

To this welcome, and warning, Agamemnon makes no immediate reply; something more important claims his first atten-

---

[1] Here too the text is doubtful. The vulgate seems to mean 'Work is
kindly to those who have completed it successfully'. Headlam cites parallel
passages to prove that εὔφρων means 'pleasant', but in all of them it is 'kindly'
except perhaps in Aesch. *Supp.* 378, where οὐκ εὔφρον means 'goes against
the grain'. In the present passage the context suggests something like what
Wilamowitz proposed: εὔφρων πόνον εὖ τελέσασιν ἐγώ. The 'ending of toil' is
one of the recurring ideas of the whole trilogy.

[2] Certainly, the verb οἰκουρεῖν means literally 'to housekeep', and the use
of the masculine participle does not preclude a generalised reference to
Clytemnestra, but the word πολιτῶν does. The audience will, of course, think
of Clytemnestra, but that is another matter—and we call it 'irony'.

tion: he addresses the gods of Argos, his 'partners' in his vengeance and in his safe return. It has been customary to speak of his arrogance and blasphemy in calling the gods his 'partners', Fraenkel has shown that this is a misconception. So too, for that matter, has Aeschylus—as he will do again; for the preludes to the first ode and to the second made it quite clear that the vengeance taken on Paris was conceived and carried out independently by Zeus and Agamemnon. The fact is plain enough; what we have to do is to understand it. Zeus and Agamemnon are 'sharers of the responsibility', which is the literal meaning of the word μεταίτιοι. As for the other half of the statement, that the gods have played their part in securing his safe return, we know that this is true; in fact, thanks to the Herald scene and its implications, we know a great deal more about this than Agamemnon does. The grim irony of this is continued as Agamemnon goes on to describe the utter ruin that he has brought upon Troy; our thoughts turn, yet again, to the hare which prefigured all this, and the anger of Artemis which was its immediate result. 'Billows of rich smoke', he says, 'are even now rising from the city. Gusty[1] ruin is still at work.' In a few moments we shall see Clytemnestra once more; she will assure us that this is indeed true.

Meanwhile he turns to the chorus: 'I agree with you ... Few are able to pay respect, without envy, to the man who is successful. They are jealous of his prosperity.' Agamemnon does indeed show blindness in this speech; what he is blind to, I think, is not a warning about Clytemnestra, but the real nature, and cause, of the 'envy', φθόνος, which attends 'success', ὄλβος. The chorus, in its address to him, has used neither word, but both have been used significantly in earlier parts of the play, and will be used again, notably in this very scene. Artemis was full of φθόνος, 'resentment' rather than 'envy', at the killing of the hare; and the ὄλβος, 'success', for which the chorus prayed (471) was one which should involve no 'resentment'. Such resentment is going to destroy Agamemnon, but all that he can see in φθόνος is the purely mundane envy or jealousy which the unsuccessful feel towards the great; and this, he says, he will be able to deal with.[2]

---

[1] If the MS. reading is correct, as I believe it is.

[2] The mirror-passage in this speech—a notorious difficulty—has I think

Agamemnon seems on the point of descending from his chariot and entering the palace, but Aeschylus will have him enter in circumstances much more impressive and sinister than these. The palace-doors open, and out comes Clytemnestra, just as in the previous scene. Her first speech is splendidly conceived: her pretence of modesty overcome by joy, the cold elaboration of the Geryon-passage, her mention of the absence of Orestes, 'pledge of our mutual faith', her enormous piling-up of similes:

> *Call him the watch-dog of the fold, forestay*
> *That saves the ship, firm pillar holding up*
> *The lofty roof, a father's only son,*
> *The sight of land to sailors in despair,*
> *A day of sunshine coming after storm,*
> *A spring of water to the thirsty traveller—*

all this puts before us, as powerfully as language can, her falseness, her hatred, her cold determination. It is almost as if she was challenging Agamemnon to see the truth, if he can. It leads to the most unexpected of climaxes: what was a metaphor, when it was applied to Paris, comes to life in startling fashion for his fellow-sinner Agamemnon, as Clytemnestra invites the 'sacker of Ilium' to 'tread underfoot the beauty of holy things'.

Agamemnon has judgment enough to reject Clytemnestra's adulation; also to know that this purple path is ἐπίφθονος, a thing to cause resentment; but she urges him to disregard the censure of men:

> μή νυν τὸν ἀνθρώπειον αἰθεσθῇς ψόγον—

a verse so constructed that we think at once of the suppressed antithesis, the censure of the gods. She urges him to accept φθόνος, envy, as the inevitable counterpart of success. So—'since you set so much store by it'—he yields, reluctantly, deprecating the 'resentment' of the gods which we know he has

been substantially cleared up by W. B. Stanford (*Classical Review*, 1954, pp. 82-85). The flatterer is a man of no independence of judgment; he is a 'mirror' because he simply reflects the mood of him whom he is flattering. But even so the passage seems to me impossibly harsh: the participle δοκοῦντας, with no substantive to explain it, and the sudden mention of Odysseus, incline me, once more, to think that something has been lost, and that the original sense was to this effect: I know that the society of men is a mirror, the reflection of a shadow. (Many of my fellow-commanders, I know, hated me,) though they *seemed* to be my good friends. Only Odysseus . . .

B

amply earned already, feeling scruples at 'despoiling' a house of some tapestries, forgetting how much he has despoiled it already, at Aulis. As he is blind to that, so he is blind to the new affront which he is offering to his wife:

> This foreign girl who has come with me, the army's choicest gift to me—take her in and treat her kindly. The gods look with favour upon the conqueror who is gentle.

So, as he walks upon purple into the home that hardly hoped to see him (v. 911), it is indeed clear that Dikê is guiding his steps. It is clear too that the second instrument of Dikê is worse than her predecessor in that office; and that when she offers her prayer to Zeus Teleios, 'Zeus par qui tout s'achève', although her prayer is answered it is very far from bringing this chain of violence to an end. Not yet does Zeus justify the title *Teleios*.

In the first three odes the chorus has moved confidently. It could understand what the sacrifice of Iphigenia portended; it saw the meaning of the destruction of Paris; it could tell us why destruction came to Troy; it could suggest to us irresistibly that Agamemnon, a sinner like Paris, may be punished like Paris. But it is not a chorus of seers. It has brought us to the edge of the precipice; we can look over, but they cannot. They stand on the edge, frightened, hardly knowing why.

The fourth ode is not an easy one, chiefly because the text is in a poor state, but a general interpretation is possible. In the main, the first two stanzas are easy enough: The King is safely home again, after so long an absence, yet I have a strange foreboding of evil. The other two stanzas are not so clear; the second half of the antistrophe, in particular, has been translated and explained in queer ways. The text may reasonably be translated as follows:

'If one lot, μοῖρα, appointed by the gods did not check another from encroaching, my heart, outstripping my tongue, would now be pouring out these anxieties. As it is, it mutters in secret, broken in spirit, with no hope of unravelling anything useful from a tortured mind.'

What is the meaning of 'lot checking lot'? Fraenkel offers a rather hard explanation. The first 'lot' is 'the lot of man in general, established by God: his fate or destiny', while the

second is 'the portion or lot (powers, possibilities, etc.) with which
the individual is endowed.' Aeschylus is sometimes difficult, but
not as difficult as this, and the interlocking phrase τεταγμένα
μοῖρα μοῖραν ἐκ θεῶν, far from suggesting that there are two
kinds of lot, in different degrees, will naturally make us think
of them as being in the same degree.[1] Mazon remarks only
'Texte obscur'. Thomson gives what in his Appendix he calls
'an unsatisfactory note', and substitutes, with hesitation: 'If it
had not been a dispensation of fate that a life once lost cannot
be recovered, my heart would have poured away these evil
tidings before my tongue could speak; i.e. I should have banished my fears without wasting words on them.'

The second part of the passage begins with the words νῦν δέ;
'as it is I can find nothing to say'. The logical framework is: 'If
so-and-so were not true, I should not be wasting words. But it
is true; therefore I am dumb.' A strange antithesis, surely?
What is this thing which, if false, would make words unnecessary, but, being true, makes them impossible? A. Y. Campbell
seems to me to be right in accepting Schutz's emendation:

$$Καρδίαν \ γλῶσσα \ πάντ' \ ἂν \ ἐξέχει$$

My tongue would outstrip my heart, and pour forth all that is in it.

If the heart outstrips the tongue, the normal result is incoherence,
but if the tongue can keep in front of the heart, dealing at once
with all that the heart produces, the result is inward ease—the
exact opposite of the real situation which the chorus describes.
Now we have a natural antithesis: easy utterance against
tortured despair.

But what is the meaning of 'lot checking lot'? This is the
important question, as this is the source of the uneasiness felt
by the chorus. Some of the explanations offered fail, as it seems
to me, because they do not give significance enough to the
words πλέον φέρειν: 'If one lot fixed by Heaven did not restrain
another from winning too much.' Surely a familiar idea? The
universe is a cosmos, an ordered whole, a balance of opposites.
'Things are always paying recompense to each other', as Anaxi-

---

[1] Fraenkel says that the word-order compels us to take ἐκ θεῶν either with
εἴργε or with μὴ πλέον φέρειν; but is this true? Surely the collocation μοῖρα
μοῖραν suggests, as the complete phrase, τεταγμένα μοῖρα μοῖραν ἐκ θεῶν
⟨τεταγμέναν⟩, where ἐκ θεῶν is naturally taken as qualifying both participles.

mander said, 'for their ἀδικία, their encroachments.' Dikè
is the force which, in the long run, preserves the balance. 'If
this were not so', says the chorus, 'I should feel easy. As it is, I
am in torment.'

The central thought is 'encroachment', πλέον φέρειν. Agamemnon's success, his ὄλβος, is so great as to cause misgiving;
anything excessive is dangerous. Over-strict pursuit of health
brings a man to its next-door neighbour, sickness; many a
richly-loaded ship, enjoying a fair journey home, has suddenly
struck a hidden reef. Even so, a well-judged sacrifice of cargo
may refloat the ship, so that all is not lost; as, in contrary fashion,
the wreck of an estate can be made good by a few rich harvests.
Only the shedding of blood is irremediable—and we have been
told often enough of the bloodshed which Agamemnon has
caused: he killed his daughter, and Greece has laid him under
something like a curse for leading so many of her sons to death.
It is not that the gods are jealous of success (vv. 750 ff); it is on
the man who is successful and unjust that retribution descends.
If any 'lot' could be absolute, independent of others, all might
be well; what Agamemnon has won by bloodshed might endure.
But it is not so; sooner or later 'lot checks lot', allowing nothing
πλέον φέρειν, to have more than its due share. Nothing can
restore the dead to life; here is something that must be paid for.
Such is 'the tangled skein of thought' which has reduced the
chorus to perplexity.

Why did Aeschylus contrive the scene that follows, the one
of which Housman made such excellent fun? There is one
apparent absurdity which can be removed by making σύ, in
v. 1061, refer not to Cassandra but to the leader of the chorus:

CLYTEMNESTRA: *If you refuse because you do not understand what
I am saying, then (Turning to the chorus-leader) you explain to
her, not in words but gesticulating like a barbarian.*

So Murray, in his Oxford text. But Fraenkel's rejection of this,
and his explanation of the text, is to me convincing: Clytemnestra is baffled and angry, and she speaks illogically, as one does
in such a case.

But this is only a detail; the major question remains: why
does Aeschylus (as Thomson puts it) 'gratuitously fritter away
the intensity of this crucial dialogue by the introduction of a

detail (viz. whether Cassandra knows Greek) which is both purposeless and incongruous?'

It sometimes helps the critic, if he will assume that the dramatist really knew what he was doing. If we will forget for a moment that Aeschylus was something of a primitive, and not quite in full control of the new art of the theatre, the scene becomes not only intelligible but also astonishingly dramatic. We have only to recreate it as the audience saw it.

Agamemnon came in a long time ago, with Cassandra sitting beside him. Throughout that long scene she remained motionless. If the audience expected Clytemnestra to say anything to her, or even about her, it has been disappointed. The only reference to her has been Agamemnon's wonderfully foolish remark: 'Take her in, and be kind to her.' On this, comment is needless, and Clytemnestra makes none. Agamemnon goes into the palace, and still nothing is said to or about Cassandra. Clytemnestra too goes in; still nothing is said. The fourth ode is sung, with not a word about this woman sitting there in the chariot. The audience must be wondering why she is there, and what Aeschylus is going to do with her.

At last the doors open, and Clytemnestra is standing there, as she was when she came to triumph over the chorus in the matter of the beacon-message, and again over Agamemnon. She tells Cassandra to come in, to play her part in the sacrifice. But nothing happens; Cassandra takes no notice. The chorus lends a hand. Still nothing happens, except that somewhere hereabouts Cassandra begins to toss and turn like one distraught. To such effect does nothing happen that Clytemnestra is reduced to saying: 'I cannot waste my time like this. The sacrifice is ready. If you will take your part, let there be no delay.' But still nothing happens; and the desperate suggestion that maybe Cassandra knows no Greek, and needs an interpreter, is a bold way of emphasising the complete *impasse* which has been reached; everyone concerned is on his beam-ends. This time Clytemnestra scores no victory; she has not succeeded even in establishing contact with her intended victim. She has to retire, baffled.

No doubt the audience too is baffled—but not for long. First, the leader of the chorus makes one more attempt, speaking gently to this strange, aloof woman. She does not reply. There is a long pause. Then at last Cassandra descends from the chariot, and speaks.

Long familiarity with this first utterance of hers has perhaps blunted its edge for us. It is one of the most astonishing moments in all drama, this sudden release of what has been dammed up for so long. For what would it be natural for Cassandra to say, when at last she speaks? Curses upon the Greeks, curses upon Agamemnon her captor, curses upon Paris, or Helen, or both; or wild lamentation for Troy, for Priam, for herself—this, surely, is the sort of thing that the audience will be expecting. What they get is something very different—that wild cry to Apollo: 'Apollo, my destroyer!'

Why Apollo? So far in the play we have heard nothing about him, except for the passing reference in the first anapaests to 'some god, Apollo it may be, or Pan, or Zeus', who hears the cry of the robbed eagles, and sends an Erinys to avenge them (v. 55). On this passage, Fraenkel reasonably asks 'Why Apollo?'—for, as he says, we know of no particular association between Apollo and either eagles or mountain-tops. No; but there is an association between Apollo and the *Agamemnon*: the god who figures there as an avenger of the oppressed behaves here as Cassandra will describe.

'Apollo! my destroyer! For you have destroyed me, with no reluctance (?),[1] a second time.' The chorus is bewildered; it turns out that it is the chorus, not Cassandra, who needs an interpreter. The audience too may be bewildered for a moment, but light begins to dawn as Cassandra continues: 'Ah! whither hast thou brought me? To the palace of the Atreidae? Say rather, to a slaughter-house, running with blood!' She, then, is

---

[1] This οὐ μόλις, 'with no reluctance', or 'not hardly', is very suspicious, both here and in the passage in the *Eumenides* (864) which is commonly cited to support the use of it here: θυραῖος ἔστω πόλεμος, οὐ μόλις παρών: 'let your wars be with foreign foes, not hardly present'. Nobody talks like this, and we should not pretend that Aeschylus did. Here (as A. Y. Campbell has observed) both παρών and οὐ μόλις are intolerable. In *Helen* 334, θέλουσαν οὐ μόλις καλεῖς is explained: 'You call me, who am willing with no reluctance', but no such sense (if this is sense) is possible in the *Eumenides* or in Cassandra's verse. In the latter I suspect οὐ καλῶς, 'dishonourably', 'shamefully'. The corruption would be an easy one, in minuscule, and οὐ καλῶς, as we shall see, would suit the sense of the whole scene excellently. It would be encouraging if the same cure could be offered for the verse in the *Eumenides*; unfortunately, it cannot.

Apollo's victim. We can see for ourselves the simple fact that she is to be the victim of Agamemnon's concupiscence and folly, and of Clytemnestra's blind hatred; but the prophetess can see further: she can see that Agamemnon and Clytemnestra are only the instruments of Apollo's anger.

Now we understand why Aeschylus kept her silent for so long, why he did not allow Clytemnestra even to make contact with her, why he almost broke his dramatic framework in order to emphasise this lack of contact. Cassandra and Clytemnestra are not on the same plane. In every way he can, Aeschylus forces on us the idea that Cassandra is really Apollo's victim. He allows her no word of anger against Agamemnon who has brought her here, nor against Clytemnestra who will kill her, lest what they do should obscure what the god is doing. We still have to explain to ourselves why Aeschylus wants to draw this sharp distinction between the divine and the human agents, but at least we can see that this is indeed what he is doing, and that it makes immediate sense of what was something of a puzzle.

The cause of it all is given in that dry and explicit stichomythia in which we are told that Apollo desired and bribed her, and that she first said Yes and then No. Aeschylus is no Euripides: he neither makes nor invites comments on the god's behaviour. The only point he makes is that Cassandra has incurred Apollo's wrath, and that the god has brought her here for punishment. She goes in to her death not when Clytemnestra tells her, but when she feels she must: and just before the end Aeschylus contrives a most imaginative restatement of the theme. In a transport of despair Cassandra tears off and tramples underfoot her prophetic insignia: then, as if coming to herself again, and suddenly seeing what she has done, she says 'Look! it is Apollo himself who has stripped me of my prophet's robes.' We are made almost to see the unseen god.

And why is Cassandra made to prophecy, twice over, not only her own death, but also Agamemnon's and Clytemnestra's, and the past crime of Atreus? For we know already that Clytemnestra is going to kill Agamemnon; and Aegisthus is coming, presently, to tell us quite explicitly about Atreus' crime. The purpose of the prophecies is therefore not simply to give us necessary information—at unnecessary length. Nor, surely, do we think so little of Aeschylus the artist as to suppose that he was simply seizing the opportunity of writing a scene, effective in an obvious way, but not an essential part of his whole design. A further question: what have these crimes to do with what hitherto has been our chief preoccupation, namely the guilty retribution which the Atreidae have taken for the crime of Paris? We speak of the Curse in the house of Atreus: what has it to do with the first two-thirds of the play? So far the abduction of Helen has been regarded as the starting-point, the πρώταρχος ἄτη; we have managed very nicely without the Curse —and it was obviously not the Curse that drove Paris to steal Helen, or Agamemnon to destroy Paris and his city.

The answer to all these questions is, naturally, one and the same. Twice, first in visions, then in definite prophetic statement, Cassandra brings before us the crimes that this house has seen and will see, all of them crimes of the same nature: bloody retribution for an earlier crime. The spirit of all these crimes is personified in that 'discordant band that ever haunts the house', drinking human blood, not to be driven out, the Erinyes. These it is who have presided, and will preside, over this savage succession of retributive murders: the Curse is simply the fact that the house has been possessed by this spirit. The connexion between the Curse and Agamemnon's war is that the war was inspired by the same spirit too. It was Wrath, that drove the Greeks against Troy (v. 701); it is as a Wrath incarnate that Clytemnestra will murder Agamemnon (155); it is in a spirit of wrath (1036) that she receives Cassandra—except that in the baleful irony of that speech she discloses her meaning by expressing the opposite (οὐκ ἀμηνίτως).

This violent, wrathful conception of Dikê is always associated with the Erinyes, later called 'wrathful hounds' (*Choephori* 924, 1054). We are explicitly told that Agamemnon was sent on his war as an Erinys (58 ff), and that Helen brought to Troy in her train an Erinys sent by Zeus (744-749). The Erinys, on the one level, is the natural agent of Zeus, as on the other level Agamemnon is his 'Minister of Justice'; and we have seen that though it was ordained by Zeus it was a 'justice' exacted in blood, through hybris, and therefore a justice that must entail a similar justice on him who executed it. But now the range is suddenly enlarged. We can now see that all the crimes that this house has known and will know are of this same pattern, all of them acts of a 'justice' that can know no end. Clytemnestra prays to Zeus Teleios, Zeus the Achiever, but there is no sign of finality, nor can there be. Yet these blood-drinking Furies whom Cassandra sees *are* the agents of Zeus, and now of Apollo. When Aegisthus enters, the most despicable and shameful of the avengers in this play, he enters with the word δικηφόρος on his lips: 'bringer of retribution'. He mentions too the Erinyes, the ministers of the divine 'justice'. He sees Agamemnon's body lying in the net in which Clytemnestra had caught him, and he says:

> ὦ φέγγος εὖφρον ἡμέρας δικηφόρου·
> φαίην ἂν ἤδη νῦν βροτῶν τιμαόρους
> θεοὺς ἄνωθεν γῆς ἐποπτεύειν ἄχη,
> ἰδὼν ὑφαντοῖς ἐν πέπλοις Ἐρινύων
> τὸν ἄνδρα τόνδε κείμενον.

Welcome, day that brings retribution! Now at last I can say that the gods above avenge the sufferings of men, now that I see this man lying in the net which the Erinyes have woven.

These guilty people, all of them, are carrying out the designs of the gods, and the Erinyes, the agents of the gods, are working in them.

But Cassandra has already made this clear. It is to this charnel house, this bloodstained lodging of the Erinyes, that Apollo has sent Cassandra for retribution, using as his means the folly of Agamemnon and the blood-lust of Clytemnestra, even as Zeus Xenios used the ambition and violence of Agamemnon. And as Agamemnon was doomed for what he was to do, so Cassandra cries:

> οὐ μὴν ἄτιμοί γ' ἐκ θεῶν τεθνήξομεν·
> ἥξει γὰρ ἡμῶν ἄλλος αὖ τιμάορος.

And yet my death will not be disregarded by Heaven, for another will come to avenge me.

All these crimes are inspired by the Erinyes, and the Erinyes are all agents of the gods.

It is tempting to suppose that the permanent back-stage buildings was in existence when this trilogy was composed, for Aeschylus makes the Palace of Atreus almost an actor in his drama. On its roof we saw the Watchman, hinting what this house could tell us, 'could it find a voice'. From this house we have seen Clytemnestra the μῆνις οἰκονόμος, the 'Wrath that dwells in the house', coming out time after time on her deadly business. We have seen Agamemnon, treading on purple, pass into it, brought home, beyond all hoping, by Justice. Now Cassandra's visions bring before us the dismembered limbs of children within this same house, and a sword that strikes through a net, and the harsh music of its ghastly inhabitants the Furies, agents of the gods: and we see how within this same house a son will kill his mother—all under the guidance of θεοὶ μεταίτιοι, 'the gods our partners'. Aeschylus, through Cassandra and her visions, makes of this building a visible symbol of the agony of humanity, as it waits for light, healing, finality, and release from toils, for a Dikê that will be bearable.

When Cassandra has gone in to meet the death that Apollo designed for her, we encounter another passage that inspired Housman: the formal debate that takes place between the members of the chorus when Agamemnon's death-cry is heard. Once more, we may find that the dramatist has not been so naïve as some of his critics. The difficulty, as commonly stated, is that Agamemnon cries for help, and that the chorus, instead of doing anything sensible, debates at some length whether to act or not, and then decides to do nothing. Some of the explanations advanced are worth examining.

The parallel scene in the *Medea* is usually cited. It is no parallel at all. In the first place, the chorus in the *Medea* has been expressly told that Medea is going to murder her children; and when the children cry out for help and the chorus says 'Shall we go in and save them?', they can hear, and they say 'Yes, in god's name save us!' In the *Agamemnon* it has indeed been made quite plain to the audience (which in any case knows the story) that Clytemnestra is going to kill Agamemnon, but the chorus has not understood it; and Aeschylus has reminded us that it was part of Cassandra's punishment that her prophecies should never be credited.

But this is a small point. A much more important difference is that the situation is handled lyrically by Euripides, realistically (within due limits) by Aeschylus. We must, after all, do justice even to Euripides. We may, and I think should, assume that the chorus there does make a symbolic attempt to break in.

The fact that it proceeds to *sing* should warn us that we must conceive the scene as resembling ballet much more than a piece of modern dramatic realism. So treated, the passage in the *Medea* becomes quite intelligible, and leaves the passage in the *Agamemnon* high and dry. The chorus here does not sing and dance; it argues.

A different defence is that the chorus in a Greek tragedy does not take part in the action, and that the audience would not expect it to here. Generalisations about the Greek Tragedy are very dangerous, since Greek Tragedy is a term that includes many types of drama, from the purely poetic to the realistic. The balance between chorus and actors was continually changing, so that a principle observed in one play is disregarded in another. Certainly if Aeschylus' audience never expected a chorus to intervene in the action, it must have been taken aback in the *Choephori*, when the chorus persuades the Nurse to alter very materially Clytemnestra's message to Aegisthus; while the chorus of the *Eumenides* must have bewildered their simple minds beyond recall. In fact, it is perfectly plain that the chorus always does participate in the action where such participation is natural. Where such intervention would be ruinous, as in the *Hippolytus*, the dramatist has to adopt the conventional expedient of swearing it to secrecy.

Desperation has pointed out that if the chorus intervened here it would spoil the play. This excuse was demolished some time ago, by Aristotle, who said, in his dry and sensible fashion, that the dramatist should not make plots like this at all.[1]

Thomson does well to warn us how much we are under the spell of Elizabethan realism—though modern realism is much more misleading. This warning is in fact relevant to the two verses which Agamemnon speaks in this very passage: there is a kind of provincialism that points out that a man being stabbed does not speak in blank verse. But in fact, as we have said already, the passage is handled realistically, by Aeschylean standards. Aeschylus might have given his chorus dochmiacs to sing: he does not. Thomson's own explanation is that the chorus is too senile to act, and that the instinct of their senility causes them to fall at once into a regular debate: ἔργα νέων βουλαὶ δὲ γερόντων.[2] But the chorus is not too senile to offer

[1] *Poetics* 1460 a 33.   [2] Proverbial: 'The young act, the old advise.'

defiance to Aegisthus later on, and the regularity of the debate is the same as the regularity of stichomythia, and this is not confined to the aged.

In fact if we assume that the chorus is debating whether or not to break in and save Agamemnon, there is no reasonable explanation of Aeschylus' procedure; but if, instead of relying on the *Medea*, we read the *Agamemnon*, we find that they are doing nothing of the kind. Some of the chorus doubt if the cries mean what they say (1366-1369); the others take it for granted that Agamemnon is already dead, so that there is no question of saving him; these assume that what they are confronted with is a *coup d'état*. The presumed assassins are always referred to in the plural, and 'tyranny' is twice mentioned as the likely outcome. That a group of twelve men should hesitate to force their way into a palace and confront, presumably, a determined band of political assassins is neither discreditable to them nor undramatic: in fact, the first speaker, in suggesting that they should summon the help of the citizens, is talking plain common-sense. This chorus does indeed deserve our sympathy—first, that they are so suddenly plunged into what looks like a danger-ous situation; and then, for being accused of senility, dilatoriness and ineffectiveness—and that, too, by professors.

But if this is what Aeschylus is doing, why does he do it? Perhaps it is natural that the murder of a King should suggest rebellion and tyranny, but it is the business of the dramatist, as of any artist, in choosing his material, to use not what is merely natural, but what is also relevant. We shall see as we proceed with the trilogy that the idea of unlawful tyranny is very relevant indeed.[1] And why, having his own reasons for intro-ducing here the idea of unlawful tryanny, does Aeschylus intro-duce it in this way, by resolving his normally solid chorus into twelve separate persons? In Euripides this was a common device. In his more naturalistic drama it was sometimes im-possible to introduce a united chorus plausibly: in such cases he pretended that his chorus was a group of fifteen individuals who had assembled fortuitously, out of sympathy, or curiosity. But Aeschylus was never reduced to this, and there is only one other

---

[1] If our suggested interpretation of vv. 783-809 is correct, that the chorus there is warning Agamemnon against disaffected citizens, not against Clytem-nestra in particular, then that passage is a natural prelude to this one.

case in his surviving plays of such a catalysis of the chorus, and that is in the Parodos of the *Septem.* There the dramatic point is obvious: Aeschylus is creating an effect of indiscipline and disorder which Eteocles is at pains to quell. The effect, I think, is not dissimilar here: this sudden breaking up of the united chorus is a very dramatic expression of the confusion into which Argos is plunged by the murder of its King.

Agamemnon is dead; Cassandra is dead. Troy and the slaughtered Greeks are avenged: Apollo's wrath against Cassandra is satisfied—by Clytemnestra; she has done what Artemis and Apollo foresaw and intended. For the last time the doors open, and we see Clytemnestra and the two bodies—Agamemnon's enmeshed in the net which, under Zeus, he himself had cast over Troy.

What remains of the play is not development, but repetition: this is of its very essence, and is the secret of its dramatic power. Only one thing is new—the revelation of Clytemnestra's cold hatred of Agamemnon, and incidentally of Cassandra. We have had hints indeed, but only enough to assure us that she will murder her husband: now we have open avowal:

> I struck him twice; twice he cried out, and then his limbs relaxed; as the body lay there I dealt it a third blow, a thankoffering to the god of Death. So he fell and poured out his life-blood; and as his wound spurted out the stream of blood, the dark and deadly shower bespattered me; and I was glad, as the swelling ear in the cornfield is glad when Zeus sends it glorious rain. (1384-1392)

Now we know how she hated him—even to that last horror of driving her sword into his dead body.

> Here he lies, this woman's seducer, the darling of every Chryseis in Troy. And here is she, his captive, seer of visions, his bedfellow, the soothsayer, his faithful lover who sat beside him on the ship's benches. Their end was worthy of them. His you know: and she, like a swan, sang her last lament, and lies beside her lover. He brought her to my bed, like dessert to grace a meal. (1438-1447)

Now we know what, in spite of her silence, we had guessed—what she felt when she saw Cassandra. And she says:

> He did not think twice; but as if she were an animal taken from a countless flock of sheep he sacrificed his own daughter, my beloved child, as a charm against winds from Thrace. (1415-1418)

No mourning rites for him! No; but Iphigenia will welcome him,
as a daughter should; she will run to meet him on the banks of the
swift River of Lamentation, and will embrace him, with a kiss.
(1554-1558)

Now we know what she thought of the sacrifice of Iphigenia.

Why have Clytemnestra's inner feelings been kept back until
now? Dramatic necessity is one answer to the question: she
could not avow her motives until she could avow the murder.
But there is something more, for Aeschylus treats her exactly
as he treated Agamemnon. We saw Agamemnon in a double
aspect, first as the μέγας ἀντίδικος, the minister of Justice, carrying out a divine mission, and then as the blind and reckless
man, guilty of hybris. So it is made clear to us that to achieve
Dikê Zeus avails himself of guilty human passions. This pattern
is now repeated. During the first part of the play, Clytemnestra
emerged more and more clearly as the agent appointed by
Heaven for the punishment of Agamemnon's hybris: 'Justice',
said the chorus (781), 'leads all things to the appointed end',
and the end appointed for Agamemnon was his wife. Now that
Heaven's instrument has acted, we are shown fully what she
is like. We are shown how her great wrong has aroused in her
pitiless hatred; and we are shown something else:

> I swear by the avenging of my child, now achieved,[1] by Atê, and
> by the Erinys, to whom I have sacrificed him, that no foreboding
> of Terror walks in my house, so long as Aegisthus keeps alight the
> fire on my hearth, and remains as trusty as heretofore, my strong
> shield and defender. (1431-1437)

Her adultery is openly proclaimed; so too, in the scene with
Aegisthus, is the plot that the two of them shall rule in Argos.
The suggestion is carefully avoided that she took Aegisthus in
order to encompass her revenge on Agamemnon. Independently
of that, she is an adulteress. Such a woman is the gods' instrument for the punishment of Agamemnon, and for the satisfaction of Apollo's anger.

In this respect, then, Clytemnestra is a repetition of Agamemnon. In another respect, too; for, like him, she has the
vain hope that the Dikê now achieved shall be final. Paris'
crime cried out for punishment: Agamemnon punished it, in

---

[1] The Greek is τέλειος δίκη, 'achieved' (or 'final') Dikê—another echo.

his fashion; having done it, he came home thanking the gods for the vengeance he had taken, and hoping that all would now be well—subject to certain minor adjustments. So Clytemnestra proclaims the justice of her deed, and hopes that all will be well. When the chorus invokes a curse upon her, she retorts 'But you said nothing against Agamemnon, when he slew Iphigenia!' (1412 ff). They utter a lament for Agamemnon and she says, 'What? did he not plot treacherous ruin upon the house? He took my child, and he has suffered what he deserved' (1523 ff). The chorus has no answer to make, except that she must pay for what she has done; and they express this conviction in a familiar rhythm—the one on which the second ode was built:

μίμνει δὲ μίμνοντος ἐν θρόνῳ Διός
παθεῖν τὸν ἔρξαντα· θέσμιον γάρ.

'This remains while Zeus remains on his throne, that the doer must pay. It is the law.' But Clytemnestra prays that the doer may *not* pay:

I am ready to make compact with the curse of the house, to accept the present evil, great though it is, and for the future that it shall leave this house and vex another with domestic murder. Enough for me to have but a small share of its wealth, if I can remove this blood-frenzy from our midst.

But Dikê is inexorable: 'Neither by burnt offerings nor libations nor tears will you soften the hard hearts of the gods.'[1] Εὖ γὰρ εἴη, 'May it be well', is a vain prayer.

The whole source of the tragic intensity of this scene is its restatement of the earlier dilemma. There is nothing new: no fresh hope. A worse crime than Agamemnon's avenges what Agamemnon did; the second instrument of Dikê is guiltier far than the first. And the third is worse than the second: Aegisthus is a real climax—the wolf, sprawling in the lion's bed, the 'woman' who skulked at home when the men were fighting. This creature, welcoming the 'day that brings retribution', claims to be the 'just contriver', the δίκαιος ῥαφεύς, of the murder; 'just' because he is avenging on Atreus' son the wrong that Atreus did to Aegisthus' father and brothers. But the 'justice' that he inflicts on Agamemnon is murder, preceded by the corruption of his wife, and followed by the usurpation of his

[1] Vv. 69-71.

crown and the banishment of his son. This Justice, inspired by wrath and carried out by crime, is intolerable; but Aegisthus is quite sincere, so far as his plea of 'justification' is concerned. The Dikê that he exacts from Agamemnon is the same in kind as the Dikê that Agamemnon exacted from Paris, and Clytemnestra from Agamemnon: it is the punishment of crime by worse crime. It is different only in degree: the Dikê of Aegisthus takes a much more repulsive and contemptible form, and he is venting his rage not on the wrongdoer but on his son. But, in spite of this, it is Dikê, as the term is to be understood in the *Agamemnon*:

> Now at last can I say that the avenging gods do look down upon the sufferings of men, when I see this man lying in the net woven for him by the Furies.

The 'black Erinyes' have presided over all those acts of Dikê; it was as an Erinys that the Atreidae punished Paris, and the Erinyes, equated with the Curse in the House of Atreus, have punished Agamemnon by the hands of Clytemnestra and Aegisthus. They are the agents of Dikê and of Zeus, and it was to this bloodstained home of theirs that Apollo sent Cassandra.

> *Alas, alas! it is through Zeus*
> *The Cause of all, the worker of all.*
> *For what is brought to pass except by Zeus?*
> *What have we here that he has not decreed?*
>
> (vv. 1485 ff)

The *Agamemnon* ends in black despair and chaos. It is built on Law: that Dikê must come to the sinner; that the doer must suffer; that hybris begets hybris. But, as Dikê is achieved only through hybris, there is no visible end to the chain of violence. As in recent European history, violent action is met by equally violent reaction, and

> κεκόλληται γένος πρὸς ἄτᾳ—
> *The house is glued firm to Ruin.*

The only ray of light comes from a long way back, from the Hymn to Zeus, which assured us that understanding comes, in our despite, from suffering, and that Zeus made for man the path to wisdom.

CHAPTER TWO

Choephori

MEASURED in one way, the interval between the *Agamemnon* and the *Choephori* is ten or fifteen years;
measured in another, it was perhaps ten or fifteen
minutes. The second measurement is certainly not less significant than the first, for when the *Choephori* begins, we are at
once aware of certain fundamental changes. We have been
contemplating the murder of the King and his paramour committed by the Queen and her inglorious accomplice, committed
in the name of 'Justice', and, as the chorus has told us (1485 ff),
by the will of Zeus. In the first two scenes of the second play
the new avengers, already foreshadowed, stand before us: they
are very different ones, seeking their vengeance not out of
guilty passions but in purity of heart. Agamemnon too is presented in a different aspect; his sins forgotten, he is now the
great King, foully slain, and outraged even in his death. Further, Apollo is surely a different god—not very obviously, perhaps in the *Choephori*, but certainly in the *Eumenides*; for the
majestic god of order, purity and light who dominates the first
part of that play is not very easy to reconcile with the god who,
from such motives, had Cassandra taken to the bloodstained
palace of Atreus, haunt of the Erinyes, to be done to death by
an adultress. If we can suppose that in these matters Aeschylus
was obediently retailing legend, and no more, then no problem
arises, but if we assume that he meant what he says, then there
is a problem, and one which we have to take very seriously
indeed. In any case we can hardly fail to observe this, that
while in the *Agamemnon* Apollo makes use of 'the discordant
band that never leaves this House' (1190), in the *Eumenides* he
can hardly find words to express his loathing and contempt of
these same Erinyes.

All these are facts for which we must hope to find some consistent explanation, and with them we must combine the

general structure which Aeschylus has designed for the *Choephori*; for the first five hundred lines of the play, culminating in the long Commos, are relatively static, but from this point the action gathers momentum and drives on irresistibly to its climax. This first part of the play, unless we are careful, we can easily misconceive. Here is Orestes, we say to ourselves, caught in this terrible dilemma: on the one hand, the inescapable duty of avenging his father; on the other, the horror that a man must feel at the prospect of killing his mother. One function, therefore, of this half of the play is to show what forces, what arguments, prevail at last over his natural repugnance; to show with what motives, and in what anguish, he brings himself to do it. But we shall see, I think, that all this has very little importance in Aeschylus' design, that Orestes is not this kind of tragic hero, that his character and his inner conflict are only a small part of the real drama.

Let us begin at the beginning. The dramatic movement of the *Agamemnon* was a spiral. It circled always around the idea of Dikê exacted through crime, leading through a gathering darkness to chaos, as the most despicable of all the avengers commits the most despicable of all the crimes, yet in exactly the same spirit as the previous agents of Zeus. More and more urgent grew the cry for finality, light, healing, release from evils. Had this movement continued into the *Choephori*, we should see new avengers seeking to requite Clytemnestra and Aegisthus in hybris—a bloody retribution hopelessly bound up with some guilty scheme of their own. Instead, in the sharpest possible contrast to Aegisthus, we see Orestes in prayer, praying to Hermes. By an unlucky chance, someone, once, lost the first page of the archetype of the *Choephori*, so that all we know of this prayer is what Aristophanes quoted in the *Frogs*, together with three short fragments cited by ancient commentators on Euripides and Pindar. This is enough to show us that Orestes is standing at the tomb, praying that his father will be his protector and ally; and that he is offering to his father's spirit the mourning-tribute which should have been offered long before: 'But I was not present, father, to make my lament nor to stretch forth my arms toward you at your burying.' Orestes is not one who is possessed with hybris; he is not looking forward with savage glee to his revenge. On the contrary, he is being driven by necessity and honour and the express command of Apollo to a task which he cannot shirk but finds repugnant; and his prayer (v. 438) is not Clytemnestra's, that he may kill and then live in peace to enjoy the fruits of crime, but that he may kill her and then die.

Lamentation for Agamemnon is very prominent in this first half of the play. Orestes and the silent Pylades withdraw before the coming of the black-robed chorus, led by Electra. If we should consider it realistically, the wild grief of the chorus, sustained over so many years, would seem hysterical; but the burden of their song is that the majesty of the dead King has been swept on one side, that the spirit of the dead man is full of wrath against his slayers, that from this wrath has come the dream which has terrified the Queen, that her attempts to appease it are impious and vain, and that for the shedding of blood, as for the defiling of a virgin-bower, there is no cure but death.

As soon as Electra speaks we see that she too is different from any of the avengers in the *Agamemnon*. Like Orestes, she prays that her father may be their ally against his murderers. She also prays for purity:

> αὐτῇ τέ μοι δὸς σωφρονεστέραν πολὺ
> μητρὸς γενέσθαι χεῖρά τ' εὐσεβεστέραν.

Grant that I may prove myself purer far than my mother, and more reverent in action (140 f).

We heard little of Purity in the *Agamemnon*.

The new spirit produces a new word. The chorus tells Electra that she should pray for vengeance, that she should pray that someone should come to Clytemnestra and Aegisthus . . . 'Do you mean', she interrupts, 'a δικαστής or a δικηφόρος?' The chorus replies 'Say simply, Someone to kill them in return.' The chorus is not interested in Electra's distinction, but *we* may be. The second word, δικηφόρος, 'bringer of retribution', we have met twice before,[1] and it affords little comfort: Troy was overthrown by 'the crowbar of Zeus who brings retribution', and we know what inevitably happened, by the designs of the gods, to the man who wielded the crowbar: he was murdered on that day which brought so much joy to Aegisthus, the 'day

Agamemnon 525 and 1577.

that brings retribution'. But δικαστής, of an avenger, is new; not 'a bringer of retribution', but 'one who shall adjudge'. There is a ray of light here, transient though it may be; and there is another in Electra's next question:

CHORUS: *Say simply: Someone to kill them in return.*
ELECTRA: *And is this a righteous thing to ask of the gods?*

This again is a thought that occurred to nobody in the *Agamemnon*; in that play they killed, and hoped for the best.

This new spirit pervades the second part of the trilogy, and it is hardly necessary to cite every scrap of evidence for it. But we may find room for one typical passage: typical, because in it, as so often, Aeschylus reveals his thought through his imagery. When Orestes is standing over Clytemnestra's body he displays the μηχάνημα, the 'contrivance', whereby she had killed Agamemnon. He shows the monstrous thing to the all-seeing Sun, and cries: 'Such a thing a footpad might use, one who follows the life of waylaying travellers and robbing them. With a cunning thing like this, many a man could he do away with, and much joy could he find in it.' To this level, now, has sunk 'the woven net of the Erinyes', which, when first we heard of it,[1] was the literal repetition of the metaphorical net thrown over Troy by Zeus himself. This too is something that we must hope to understand; clearly, it will not be surprising if it proves to be part of the same design which makes the Erinyes, once Apollo's agents, so loathsome to Apollo in the *Eumenides*.

We find, then, avengers who are very different from the old ones. We find also a different presentation of Agamemnon. In the first play he was the blind sinner whose successive acts of hybris made his punishment more and more certain; in the rest of the trilogy his sins are forgotten. Now he is always the mighty King, 'dignified by the sceptre that Zeus gives; killed by a woman, and that, not in war, as if by the Amazons, but treacherously.' Thus Apollo, to the Erinyes (*Eumenides* 625). In the *Agamemnon* his sacking of Troy was hybris; twice at least in the *Eumenides* it is a glorious achievement. The passage just quoted continues: 'For when he returned from the war, bringing home more than he had lost . . . '; and when Orestes is declaring himself to Athena he says 'I am from Argos. Thou knowest my

[1] *Agamemnon* 1580.

father Agamemnon, commander of the host, with whom thou didst sack the city of Troy.' It is now a great exploit, and Athena shared in it. What is the reason for this change of front?

It would be superficial to say that oblivion descends on Agamemnon's sins because we now see him through the eyes of his friends. This would not explain why Clytemnestra and the Erinyes say nothing about them; and it may be observed that the one reference to the sacrifice of Iphigenia is made not by Clytemnestra but by Electra (*Choephori* 242). Moreover, if Aeschylus were thinking of ordinary dramatic plausibility, we should expect hostile references to Agamemnon from the chorus of Asian captives. This chorus does once (*Choephori* 80) refer to the destruction of the city and the bitterness of exile, but it is very far from suggesting that this was a crime which Agamemnon justly had to expiate; on the contrary, it consistently speaks of his death as a foul crime that will infallibly be avenged.

The true explanation will take us very much deeper than personal dramatic motives of this kind, but before we look for it, perhaps it would be well to justify an assertion made above, that the first part of the play is not particularly concerned with the personal tragedy of Orestes.

In this connexion a certain editorial aberration is worth considering. A surgical operation on the commos was proposed by Schütz and Weil, and accepted by Wilamowitz: the stanza 434-438 should be transferred from the position which it occupies in the MSS. to the end of the commos. Wilamowitz declared that the sense alone is enough to justify the transposition; in its traditional position it renders the stanzas that follow pointless.[1] The sense is this: Orestes, in response to Electra's description of the dishonourable burial of their father, says, 'For this dishonouring she shall pay, with the help of the gods and by my right hand; and when I have killed her, let me die.' 'This', the argument runs, 'must be the climax and the end of the commos; it is to this terrible decision that all has been leading.'

It is indeed a strong argument—if we have mistaken the nature of the drama. If we have made for ourselves, throughout the first part of the play, and particularly in the commos, an Orestes who is being subjected to the pressure of religious and other considerations, coming whether from himself or from

[1] *Interpretationen*, 205.

Electra or from the chorus, such that he can see no escape from his repugnant duty, then naturally we shall want to make this declaration of his the climax of the whole development. But if we watch what Aeschylus is doing, and put from our minds the assumption that he must necessarily be doing what any nineteenth or twentieth century dramatist would do with such a situation, then we see that such a development was no part of his design. Schadewaldt has pointed out, in an important article on this commos,[1] that nowhere in this first half of the play is there the slightest suggestion that Orestes' decision is not already firm. It is true that he is terribly shaken later, when he is face to face with Clytemnestra; but it is not for us to anticipate that, as if Aeschylus had made a mistake in not mentioning it earlier. What Aeschylus chooses to tell us here is that Orestes has received Apollo's command, which he does not and dare not question; that he has too his own personal motives in seeking vengeance. He prays to his father, to Hermes, to Zeus, to the gods above and the gods below, and his prayer is always the same—that they will be his allies in what he is going to do. Never does he pray for the guidance or for the approval of the gods. Schadewaldt is perfectly correct when he says: 'Nicht ein psychologisches Ob reizt Aischylos; er fragt nach dem faktischen Dass.' It is not the question *whether* he will do it that interests Aeschylus, but the fact that he must.

We may go further. If we would construct, out of these scenes, an Orestes who is tragically torn between the necessity and the horror of matricide, we do it with singularly little help from the dramatist. Up to the beginning of the commos there is not a single hint of it, and in the commos itself there is nothing but what we may infer from the one remark 'May I kill her and then die'; and certainly this does not bring his horror of matricide into any great prominence. If we say to ourselves 'Ah, but he *must* have been feeling this', we are in effect treating Orestes as a real person, not as a figure in Aeschylus' design; and by bringing into his design something that he has not put there, we are altering it. Obviously, we cannot remove the idea from our own minds, and we should be very silly to suppose that so elemental a thing as horror of matricide was not also present in the mind of Aeschylus; what we may not do, if we wish to

[1] *Hermes*, 1932.

understand the play, is to inject it, despite the dramatist, into
the mind of Orestes. Orestes will feel it, in due course.

A development from hesitation through conflict to a decision
is not in the picture at all. That is what I meant in calling this
part of the play 'static'; all its elements are there from the
beginning: the decision, the prayers for help, the hatred of the
murderers and usurpers, the indignation of the two children of
Agamemnon that they are excluded from their rights, the living
wrath of the dead man, their hope that this wrath will come to
their aid. I think it is true to say that the commos produces
only one thing that has not been already stated or fully implied,
and that is the statement that Clytemnestra mutilated Agamemnon's body after his death.

But this is not something urged by the chorus upon Orestes, a
new horror, for the purpose of increasing or confirming his
desire for vengeance; it is in fact part of a funeral rite—the
second, in this half of the play, which is performed to Agamemnon.[1] It is not a detail which is meant to bear directly on the
mind of Orestes, becoming, to him, the very last straw. It is a
part of the same picture that we have been contemplating since
the beginning: the crime, the dishonouring of Agamemnon, the
existing intolerable situation, the impossibility that it shall
continue for ever. She mutilated him, hoping to escape his
vengeance; the hope is vain. We see before us, in the orchestra
around Agamemnon's tomb, what the chorus calls (458) a
στάσις πάγκοινος, the 'united company' of Agamemnon's friends,
now made complete by Orestes' return; and they sing their
threefold hymn not at all for the purpose of influencing or confirming one of their number—the very form of the commos
protests against that, for it is a joint hymn—but of making
themselves heard by the spirit of Agamemnon, of imploring his
help, of paying to him at last the honours which he should have
had years before, of demonstrating their loyalty to him and so of
winning his help,[2] of exciting his wrath against his murderers,
of displaying to him the unprotected and dishonourable position
of his own children and the danger that the line of Atreus may

[1] ἔκοψα (423) is surely a momentary aorist: 'I now begin my lament.'
[2] Orestes said at the beginning (vv. 8-9) 'For I was not present, father, at
your burying'; and so Electra says, in the commos (445 ff) 'I was not present;
they shut me up like a mad dog.'

come to an end, of declaring to him and to all the gods the past and present iniquities of their common enemies.

The whole of this part of the play is devoted to the steady presentation of these and related ideas; the situation is, by implication, complete at the beginning. The dramatic movement is simply that at last Agamemnon's friends come together; that at first, in the dialogue-section, they declare their motives and their firm resolution separately, and then, in the commos, all together, with the increased intensity and solemnity which comes from lyric utterance and the use of ritual forms. Character-drawing is of the simplest. We could no doubt compile a short list of the qualities displayed by Orestes and Electra,[1] but Aeschylus has no particular interest in them, beyond the fact—the only one which matters—that here are two avengers, pure in heart, who, for this reason and that, have no choice but to punish the criminals. Certainly the idea that Orestes is being driven, or drives himself, to his dreadful decision, is an incongruous intrusion from drama of quite a different kind.

The dramatic movement that we do find here is akin to what we find elsewhere in Aeschylus—for example, in the middle parts of the *Supplices* and the *Septem*: a vertical rather than a horizontal movement. But there underlies it a tension, a contradiction, which is in the highest degree tragic: the contradiction between what is new—the pure motives of these avengers—and what is old; for the old bloody and hopeless conception of Dikê remains unabated, and is set before us time after time, both in plain statement and in imagery. Blood for blood, slay in return, a blow for a blow, this law is proclaimed throughout by the chorus; Apollo enforces it; Orestes and Electra fully accept it, except when, at the beginning, Electra asks her question 'Is this a lawful thing to ask of the gods?' It is—in this play. There is no cure (ἄκος) for bloodshed except δι' ὠμὰν ἔριν αἱματηράν, 'cruel, bloody strife' (474). In this passage we are told, with emphasis, that the cure can come only through the family. The significance of this is unmistakable—unless we dissipate our attention by directing it far outside the play to Tribal Customs and other such fascinations. If the vengeance must be inflicted, as the chorus says, by a kinsman, then the Curse in

---

[1] For example, we could say that Orestes is courageous, and cite v. 179, where the chorus says 'And how would Orestes dare to come here?'

the House can never end. The passage points forward to the
end of the trilogy, where part of the solution of the whole
problem of Dikê is that retribution for wrong-doing shall be
inflicted by the disinterested hand of the city.

But this old law, which led to chaos in the *Agamemnon*, is
restated here in imagery too, and verbal reminiscence is called
in aid. The eagle reappears: three times (247 ff, 256, 501)
Orestes and Electra call themselves the 'nestlings' of an eagle
which a serpent has destroyed. Our minds inevitably go back
to the beginning of the *Agamemnon* (49 ff). There, an eagle
robbed of its young cries to Zeus or some other god, and Zeus
sends an Erinys, ὑστερόποινον, 'bringing vengeance soon or late'.
In that case, Agamemnon was the avenger, and in his turn he
became the eagle who ripped open the body of the hare; and for
this, Artemis, with the full consent of Zeus (v. 1485) had him
destroyed—by the serpent. Now the eagle's offspring cry to
Zeus, imploring him to avenge the eagle and to protect them;
Orestes invokes against the murderess ὑστερόποινον ἄταν, 'destruction soon or late' (383). Zeus will no doubt do it, as before.
Will he also, as before, destroy the avenger? The whole cycle
promises to begin afresh, and the prospect is the more terrible
inasmuch as the new avengers are so different from the old ones.

To the same effect, Electra prays that Zeus may strike the
criminals: 'O when will the all-powerful arm of Zeus fall upon
them?' (394-395). This recalls the beginning of the second ode
of the *Agamemnon*: the sinner Paris was struck down by Zeus
—and thereafter Agamemnon, who had done the striking. Now
Electra is praying to the same god to manifest himself a third
time. Will he do it a fourth time too? Similarly, the chorus
prays that it may be theirs to sing the ὀλολυγμός, the cry of
triumph, over a man and a woman lying dead (385 ff)—the
same ὀλολυγμός that Clytemnestra sang when the fall of Troy
promised the return of her husband and her own revenge
(*Agamemnon* 587 ff and 1236); the same cry that the Erinyes
raised when she slew him. We cannot escape the question:
Will this new triumph-cry prove equally transitory?

The same thought is prompted by the prayers for Victory—
and 'victory', as Schadewaldt has observed, becomes something
of a key-word in the *Choephori*. Electra (148) invokes the help
of 'the gods and Earth and Dikê that brings Victory'. The

commos ends (478): 'Blessed gods, hear their prayer, and graciously aid them to victory.' Later, when Aegisthus has entered the palace where Orestes is awaiting him, the chorus again prays for victory:

> Zeus, now must either the bloodstained swords of the murderers lay the house of Agamemnon in final ruin, or Orestes kindle the blazing light of freedom and recover his lawful throne and his father's wealth . . . May his be the victory!

So far, Dikê the Bringer of Victory has brought victories that have been ruinous to the victors. It is a key-word not only in the *Choephori* but also in the *Agamemnon*. We cannot forget how Agamemnon returned as a victor, and entered this same palace with a prayer that his victory might endure (854); nor how, in the last line of the play, Clytemnestra said: 'We are masters now in the palace (κρατοῦντε); we will order all things well.' The victory for which the chorus now prays is associated, like the earlier ones, with a αἱματόεσσα πλαγά, the πόνος ἐγγενής, the δυσκατάπαυστον ἄλγος, of the race (466 ff):

> *Ah! the misery that clings to the race, dire bloodshed of Atê!*
> *Anguish and woe unendurable, suffering without end!*

Such, then, is the contradiction, and the tension, which underlie this static part of the play; and such is the background which Aeschylus is constructing for it; a background of seemingly unalterable law, and of gods who rule, but seem powerless to direct things to anything but chaos. Apollo has indeed promised Orestes his protection; this is the one reassurance that we can find among so much that is black and menacing.

'Electra's wish is to get married.' This is part of Thomson's comment on *Choephori* 480. Does it not jar? How can it not seem banal and incongruous in this setting? But the text justifies it—or something very like it; for at the end of the commos Electra says:

> I, father, will bring tribute to you, at my wedding, from the full dowry that I shall receive from my father's house.

If we leave it at this, that Electra is anxious to get married, we shall hardly acquit Aeschylus of mixing dramatic styles in a way which is little short of offensive. But we may not leave it at this; and in fact I have not been fair to Professor Thomson, for the note in full runs: 'As Orestes desired possession of his father's house (478), so Electra's wish is to escape servitude (155) and get married (484-485).'

How are we to take these details? Perhaps a point of some critical importance is involved. Did Aeschylus design them as bits of character-drawing? If so, what do they contribute to the characters, and through them to the play as a whole? It is perfectly natural that Electra should want to escape from servitude, and to be married—though she does not actually say that she wants the latter; it is only an inference. Why does Aeschylus introduce this trait, and that, so very distantly, in a character whom otherwise he draws in no detail at all? Is it only a very tentative approach to the much more assured character-drawing that Sophocles and Euripides were to achieve later?

No. If we trust Aeschylus, all makes both sense and good drama. He has drawn his background, and these details are a coherent part of the whole structure—provided that we do not try to take them as gratuitous character-drawing, unconnected with that structure. We might think of them in Shakespearean terms: a son disinherited, a daughter treated like a slave, robbed of her dowry, kept unmarried—these are signs that 'Degree has been shak'd', as Ulysses remarks in *Troilus*. So too is another detail, which now we can fruitfully associate with these; Orestes says (233): 'Those who should be dearest to me are my enemies.' 'Injustice', ἀδικία, prevails; injustice not only as a moral state but also as something contrary to Nature (as again Shakespeare would say); and such a thing, being the negation of Dikê, cannot persist, and must be the concern of the powers that order the Universe. Electra is not at all hinting at a desire for a husband, home and children; so personal a matter would be obtrusive and meaningless here. Her servitude, Orestes' poverty, the murder and the dishonouring of a King, his unsleeping wrath, the danger that the House may be blotted out, and Zeus fail of its rich tribute to him—all this coheres to make irresistible the demand for vengeance, for Dikê; though it is a demand which excites in us nothing but misgiving, tempered by Apollo's promise.

In all this there is certainly no lack of dramatic tension, but it is not of the kind that expresses itself in overt action, or even in conflicts or strains between or in individuals. But the second half is full of dramatic movement of this kind; here, the tragic contradiction that we have been contemplating on a cosmic scale is translated into particular terms: we see what in fact it meant to Orestes—and so does Orestes. The action moves swiftly; there are the dream, the stratagem, then a completely new character, the Nurse; the killing of Aegisthus, and of Clytemnestra; and finally the denouement. But we shall still find that Aeschylus does not manage the matricide as the unwary reader might expect; he does not try to make it an event which grows in horror within the mind of Orestes—rather, in the mind of the audience. There is no psychological preparation; instead of that, a sudden revelation, contrived by a typical stroke of Aeschylus' stage-technique.

Aeschylus begins by making the chorus-leader tell Orestes about Clytemnestra's dream: she had given birth to a serpent, and while she was suckling it, it bit her breast and drew blood. We observe Orestes' response: it is a sign which, he prays, he may fulfil; he will turn himself into a serpent (ἐκδρακοντωθείς, v. 549), and kill her. We recall that Clytemnestra has herself been likened, by Orestes, to a serpent, the serpent that killed the eagle (248 f); now he in his turn, in the unendurable world in which 'Dikê fights with Dikê, Violence (Ares) with Violence' (461); he must himself become a serpent, like his mother. Whereupon he expounds his stratagem. Nothing specific is said about Clytemnestra; the speech is mainly of Aegisthus, how he shall be killed. It is the chorus, in the ensuing ode, that lays all the weight on Clytemnestra, in comparing what she has done with the 'Lemnian crime'.

Orestes returns, knocks at the doors and asks admission to 'the House of Aegisthus'. We do not know who will answer—but it is Clytemnestra who comes to the door. The supreme crisis therefore is postponed; the absent Aegisthus must be dealt with first.

Now Aeschylus invents his new character, the Nurse. Why? She is by no means necessary. A message has to be sent to Aegisthus, but it would have been entirely consonant with the spirit and style of early Greek Tragedy if a quite impersonal agent had been invented; and further, there was no necessity that one message should be sent by Clytemnestra and a different one substituted; for had Aegisthus been simply told to come, and had come unattended, nobody would raise any question about it. But instead of being austere, in the famous Greek manner, Aeschylus sketches a character almost Shakespearean in her vividness, and arranges that the original message shall be altered, even though that involves defying the canon, laid down in many books, that the Greek chorus does not involve itself in the action. About this scene, have we said all that we should when we have remarked that the character-drawing is vivid, that the scene brightens up this part of the play, and that Greek Tragedy is obviously getting along quite nicely and will soon be positively dramatic? The scene is indeed dramatic—but upon what level?

Certain facts may be observed. One is that immediately before the appearance of the Nurse the chorus is praying, to Earth and to the Royal Tomb:

> Hear our prayers; send your aid. Now is the time for Guile ($\Pi\epsilon\iota\theta\grave{\omega}$ $\delta o\lambda\acute{\iota}a$) to descend and help Orestes; for Hermes the Deceiver, Hermes Guardian of the dead, to direct this bloody conflict.

Out comes the Nurse. The juxtaposition makes it legitimate to doubt if those critics are on the right track who hail her as one of the few comic characters in Greek tragic drama.

Then we may notice what in fact the Nurse says. The news of Orestes' death is a secret joy for Clytemnestra, but a disaster for the house, particularly for herself, the Nurse, who had lavished all her care on Orestes when he was a baby—all in vain, since he is dead. Now she must go to the hated defiler of the house with a message that will bring him joy too.

How much Sophocles was indebted to this passage only Sophocles could tell us, but in the *Electra* he writes a comparable speech at a comparable moment: the long speech that Electra makes when she supposes herself to be holding in her hands the ashes of her dead brother.[1] She says, to put it briefly:

> The loving care that I spent on you was, then, useless. One single day has blotted everything out. My father has gone, you are dead, and your death is my death. Our foes laugh, and you are a useless shade. Let me join you in death; you are nothing, and I am nothing.

Here we may find a clue in the repeated word $\dot{a}\nu\omega\phi\epsilon\lambda\acute{\eta}s$,

---

[1] I formerly took this whole scene to be simply a development of the situation and of Electra's character: 'Electra is now complete.' Not perhaps a stupid comment, but not the important one.

ἀνωφέλητος, 'useless'. If it were true that all this love, loyalty, courage were useless and brought to nothing, then we might indeed despair of life. But it is not true. Certainly, Orestes' enemies are laughing—but it is Orestes who has made them laugh, to further his own grim purpose. Sophocles is no pessimist. He makes Electra look into an abyss in which life seems meaningless, in order to suggest that it is not: Orestes has come Διὸς εὔφρονι βήματι, 'with the favouring escort of Zeus' (*Electra* 162 f), and triumph is near at hand.

In each case the false news underlines the truth, and the truth is that evil is not victorious for ever but defeats itself; and one reason why it defeats itself here is that this lowly creature, out of her loathing of the criminals, is anxious to do anything she can to defeat them. When Aegisthus does come, his first line has significance—as his first line had in the *Agamemnon*:

> I have come, not of my own accord, but upon a summons.

We recall that the summons was reshaped and delivered by those loyal to Agamemnon. Hermes the Deceiver has done his work; the divine powers are assisting the avengers. This, surely, is the real reason why Aeschylus contrived the scene:

Later, another slave in the palace, the Porter, contributes his little to this impression that Justice is working against the guilty. In something like a frenzy he calls for the doors to the womens' quarters to be opened:

> Are they deaf? asleep? Do I shout in vain? Where is Clytemnestra? What is she doing? Her neck too, I think, will soon be at the sword's edge; and justly will she fall.

We are now at the crisis of the play. Clytemnestra confronts Orestes with her cry for 'a man-slaying axe'; but she recognises that this time the Guile (δόλος) is working against her. Orestes confronts her with an ambiguous threat: 'The dead are slaying the living': ambiguous, because τοὺς τεθνηκότας, 'the dead', can mean both Orestes, reported dead, and Agamemnon, whose aid the avengers have so long and so earnestly been invoking.[1] He confronts her too with the same determination—the same unreflecting determination, one might say, if one chose to be inept —which he has shown throughout the play. Like Hamlet, he'll sweep to his revenge.

[1] So also Sophocles, in the *Electra* (1417-1421).

But Aeschylus has not been showing us an Orestes who takes no account of matricide. He has not been showing us Orestes' mind at all, in this regard; he has shown us a man who is necessarily linked with certain cosmic forces and principles; and not until this moment has the time come to translate these into human and personal terms. Clytemnestra bares to him the breast of which we have heard already—and suddenly Orestes doubts if he can play his allotted part of serpent.

At this point Aeschylus repeats, but in reverse, a powerful effect which he had used in the *Agamemnon*. There, to enforce the idea that Cassandra was the victim of Apollo, he imposed on one of his three actors an obstinate silence, and maintained it until the play seemed on the point of exploding into futility; here he does the opposite. Pylades has been on the stage, at Orestes' side, most of the time, a mute 'super', the faithful friend and companion. We have fully accepted him as such; nothing is further from our minds than that he should speak. Therefore when he does, the effect is like a thunderclap.

ORESTES: *Pylades, what am I to do? Can I kill my mother without mercy?*

PYLADES: *What then of the oracles that Apollo delivers? What of his sure and sworn ordinances? Make all mankind your enemies, but not the gods.*

The theatrical effect of this sudden breaking of an established silence is almost as if the god himself had spoken, and, as in the other instance, it makes us feel that in this trilogy the real protagonists are the gods.[1] But what the god says is intolerable —that Orestes must kill his mother, and that he has no choice but to be destroyed either by his mother's or his father's avenging Furies. Such is the conflict which the *Choephori* bequeaths to the *Eumenides*, a play in which the gods step out from the background in which they have been hitherto, and take the stage themselves.

---

[1] Professor Fraenkel gives a different explanation of these two passages: there is a canon in early Greek tragedy that no notice should be taken of a person or object on the stage until attention is drawn to him, or it, by some explicit phrase. Cassandra does not exist, theatrically, until she is mentioned. Of the many objections that could be brought against this canon the chief is that it would obliterate two of Aeschylus' most telling, and intelligible, dramatic strokes.

CHAPTER THREE

Eumenides

AT THE beginning of the *Choephori* we felt a sudden lightening of the atmosphere when we realised the new spirit in which the new avengers were going to act. But the hopes we may have had have been dashed. At the end of the play the Chorus raised its ὀλολυγμός, its 'cry of triumph', as Clytemnestra had done before, but their triumph is even more evidently hollow than hers. The *Eumenides* also begins with a great change in atmosphere, and this time the new light is one that is not to be extinguished at the end of the play.

The sombre background on which our attention has been so long concentrated is replaced by a symbol of light, purity and order; of power too, for, as the poet reminded us in his first ode, Zeus came as a conqueror. Instead of looking at the Palace of Atreus we are looking at the temple of Apollo at Delphi.[1] The Prophetess, in her opening speech, almost goes out of her way to assure us that Apollo took possession of the shrine not violently, as one story had it, but peaceably, by the free gift of Phoebe, the last Titan occupant. A smooth road to Delphi was made for him by the sons of another Olympian, Hephaestus; Zeus gave him the gift of prophecy; and Athena Pronoia (Forethought) is honoured here too, and Dionysus and Poseidon. All is peaceful, orderly, Olympian.

But the peace is soon shattered, for at one moment we see the Priestess enter the temple to discharge her holy office, and at the next she comes out again, terror-stricken, and on all-fours. Her second speech is studded, not with the names of Olympian gods, but with names taken from the remotest and most savage layer of Greek mythology—Gorgons and Harpies. The radiant

---

[1] I do not mean that Aeschylus contrived some transformation-scene here. The Elizabethan and the Chinese theatre should assure us that the imagination of the audience can be at least as effective as the resources of stage-carpenter and the electrician.

purity of the temple is defiled by loathsome creatures whose horrible aspect the Priestess can hardly describe. Moreover, the loathing and contempt with which Apollo treats them is in keeping with the terror of the Priestess. To Apollo, the Erinyes are obscene visitants from a world of darkness; his temple is no place for them; they belong to places where justice is executed with the cutting off of heads, blinding, castration, mutilation, stoning, impalement; they are a disorderly rabble, 'a flock without a shepherd' (196), and a pollution of his holy place.

As Apollo begins, so he continues: in the trial-scene (644) the Erinyes are still 'You hateful monsters, loathed by the gods.' But Apollo's part in this play is a remarkable one. It begins most impressively with a display of his power and splendour, but it ends much more modestly—so modestly indeed that it is impossible to tell where he makes his exit.

> *Sirs, count the issue of the votes aright;*
> *Divide them as you honour what is just.*
> *If judgment fail, great harm shall come of it;*
> *And oft one vote hath raised a fallen house.*

This is Apollo's last speech, but his cause does not even triumph by the 'one vote', it triumphs by an act of grace, the votes being equal. Οὔτοι προδώσω, he had assured Orestes: 'I will not forsake you.' Nor does he—but he comes as near as possible to failing, and in the light of the result the superb opening scenes seem to lose a little of their solidity. The Apollo who is so magnificent here leaves the play in silence, justified indeed, but with nothing to spare. He has 'satisfied the examiners'.

This treatment of Apollo, Apollo's treatment of the Erinyes, and the arguments he uses are all, naturally, coherent parts of one plan, and this plan is an integral part of the whole trilogy. It is necessary to emphasise this, because in the *Eumenides* there is an unusual number of openings which tempt the explorer, holes down which more than one critic has disappeared in pursuit of the White Rabbit, to find himself in a wonderland of totems, tribal customs and the like, which have nothing to do with the trilogy, and may, for all we know, not have interested Aeschylus at all.

We saw how one dominant theme in the *Choephori* was that a King and the head of a House has been murdered. Clytemnestra has delivered Agamemnon's house to an alien plunderer, and the city has fallen into the hands of a tyrant. Since the Polis is but the family writ large, the two ideas combine to make the wider picture of a threatened social structure. This is the reason why the poverty and the exile of Orestes are so often mentioned. 'My brother is an exile from his estate, while they revel greedily in what your labours amassed' (135); 'We have lost our father, and bare famine is our lot' (249); 'The god's command impels me, and my great grief for my father; moreover my own poverty oppresses me . . .[1] for my most renowned fellow-citizens not to be subjected like this to two women' (300-304); 'Lighting a flaming torch of freedom and lawful rule, he shall possess his father's great wealth' (863 ff); 'Sing triumph! our master's house is delivered from woe and the wasting of its wealth by two murderers' (942 ff). We must not speak of the charming Greek simplicity which mingles Orestes' financial embarrassments with tremendous religious issues. The wealth of the King is the natural counterpart of his royal authority. When Orestes prays to Agamemnon δὸς κράτος τῶν σῶν δόμων, 'establish me as master in your house',[2] he is praying for the renewal of order, 'degree', in the state of Argos as well as in the house of its King.

Turning again to the *Eumenides*, we may reflect how closely the Olympian deities were connected with the Polis and with the usages of civilised life: Zeus himself, Apollo Aguieus, 'god of the streets', Hermes, whose stone stood in front of houses, and who guarded the ways and the travellers who used them, and Athena Polias. Apollo, in defending the interests of the King, father and husband, is in fact defending the very fabric of civilised society. He is vindicating, like Zeus in the *Prome-heia* no doubt, the necessary principle of order and authority; and he is doing it, like Zeus in thé other trilogy, by methods that can be, and are, called tyrannical. Apollo's concern for order is clearly expressed in his speech to the Erinyes (213 ff):

You have set at naught the pledges exchanged by Zeus and Hera. By this plea of yours Aphrodite is rejected and dishonoured; and

---

[1] There must be a lacuna in the text here, though translators usually do their best by inserting an 'and' which is not there. The sense of the missing verse would be something like: 'further, I must try to end this usurpation.'
[2] *Choephori* 480.

she is the source of all that men hold most dear, for the ordained marriage of a man and a woman, guarded by Dikê, is stronger than any bond.

Marriage is the key-stone of civilised society, and if Clytemnestra's crime is not punished this key-stone is knocked away. It is the same argument that we found in the *Choephori*, to present which, Agamemnon's own sins were passed over. Agamemnon was the lawful King and the head of the house; the murder of such a man introduced an entirely new problem.

The argument is developed in the trial-scene. Orestes puts his case briefly when he says (602):

> ἀνδροκτονοῦσα πατέρ' ἐμὸν κατέκτανεν —
> *She slew her husband and my father.*

Apollo puts the case more fully (625-640):

> It is not the same thing, the death of a noble man invested with the sceptre which Zeus gives, and that too at the hands of a woman, not in war, as if with the Amazons, but treacherously . . . Such was the death of a man whom all honoured, the captain of a fleet.

It is the same argument that Orestes had used against Clytemnestra in the *Choephori* (918 ff), when her adultery came into question:

> CLYTEMNESTRA: *But remember too the wantonness of your father.*
> ORESTES: *You sat at home; do not accuse him who toiled abroad.*
> CLYTEMNESTRA: *It is a bitter thing for a wife to be kept from her husband.*
> ORESTES: *Yet it is a man's labours which sustain the woman at home.*

It would be a mistake to dismiss this as a naïve intrusion of contemporary social standards. There was no need for Aeschylus to introduce the topic, except to make his point that 'it is not the same thing'. The man is in a position of greater responsibility and therefore of authority, and he must be judged differently—exactly as Apollo judges differently the murder committed by Clytemnestra and the murder committed by Orestes. The argument is Apollo's. Aeschylus himself does not necessarily accept it as valid.

It is natural that Zeus, through his son, should vindicate the authority of the King to whom he gives the sceptre. The old instinctive working of the law of Dikê has ended in a knot which

cannot be untied: it can only be cut. Dikê is in conflict with
Dikê: Δίκα Δίκα ξυμβάλλει. The Erinyes, those ancient servants
of Dikê, could promise no way out, for if Orestes killed his
mother, then his mother's Erinyes would pursue him, while if
he did not, then his father's would. The problem is to accommodate the demands of Dikê to the requirements of ordered
society. One element in the eventual solution is provided by
Apollo and the new avengers working together, μεταίτιοι: blind
retribution through ὕβρις is renounced. It is accepted that Dikê
must be sought in purity; and because it is sought in purity,
Apollo undertakes to purify and protect his agent.

But neither have the Olympians found the way out. Order
and authority are vindicated—but at what a cost! It is the
function of the Erinyes, in contest with Apollo, to point out the
cost. Each party is defending something essential; each over-
looks something essential. Therefore neither can, or may, carry
conviction in argument, or win a majority verdict.

Aeschylus having made his bold decision to bring the divine
quarrel before a human jury, was faced with the problem of
inventing pleas for the two parties, The positive and necessary
part of each of the opposing cases must be emphasised, and so
must the negative and impossible part. We have seen how the
necessary part of Apollo's case is presented, how he is made to
appear as the champion of authority and order. The impossible
part of his case is that it was right to allow Orestes to kill his
mother. Apollo must attempt to argue this in court. The argument cannot be cogent, but it must be found. Aeschylus saw
exactly what he wanted in current biological speculation: the
only true parent is the father. We should not suppose that he
believed it, or was even interested in it. Perhaps he was; but
all we *know* is that he saw its dramatic possibilities here; it gave
apparent justification to Apollo for making the father's claim
paramount.

As for the Erinyes, the positive part of their case is quite
straight-forward: it will never do to allow sons to murder their
mothers. The negative part of their case, the impossible part,
is that the structure of civilised life is of no importance. This
too is presented partly by statement, partly by sheer spectacle.
Their savage inhuman appearance marks them as creatures
strange and indifferent to the familiar world shared by gods and

men, the world of the Polis. The intellectual presentation of this is their argument of blood-relationship: Clytemnestra's crime was as nothing when compared with the crime of Orestes, since in killing Agamemnon she was killing a 'stranger', whereas he killed one who was nearest to him in blood. It is the exact counterpart of Apollo's argument about parentage. That was chosen to show how one-sided Apollo's case is; this is chosen to show the same of the Erinyes. To disregard the mother's claims is to flout one of the deepest human instincts; conversely, to exalt the mother's relationship over the father's, and in any way to palliate what Clytemnestra has done, is to destroy the basis of civilised society. Aeschylus knew of matriarchy: he treats it as the equivalent of barbarism. It is the antithesis of the polis. As with Apollo's biological argument, we are not obliged to suppose that Aeschylus' interest in it went any further than this, that it was a convenient and dramatic rationalisation of a claim which was in part true but as a whole false. The truth will be found by combining half of each and rejecting half.

The strong part of Apollo's case is put first, with the result that Apollo's part in the play, as we have seen, tends to fade out. Apollo on Ares' Hill is perceptibly less impressive than Apollo at Delphi. But his fellow-Olympian Athena gains what he loses, and more. It is she, another embodiment of the mind of Zeus, who brings about the reconciliation and the harmonious triumph of Zeus. The manner of its doing is plain enough.

The essential point is the superior wisdom of Athena. When Apollo is confronted by the Erinyes he reviles them as obscene interlopers, and he never once recognises that they have a case at all. Their claim to an ancient office he receives with a civilised disdain:

τίς ἥδε τιμή; κόμπασον γέρας καλόν. —
What is this high privilege of which you boast? (209)

They tell him that it is to punish matricide—a statement which is later expanded to include the punishment of all wanton bloodshed (336, 421). His reply, that they ought also to punish what Apollo considers the more serious of the two acts of vengeance, misses the point. Orestes' act brings him within their jurisdiction: Clytemnestra's does not concern them. In fact, Apollo, in protecting Orestes, has gone too far. It is an en-

croachment on the domain of the Erinyes, and they denounce
it as such, in terms that recall the *Prometheus*. They denounce
the son of Zeus as a 'trickster', ἐπίκλοπος, a young god who has
trampled ancient goddesses underfoot (149 f):

> ταῦτα δρῶσιν οἱ νεώτεροι θεοί,
> κρατοῦντες τὸ πᾶν δίκας πλέον —
>
> *This is what the younger gods do,*
> *Seeking all power, beyond justice.* (163 ff)

And not for the first time; for Apollo warded off death from
Admetus, transgressing 'the old dispensation', παλαιὰς διανομάς
(723-728). 'O you younger gods, you are trampling the old
gods underfoot' (808 ff). 'This is the overthrow of ordained
law,[1] if the cause of the matricide prevails' (490 ff). It is a
perfectly clear-cut situation. The Erinyes take their stand on
ancient law, and accuse the Olympians of aggression; and to
this accusation there is no direct answer, nor can there be, for
it is true. What is obvious is that the old law, or the law as
hitherto administered, has broken down; it has led to chaos, and
has plunged Orestes into the fearful dilemma of which this
divine conflict is the counterpart. But Apollo makes no constructive reply to the accusation of the Erinyes; he treats them
with contempt, and insists on his one point, that at all costs the
King must be avenged. Here there is no hope of compromise;
no hope, that is of an orderly universe.

But Athena brings something new, and in doing it she throws
into relief the one-sidedness of Apollo. She, like him, is astonished at the appearance of the Erinyes, but, unlike him, she
treats them with studied courtesy.

They, in return, formally introduce themselves to the daughter of Zeus: 'We are the daughters of Night; in our home below
the earth we are called ᾿Αραί.' ᾿Αρά is commonly translated
'curse'; an equally accurate translation would be 'cry for vengeance'. The Erinyes of this play are the Curse or Cry for
vengeance of Clytemnestra (*Cho.* 911, 923); this is the reason
why they claim the punishment of matricide as their peculiar

---

[1] Accepting Ahrens' νόμων for νέων. Νέων would indeed be surprising here,
for it would imply that the Olympians, besides being unjust, did not even
know their own business, and defeated their own new laws in the act of
making them.

office. But they are of the same nature as the Erinyes of whom we have heard before. There are the Erinyes of Agamemnon (*Cho.* 924) whom Orestes must equally fear (*Cho.* 924); these would not punish matricide, but would pursue Orestes if he did not avenge his father. There was the Curse in the house of Atreus, which in the *Agamemnon* was identified with the Erinyes whom Cassandra could see; this was the Cry for vengeance first of Atreus then of Thyestes. Equally, the robbed eagles cried to Heaven, and the gods heard them, and sent an Erinys. They are all of the same company: this is the reason why the Erinyes in this play can declare (333 ff) that their office is to punish not matricides only but 'those guilty of wanton slaying of kindred'. This is the traditional translation of the word αὐτουργία, found in this sense only in this passage: but as it means literally 'doing a deed with one's own hands', and as some of these earlier Erinyes—the army, for example, which came to Troy 'as an Erinys'—had nothing to do with the shedding of kindred blood, it seems legitimate to doubt if this traditional translation is correct. 'Act of wanton violence' would suit the Greek as well, and the context better.

However that may be, it is as ᾽Αραί that they present themselves to Athena, and Athena receives them with dignified consideration. What is much more significant, she agrees with them in an important point. Not indeed with their methods. There is perhaps a hint of disapproval here:

ERINYES: *We drive murderers from their homes.*
ATHENA: *And where does the slayer's flight end?*
ERINYES: *Where joy can never be found.*
ATHENA: *And is your hot pursuit of this man of such a kind as that?*

But more weighty is her objection that the hunted man must be allowed to plead:

ERINYES: *Yes: he took it upon himself to kill his mother.*
ATHENA: *Fearing perhaps some countervailing wrath?*
ERINYES: *What goad so sharp as to drive a man to do this?*
ATHENA: *Two parties are here: only one has spoken.*
ERINYES: *He would not take our 'oath', nor give his own.*
ATHENA: *You claim the title of Justice, but are you doing justice?*
ERINYES: *Explain your meaning; you have wisdom enough and to spare.*
ATHENA: *Do not try to win an unjust victory by 'oaths'.*

ERINYES: *Then do you try the case, and give a straight judgment.*
ATHENA: *Would you indeed entrust the decision to me?*
ERINYES: *We would indeed, paying respect to you, as you have to us.*
(421-435)

This is a critical passage. The Erinyes cannot conceive of any justification for Orestes. That one of his motives was to vindicate authority and order in his house and city means nothing to the Erinyes of Clytemnestra, and indeed the stability of the social fabric has not been the concern of any of the Erinyes we have met: the first one plunged Greece into mourning for the sake of Dikê, and the incessant crimes of vengeance in the house of Atreus have brought it down in ruin. The Erinyes are daughters of Night, instinctive and blind.

But not only can they imagine no justification: they do not admit that justification should be taken into account. Nothing matters but the act itself. This is the point of the 'oath', ὅρκος, which binds the swearer to certain penalties if his statement is untrue. Orestes refuses to submit to this procedure, because his defence is not a denial of the act but a plea of justification. In claiming judgment forthwith, because Orestes will not accept or give an 'oath', the Erinyes are (says Athena) trying to snatch an unjust victory. Athena in fact is standing for reasoned Dikê, not blind, automatic punishment.

The last verse of the passage translated above is important; the text however is disputed. What the MSS. give, αξιαντεπαξιων, is most easily read (as by Hermann) ἄξι' ἀντ' ἐπαξίων: 'We pay you honour worthy of the honour you have paid us.' But a scholium explains: ἀξίων οὖσαν γονέων, which assuredly points to a variant ἀξίαν κἀπ' ἀξίων (Arnaldus): 'for you are worthy, and of worthy lineage.' Between the two readings one surely cannot hesitate; the former is right. There is no point in accumulating parallels to the other to show that 'You are a good man and so was your father' is a common sentiment, and that ἄξιος κἀπ' ἀξίων is an idiomatic way of expressing it. Of course it is; but we have just heard the Erinyes bitterly denouncing the Olympians, so that it would be a little surprising if they now made concessions to Athena because Zeus was her father. This reading is impossible. The other is extremely dramatic and illuminating. The Erinyes are doing something of great moment; they are abandoning their claim to instant execution of

Dikê, and submitting their case to the judgment of reason. It
is true that they are so sure of the justice of their case that they
think it makes little difference, and are exceedingly angry when
judgment goes against them. (This is still a fairly common
result of arbitration.) Nevertheless they have accepted the
principle, and their acceptance is the first sign that reconciliation
between the divine contestants is possible; or, to put the same
fact on the other plane, that a way may be found of reconciling
the Law of Dikê with the survival of human civilisation. And
what leads the Erinyes to make this concession is that they
respect Athena ἄξι' ἀντ' ἐπαξίων, as a worthy return for the
respect which she has shown to them. So that perhaps we should
say that this is not the first but the second sign that reconciliation may be possible, the first being Athena's courteous reception
of them. Apollo was indeed vindicating something that had to
be vindicated, but in far too autocratic a spirit. The reasonable-
ness of Athena at once sensibly changes the situation.

Athena does not approve of the automatic and unregulated
way in which the Erinyes pursue their victims, but in another
important matter she supports them against Apollo.

In the ode which is sung while the court is being summoned
the Erinyes say that Justice is at stake. 'There is a place for
Fear, securely seated to watch over the heart. He who fears
nothing will not be just. Accept neither anarchy nor despotism;
the middle road is always best. Hybris always comes of impiety;
prosperity comes from virtue':

> μήτ' ἀνάρχετον βίον
> μήτε δεσποτούμενον
> αἰνέσῃς.[1]

What does this mean? We must of course take it in its context,
and the context is a protest against Apollo. The ode begins:
'Now is lawful ordinance overthrown, if the cause of the matricide prevails.' The meaning of the Fear, τὸ δεινόν, is clear
enough: this it is that the Erinyes represent, the fear of certain
punishment. If Apollo has his way (so the Erinyes argue) and
the Erinyes are trampled underfoot and made impotent, then
restraint will be removed and hybris will be unchecked. Anarchy
or despotism will follow, both of these being expressions of

---

[1] *Eumenides* 526-528.

hybris—anarchy, the hybris of the many; despotism, the hybris of the few. Apollo, countenancing matricide, is flouting Law; violence, anarchy, despotism must follow.

Such is the doctrine of those whom Apollo presently denounces as 'hateful monsters', but, in spite of Apollo, and his disdain, it proves to be the doctrine of Athena too:

> This Council of Judges I establish for ever, on this Hill of Ares, on the spot where the Amazons encamped and imperilled our young city. As it was saved then, so it will be kept safe now, so long as piety and inborn Fear, ξυγγένης φόβος, restrain the city from injustice and from corrupting the purity of the laws. I bid my citizens to practise and revere neither anarchy nor despotism, and not to banish Fear, τὸ δεινόν, from the city. For what man is just, if he is afraid of nothing?' (686-702)

Apollo sees only that the authority of the King and the Father must be defended; and he would sweep away the Erinyes as uncivilised monsters; he sees that true Justice is possible only in an ordered society; and that ordered society has proved to be incompatible with Dikê as it has been pursued hitherto. Yet what Apollo is doing now is dangerous; the authority of a god can hardly be allowed to condone matricide. Athena agrees with the Erinyes in their main point, that Apollo, in his zeal to vindicate order, has overlooked something of equal importance —the instinctive fear and reverence which deters men from deeds of violence. The daughters of Night have something to contribute as well as the god of Light. Seeing this, Athena brings nearer the reconciliation not of Apollo with the Erinyes —for Apollo concedes nothing, and disappears—but of the Erinyes with Zeus.

To appreciate the significance of the Trial Scene and what immediately precedes and follows it, we may try to imagine ourselves in Aeschylus's audience as citizens of Athens.

As the Erinyes end their Binding Song, which they have danced around the fugitive in the middle of the orchestra, Athena appears. Her first words, with their reference to recent Athenian history, assure us that this is indeed Athena Polias, our own Athena. We hear the preliminary pleas, couched in dramatic and poetic form, but close enough to everyday legal process at Athens to suggest that this divine dispute about Orestes is in some way to be brought very near home. Indeed it is, for the dispute which was to be referred to Athena is by her referred to the wisdom of her wisest citizens; she will not judge, since Orestes brings no pollution with him and may not be repulsed out of hand, while the Erinyes' case is a strong one, and she will not herself bring upon her people the wrath that the Erinyes threaten if they are disappointed.

But how many judges does Athena assemble, eleven, or twelve? And in what capacity does Athena vote? Is it a casting-vote, the jury being equally divided? As Thomson says, a whole literature has sprung up around this question.[1] It is, I think, a question which is worth considering.

Thomson rightly observes that three passages in Euripides (*I.T.* 1469-1472, 965-969, and *Electra* 1265-1269) imply that twelve human jurors were equally divided, and that acquittal was secured by the casting vote of the goddess. He cites Aristeides (*Orat.* 11, 24), who says explicitly that in the *Eumenides* the votes turned out equal, and that Athena added hers and saved Orestes. The tradition, Thomson adds, is perfectly clear and consistent; what is not clear, 'in the absence of stage-directions', is 'whether Athena actually records her vote, or regards it as added symbolically to those of the judges after the result has been declared.'

It may seem reckless to suggest that this tradition is wrong, but I believe it is. We have no stage-directions, neither perhaps had Aristeides; but as it happens we have something just as good —the text; and I think it is decisive. There were eleven jurors, with Athena as the twelfth. Moreover, I think that we can see a fine dramatic point in Aeschylus' arrangement.

The text, from v. 711 to v. 733 consists of eleven couplets, except that the eleventh, in defiance of the normal Greek principle of symmetry, is a triplet. It is impossible to fit twelve human voters into the design of the text. If Aeschylus had designed a jury of twelve Athenians, with Athena as president, having a casting vote, it would certainly have occurred to him to write twelve couplets, one of them to be spoken as each jury-man approached the voting-urn. But he writes ten couplets, and then a triplet; and then Athena says 'It is now my task to give the last vote.' This makes stage-sense only if we suppose

---

[1] In his note to *Eumenides* 737-746, which conveniently summarises the evidence.

eleven citizens to be sitting with Athena. During each of the
ten couplets one citizen comes to the urn, drops his pebble, and
returns to his position. Why is the eleventh speech a triplet?
In order, I suggest, to give time for the eleventh juror to
come to the urn and go back to his seat, and then for Athena
herself to come to the urn before beginning her speech. It is
certainly impossible to suppose that Aeschylus would gratuitously have made nonsense of his stage-picture, so formal up
to this point, by having *two* human jurors vote during the
triplet.

If this is accepted, then we may ask what is, after all, the only
interesting question: Why did he do it? A jury of twelve, with
Athena as President, would seem to be the obvious arrangement
—but Aeschylus does not always do the obvious thing. We
should consider this: that Aeschylus is here putting on the stage,
effectively, the Polis, and what the Polis means, in this matter
of civilised Justice. The assembled Athenian citizens are looking
at the archetype, so to speak, of all their familiar courts of law.
Athena herself, Divine Wisdom, has convened it; and Athena
herself sits with her citizens as a member of the first jury—
θεὸς μεταίτιος, the goddess their partner. How true it is that the
Poet was the Teacher of the people! Certainly it would be no
trivial lesson, if, the next time these citizens served as jury, they
felt that the unseen goddess was one of their number, judging
in a spirit of reason and mercy.[1]

We have already sufficiently discussed the major arguments
used by each side in this dispute. They are necessarily conventional, not to say absurd, if we should consider them realistically.
Nothing but an absurd argument is possible if one has to argue
either that it is worse to kill a husband than a mother, or vice
versa. Aeschylus may not have had the slightest interest either
in matriarchal tribalism or in theories of parentage. The value
of these arguments to him here is purely dramatic: they enable
him to present the two parties to the conflict as utterly one-
sided, and irreconcilable.

But there are two subsidiary arguments which demand notice.
Apollo (625-639) speaks of the treacherous way in which Agamemnon was murdered. The Erinyes retort on him that Zeus

[1] For Athena's speech, and her reason for voting as she does, see below,
p. 85.

has little justification for being so touchy of wrong done to a father, considering what he did to his own. Apollo's reply is weak: he says only that there is remedy for imprisonment, but none for death. To which the Erinyes might have replied: Zeus has not in fact released Cronos; but the reply they do make is stronger: Death indeed is irreparable. Yet it is precisely this injury which Orestes has inflicted on his mother.

Now, why does Aeschylus make his Erinyes bring up this damaging legend about Zeus, and then fail to provide Apollo with a satisfactory answer? Thomson has suggested (in his note *ad loc.*) that Aeschylus had not yet arrived at his own answer to the question, but does give it in the (later) *Prometheia*; and that it is, in brief that Zeus himself was subject to development. That this indeed is Aeschylus' answer is, I think, beyond question, but surely it is impossible to suppose that Aeschylus had not yet thought so far. Certainly nothing prevents a dramatist from making a character ask a question to which neither the dramatist nor anyone else knows the answer. But what we have here is a forensic dispute, and if in such a dispute one party asks the other a question which he cannot answer, we immediately draw conclusions, and they will concern not the author of the play but the character who cannot answer the question. Unless Aeschylus had wanted to put Apollo into a hole, he would not have made the Erinyes ask this particular question. But he does wish, in this scene, to show Apollo to no great advantage. The strong side of Apollo's case we have seen already, in the *Choephori* and in the first scene of the *Eumenides*: now it is the turn of the Erinyes. Now we are to see that those who were presented as obscene monsters have indeed something to say for themselves, and that the majestic god does not represent the whole truth. If Apollo were given a conclusive answer to all the questions, the inconclusive verdict of the court would be unintelligible. Therefore we may not conclude that Aeschylus himself could not yet answer the Erinyes' question. In fact, we shall see ample reason presently for supposing that he could—which indeed we ought to expect.

The second of the two arguments mentioned above bears on the same point. It is in fact advanced not during the trial, but in the earlier scene (71-73), though this makes no difference. Apollo says of the Erinyes:

κακῶν δ' ἕκατι κἀγένοντ', ἐπεὶ κακόν
σκότον νέμονται Τάρταρόν θ' ὑπὸ χθονός,
μισήματ' ἀνδρῶν καὶ θεῶν 'Ολυμπίων.

*They were made for evil, and they inhabit the evil darkness of
Tartarus, hateful to men and to the gods of Olympus.*

We saw enough in the *Agamemnon* of the Erinyes and their
works to know that the first part of this is substantially true.
Yet now it appears, in the Trial scene, that these evil doers,
hated by gods and men, discharge a function without which
violence will reign and society will perish. There is a discord
here, and we will leave it unresolved until Aeschylus resolves it
for us.

But this passage raises another problem which we cannot
afford to shirk. We might say to Apollo, if he would allow us
to be so familiar: 'It is all very well for you to denounce the
Erinyes as evil denizens of Hell, but did you not, in the *Agamemnon*, for private reasons of your own, send Cassandra to
meet her death at the hands of these same Erinyes, quartered
in the palace of Atreus? And did not Zeus your father time after
time make use of these same Erinyes? How then can you say
that they are evil and made for evil deeds, without condemning
yourself, and Zeus?'

With this question goes another, which equally we may not
shirk: What relation are we to imagine between the Apollo of
the last two plays and the Apollo of the Cassandra-episode? The
Apollo of Delphi, though he does not possess all wisdom, is at
least a god of purity and light. The Apollo of the *Agamemnon*
is one whose behaviour, in contemporary Athens, would rightly
have put him within reach of the law. How can we reconcile
the two?

It has been argued by Professor Rose (*Harvard Theological
Review*, 1946) that we can draw a distinction, in Greek poetic
literature, between religion and mythology: that in a play the
dramatists' religious thinking and his mythology are, or can be,
two quite distinct elements. But this lands us into incredible
difficulties. What happens to the integrity of the work of art, if
it is not a ζῷον, a living organism, but an animal with a pack
on its back? How is an audience to distinguish between mythology which does express thought, and mythology which is simply

mythology? The difficulty of the two Apollos is great, but not as great as this.

Moreover, even if this distinction removed from our path the difficulty of the two Apollos, it would leave others which are just as great, and evidently connected with this. We should still have the problem of Zeus—for the god whose mercy and wisdom are revealed in Athena is very different from the god who avenged Menelaus by means of a bloody 'war for a wanton woman'—a war which was condemned even by the Argive Elders (*Agam.* 799 ff)—and who then, in precisely the same way, used Clytemnestra as the means of punishing his own 'minister of Justice'. We shall still have the problem of the Erinyes, who, having in the *Agamemnon* been the willing agents of Zeus, rise up in revolt against him in the *Eumenides*, and not without reason, or success. Here at least we cannot say that Aeschylus is not strenuously thinking, but only purveying mythology, for the simple reason that this particular myth was itself invented by Aeschylus.

The explanation which I believe to be the true one may seem at first sight more difficult than the difficulties which it is meant to explain. It is that the *Oresteia*, like the *Prometheia*, is based on the idea of a progressive Zeus, and of a progressive Apollo. The idea is not new (see, for example, Thomson, *Oresteia*, I, 2). But, it has not, I think, been fully argued.

It may well seem a formidable idea. The very conception of a god who, as it were, improves is foreign to our way of thinking, and even if we are persuaded that Zeus develops in the *Prometheia* from a harsh tyrant into a wise and merciful sovereign, we may well hesitate before accepting such an idea in the *Oresteia*, since the time-scale of the two trilogies is so different. On top of these general difficulties is the particular one, that whereas the *Prometheus* insists on the newness of Zeus's rule, the *Agamemnon* not only does nothing of the sort, but actually confronts us with the Hymn in which Zeus figures as the supreme god, long-established, the ultimate source of all wisdom. We may however bear in mind some of the countervailing difficulties. Zeus for example lays on Agamemnon a mission which is not only condemned by the judgment of men but is also punished by the gods, who 'are not regardless of men of blood'. We might try to persuade ourselves that Zeus was doing this, in his wisdom, in order that humanity might learn by its own mistakes, were it not for the fact that Apollo, in the same play, behaves in much the same fashion. Aeschylus was not compelled to present Cassandra as the victim of Apollo rather than of Agamemnon, nor to present so baldly the story—which Pindar would never have admitted in so crude a form—of her dealings with the god. The poet, like the citizen, must be held to have intended the natural consequence of his acts, and the natural consequence of this scene is that we find Apollo seeking revenge through blood—just like Clytemnestra herself.

The only possible alternative to the idea of a 'progressive' Zeus seems to be this, that Zeus, being all-wise, is biding his time until mankind, taught by suffering, is ready to accept his wisdom. But this is not a possible interpretation of the trilogy. I cannot see that Aeschylus anywhere suggests it, and his treatment of Apollo excludes it. One of the longest scenes in the trilogy, and the most carefully-prepared surprise in Greek drama, are dedicated to the statement that Apollo's conception of 'justice' is as violent as Clytemnestra's, so that we should have to argue that Zeus has to bide his time until Apollo too is ready to accept this higher conception of justice. Moreover, when the Erinyes rise in revolt against the 'younger gods', and protest, neither unreasonably nor without effect, against their high-handed action, it surely destroys all sense, to say nothing of dramatic tension, if, without any warrant from Aeschylus (other than the Hymn, which we have not yet properly examined), we picture in the background an omniscient, all-wise Zeus, who had foreseen all this, and its outcome, from the beginning. Besides, such a Zeus as this, having from the beginning his conception of perfect justice, but waiting until mankind—and Apollo—were ready for it, would make nonsense of Artemis. She protests against the indiscriminate slaughter involved in the plan of Zeus. If Zeus is only biding his time, we must conclude that she is being too impatient; that she intervenes only because she has not understood the deep wisdom of Zeus. But nothing in the trilogy entitles us to draw such a distinction between Zeus and the other Olympians; the distinction that is drawn is the one between the Olympians as a whole and the older deities. Artemis in fact proves to have exactly the same conception of

Justice as Zeus, even though she hates his winged hounds: she
makes it a condition that Agamemnon shall do something which
shall call into existence a 'treacherous wrath' for his destruction;
in fact, to punish Agamemnon she uses the bloodthirstiness of
Clytemnestra, just as Zeus uses the ambition and violence of
Agamemnon in order to punish Paris.

I hope to show that the idea of a 'progressive' Zeus, properly
understood, removes all these difficulties, and explains perfectly
the structure and treatment of the trilogy; further, that it is a
conception perfectly natural to Greek thought, one which would
not in the least dismay or puzzle the audience for which
Aeschylus wrote.

Let us begin by considering once more the dual plane on
which the action is so often presented. The war was, first of all,
a plan of Zeus Xenios, who 'sent' Agamemnon, like an Erinys,
to avenge in blood the wrong done by Paris to Menelaus. But
the eagles of Zeus anger Artemis: she will allow the two Kings
to proceed only on terms that will ensure the destruction of the
leader. Then we see the war as a political action on the part of
Agamemnon: he is sure that he is right, and when successful
he thanks 'the gods, his partners'; but he is quite unconscious
that he is being 'sent' by Zeus; he is an entirely autonomous
agent. The indignation of Artemis we may call the reflection,
on the divine plane, of the indignation felt by the Greeks at the
destruction of life caused by this wanton war. Her anger does
not mean that she is 'better' than Zeus, standing as champion of
a higher conception of justice; she is not an enlightened rebel;
her anger is simply the counterpart of Zeus' own plan, that
wrong shall be avenged by violence, and that in consequence the
avenger must pay.

Clytemnestra too is both the divinely appointed avenger of
the slain, and an entirely autonomous and therefore responsible
agent: murdering her husband, conspiring with her lover, and
banishing her son. She does indeed see herself as an agent of
some higher power; but it is Cassandra, the prophetess, who is
able completely to remove for us, the veil between the two
planes. Once more, her story is complete and clear on the lower
plane: Agamemnon, like a fool, brings her home, and Clytemnestra, like the vindictive, bloodthirsty woman she is, kills her.
That is all there is in it—on the human plane. But Cassandra

herself sees it on another. To her, it is all Apollo's work, Agamemnon and Clytemnestra being only his tools.

So too, the crimes of Thyestes and Atreus, continued by Aegisthus, are at once the crimes of violent men and the work of the Erinyes. And the double plane is continued in the other two plays. The new avengers show an entirely new spirit, and this they have not from any divine instruction. It is their own; it is simply something that happens. But something else happens, parallel to this: the Apollo in these plays is different from the Apollo of the *Agamemnon*. Moreover, on the human plane we see that human society is thrown into confusion by Clytemnestra's act, and that one of Orestes' compelling motives is to rescue his city from a lawless tyranny and his patrimony from a robber. This, on the divine plane, becomes Apollo's championing of the King, Father and Husband. The clash between Apollo and the Erinyes is, on the divine plane, the expression of the clash between the two complementary principles in human society, eventually reconciled, by Athena, in the forms and the ideals of the Athenian polis.

This use of two planes was not invented by Aeschylus. We find precisely the same thing in Homer, where repeatedly (as Jaeger has pointed out[1]), the same event is seen first as the result of divine action, then as the result of human effort. We find it too not only in Aeschylus but also in Sophocles and Euripides—which obviously means that it was a natural expression of Greek thought. The essence of the dual plane, or double perspective, is always the same: an action is complete and self-explanatory on the human plane, and the actors are autonomous and unprompted—except that the story may sometimes require direct divine intervention as a *terminus a quo*; but at the same time it is presented as a divine action.

As these statements may demand justification, we may examine a few typical cases, in order to see that it is a normal dramatic device, and one which is used for a very definite and important purpose. We shall see that it implies a theology rather different from the one which is sometimes attributed to the Greeks, and, I hope, that it makes the *Oresteia* completely intelligible.

We may begin with what is perhaps the clearest case, the

[1] *Paedeia*, 1, 52 (English edition).

Electra of Sophocles.[1] In this play Sophocles takes great pains to show that both by character and circumstance Electra and Orestes are impelled to seek vengeance. Being what they are, placed where they are, they can do no other. They do indeed believe that what they are doing is right, and they are confident that the gods, as well as the spirit of their father, will help them; but it is also true that Orestes cannot endure to be kept out of his patrimony, and that Electra cannot endure much longer to live with her father's murderers—nor indeed will she be allowed to, since Aegisthus will do away with her. It is not true that they are commanded by Apollo to avenge Agamemnon. Orestes goes of his own accord to Delphi, not to ask what his duty is, but to ask how he shall prosecute this just act of vengeance. The answer he receives is, virtually, 'Do it yourself, as best you can'; and this is precisely what he does, for Apollo does not assist him in any particular. There is no divine intervention whatsoever. Clytemnestra indeed has a very significant dream, but that does not help Orestes. Orestes may perhaps be considered lucky in finding Aegisthus abroad, but this is not represented as the work of a benevolent Apollo. The actors and the action are entirely autonomous, self-sufficient, self-explanatory. It would be perfectly easy to remove from the play all traces of Apollo; the play would lose nothing—except its meaning.

For though Apollo does nothing to forward the action, he does as it were accompany it on his higher plane, enlarging its reference, certifying its universal truth. Sophocles has his own way of presenting his dual plane, and a most imaginative way it is. As Orestes returns home from his long exile Clytemnestra has a dream which accurately predicts what is about to happen: Agamemnon's sceptre planted beside his hearth grows into a tree that overshadows the whole country. The dream was manifestly sent by the god. Any dramatist could have contrived this stroke; the next is Sophocles' own. Clytemnestra, thoroughly frightened by the dream, prays to the god who sent it that he will avert the omen; she prays that she may continue to enjoy what her foul crimes have won for her; and the rest of her prayer is so terrible that she dare not put it into words: 'but thou, being a god, wilt understand.' Apollo does understand.

[1] These remarks on the *Electra* and the *Oedipus* are a short restatement of what I have argued rather more fully in my *Greek Tragedy* (2nd edition).

Immediately there comes into the theatre Orestes' old slave, with his false tale which is designed to lure Clytemnestra to her death. But he was not sent by Apollo; he was sent by Orestes—we saw Orestes doing it. He was coming in any case; but his coming at this precise moment reveals the unseen hand of the god.

There is the dual plane: the autonomous human actors and the divine actor working on parallel paths. What is the meaning of it? As Jaeger says of the dual plane in Homer, it universalises the action. Orestes and Electra are doing what they feel they needs must do, and they do it without any divine prompting or help; but the fact that the god moves along with them certifies that what they think is· Dikê really is Dikê; they are not mistaken. It shows too that the action is not merely a particular event; it is a manifestation of Law. The dual plane generalises it. What Electra and Orestes do to Clytemnestra and Aegisthus is horrible, and Sophocles does not pretend that it is not, but it is Dikê, the inevitable recoil of what its victims themselves had done. This is the way in which things work. 'If the Sun should depart from its path, the Erinyes would bring it back.'

The theological implications too are important. We find it difficult not to think of the 'gods' as transcendent deities, not only all-powerful but also all-wise, beneficient, and in every other way perfect. Thinking like this we find the *Electra* puzzling. How could Apollo, a god of purity and light countenance such a thing as this? Is this Apollo a god or a devil?

He is neither, he is a θεός, and in Sophocles this may mean that he is something that resembles a law of nature rather than what we think of as a god. A θεός may typify what does happen rather than what 'ought' to happen; morality may perhaps enter into the question hardly at all. In this play, Dikê has a sense very close to the sense in which the Ionian philosophers used the word: the general balance of things. If we have a fortnight's warm and sunny weather in February the countryman shakes his head and says: 'We shall pay for this.' He believes in Dikê. Clytemnestra and Aegisthus did certain things. They had to pay for them. The elaborate study of character and circumstance which the *Electra* presents on the human plane shows us how natural and inevitable it was that they should pay; the remote Apollo who accompanies the action on the divine plane signifies

that what happens below is the working of a universal law. We
do not have to pretend that the matricide is edifying or glorious,
or that it serves some further and undisclosed divine purpose, or
that a holy god is unaccountably blind to the horror of matricide,
or that Sophocles, because he was an artist, spared himself the
responsibility of thinking.

The *Tyrannus* is built within the same philosophic framework. The oracle given to Laius and Iocasta is indeed an intervention from Heaven, but it is simply the necessary ἀρχή, a
datum. From this point onwards Apollo does nothing to influence
the action. He refuses indeed to solve Oedipus' difficulties for
him by telling him who his parents are: instead, he merely
repeats the warning already given to Laius. The god does
nothing to bring about the catastrophe. This occurs because
everybody concerned is just what he is, and not something
different. On the human plane we have a very complex web of
character and circumstance, complete in itself. Once more, we
could remove Apollo entirely—but for the original warning—
and all we should lose would be the significance. But, once
more, Sophocles makes us see the god accompanying, and fore-
seeing, the action on the higher plane; and he uses the same
means as in the *Electra*. Iocasta prays to Apollo that he will
avert what he has just said must happen, and she has her immediate answer: the Corinthian bustles in with the happy news
that Polybus is dead. We cannot help taking this as Apollo's
answer to the prayer, yet Sophocles makes a point of explaining
that this Corinthian has come not because a god has sent him—
though a god *has* sent him, as Zeus Xenios 'sent' Agamemnon
—but for very good private reasons of his own.

But if the god does not control the action, what does his
presence contribute to the play? Briefly this, that when it is
over, when we see Oedipus blind, Iocasta dead, their children
with their lives blasted, and the good intentions of the two
shepherds thus rewarded, we feel that this is not a private,
accidental horror, but part of the whole pattern of life; that in
spite of things like this—things that we can neither understand
nor justify—life is not chaos; that there *is* a λόγος, a world-order;
that Iocasta's doctrine of the random life (vv. 977-9) is false, even
though human forethought is a feeble instrument; that of this
pattern, righteousness and purity and prudence are an important

part, even though the whole is hidden from us. Apollo, in this play, is not a malignant fate who pulls the strings; the character-drawing, if nothing else, cries out against this absurdity. Nor is he a Superior Being who arranges these things for the ultimate good of mankind; Oedipus is not punished for sin, nor does his fate teach any clear moral lesson. It simply shows us what life is like; such things happen, yet Law is not disproved nor morality discredited.

It is this conception of an underlying Law that explains the prominence, in Sophocles' work, of prophecy, oracles and omens. Whether Sophocles himself believed literally in oracles is a question of merely biographical importance. What concerns his interpreter is this, that in his plays prophets can prophesy for the same reason that astronomers can prophesy: Law prevails. A prophecy is not a special and arbitrary decree—though Sophocles may on occasion[1] use it as such, if that is convenient to the mechanics of the plot; it is a prediction made by a god who, unlike men, knows all the facts and can therefore see in advance how the situation must necessarily work out. If life were random, as Iocasta says it is, then not even a god could prophesy.

Euripides uses the double plane disconcertingly (at first sight) in the *Medea*, formally and explicitly in the *Hippolytus*. If we read the *Medea* as a character-study and no more, then it is difficult not to say that the Sun sends the magic chariot to rescue the dramatist from his plot rather than to save the murderess from vengeance. If however we judge it unlikely that Euripides was incapable of winding up the plot without a miracle, and if we have come to suspect that the play is more than the study of an exciting individual, and has a much wider field of reference, then we may judge differently of the chariot: it suggests that there is in the universe something elemental, even as Medea is elemental, which does not necessarily accord with what we ourselves think just and comforting.

Misunderstanding of Euripides' use of the gods disables criticism. When the *Hippolytus* was last produced in London, one of the leading critics wrote that it is one of those grim old Greek plays which, since they represent humanity as the helpless play-things of omnipotent and capricious deities, have nothing of interest to say to us now—a criticism which, however ludicrous,

---

[1] As in the *Philoctetes*. (Below, p. 156.)

is inevitable if one makes the assumption which is natural to us that Aphrodite and Artemis are transcendent deities, outside the world of man; though it is not more ludicrous than the idea which has found favour with some scholars, that Euripides, like some adolescent atheist, was 'denouncing' these gods as an unworthy superstition—an interpretation which would leave the *Hippolytus* not a tragedy, but a pamphlet embodying a pathetic human story.

From this excursion we return to the *Oresteia* with the knowledge that the use of two planes at once was usual in serious Greek poetry, not a phenomenon that would confuse the vision of Aeschylus's audience; that the higher plane is used to universalise the action on the lower plane; and that the gods can be an immanent rather than a transcendent force. What we have not brought back with us is any knowledge of such a 'progressive' deity as we have postulated for Aeschylus. But we are now in a position to tackle this difficulty.

We have been contemplating two of Sophocles' plays and two trilogies of Aeschylus, the *Oresteia* and the fragmentary *Prometheia*. There is one general difference between the two pairs, and it is a fundamental one: we may provisionally put it thus, that Aeschylus is dynamic, Sophocles static. The *Tyrannus* and *Electra* grapple with the conditions of human life without essential reference either to place or time; the principle of Dikê in the one play, the conception of pattern or λόγος in the other, are absolute and timeless; they remind the modern reader of scientific thought. Aeschylus too, being Greek, has this same conviction that there are fundamental, unchanging laws; this is shown by the *Persae*. But in these two late trilogies he is concerned with the growth of human society within this unalterable framework. In the first play of the *Prometheia* mankind has, so to speak, just emerged from the Early Stone Age. Prometheus has taught man the arts of life; Heracles (we may surely infer) makes the world habitable for him: the reconciliation of Zeus with Prometheus implies that means are found of reconciling the necessary principles of order and authority with liberty and progress; and since the little we know of the end of the trilogy —the reception of the Athenian cult-god into Olympus—is so like the end of the *Oresteia*—the reconciliation of the ancient Erinyes with the Olympians, and their acceptance of a home in

Athens—it is permissible to infer that in this trilogy too Aeschylus saw in his own city, in his own time, the climax of a long growth and a long struggle. The Athenians now have in their hands the means of avoiding both anarchy and despotism; of combining freedom and order. In the *Oresteia* there is an unalterable framework of law: the law of Dikê, that wrong must and will be avenged, and the law that hybris breeds hybris, and issues in ruin. Within this framework we are to see how mankind struggles, morally and politically, out of chaos into security, or at least, the possibility of security, by learning how to satisfy the law of Dikê without infringing the law of hybris.

If with this we combine what we have learned about the dual plane and the function of the gods in Greek drama, the conception of a progressive Zeus becomes immediately intelligible, and the fact that Zeus and Apollo 'improve' within the space of one human generation will trouble nobody but those incorrigible realists who read poetic drama with Whittaker's *Almanac* in one hand and *Bradshaw* in the other.

Throughout the *Agamemnon* Dikê is accomplished, as it must be; but only through hybris. This is put to us on the two levels, which are distinct, but will sometimes make contact. On the human level, Agamemnon, quite unprompted by Zeus, begins a reckless war for 'a willing wanton'. The bloodshed caused such indignation in Greece that the chorus fears 'something done under cover of night' (459 ff), for 'the gods are not regardless of men who shed blood'. What the chorus fears is obviously something like a political assassination. He is murdered, though by private, not public enemies, and their hybris is worse than his.

All these events have their counterpart on the divine plane. Aeschylus takes some trouble to tell us that the war 'for a wanton woman', with its destruction of life, was planned by Zeus, in order that Dikê might be exacted from Paris (40-71). But although Zeus planned this, 'the gods are not regardless of men who shed blood'; an Erinys awaits them (461 ff). This plan of Zeus, which will involve both Greeks and Trojans in many a struggle, as the lances are shivered in the first onset (63-67), will necessarily involve his agent in retribution. Hence, on the divine plane, the anger of Artemis against 'the winged hounds of her father'. We may say that she is in revolt against Zeus, but we may not think of her as a rebel; Aeschylus never says another word about her, and the rest of the play consistently implies that what is done to Agamemnon is done according to the plan of Zeus. The gods punish men of blood; Clytemnestra is as much the agent of Zeus—and of Apollo—as Agamemnon had been; Zeus threw his net over Troy (355-361), and Clytemnestra throws a net over Agamemnon. Artemis is not a rebel; as we have seen already,[1] she has the same conception of Dikê as Zeus. She is, so to speak, an extension of Zeus. His plan is already self-contradictory inasmuch as it must involve his agent in destruction; the anger of Artemis is simply one limb of this contradiction. It is 'the gods' collectively who punish men of blood, not Artemis who does it against the will of Zeus. What the anger of Artemis does is, first, to make it clear to us, even if not to Agamemnon, what manner of thing he is proposing to do; second, to ensure that he shall be destroyed through the Wrath which this bloody deed will create; and third, to make it quite plain that the gods are using the wrath and the guilty passions of Clytemnestra as their agent, even as Zeus employed the folly of Agamemnon. The resentment of Artemis is the counterpart, on the divine plane, of the anger felt by Clytemnestra at the sacrifice of her innocent daughter and the anger of the Greeks at the slaughter of their men.

The dual plane has the same function here as in Sophocles and Euripides and (occasionally at least) Homer: it is the poet's way of universalising the particular event. What we are dealing with is nothing less than a universal conception of 'justice'—though a disastrous one: 'justice' pursued through blind retaliation.

Apollo's treatment of Cassandra is the climax of this universalising statement; the consummate dramaturgy of Aeschylus here, once it is understood and not mistaken for incompetence, brings the two planes so close together that they become one. If Euripides had written a play in which Apollo carnally desired a woman, bribed her, and then, when she recoiled, punished her first by annulling his gift of prophecy and then by having her appropriated as concubine by Agamemnon and murdered by his wife, we should never have heard the last of it: the play would have been hailed, or denounced, as Euripides' most savage and outspoken attack on an effete and immoral Olympian reli-

[1] Above, pp. 5, 70 f.

gion; but as it is Aeschylus who presents all these facts, quite explicitly and with considerable power, nobody seems to mind. Of course Aeschylus is not attacking a conventional religion; he had more important things to do—and so had Euripides. We must think of this Apollo as we thought of Apollo in the *Electra*, as the embodiment of a universal principle—though not, in this case an eternal one, for there is to come a higher conception of Justice which will sweep away this blind and crude system; and this advance too will naturally be represented on both planes. But meanwhile Apollo avenges himself in the same spirit as Agamemnon, Clytemnestra and Aegisthus, and as it happens he uses the same foul instrument as Zeus and Artemis.

The *Agamemnon*, then, pictures a world of moral violence ending in social and political chaos, and this chaos and violence involves the gods as well as men. It is emphatically not the case that the gods have higher ideas towards which they are waiting to lead mankind. But does not the Hymn to Zeus say the opposite? So much has been said, and justly, about the 'Hebraic intensity' of this Hymn, placed by Aeschylus at the very beginning of this chaos, that it becomes necessary to examine it carefully, and to see that its Hebraic intensity does not imply any Hebraic theology.

'Zeus, whoever he is, if that name is acceptable to him, by that name I call him.' Clearly, Aeschylus is no simple believer in a personal deity: the name 'Zeus' is simply the best symbol he can find to represent what he means. 'When I weigh all things I can form no image but Zeus, if a man is to rid himself of his baffling anxiety.' That is to say, it is Zeus, 'whoever he is', who is the sole warrant for not despairing among all the πόνοι, woes, that surround us, in this play as in life itself.

The next stanza abruptly reminds us of the difference between the supreme Greek god and the God of the Hebrews, who is from everlasting to everlasting. There was a time when Zeus was not. He came as a conqueror; his predecessors, unnamed though not unknown, are as if they never had been. To acclaim the triumph of Zeus, that is the sum of wisdom.

As to this stanza, if we can believe that Aeschylus, or any other serious Greek poet, recited myth in a spirit of pious commemoration without meaning by it anything in particular, we shall raise our hats politely and pass on. If we think however that this is a misconception both of mythology and of the poets, we shall not pass on so quickly. We shall reflect that since the first stanza virtually dismissed the Zeus of legend, Aeschylus is not likely to continue in mythological vein unless the mythology means something to him. But what does it mean? He is telling us that Zeus, supreme in power, has remained firm in the seat from which his two predecessors were flung headlong, and that Zeus is the only refuge from the oppressive burden of thought. Why so? Did Zeus come as the perfect god, not only all-powerful but also all-wise and all-knowing? If he did, Aeschylus does not say so, nor could he, without contradicting what he makes Zeus do in the rest of the play. What he does say is that Zeus, 'whoever he is', 'opened the road for man to become wise', by establishing the law that out of suffering shall come understanding. Pain keeps a man awake at night, reminding him of his hurt, and prudence comes to him in his own despite. The favours that Heaven gives are not given easily.

Before proceeding, we should observe that this has no reference to any individual person in the trilogy. Agamemnon, for instance, has little opportunity to lie awake at night and to understand at last where he went wrong. The reference can only be a universal one.

Zeus 'opened the road for man to become wise'. Clearly, it is in this, as well as in his power, that he surpassed his unnamed predecessors. Under their dispensation, we may conclude, suffering led to nothing, but was barren; under Zeus, it leads to wisdom.

Now, Aeschylus was not trying to create a system of speculative theology. In this play he was addressing his fellow-citizens —nearly twenty thousand of them. By this religious symbolism, which he has told us *is* symbolism, he presumably meant something of direct importance to his audience. The interpreter of symbols can make their meaning clear only at the risk of contracting their significance, but this is a risk that the critic cannot avoid. We repeat the question therefore: what does this mythology mean?

We know where the trilogy ends: in the institution of the Court of the Areopagus, and, on the divine plane, in the acceptance by the ancient Erinyes of the new ordinances of Zeus. The conflict between the Law of Dikê and the Law of Hybris is resolved in the ordered system of the Polis, for now Retribution can be administered without moral guilt and violence. We may remind ourselves that such a Polis which had come to witness the *Oresteia* was a relatively new thing in human history; it was the summit, so far, of human achievement: spiritual, moral, intellectual, political. Not that Aeschylus was complacent about it, for the closing scenes of the *Eumenides* are full of warnings against that moral violence which this earthly *Civitas Dei* was designed to supersede. In the *Prometheia*, it seems, Aeschylus looked back over the whole range of human civilisation, from its present triumphs to the time when mankind was no more than a weak and ignorant child; in the *Oresteia* his concern is with a specific but fundamental aspect of this advance: the problem of Dikê is solved, in the mature Polis, if men will, under the awful sanctions of the Eumenides, match its high conceptions with their own conduct. Again the poet is looking back: past ages have been long, and the stable Polis is relatively new; how has it come about? Aeschylus, being a poet and not a sociologist, speaks in myth. He reminds us that there were earlier gods; that these were swept away by Zeus the Conqueror; that Zeus brought with him the law that wisdom should come out of suffering. So at last, wisdom being accessible to man, progress became possible. These two facts, the coming of Zeus and the new ability of man—of *Greek* man—to learn, are each the counterpart of the other in this double perspective. As in the other poets, the god is no external, transcendent power, but an immanent force or principle; in this case, the force, 'whatever it is', which has led man out of chaos into order. It is prefigured therefore as a progressive deity.

So that there is no contradiction at all between the Zeus of the Hymn and the crude Zeus Xenios of the rest of the play, or Apollo who vindictively destroys Cassandra, or the merciful Artemis whose mercy is slaked by the bloody revenge of an adulteress; because the Zeus of the Hymn is not the ultimate wisdom, only the possibility of wisdom. At this stage the ultimate wisdom is not to be expected in the actions of the gods, for it is yet the universal principle that crime is punished by the blind retaliation of the party injured. Nevertheless, mankind can learn from its errors, and the expression of this on the divine plane is Zeus Teleios, 'Zeus who brings fulfilment'.

We have already observed, among the new features which the *Choephori* displays, that Apollo is different, and that the spirit of the new avengers is different. We must now observe that these two features are presented quite independently, and that this is entirely consonant with the theology which we have been using. It is nowhere suggested that the disinterestedness and the piety of Electra and Orestes are due to the guidance or the prompting, still less the direct command of the god, whether of Zeus or Apollo. We merely find an Orestes who is undertaking his task not in ὕβρις but as an inescapable and repugnant duty—and is informed by Apollo simply what the consequences of either action will be: we find too an Electra who prays that she may be more 'wise', σωφρονεστέρα, than her mother, and purer in action. This new spirit, as it were, simply happens. We are compelled to see it as part of a general movement which culminates in the last scene of the *Eumenides*, when the Erinyes, now the Kindly Ones, promise blessings to the people of Attica:

σωφρονοῦντες ἐν χρόνῳ —
Wise at last (Eum. 1000).

All this means that the 'double perspective' is being continued. The difference between the two Apollos is exactly parallel to the difference between the two sets of avengers, those of the *Agamemnon* and those of the *Choephori*. What Aeschylus is doing is, as it were, to condense into this Orestes-legend his conception of the gradual achievement of true Justice, or rather, the possibility of it. In the *Choephori* mankind has sufficiently 'learned by suffering' to break free from the apparently endless chain of retribution by Hybris that binds everybody in the *Agamemnon*; it has learned that Dikê must be sought in purity of spirit. On the lower plane this advance is exemplified in Orestes and Electra; on the higher, it is exemplified in the god of Delphi, pure as they are pure; a god therefore who will purify and protect his agents instead of destroying them, as did Zeus in the *Agamemnon*. If anyone should object that such changes do not come about in this clear-cut way, nor within the space of one generation, it would be possible to make a long reply or a short one. The short reply would be 'Poetic drama was not intended for *you*.'

But something more than a new spirit is necessary if the

absolute law of Dikê is to be reconciled with what the innocent Greeks thought 'social security' to be. A new political idea is as necessary as the new moral idea. Orestes' duty may be inescapable, but it is still intolerable. It may be his bounden duty to avenge his father, the King, and to rescue both himself and his city from the hands of interlopers and usurpers; it may be a necessary step in the establishment of true Justice that order and authority should be vindicated in this violent way; but it cannot be a permanent solution that the vindication of order should be left to an individual. The cost to him is too great, and it may—as it does in this case—conflict with even more sacred and necessary obligations.

This too we see in double perspective. What is, on the one plane, the intolerable dilemma of Orestes, compelled to satisfy Dikê by matricide, becomes on the other plane the desperate conflict between Apollo and the Erinyes, each of them the champion of something that is necessary, each neglecting something that is necessary. Apollo's defence of the male is a defence of the authority and stability of the fabric of society. His disregard of the female, of the mother, threatens society in another way, and justly exposes him to the implicit charge which the Erinyes bring against him, the charge of countenancing despotism and anarchy: for it is despotism if authority is so to trample upon instinctive sanctities, and anarchy if such violence is not to be punished and suppressed. The Erinyes' defence of the mother is a defence of these instinctive sanctities, outraged by Apollo, which must be an essential part of Justice. On the other hand, the Erinyes do not promise, as Apollo does, what must be another essential part of Justice, namely that it shall be final, and that he who executes it shall be secure.

To the two powers arrayed in conflict—the civilised, forward-looking god of Delphi, and the immemorial Erinyes, as old as the universe itself,—is added a third: Athena; and it is noteworthy that she does not decide the conflict on her own authority. The responsibility must be left to the Athenian people. Once again, the θεός is μεταίτιος. What Athena does is to institute the means of resolving the issue, the most acute conflict of Dikê that can possibly arise.

What we have seen already, in this trilogy and elsewhere, of the significance of divine action will enable us to interpret

Aeschylus' symbolism in security, if we wish to. Athena—ἥτις
ποτ' ἐστίν—establishes that Court which surely we must take
as being, firstly, the Court of the Areopagus, and secondly as
the type of all Athenian courts of law, where disputes are sub-
mitted to reasoned judgment, and where punishment, when it
is necessary, is inflicted not by the party who has been wronged,
but by the impersonal hand of the 'judge', δικαστής.

These institutions of the ordered Polis are the indispensable
condition of Justice. That is the reason why Athena votes for
Orestes, and is given a reason for so voting which may seem
frivolous but is in fact very serious. She votes for the male
because she had no mother: that is to say, although she recognises to the full the strength of the Erinyes' case, she recognises
too that the authority of the social order is logically prior. No
instinctive Justice can be successfully defended if society itself
is in chaos.

This being established, by the equal vote which acquits
Orestes, Apollo disappears without a word. He is now superseded, as Zeus Xenios and his methods have been superseded.
Now Athena addresses herself to his opponents—and in terms
which make it clear that the question of homicide is the occasion
but not the substance of the dispute. The climax of the trilogy
is not the institution of the Court of the Areopagus, but the
migration of the Erinyes from their old home in the darkness
of Tartarus (*Eum.* 72) to their new home in the soil of Attica,
and their conversion from blind and bloodthirsty persecutors
(*Eum.* 186 ff) into awful defenders of that true Justice which is
the only source of spiritual and material well-being. In particular, when they consent to enter the civilised structure which
is the especial care of the Olympian gods, their special function
of avenging bloodshed within the family is enlarged; it is made
to include acts of violence within the Polis. As Athena says, in
a preposterous verse which too many editors accept without
comment:

θυραῖος ἔστω πόλεμος, οὐ μόλις παρών —
Let war be with foreign foes, not hardly present (*Eum.* 864)

which is not Aeschylus' way, nor anyone else's, of saying 'not domestic strife'. The Erinyes themselves later invoke this blessing
upon Attica in language that is redolent of the *Agamemnon*:

τὰν δ' ἄπληστον κακῶν
μήποτ' ἐν πόλει στάσιν
τᾷδ' ἐπεύχομαι βρέμειν·
μηδὲ πιοῦσα κόνις μέλαν αἷμα πολιτᾶν
δι' ὀργὰν ποινὰς
ἀντιφόνους ἄτας
ἁρπαλίσαι πόλεως.
χάρματα δ' ἀντιδίδοιεν
κοινοφιλεῖ διανοίᾳ,
καὶ στυγεῖν μιᾷ φρενί.
πολλῶν γὰρ τόδ' ἐν βροτοῖς ἄκος.

I pray that civil strife with its endless misery may never rage in this city; nor may the dust drink the dark blood of the citizens and then, greedy for requital, demand from the city destruction to avenge slaughter. May they exchange joys in common love, and hate with a common hatred. This is the healing of many woes among men.

Their function now is 'to dispense all that concerns man':

πάντα γὰρ αὗται τὰ κατ' ἀνθρώπους
ἔλαχον διέπειν.

He who reveres them will prosper; on the impious, who do not, they will inflict sudden disaster—unless this is reserved for their descendants (930-937). The Erinyes have great power among the gods of Olympus, the gods of the Underworld, and mankind: the rift between them and Zeus is closed, and they are once more his Ministers of Justice. Only it is a much profounder Dikê, not mere retribution. Persuasion has prevailed; Zeus Ἀγόραιος, Zeus the eloquent speaker, has conquered (970-973).

In fact, not only has Zeus 'progressed', but the Erinyes too, both of them reflecting on the divine plane the advance that has taken place on the human plane, and they meet once more in a conception of Dikê which is much wider and deeper than the old one which they carried out in concert. No longer is it blind retribution; it is now Justice, rooted in holiness, governed by reason, defended by awe of its august protectors. This is the fruit of the law established by Zeus, that suffering shall bring wisdom. Now, on condition that the Athenians revere their new divine partners, blessings of every kind will be theirs. Mankind has found light, healing, release, ἀπαλλαγὴ πόνων. Zeus *is* 'the Achiever', Τέλειος.

CHAPTER FOUR

Philoctetes

ROM the *Oresteia* to the *Philoctetes* may seem to be a desperate leap, but there is a reason for making it. If there is
anything of value in the foregoing treatment of the *Oresteia*
it was arrived at by following a very simple hypothesis, namely
that Aeschylus knew what he was doing, and that everything
that he does in the trilogy is a logical part of a coherent plan.
But Aeschylus is not the only Greek dramatist who does things
which, at first sight, seem odd, and which tempt the critic to
propose *ad hoc* explanations, such as incompetence on the part
of the dramatist, or the hampering effect of tradition, or of the
theatrical conditions. Sophocles does nothing so startling as
what Aeschylus does with Cassandra, but he does many things
which, calmly considered, are even more difficult to explain
away. Considering what renown he has always enjoyed as a
master of construction, he makes a surprising number of elementary mistakes. He allows the *Ajax* and the *Trachiniae* to
fall into two distinct parts, and it does not occur to him to
tighten the unity of the *Antigone* by bringing back the heroine's
body with Haemon's, at the end of the play. In the *Antigone*
there is also the problem of the Second Burial, for which some
surprising solutions have been proposed. The *Tyrannus* has its
well-known 'irrationality' which attracted the notice of Aristotle.
In the *Coloneus* there is the curious uncertainty about the
banishment of Oedipus from Thebes: four references to it, each
of them implying a slightly different version of the event.
Finally, there is the *Philoctetes*, which is just as uncertain about
something much more important to the play, namely the exact
terms of the oracle about the taking of Troy. Only the *Electra*
has escaped criticism on the grounds of construction—for the
casual, and perfectly natural, anachronism about the Pythian
Games is different from these constructional blemishes.

It is surely a remarkable list; and if it should be objected that

one or two items are so unimportant as hardly to be worth
mentioning, the answer is that it is precisely the unimportant
ones which are difficult to understand. In the matter of Oedipus' banishment, for example, what could be more natural than
that the dramatist should imagine one version of the event, and
stick to it? Or that, in beginning to work on his *Philoctetes*, he
should first make clear to himself, and subsequently to his
audience, what the terms of the oracle were? But in any case it
is not merely that Sophocles is not logical about matters that
might be thought 'outside the play'; in matters within the play
he can show himself apparently quite indifferent to Aristotle's
law of 'logical sequence' (κατὰ τὸ εἰκὸς ἢ τὸ ἀναγκαῖον). If there
were only one instance of this, as, for example, the second burial
in the *Antigone*, one might be disposed to accept a mechanical
explanation—that Sophocles, for once, made a blunder, or that
the present play is a revision of an earlier draft incompletely
carried out. But as nearly every plot contains something to be
explained away, the number and variety of these *ad hoc* explanations would become alarming. One explanation is better
than a dozen different ones, and in fact one explanation seems
to suffice. Once more, it involves the assumption, perhaps not
too extravagant, that the dramatist knew precisely what he was
doing, and why he was doing it.

We censure this or that detail in a play as being ἄλογον,
'irrational': what is the λόγος, 'logic' against which the detail
offends? Presumably it is the logic of ordinary life. Aristotle
finds it 'irrational' that Oedipus should now for the first time
relate his past history to Iocasta: in ordinary life he would have
done this long before. Aristotle's rather uneasy defence is that
this ἀλογία concerns something which is ἔξω τοῦ δράματος,
outside the play, or, outside the plot.[1] But is it? We cannot in
fact draw a circle around the play, or its action, and say that
everything inside the circle is 'within the play' and everything
else is 'outside the play'. Everything that is implied by the play
is in the play, and if Aristotle's rules of logic are to prevail, they
should prevail over what is implied just as much as over what
is actually done on the stage. To a limited extent Aristotle's
defence of this ἀλογία is valid. He says elsewhere[2] that there are
improbabilities (such as Achilles' pursuit of Hector) which may

[1] *Poetics* 1454 b 8.　　[2] *Poetics* 1460 b 14.

be successfully narrated, although they could not possibly be acted. In this sense the silence of Oedipus is indeed 'outside the the action'; it is more acceptable in the existing play than it would be if we saw him being silent in circumstances in which he would naturally speak. But this does not touch the heart of the matter; it says only that the ἀλογία might have been much worse. The real problem is that time after time Sophocles does 'irrational' things, that some of them are in no sense 'outside the play', and that most of them could have been avoided very easily indeed. We can go further: some of them are obviously contrived, with great care. My argument indeed will be that all are. An illogicality that is obviously contrived is the one in the *Coloneus*. Méridier points out (ed. Budé, p. 149) that at v. 367 Oedipus' two sons had no royal authority when Oedipus was banished; at v. 427 it is implied that they acquiesced in the banishment; at v. 599 Eteocles and Polyneices are jointly responsible: finally, at v. 1354, Polyneices alone is responsible. As Méridier says, 'La progression est trop regulière pour ne pas être calculée'[1] and he adds 'A la représentation elle ne risquait guère d'être aperçue'; which is a point to which we shall return.

Here, in the *Coloneus*, we have an ἀλογία which, though not 'outside the play' in any real sense, is at least on the outskirts of the action. Since Sophocles seems to have been so careful about this one, it is not enough to say, about an ἀλογία which is very near the centre of another play, that it does not matter much because it is 'outside the play'.

The source of the difficulty is that we are thinking of the wrong *logos*—the logic of ordinary life and not the logic of artistic representation. The two may roughly coincide: how far they should coincide is a matter of judgment, or of fashion; but they are not identical. A work of art is something designed for a particular end—to express a certain conception, or mood. This conception (for students of Greek drama need not worry much about moods) is the logic of the work, and this is the logic which the dramatist obeys. The fact is demonstrable, and I hope to demonstrate it in what follows. How far the logic of the work may diverge from the logic of ordinary life is a matter for the artist's judgment to determine; the more powerful the artist, the further he may safely diverge, for the simple reason that

[1] See also my *Greek Tragedy*, pp. 395 f.

the more powerful the artist is, the more successfully can he impose the logic of his work on the mind of his audience. If the hearer, or beholder, will in no case accept divergence from the logic of ordinary life, then let him stick to Landseer and be happy.

These illogicalities in Sophocles have something in common with distortion in painting, for distortion is also a divergence from the logic of ordinary life in the higher interests of the design of the picture. To take a familiar example from a 'modernistic' painter, the one who designed the Cup-bearer frieze at Cnossos. This painter gives the cup-bearer a quite impossible twist at the hips, and the result is a parallelogram— back, arm, hips and cup—which gives the design its impressive strength. This man was a designer, not a photographer—and so was Sophocles. When we look at the painting we do not ask ourselves what hip-disease or what dislocation the cup-bearer was suffering from. We do not look outside the painting at all, for an explanation of its form; we allow the design to make its own effect, and assume that the painter knew what he was doing, since he seems to have been quite competent at drawing.

Surely we should do the same with Sophocles, if we have reason to think that he too was competent. If a clever sixth-form boy should point out how Sophocles might have bettered his plot here or there, we ought not too hastily assume that he has seen something which was hidden from Sophocles; rather, that there is a significance in the total design of the play which the impetuous critic has not yet seen, and that the illogicality is a necessary part of it. If this is so, it may not be a bad idea to consider the illogicalities carefully. They are details of the design which challenge our understanding, if we care to approach the plays as critics; and if they appear to be purposeful distortions, logical parts of the complete design, then we shall know what the play is about. We may of course find that the play 'means' what everybody has always supposed it to mean, but even so we shall have gained a little, if we can show how intimately the meaning and the structure interlock.

But in fact there are few plays in which everybody has always found the same meaning. Bowra has said, 'There is uncertainty about almost every play of Sophocles, not merely about matters of language and text, but about the whole meaning of an episode or even of a play.'[1] This is true, and, I think, unnecessary. The more extravagant interpretations give the impression that the critic has used the play as mere raw material, determined to make it mean what he would like it to mean. Others have obviously been influenced by transient fashion; and the fact that one interpretation is succeeded by a quite different one is cited to prove that 'the play is still alive'—a metaphor which no doubt conveys some truth, though to enquire how much would take us too far from the *Philoctetes*. Perhaps there are two separate questions: What does the play mean to this generation? and, What did it mean to the dramatist and his generation? The answer to the first must be indeterminate; the answer to the second, in the nature of the case, can never be exact, but the area of eccentricity can be much reduced, if we will give proper attention to Form. Bowra declares that in order to understand the classical Greek drama we must seek to understand fifth-century Greek ideas as fully as possible. It is, I suppose, the chief contribution that present-day scholarship has made to the understanding of art, that it has tried to set it in its contemporary intellectual and social context. This is the contribution which scholarship ought to make; but scholarship should remember that it is *only* a contribution; the interpretation of art is not itself a work of scholarship but of criticism, and when the critic has absorbed what scholarship can tell him, he still has all his work to do. Indeed, I am not sure if the critic, even though he worked independently of scholarship, could not in the end tell the scholar more about fifth-century Greek ideas than the scholar could tell him about the play. His task would naturally be more difficult without scholarship than with it, but, at least ideally, it would be possible for him, after he had pondered on the style and form of the drama as being the outward expression of its inner meaning, to say: In matters concerning Man, and the Gods, the nature of the Universe and of human life, this and this and this are what Sophocles meant and expected his audience to understand.

Some, no doubt, will think that the following chapters on three plays of Sophocles rest on the tiresome old assumption that a Greek artist is necessarily perfect. They do not. They do assume, as I have already suggested, that Sophocles was at least

[1] *Sophoclean Tragedy*, p. 2.

as competent a technician as, say, Pinero; and this, I think, is not too wild an assumption to serve as a working hypothesis. My submission is that it does work—and that, I hope, without any kind of special pleading. To assume the perfection of the plays as an axiom would of course be unscientific, but if it emerges as a result of inspection, why should we be incredulous? We have a small selection, made apparently not without intelligence, from the works of those three dramatists who, in the judgment of their contemporaries, stood head and shoulders above the scores of other dramatists writing at that time. If we had a selection of seven of Bach's works, seven of Mozart's, and seventeen of Beethoven's, and competent critics declared them flawless, should we smile? On this point (as on many others) Donald Tovey is worth quoting.[1] He observes that there is nothing in the nature of art that makes absolute perfection impossible, seeing that all its material is invented by, and is under the control of, the artist; and that perfection is in fact the normal condition of such art that possesses permanent value. We are indeed astonished, but we have no right to be incredulous, when those who know expound the extreme virtuosity in composition displayed in a work like the Goldberg Variations of Bach (which are also extremely beautiful); what reason have we for expecting a lower standard of integrity and skill from Sophocles? That he wrote dull and perfunctory plays is likely enough; some of Beethoven's large output is dull—perhaps some even of Bach's. What would be surprising is that either of these composers should make elementary blunders in form or technique which an intelligent music-student could at once remove. In fact, analogy suggests that it is in the greatest plays that we should expect not only the greatest skill and care in technique, but the greatest daring too; it is the pressure of great ideas and intense feeling that stimulate the artist's technical resource to the uttermost—except in periods when the artists have had nothing of great importance to say, and have in consequence exploited technique for its own sake.

We need not then be nervous if we make considerable drafts on Sophocles' credit as an artist; his credit is very good. If it appears that every single detail in a play, like every single detail in a Mozart symphony, or in the Parthenon, is a significant

[1] *The Integrity of Music* (Oxford, 1941), pp. 6, 13, 18.

part of a coherent and intelligible design, I for one see no reason
to take fright.

Writing on the double-burial in the *Antigone* Dr Rouse said:
'If I were a Homeric critic I should now pitilessly cut out all
that relates to the first burial, and point in triumph to the later
part of the play, where nobody ever mentions two burials. Not
a word in the dialogue of Creon, Ismene and Antigone need be
altered if there were only one burial. Surely this is a clear case
of a Dunciad within the Antoniad; and how happy we shall all
be when the malignant growth is cut away, although it contains
some beautiful passages, well worthy of Sophocles. Another
Sophocles—or was it Socrates? no matter—is mentioned in
Apuleius's *Golden Ass*; perhaps he wrote them, and Pisistratus
put them in, with his well-known mania for editing.'[1]

It would be even greater fun to turn certain Homeric critics
loose on the *Philoctetes*—and for that matter it would have been
interesting to hear realistic critics like Dr Rouse explain it: for
in two respects, one of them at least important, the plot is
almost inconceivably illogical. To prove this statement, we will
go through the play with our attention fixed on two things
only: the prophecy about the capture of Troy, and the history
of Philoctetes' malady. In doing this we shall of course be doing
something which, in one sense, is both illegitimate and silly.
The reader will understand this, but as certain Homerists may
not, I will explain. Sophocles did not write the *Philoctetes* for
me, sitting in my study, with a microscope, but for the Athenian
people, sitting in the sunshine, with a wide spectacle of theatre,
mountains and sky before their eyes. More important still: he
did not write for people who either would or could do what we
are about to do; for we are going to neglect entirely the dramatic
picture that Sophocles unrolls before us, in order to watch
narrowly two details in this picture. A dramatist who knows his
business can direct the attention of his audience to what quarter
he will; a reader, if he chooses, can look somewhere else—as
many readers habitually do, because they find it either easier or
more interesting. We however shall be doing this quite deliberately, for a set purpose; and the purpose is to show how
'illogical' the plot is in these two particulars.

[1] *Classical Review*, XXV, 41.

When we have done that, we shall stand back and contemplate the situation. We shall see that the illogicalities are there not because there was any difficulty in making a tidy plot out of the material used. We shall find, on the contrary, that they are essential parts of a coherent plan, very carefully designed, to the minutest detail; and when we have found the interpretation of the play—and there is likely to be only one such—which explains why Sophocles did these illogical things (as well as the other things that he does in the play), we shall know what the play is about; the examination of the form will have established, for us, its meaning.

I say deliberately 'for us', because the meaning was presumably plain at first sight to those for whom Sophocles wrote. But we, not being fifth-century Athenians, are under certain disadvantages. The world has changed considerably, and has found dramatic interest in themes which did not especially interest the Greeks. We think, for example, that a play can be simply a study of individual character, as it obviously can; and therefore, seeing character-study in a Greek play—and often greatly exaggerating it—we may bend our gaze on this and see nothing else, as indeed I myself did in an earlier criticism of the *Philoctetes*.[1] Or, since our approach to these plays is naturally apt to be bookish and literary, we may assume that their writers too were bookish and literary; that Sophocles wrote one of his plays in order to show Euripides how he ought to have written one of his. Or, because we have constructed out of Sophocles' other plays a systematic religious doctrine, we try to impose this on the *Philoctetes* in defiance of the dramatic facts. Or we interpret the plays in the light of our own philosophy. It is very easy to see in a play what you see everywhere else; a Marxist interpretation of the *Philoctetes* may be expected at any moment now, to be followed by another inspired by modern psychology. We have one safeguard against our own enthusiasms, misconceptions and inevitable ignorance: it is to assemble all the dramatic facts we can find in the play—facts of structure, treatment, style—and then ask ourselves what interpretation makes complete and immediate sense of all these facts. If, after prolonged consideration, no such interpretation presents itself, then it may be that we are dealing with an ill-made play, and if the

[1] See my *Greek Tragedy*.

play *is* ill-made, we shall probably have felt the fact long before we prove it. Then we must do the best we can; though we should not be too quick in assuming that the poet is at fault. The critic's most essential tool is a decent humility. And when the interpretation is found, if it is an ingenious one it is probably wrong; for we must assume, until it is disproved, that the Greek dramatists, like any reasonable artist in a reasonable society, thought that they had something of importance to say to their fellow-citizens, and strove to say it clearly.

If it is objected that no audience could possibly notice such refinements of structure as will be propounded here, the answer is that they were never intended to, any more than those who admired the new Parthenon were expected to admire also the careful placing and tilting of the columns. Each tiny detail contributes to the total impression. It was for the audience to receive the impression; to find out how it was created is the pastime of the critic. But both analogy and experience suggest that it is prudent to set no limits to the intelligent control of his art exercised either by Sophocles or by any other first-rate Greek craftsman.

Now we will examine what Sophocles says, or implies, first about the capture of Troy, then about the origin of Philoctetes' malady. We will imagine that we are stupid people watching and listening to the play for the first time, in Greek. We must be stupid; if we are not, we shall get interested in the play, and lose sight of the problem. At the same time, in order to carry out the investigation properly we must have a measure of that narrow intelligence which modern education so successfully fosters. Thus equipped, we begin listening to the play, and when it is over we shall have recorded what follows.

The first scene implies that Neoptolemus has only the vaguest idea why he has been brought to Lemnos. He has been told that he alone was to take Troy, and what Philoctetes has to do with it he cannot see:

ODYSSEUS: *When you are seeking your own advantage, you must not hesitate.*
NEOPTOLEMUS: *Advantage? How does his coming to Troy help me?*
ODYSSEUS: *This bow, and nothing else, will capture Troy.*

NEOPTOLEMUS: *Then the city is not to be taken by me, as they told me?*

ODYSSEUS: *Not by you without the bow, nor by the bow without you.*[1]

Whether Philoctetes himself must be taken to Troy is not very clear. In the passage just quoted Neoptolemus assumes that they must try to bring him; in v. 14 Odysseus talks of the 'clever trick' by which he hopes to take him: τὸ σόφισμα τῷ νιν αἱρήσειν δοκῶ; in v. 90 Neoptolemus is ready to 'bring the man' by open force, though not by fraud. On the other hand, all the emphasis is laid on the possession of the bow, as in the passage rendered above, and in vv. 68-69: 'If his bow is not secured, you can never sack Troy.' We are given to understand that Philoctetes himself must somehow be tricked into coming to Troy only because it will not be possible to get the bow in any other way.

Naturally, we shall not be surprised if we find that Odysseus is playing a deep and dirty game, and has told Neoptolemus much less than the whole truth. But that is another matter; what we are concerned with here is the way, true or false, in which the situation is propounded to Neoptolemus, and through him to the audience; and the situation is that the bow is necessary, and that Philoctetes must be abducted because this is the only way of getting the bow.

Neither Neoptolemus nor the audience is told any more about the situation until the pseudo-merchant, at v. 603, begins to relate circumstantially a prophecy which had been delivered to the Greeks about the capture of the city. Helenus 'prophesied everything to them; among other things, that they would never capture Troy until they won over this man here by persuasion, and brought him from the island where he now is.' This is entirely new. We have heard nothing yet of any prophecy, still less that the Greeks must 'persuade' Philoctetes. 'Persuasion' has indeed been mooted, by Neoptolemus:

ODYSSEUS: *I tell you that you must get hold of him by some trick.*
NEOPTOLEMUS: *Why by a trick, rather than by persuading him?*
ODYSSEUS: *He will never be persuaded, and you cannot get him by main force.*[2]

In this passage 'persuasion' was sharply distinguished from 'trickery'. Now the Merchant enters, to tell us—and Neopto-

---

[1] Vv. 111 ff.   [2] Vv. 101 ff.

lemus—that Philoctetes must be 'persuaded'. Certainly the Greeks had conveniently elastic ideas of what might constitute persuasion; or, to put it more accurately, the essential meaning of the verb πείθειν is not 'to persuade' but 'to win over'; but this phrase πείθειν λόγῳ can mean only 'persuade' in opposition to 'trick' or 'compel'—'to persuade', as Philoctetes himself says presently, 'by soothing talk'.

However, there is no reason at all to believe this story about Helenus and the prophecy. The Merchant is bogus, and we know that he is bogus. We know that he has been sent by Odysseus to help in the abduction of Philoctetes by improvising what he thinks may help. We know that nearly every other statement he makes is a lie. A worse witness cannot be imagined. The only person in the whole theatre who does not know him to be a liar is Philoctetes; and in fact no one else takes any notice of this 'prophecy'. The chorus is not deceived for a moment; otherwise, when it is alone (between 676 and 717), if not earlier, it must have said something about the prophecy and the new condition which it introduced, namely that Philoctetes must be 'persuaded'; especially since there does not seem the slightest chance that this condition can be satisfied. But the chorus knows as well as we do that the pretended Merchant is a liar, like his master. Therefore when Philoctetes falls asleep the chorus very sensibly urges Neoptolemus to pick up the bow and make off with it.

But Neoptolemus replies (839 ff):

> ἀλλ' ὅδε μὲν κλύει οὐδέν, ἐγὼ δ' ὁρῶ οὔνεκα θήραν
> τήνδ' ἁλίως ἔχομεν τόξων, δίχα τοῦδε πλέοντες·
> τοῦδε γὰρ ὁ στέφανος, τοῦτον θεὸς εἶπε κομίζειν.

True, he can hear nothing; but I can see that we are taking the bow all to no purpose, if we sail without him. His is the glory: him the god has told us to bring.

This is quite unintelligible.[1] It may be true, but Neoptolemus has no reason to suppose that it is true. Yet not only does this simple-minded youth take seriously the bogus Merchant's story; he actually goes even beyond this evidence, worthless though it is. For the Merchant said nothing about any 'glory' that was to come to Philoctetes; only that he was to be fetched back, with

---

[1] The reader will remember that, for the moment, he is being stupid.

his own consent, from Lemnos to Troy. The 'glory' is a possible inference, perhaps not an unreasonable one, from what the Merchant had said—but why believe the Merchant at all? This, surely is what any intelligent chorus would immediately point out in reply to Neoptolemus' declaration; but instead of doing this the chorus seems to accept it. At least, it says 'The gods will see to this'—and then it repeats, in guarded language, its advice that Neoptolemus should take the bow while he can. The difference between the chorus and Neoptolemus is that the chorus takes a more optimistic view of the situation: 'The gods will see to this.' Neither of them realises what any Verrallian audience would see at once, that there is not the slightest reason to suppose that the situation exists at all.

The next thing that happens is that at 915 Neoptolemus tells Philoctetes that he must come to Troy and help him capture it. This is indeed consistent with what the bogus Merchant had said, but we still have no explanation why Neoptolemus should believe it. However, the story seems to be confirmed a little later by Odysseus himself. He says to Philoctetes (982):

> ἀλλὰ καὶ σὲ δεῖ
> στείχειν ἅμ᾽ αὐτοῖς, ἢ βίᾳ στελοῦσί σε.

You have to go with them, or they will carry you off by main force.

Since Neoptolemus is now holding the bow there is no reason why Odysseus should still want to carry off Philoctetes unless the story about Helenus' prophesy is true. That it is true is confirmed a moment later, for when Philoctetes absolutely refuses to go, and threatens instead to dash himself to death from the cliff, Odysseus forcibly prevents him. Since Odysseus is not conspicuously humane, his reason must be that the presence of Philoctetes at Troy is indeed necessary. Therefore Odysseus must be bluffing at 1055, when they go off without Philoctetes but with the bow, and Odysseus says: 'We have no need of you, now that we have the bow. Teucer is as good an archer as you —and so am I.'

It is now quite clear that Odysseus was lying in the prologue. That need not disturb us. What is quite unintelligible is the way in which the truth is revealed to Neoptolemus. But worse is to come. For in the speech that begins at 1314, when Odysseus has been driven out of the play with ignominy, and Neoptolemus has handed back the bow, Neoptolemus informs Philoctetes that he, Philoctetes, is destined to take Troy with the bow, with the help of Neoptolemus; also that he will be healed if he comes to Troy, not otherwise; also that Troy is destined to fall this very summer. All this, says Neoptolemus, was explicitly declared by Helenus. Moreover, he now knows the picturesque detail that Helenus offered to stake his life on the accuracy of his prophecy.

An old *Punch* drawing portrayed a street-scene in which a dignified old gentleman was skidding dangerously on a bit of orange-peel. 'Mummy', said the little girl, 'how did he *know* it was a blood-orange?' That is what we should like to know here; how does Neoptolemus *know* all this? At the beginning of the play he did not even know that Philoctetes was to be concerned in the capture of Troy at all. The Merchant, even if he were worth believing, had not mentioned the healing of Philoctetes, or the time at which Troy was to fall. No one else has said a word about Helenus or his prophecy. Yet when Heracles appears and rapidly outlines the immediate future, he confirms in every particular what Neoptolemus has just said. Neoptolemus cannot possibly know, yet he does know. It is quite inexplicable. One wonders if Aristotle ever noticed this, and if so what he said about it when lecturing on the *Poetics*, for assuredly this sequence of events is not κατὰ τὸ εἰκὸς ἢ τὸ ἀναγκαῖον, probable or inevitable.

When we turn from this matter of prophecy to the history of Philoctetes' malady, we find that this—a simple enough matter—is handled in the same illogical way; so that it may fairly be demanded of an interpretation that professes to explain the one difficulty that it should also explain the other. This time our examination will be brief.

From the first ten verses of the play it is evident that Neoptolemus knows nothing whatever about Philoctetes' personal history—a state of things which, though not inevitable, is perfectly natural. Let us observe what Odysseus tells him in these ten verses:

This is Lemnos, where on the orders of my commanders I once deposited Philoctetes, because he had a running sore on the foot, so that he filled the whole camp with his cries, and we could not sacrifice in silence.—But why waste time talking? We have now to act . . .

There is no explanation how Philoctetes came by his wound, although one verse, consuming perhaps five seconds of Odysseus' valuable time, would have been enough to give the essential facts. But they are not given; in spite of which Neoptolemus is able to impart a surprising amount of information to the chorus next time the topic occurs (191-200):

> None of this (i.e. Philoctetes' sufferings) is surprising to me. It is from the gods, if I have any understanding, that his woes come— from savage Chrysè. What he now suffers, with no one to cure him, must have come by the contrivance of the gods, that he should not bend his irresistible bow against Troy before the time is fulfilled in which it is said the city must be subdued by it.

We may perhaps think that the gods are rather amateurish if they have to treat a man in this unconscionable way in order to prevent him from upsetting their plans, but this is not a point that we will examine just now. We are pursuing another hare, and what we should like to know—once more—is how Neoptolemus can possibly know the detail about Chrysè? He can't. Odysseus might so easily have told him—but Odysseus has not. Of course, we can think out excuses for this. We can say (if we think little enough of Sophocles' technique) that in the first ten verses Neoptolemus is not really ignorant of the story; Sophocles is merely conveying information to the audience. To such an explanation there would be at least two rejoinders: Why did he not give enough information? And will this or any similar consideration explain the precisely similar outcrop of unexplained knowledge which we have found at the end of the play? No we must hope to do better than this.

The next point to observe is that at v. 265 Philoctetes himself relates that he got the malady from the bite of a serpent. Finally, to conclude this curious history, Neoptolemus finds himself empowered, at v. 1326, to explain to Philoctetes that the serpent bit him because he was trespassing on Chrysè's domain, of which the snake was the guardian. The ways of the gods are mysterious, but those of the dramatist are hardly less so. If, for some unexplained reason, Sophocles wanted to keep back the detail of the trespass until late in the play, why did he not wait five minutes more, and allow Heracles to tell us? Why, for that matter, did he not do the same with the much more important

point of the healing of Philoctetes and the fall of Troy? Heracles, being a god, knows everything; Neoptolemus cannot know
about either of these things. Heracles is already waiting in the
wings to come on—yet Sophocles makes Neoptolemus anticipate
him.

This is what a prosaic review of the play can disclose. It has
been there all the time, since 409 B.C., and yet until Bowra's book
on Sophocles appeared no one seems to have given any but the
most perfunctory attention to what is a most unconventional
piece of stage-craft. It might be a pleasant occupation to work
out a strictly rationalist interpretation of the play. We should
very likely prove that the Merchant was Helenus in disguise,
and then we should only lack a Verrall to write for us a convincing account of what Neoptolemus, Odysseus and the dis-
guised Helenus said to each other, off-stage, between 1081 and
1217.

Bowra has offered a general explanation of the oddities of
construction that we have been examining, and since a totally
different explanation will be offered here, it would perhaps be
well to show cause for not accepting his. In brief, his interpretation is that the *Philoctetes*, like Sophocles' other surviving
plays, is based on the conception of two worlds; there is the
world of men, who are blind, weak, full of illusion, and try to
oppose what the gods ordain; and there is the perfect world of
the gods. In this opposition the will of the gods, of course,
prevails, and in one way or another, through suffering it may
be, men are brought to see that they must submit. In the
Philoctetes we have on the one hand the plan of the gods for the
capture of Troy and the recompensing of Philoctetes; and, in
the usual Sophoclean way, men, for their own blind reasons, try
to oppose this plan. First Odysseus thinks that he can have Troy
captured by other means—by abducting, not by persuading,
Philoctetes. He is made to see that this cannot be done. Then
Philoctetes obstinately sets himself against the divine will, but
he too finds that this is useless; he is brought to a due state of
modesty by Heracles, and so accepts the destiny which the gods
have planned for him. We naturally ask why Sophocles reveals
the divine plan so gradually and obscurely. The answer is that
this is his way of emphasising the darkness and illusion in which
men live. Sophocles is deliberately creating an apparent muddle

in order to reflect the muddle which men make for themselves by trying to oppose or circumvent the divine will.

The play is therefore essentially theological: something much more serious than I, for one, had supposed it to be in calling it an elegant study in character and dramatic intrigue. That it is more serious than this I now agree, but such a theological interpretation seems impossible.

In the first place, we must remember the Law of Parsimony. The illogicalities which we have discovered are of the same general kind as those in the *Antigone*, the *Tyrannus* and the *Coloneus*: in each case the dramatist does not obey Aristotle's canon of 'the probable or the necessary', but gives himself licence to use 'the improbable or the impossible' instead. If we are content to regard all these phenomena as random blunders, well and good—except for Sophocles' reputation, or possibly the critic's. If we reject this easy way out, as I think the facts compel us to, then a theory which explains all these illogicalities must *prima facie* be better than a theory that explains only one of them. The naturalistic critics of the *Antigone* may properly be asked to apply their critical principles to the similar ἄλογα in the other plays, and the theological interpreter of the 'muddle' in the *Philoctetes* may fairly be invited to explain similarly the 'muddles' in the *Antigone* and the *Coloneus*. Failure to do this will not indeed disprove their particular interpretations, but it will not commend them.

But apart from this general consideration, the obstacles in the way of Bowra's interpretation are formidable. One of them is very clearly stated by Bowra himself, namely that the play must have been nearly as baffling to Sophocles' audience as it is to us, since Sophocles not only wraps in obscurity his real theme, namely the divine plan and human opposition to it, but makes it even more difficult of access by putting in the foreground 'exciting personal issues' which would be bound to attract the attention of the audience. But if Sophocles had something to say to the Athenians which he thought important, what conceivable motive or calculation could lead him deliberately to make it almost unintelligible? Would such a master of stage-craft, if he had something difficult to say, first of all put it in the background, and then, in the foreground, erect a very lively drama full of 'exciting personal issues'? This hardly sounds like

Sophocles, or indeed like any other artist. And the difficulty is even greater than this, for the action which fills the foreground, and indeed dominates the play, is much more than 'exciting personal issues'; it raises immediately and directly, as we shall see, a question of most profound interest and importance for this very political Athenian audience. Sophocles could never have hoped or intended that his audience should look past this to something very obscure lurking in the background.

This objection can be made more specific. The Chorus conferred many advantages on the Greek dramatist, not the least being that it could bring to the surface, when necessary, the broad general principles underlying the particular action of the play. If Bowra is right, there is no surviving play in which it was more necessary that the chorus should do this. The audience is admittedly baffled. Sophocles creates his opportunity to explain things when, at 675, he removes from the stage Philoctetes and Neoptolemus, and, for the only time throughout the play, leaves the chorus alone in the orchestra. Now is the time to give the clue that the audience so badly needs. It is not in the least necessary that these sailormen should suddenly transform themselves into theologians; a mere hint will at least do something —an ode on the simple theme 'O God, what a muddle we are in!', something to point to the idea how futile it is to try to oppose the divine will. But instead of doing anything so sensible, and indeed necessary, Sophocles throws away the opportunity which he has made for himself, and consumes the precious minutes by telling us nothing but what we know already, namely that Philoctetes is in utter misery.

In this and in many other ways the theological interpretation fails in what is the first duty of an interpretation, namely σώζειν τὰ φαινόμενα, to explain the dramatic facts. Take the *deus ex machina* for example. It is to be the function of Heracles to bring Philoctetes to a state of proper modesty, so that he will accept the will of Heaven and go to Troy. Now, in the first place, Sophocles has most inconsiderately done all he can to make things difficult for Heracles, and for his own audience, by representing Philoctetes, throughout the play, in every detail, as the victim of a barely credible inhumanity. The Greek leaders had indeed some reason for not allowing him to proceed with them to Troy; they had no reason whatever for marooning him as they did on this uninhabited island, instead of sending him home as an honourable ally who had become incapacitated; and now that they need him, they try to entrap him as if he were a wild animal, or in the alternative to steal from him his only means of maintaining life. Nor is any hint given of any fault in Philoctetes that might incline us to the view that he too was in the wrong.

If, after all this, we are to see that there is a divine plan, and that the tortured Philoctetes needs a lesson in humility, then Sophocles has set himself a serious task. Heracles, in one speech, must convincingly set all that has happened and will happen on a broad philosophic foundation. It will not be enough simply to make Philoctetes submit—a thing which any fool of a dramatist could contrive. Simple submission may save Philoctetes' soul, but it will not save the play. It is not Philoctetes that matters, but the audience: unless the audience is overwhelmed by the power, the majesty, the wisdom or the *something* of the gods, the play fails.

Heracles has been given a difficult task, but if any poet can bring him through it safely, then Sophocles is the man. As it happens, this is his particular field. The thought is habitual with him that though human circumstance is baffling in its complexity and mutability, nevertheless it is ruled by λόγος, δίκη, rhythm. The play will end—it *must*—in a revelation of the majestic pattern of life, a revelation so impressive that Philoctetes' past sufferings and future glory will be given some universal significance. We know that Sophocles can do it. We remember, from the early *Ajax*, that magnificent speech in which Ajax brings himself to break his stubborn resolve:

> *All things doth long, innumerable Time,*
> *Bring forth to light and then again conceal . . .*

We remember, from the not yet written *Coloneus*, the even more magnificent speech:

> *Dear son of Aegeus, to the gods alone*
> *Do age and death not come. All other things*
> *The power of Time subdues and brings to nothing.*
> *Earth's strength decays, and human strength decays . . .*

We confidently expect a speech of this calibre here: grave, spacious, profound. Sophocles can do it, and nothing less will bear the weight of Bowra's interpretation. Do we get it?

Nowhere in the whole of Sophocles is there a speech less impressive than this one which he wrote for Heracles. The first five verses are to this effect:

> First I will mention my own sufferings, the heavy labours that I endured before winning the immortal glory that you behold. Such a lot is to be yours also, to make your life glorious after this suffering.

This is a sensible opening. We may go further, and say (in Aristotle's word) that it is φιλάνθρωπον; it satisfies our sense of justice: recompense is coming to Philoctetes. But does it make us shiver, as those other speeches do? No. Then we find seventeen verses which rapidly outline the immediate future. Dr Baedeker might have written them, if he had enough Greek. Nothing is said in them about any divine purpose. If we hope to discover why the gods brought all this misery upon Philoctetes, why they now relent, why they now decree that Troy shall fall, we are disappointed. Heracles makes no reference to the gods until, in his last sentence, he reminds Philoctetes and Neoptolemus of what happened to the Argive host in the *Agamemnon*: 'When you capture Troy, respect the shrines of the gods. Reverence is what the gods prize above everything.' And what has this to do with the sufferings and the healing of Philoctetes? Nothing whatever.

On the other hand, this moral sentiment, like the assurance that all will be well now with the hero, does give an air of finality —which is what the end of a play must have. But surely it is an ending of quite a different kind from the ending of the other plays: not the inevitable conclusion of a tragic action which finds its catharsis in the illumination that it brings, but simply a satisfactory ending. If Sophocles wanted to round off the action, to reverse Philoctetes' decision without giving any theological or intellectual or psychological reasons for the reversal, the speech is excellent. As religious or philosophical poetry, illuminating one of the dark corners of life, justifying, or even illustrating, the ways of the gods, not only does it fail, but it also gives the impression that Sophocles is not even trying.

This theological interpretation, then, fails time after time to give a reasonable interpretation of the form of the play. In what follows it will become apparent that my own earlier interpretation also fails, for much the same reason: the idea that the play is an interesting study in character based on a well made dramatic intrigue leaves too much either unexplained or uncoordinated.

The process of interpretation is an inductive one. The critic has to assemble all the dramatic facts he can see, and then try to find the conception which will best explain them. It is not a method which lends itself to exposition, since the business of collecting the facts, setting them down, and testing various hypotheses, would become tedious. For the purposes of exposition the process must, to some extent, be inverted: we must state, as a working hypothesis, the conclusion arrived at by induction, and show that it is confirmed by as many of the facts as the reader's patience may be presumed to endure. Among these dramatic facts will be those already mentioned—the choice of material for the only 'free' stasimon, the tone and content of Heracles' speech, the 'irrationalities'—with many others. As a provisional statement, let us say that the unifying idea is not that of the two worlds of gods and men, nor that the play is a delicate study of character with the spiritual experiences of Neoptolemus as its centre-piece, nor a study in morbid psychology, nor an attempt at Euripidean realism, but a profound study of political morality set against a universal background of divine justice.

It may be asked: Is not an unreal rigidity implied in this statement? Is it not possible that a play should have a question of political morality as its theme, and still be a study in dramatic realism, full of character-drawing? The answer of course is Yes; in the classical Greek drama we do find character-drawing, and the exploitation of many other aspects of the dramatic art; but they are always found in strict relation to one dominant conception. This is what makes the plays classical. Free character-drawing, the exploitation of dramatic effects for their own sake, are not found until we come to plays like the *Helen* or *Phoenissae*, and in these the absence of the classical logic and concentration are at once apparent. If, in this play, we find that the realism and the character-drawing are necessary for the deployment of this politico-religious theme, and that there is no more of either than the theme requires, then we are right in saying that 'study in realism' or 'character-study' is not a proper description of it, and that on this level it will not be securely interpreted. We shall not have seen what Sophocles meant.

Suppose, for instance, that there turned up tomorrow, in Egypt, the complete work of Ion of Chios, and that it contained the statement that in 410 B.C. Euripides bet Sophocles ten minae that he could not write a play in which the hero was a cripple dressed in rags: what would be the importance of this to the critic of the *Philoctetes*? None whatsoever. It would be an interesting biographical fact, but it would have nothing to do with the interpretation of the play unless criticism had hitherto found the realism in it quite inorganic, and was at its wit's end to explain how it got there. But if we find, as I think we shall, that the realism is purposeful and strictly related to the theme, then to say that it was induced by the influence of Euripides is only an idle guess, which does the disservice of diverting our attention from its real purpose.

Now we must review the play, not, this time, in blinkers, fixing our eyes on its improbabilities, but on the contrary opening our minds as widely as we can to its varied impact, and hoping, in the end, to find some unity of impression.

It begins with a scene of easy naturalism: no palace-front, but a hill-side[1]; no long speeches, but easily-moving dialogue, during which Neoptolemus climbs up the slope, discovers the cave, and sees in it some stinking rags. We can dismiss the naturalism as an adventitious effect added by Sophocles in deference to contemporary taste; so might a man explain away the large buttresses which fourteenth-century builders applied to their churches —if he were ignorant of the fact that without the buttresses the churches would have fallen down. In fact, the stinking rags and the rough-hewn cup are part of a consistent building-up of Philoctetes' part, and are essential to the structure and the idea of the whole play.

We find too, in this first scene, a fine piece of character-drawing: the contrast between the experienced, wily and un-scrupulous Odysseus, and the honourable but inexperienced son of Achilles. Here too it is easy for us, as I well know, to lose ourselves in one part of the drama at the expense of the whole,

---

[1] See the footnote above, p. 54.

and to see in this character-drawing the chief interest of the play. But it is not; like the naturalism, the character-drawing is ancillary to something more important, carried as far as the real theme demands, and not a step further.

For if we try to put from us our natural bookishness, our interest in literary theory, dramatic history and the rest, and think of Sophocles' audience sitting below the Acropolis in the spring sunshine; and if then we ask ourselves 'What in this first scene would grip the attention of the audience?'—what answer must we give? We may of course give the wrong answer, but if we do, the future course of the play will show us that our answer was wrong, because the play will not make complete sense. Surely the simple answer to our question—and an answer which is not simple is not likely to be correct—is the apparent dilemma into which Neoptolemus is placed by Odysseus. On the one side, an act of revolting meanness and inhumanity, particularly so to the son of Achilles, proud and jealous of his father's name; on the other side, every argument of honourable private ambition and of urgent public interest too. We know that this audience met regularly in another place as the sovereign Assembly of Athens: surely it would be perverse to suppose that Sophocles expected anything else than this challenging problem in political morality to seize the minds of those watching the scene? But we shall have our controls to check us if we are wrong.

Let us observe Odysseus' language. His plan is a σόφισμα, a 'clever stroke' (14). The theft of the bow must be σοφισθῆναι, 'contrived intelligently' (77). If Neoptolemus succeeds he will be hailed as σοφὸς κἀγαθός, 'able and reliable' (119). Neoptolemus dislikes the scheme very much indeed: 'You are simply asking me to tell lies!' (100).—Not quite 'lying': it is δόλος, 'a stratagem'—'But don't you think it wrong to tell lies?'—'Not if our safety depends on it.'—'Even so, how can one have the face to utter such lies?'—'When you are doing something for your advantage you mustn't hesitate' (108-111). You must be γενναῖος, you must show what you are made of (51). 'I know it is not like you to tell a false tale and to contrive a low trick—but think how precious victory is! You must bring yourself to do this. We can prove some other time that we are honest men. Now, for one brief day, lend yourself to knavery, and then for

the rest of your life be known as the most upright of men (79 ff).
Yes; when I was young I too was quick to act and slow to talk.
But experience of life has taught me that the tongue, not the
hand, wins the day everywhere (96 ff). If you fail to do this, it
will be a great blow to all the Greeks, because if this bow is not
secured, you cannot possibly take Troy.' Odysseus explains quite
convincingly why he himself cannot undertake the task; and
there are equally convincing arguments to show that Neoptolemus can rely neither on persuasion nor on open force.
Neoptolemus does his best to escape, but all the earths are
thoroughly stopped. There is no alternative. 'If that is the
case', says the young man, 'it seems I must be quite shameless,
and steal them' (vv. 116, 120).

It would probably be a mistake to try to 'identify' Odysseus,
the smooth-spoken rogue who could justify any villainy as a wise
stroke of policy imposed by political necessity, but we need go
no further than the pages of Thucydides to assure ourselves that
this type was familiar enough to the Athenians, and this situation too. Here is the type, brilliantly portrayed, and here is one
of the fundamental problems in political morality, put as forcibly
and as clearly as it can be. It would be indeed strange if this
important theme, so firmly stated at the outset, were something
irrelevant to the main issue of the play.

We have now recorded the major dramatic fact in the prologue, but several others demand notice.

The first eleven verses explain the situation to us—and they
explain it in a certain way, not, for example, in the Euripidean
prologue-style. Odysseus is brief, and, as we have noticed
already, Sophocles keeps back certain relevant facts, even at the
cost of imparting them later through Neoptolemus, who has no
ascertainable reason for knowing them.

Philoctetes, Odysseus tells us, was marooned on Lemnos.
Why? Because his malady caused him to interfere with the
sacrifices, with his continuous cries of pain. Odysseus did it, but
the orders came from the Atreidae. Does this detail mean anything? Of course we have no time to ponder on this, for the play
goes on. We note simply that the orders came from the Atreidae.
The story, as Odysseus presents it, is one of stark brutality on
the part of the Greek commanders. There is no hint of a wider
background, of any divine agency at work.

Another detail: we note the amplitude of Odysseus' address
to Neoptolemus:

> ἀλλ' ὦ κρατίστου πατρὸς Ἑλλήνων τραφείς
> Ἀχιλλέως παῖ Νεοπτόλεμε . . .

> *Neoptolemus, son of Achilles, offspring of him who was foremost
> among the Greeks . . .*

With this we may compare the opening of the *Electra*:

> ὦ τοῦ στρατηγήσαντος ἐν Τροίᾳ ποτέ
> Ἀγαμέμνονος παῖ . . .

> *Son of Agamemnon who once led the host to Troy . . .*

or the opening of the *Antigone*:

> ὦ κοινὸν αὐτάδελφον Ἰσμήνης κάρα . . .

> *My dear sister, my own sister Ismene . . .*

In each case the amplitude of the address has a special point.
Ἀγαμέμνονος παῖ, 'Son of Agamemnon' would have been enough
to tell the audience who the silent actor is, as in the first line of
Ajax Athena says simply 'Son of Laertes'. But the *Electra* presents an Orestes one of whose chief motives is to recover his
crown and patrimony. Therefore he is not, for example,

> Ἀγαμέμνονος παῖ, τοῦ φονευθέντος πάλαι,
> *Son of Agamemnon, murdered of old . . .*

though this might have been a suitable introduction of Electra,
whose motives are much more personal. The emphatic mention
of Achilles here has, as we shall see, dramatic point. It is not
merely ingratiating for the moment, but is a tiny touch of colour
which plays its part in the whole design.

Then comes the naturalistic passage in which Neoptolemus
finds the cave and describes its pitiful contents. Not idle 'realism', for it brings vividly to our minds, before ever we see
Philoctetes, the misery to which he has been condemned by this
casual act of brutal indifference. One of the most important
structural features of the play is the building-up of our sense of
what Philoctetes has endured and is still to endure. This has to
be built up and buttressed firmly, since a great strain is going
to be put on it. The process of building-up begins here: the
influence of Euripides has nothing to do with it.

When Odysseus retires, with his glib prayer to 'Hermes the

Deceiver and Athena Polias giver of Victory', we are left with Neoptolemus and the chorus. The young man has not been corrupted easily, but Odysseus' arguments are unanswerable. It is clearly one of those situations in which it is impossible to be honest and straightforward: politicians know how frequent they are. Since it is so, Neoptolemus is ready to play his part resolutely, and in the lyrical passage which ensues he gives suitable instructions to his men.

It is in this passage that the first of our 'illogicalities' occurs— the sudden mention by Neoptolemus of Chrysê. It is not a point that will trouble the audience, but the critic should take notice of it, because, as readers of detective stories know, anything unusual, however unimportant it seems, may be significant. It would have been normal procedure for Sophocles to have made Odysseus give us this detail: but Odysseus has told us the minimum, on the plea that time is precious. Why does Sophocles give the information through Neoptolemus, who, when you come to think of it, ought not to know it? If we can think of no better explanation we will say that Sophocles is 'distributing his exposition'; though so slight an exposition is not worth distributing, especially at the cost of a slight technical blemish.

But when we look at the context we find an interesting fact. Sophocles has just given the chorus two consecutive stanzas, a little stasimon within the lyrical dialogue; and in these two stanzas the chorus has said: 'I am sorry for this man, sick, in pain, alone, helpless, a man of noble birth, but living in the extremity of misery.' This is natural, but not inevitable. Sophocles could have made his chorus say something quite different. It would be equally natural if the chorus should speculate about the prospects of success, for if the bow can be stolen and Troy captured, then these sailors can go home to their wives and children. Their own fortunes are very closely connected with the present venture, an obvious point which Sophocles never once allows them to make. Instead of saying this, they reflect on the acute misery in which Philoctetes has been living so long.

It is in reply to this that Neoptolemus says: 'There is nothing here that surprises me. His sufferings, if I can read them rightly, come from Heaven, from cruel Chrysê. The gods have ordained them, to prevent him from shooting his irresistible arrows against Troy before the time is fulfilled when Troy is fated to fall before them.' Now, the actor who plays Neoptolemus might deliver these lines in a tone of high earnestness, but the producer who allowed him to do it would be a fool. The justification for this statement is not simply that the theology is so unintelligent, implying as it does that the gods had to treat Philoctetes in this barbarous way lest he should capture Troy at the wrong time. The real reason why we must not take this statement seriously is much more weighty: if Sophocles meant us to believe this, he would be raising in its acutest form one of the most profound of problems, the problem of suffering and Divine Providence. Once raised, this problem must dominate the play. But it does not: it drops stone-dead. Therefore Sophocles, not being incompetent, does not intend to raise it, and Neoptolemus must not speak these lines as if he had just descended from Mt. Sinai. In any case Odysseus has made quite plain the real reason why Philoctetes has suffered like this: it was because he was a nuisance to the army, and because the Atreidae and Odysseus did not mind behaving like blackguards.

These lines must be spoken defensively. Neoptolemus has himself expressed his natural pity for Philoctetes (162-168); this theme is immediately taken up by the chorus in its two stanzas, and developed through the superior eloquence of music and the dance. Neoptolemus, not being a brute, is extremely uncomfortable. He dislikes the idea that the men he is now serving are a set of unconscionable villains, and therefore he blames the gods—as many other characters do in Greek tragedy, always wrongly. He says, in effect, 'But these things happen, you know. It was all intended for a purpose.'

This explains the mention of Chrysê: Philoctetes' past history has to be completed some time, but Sophocles was not a dramatist who regarded the necessary past story as so much inevitable lumber, to be stowed away somewhere as neatly as possible, like suit-cases when the holidays are over. He preferred to use it positively and constructively. The mention of Chrysê is just enough to give plausibility to Neoptolemus' optimistic theology. Sophocles did not want Odysseus to mention her, for a very good reason: this would have suggested that there was divine agency in the background, when Sophocles wants us to see nothing but the cruelty of the Atreidae and Odysseus. For the same reason he now keeps back the detail of Philoctetes' trespass on holy ground. This will come in very effectively later (1326); produced now, it would only tempt us to take Neoptolemus' defensive theology seriously.[1] We should suspect that there was a divine agency behind Philoctetes' sufferings, which is precisely what Sophocles wants us not to do. The exact timing of these details is much more important to Sophocles than the mere observing of prosaic logic.

Immediately after the end of this speech the 'building-up' process is resumed, accompanied by a great intensification of that purposeful realism. Neoptolemus has seen the home-made wooden cup and the stinking rags; he is now to be exposed to the full impact of what the Atreidae and Odysseus have done. Once he has seen it he is not quite so ready with his theological explanations. Cries of pain are heard, first distant, then nearer. Sophocles takes his time over this first entrance of the victim.[2] This mental impact is completed by the sheer physical impact, as Philoctetes comes in, 'ploughing his painful way along' (163). The revolting sight is an essential part of the whole design: *this* is what the clever and plausible Odysseus has done; *this* is the pitiful creature from whom Achilles' son has promised to steal his only means of remaining alive. Excitedly Philoctetes asks them who they are. No answer comes. 'Do not shrink from me in horror, if you have come as friends.' Still Neoptolemus can find nothing to say—'Ἀλλ' ἀνταμείψασθε: 'Nay, do answer me! This silence is not fair to you or to me.'

The strain on Neoptolemus, and on us too for that matter, was already considerable; Sophocles now turns the screw hard, and continues to turn it for quite a long time. The σόφισμα, the politicians 'astute move', sounded rather unpleasant even in the abstract; now we can all contemplate it in the terrible reality. The next turn of the screw comes immediately; first in Philoctetes' joy at hearing himself addressed in Greek:

> *O welcome sounds! To think that after all these years I should be greeted so!*

[1] It is of course no objection to the present argument that Sophocles' audience knew the story beforehand. They did not know what modifications he was going to introduce.

[2] We should remember here that the entrances, πάροδοι, to the orchestra in the Athenian theatre were some thirty yards long.

then in Philoctetes' excited response to the name of Achilles:

> *Son of my dearest friend! From the country I love so well! Ward of old Lycomedes!*

We have heard Neoptolemus speak before of his father, that pattern of Greek chivalry, of whom he has seen so little: 'It is not my way to stoop to trickery, nor, I believe, was it my father's way either' (88 f). But 'the exigencies of the existing situation' have made him so to stoop—and now the man whom he has undertaken to ruin turns out to be an old friend of his father's.

The prominence given to Achilles' name throughout the play is notable and deliberate. Achilles is 'the mightiest of the Greeks' (3); honourable (91); brave (96); Philoctetes' greatest friend (242, 332 ff). When Neoptolemus has stolen the bow Philoctetes protests against 'what this son of Achilles has done to me' (940), 'most contemptible son of the noblest of fathers' (1284); when he restores it, he 'gives proof of the stock from which he comes, no son of Sisyphus, like Odysseus, but of Achilles, best of men while he lived, and now best among the dead' (1313. Add incidental references: 30, 260, 358 ff, 468, 542, 582, 874, 904 ff, 1066, 1298.) Parallel to this re-echoing of Achilles' honourable name is the constant denunciation of the Atreidae and Odysseus (feigned or not makes no difference, since we know what Neoptolemus must be thinking of them): 257, 262 ff, 314 ff, 321, 361 ff, 384, 396, 406 ff, 417, 429, 441, 455, 622, 633 ff, 791, 793 ff, 872 f, 971, 1004-1044. The effect of all this is twofold. Neoptolemus, continually reminded of his father's honour and the dishonour of his present associates, becomes more and more uncomfortable; while we, the audience, are continually reminded of the difference between real nobility and these agents of 'political necessity'.

If the first scene of the play engaged our sympathetic interest in Neoptolemus as the inexperienced youth overwhelmed by Odysseus' exposition of high politics, we shall follow the rest of the present scene not as the simple exposition of a Robinson Crusoe story, but (through the mind of Neoptolemus) as a relevation of what high politics, in this instance, really mean. We notice again how careful Sophocles is not to put Philoctetes' sufferings in a religious or philosophical frame: when Philoctetes refers to the origin of his wound (266 f) the supernatural element is entirely avoided; for all we yet know it may have been a perfectly accidental occurrence. This matter will not be mentioned again for over a thousand verses. Sophocles tells us here enough to satisfy our immediate curiosity; it is not a point in which he wants us to interest ourselves.

It is an improbable assumption that the busy Aegean could conceal a marooned man for so long, or that the few Greeks who saw him should be so indifferent to gain as to leave him there, but Sophocles is too wise to try to justify it. He could have spared himself the second of these two improbabilities; his reason for admitting it is obviously that it notably increases our sense of Philoctetes' anguish. It contributes to the building-up process; it contributes something to the whole design; therefore Sophocles uses it, probable or not. The long and pitiful story to which Neoptolemus has to listen ends with the words: 'That, my son, is what the Atreidae and the violence of Odysseus have done to me. May the gods do the same to them.' By Greek standards, a most reasonable prayer.

Neoptolemus, we may suspect, is not very happy. Still, he tells his false story manfully—effectively interrupted at the very beginning by Philoctetes' grief at the news that Achilles is dead. Sophoclean irony is not very prominent in this play, but, knowing what sort of man Neoptolemus is, may we not see something of the sort in the conclusion of this speech? Odysseus gave him full permission to revile him and the Atreidae as much as he liked. He avails himself of this permission. Is it not conceivable that his denunciation of them is not entirely feigned? Certainly there is irony enough in the last sentence:

> . . . cheated by Odysseus, that villain from a race of villains. Yet I do not blame him so much as his superiors. A city, like an army, is in the hands of its leaders. When men behave ill, it is through the words of their teachers that they are made bad.

Neoptolemus is surely thinking of himself—and Sophocles, of his audience.

At this point the chorus sings a short stanza which as it were ratifies the concord to which Neoptolemus and Philoctetes have ostensibly come. It also gives the long scene its second wind, and gives Philoctetes occasion for another denunciation of Odys-

seus and the Atreidae: 'I know his tongue would stop short of
no false and villainous speech, if thereby he could accomplish
some dishonest purpose.' Neoptolemus' dilemma, and ours, is
that he knows well enough that Odysseus' tongue is false:
Neoptolemus is at this moment telling Odysseus' own lies; but
this time the purpose, the capture of Troy, is very far from
being dishonest.

Now comes the long passage in which Philoctetes asks about
his old associates. Why this? It is indeed perfectly natural—
but Sophocles was no innocent 'realist', and the fact that this is
natural is not necessarily the complete explanation of its presence in the play. If we watch Neoptolemus we shall see that
there is a much more important reason. For Philoctetes begins
again with renewed, and accurate, denunciation of Odysseus
(407 ff), then asks how Ajax could have allowed Neoptolemus to
be defrauded of his father's armour.—But Ajax is dead; Anti-
lochus is dead; Patroclus is dead. 'But the villain Odysseus is
still alive!' 'War always takes the good man, and spares the
rogue.' This might have been said by Philoctetes; the interesting fact is that it is said by Neoptolemus; and again, Neoptolemus must feel that it is uncomfortably true. 'There was
another fellow—No, not Odysseus, but . . . Thersites was the
name. What of him?' 'He is still alive.' 'He would be! The
gods seem to look after villains like him.'

Is all this the result of Sophocles' bitter reflections on the
Peloponnesian War? It is very probable—but let us not fly off
at a tangent and try to identify 'Thersites' with some contemporary demagogue. Sophocles is not using drama to comment
on current events: he is using common experience to make
drama—and thereby illuminating that common experience.
The dialogue turns the screw still more on Neoptolemus by
making him realise the more that those he is trying to serve are
not the noblest of those who sailed to Troy; and if Sophocles'
audience cares to see any parallel with its own situation, it will
encounter the suggestion that scoundrels survive, and that base
pleas of political necessity are put forward by such scoundrels.
'What can I think of this? How can I praise the gods, when I
find them evil?' An impious remark? No doubt, but it is one
wrung out of Philoctetes by the bitterness of his suffering.
Sophocles allows him this cry of despair, and then immediately

changes the subject. We are not encouraged to think theologically.

Neoptolemus' pretence that he must now leave produces the desired result—almost certainly more than the desired result; for Philoctetes' humble and passionate appeal must move anyone who is not an Odysseus. However, Neoptolemus stands fast, and we think that his scheme for abducting his victim is about to succeed, when Sophocles makes a diversion by sending in Odysseus' man in the guise of a merchant. Why does he do it? We have to consider the merchant as an actor in two plots at once—those of Odysseus and of Sophocles. As a part of Odysseus' plot it is a very clever move. The true story that Odysseus is coming in search of Philoctetes makes Philoctetes the more eager to sail with Neoptolemus. The false story that other Greek leaders are looking for Neoptolemus confirms, in Philoctetes' mind, the story which Neoptolemus has told him; while the conspicuous detail that Neoptolemus is being sought by such eminently noble figures as Phoenix and the two sons of Theseus guarantees the respectability of Neoptolemus. In every way it is made to seem advantageous that Philoctetes should sail with him.

This is cleverly devised, but of course Sophocles was at the same time devising something much more important. The great reason for inventing the merchant is seen in the fact that it is he who introduces the idea that Philoctetes must be persuaded to go willingly. Is his story true? It is not consistent with what Odysseus said, or at least, implied at the beginning, and we know that the man is a liar. But then, so is Odysseus.—But Sophocles allows us little time to ponder over the problem, for soon Philoctetes is shouting: 'What? that villain persuade me to go to Troy? I could as easily be persuaded to come back from Hades when I am dead—like that man's father.' Persuasion, if it *is* necessary, is obviously out of the question: and we cannot be surprised. After which, Sophocles writes one of his most astonishing couplets:

> οὐκ οἶδ' ἐγὼ ταῦτ'· ἀλλ' ἐγὼ μὲν εἶμ' ἐπὶ
> ναῦν. σφῷν δ' ὅπως ἄριστα συμφέροι θεός.

The couplet begins in the most perfectly off-hand style, and ends in normal tragic diction, with not the slightest sense of effort. 'I don't know about that. I'm off to my ship, and God be with you both.' Shakespeare could have translated it; I cannot.

Now Philoctetes is desperately anxious to be gone, but Neoptolemus is in no hurry. Why not? Is he too uncomfortable about the whole business? Uncomfortable or not, he succeeds in getting the bow in his hand for a moment, and then with a very natural excuse leaves the stage free for the chorus.

We have already noticed that this solitary opportunity is not used by Sophocles to direct our minds to theological questions. What is perhaps more surprising is that he does not allow the chorus to say anything about Helenus and his prophecy. The chorus does not say, in effect: 'If he has to be persuaded, then it's a poor look-out for all of us.' If they did say this, we should begin to wonder if it were true, and that would only direct our attention to the illogicality that is coming. What they do say is, simply, that Philoctetes has been abominably treated, and has had ten years of almost unbearable misery. But we know this already: the chorus cannot tell us anything new on this subject. Isn't Sophocles wasting an opportunity, and being a bore into the bargain?

It is not like Sophocles to waste opportunities, nor is he doing it here, if we are on the right lines. In the last of the four stanzas, when Philoctetes is again within ear-shot, the chorus takes up its rôle of Assistant Conspirator; in the first three it sings of nothing but the prolonged and utterly undeserved misery of Philoctetes. Sophocles makes his chorus harp on Philoctetes' sufferings because he does not want our minds to be occupied by anything else. The ode is positive, not negative. The point is that these sufferings which fill the minds of the chorus are also filling the mind of Neoptolemus, and must fill our minds too. Sophocles is making us all feel the impact and the strain of it. *This* is what Odysseus and the Atreidae have done to a helpless ally.

The inward struggle of Neoptolemus is intensified by the next scene. Philoctetes' physical agony, utter helplessness, and complete trust in Neoptolemus are the last straw. Philoctetes gives the bow to Neoptolemus; Neoptolemus has won.

But has he? Since the visit of the merchant we have been wondering, perhaps, if Neoptolemus is not only crawling through mud, but also doing it to no purpose. The idea has been dropped into our minds that Philoctetes must go willingly. The idea has not been confirmed, nor denied, but it is there. Now it is confirmed. We have spent some time in pointing out how illogical it is, from the prosaic point of view, that this confirmation should come from Neoptolemus. But on the other hand, how prosaic it would have been if Sophocles had accommodated his plot to the ideas of the man in the street. This good man may be an excellent judge of a play, but he does not necessarily know how the effects are produced which he so much admires. The man in the street might think, for instance, that Sophocles might have done better to produce a new character at this point, an eminently trustworthy person from Troy, who should give Neoptolemus an indisputable account of what Helenus had said. But if Sophocles had done this, the man in the street would wonder why the play was slow-moving and cumbersome in comparison with Sophocles' other plays, and why it seemed suddenly to lose its dramatic tension. Sophocles' method here combines daring and skill. When Philoctetes is asleep, and the chorus urges Neoptolemus to make off with the bow, Neopto-lemus says something that he has no business to know. Why does Sophocles make him do it? Simply because it is the most 'logical' thing to do. This is the moment when we must be made to realise that Neoptolemus' easy and dishonest victory is no victory at all, only intolerable shame. The way in which it is done is interesting. If Neoptolemus said to the chorus, in plain iambics, 'But you know as well as I do what Helenus said', it would merely make us reflect that what the merchant had said was not evidence. Sophocles is far too good a dramatist to make a mistake of this kind. He knows, no less than Aristotle, the value of a παραλογισμός, a false syllogism; and he knows how safe and how economical it is, in the appropriate circumstances. The implied παραλογισμός here is as follows: Oracles speak in hexameters, and what oracles say is true; Neoptolemus speaks in hexameters, therefore what he says is true. It is perfectly safe, because we are entirely absorbed in something much more im-portant than the mechanics of the plot, namely in Neoptolemus' growing shame, in the 'attack' on him which has been going on for so long, and now proceeds to its climax without a break. An inferior dramatist might have made the plot impeccably logical here, and dissipated our interest; Sophocles' 'illogical' design avoids a lot of lumber. And we may observe once more that as soon as he has made his point he sheers away from it; he knows

E

that the ice is thin. Neoptolemus ends his hexameters with a line that expresses his embarrassment most forcibly:

κομπεῖν δ' ἔστ' ἀτελῆ σὺν ψεύδεσιν αἰσχρὸν ὄνειδος
To boast of failure and lies together is disgrace indeed.

That is where our thoughts are. We know now that Odysseus' clever scheme was futile as well as revolting, and anyone in the theatre who, at this moment, began to ask himself questions about the evidence would not in any real sense be in the theatre at all, but in some foolish little world of his own.

Naturally, Sophocles does not allow the chorus to say anything which would prompt us to ask the fatal question: 'How does he *know* it was a blood-orange?' Without a word being said, he gives us the impression that the chorus, as well as Neoptolemus, knows the new truth, while it can still urge upon Neoptolemus the course which we now know to be futile. The means whereby this is done are very simple. The chorus merely says:

My son, the gods will see to this.

We know perfectly well that they will not; it is not their way. This is a vulgar error, natural enough to this chorus of sailors —but, without our thinking about it, what Neoptolemus has just told us is confirmed: Philoctetes must be persuaded to come willingly. Sophocles may take risks, but he calculates them minutely.

When Philoctetes awakes, Neoptolemus is hard pressed indeed. He goes through the motions of starting for the ship, but it is the hollowest pretence, and it brings him to the heart-broken cry of 903-904:

῞Απαντα δυσχέρεια, τὴν αὑτοῦ φύσιν
ὅταν λιπών τις δρᾷ τὰ μὴ προσεικότα.
When a man is false to his own nature and does what ill-befits him, then all goes wrong.

We should observe that the word δυσχέρεια is echoed from Philoctetes' previous speech. There it meant the unpleasant smell of his wound. Neoptolemus, in effect, is saying: when a man abandons his sense of honour, he finds himself in a world that stinks.

Now we come to the second part of the play. This contains

the illogicalities already noticed, and it prompts many other questions. Why did Sophocles want a *deus ex machina* at all? Why are the several attempts to persuade Philoctetes disposed as they are? For instance, if Neoptolemus knows that Philoctetes is to be healed at Troy, why does he not say so at once instead of waiting until the end of the play—and then producing the information just in time to take the wind out of Heracles' sails? There is an answer to all these questions, and it is always the same answer. The structure of the play is quite intelligible and coherent.

We will continue from where we left off. Neoptolemus can, if he likes, march off with the bow and the pathetically grateful Philoctetes, as if going with him to Greece, but he knows that it will be useless. He must therefore confess the truth and try to persuade him to come to Troy. There are five attempts to persuade him. If we watch them carefully they will help to show us what Sophocles thought his play was about.

The first attempt runs like this (915 ff):

NEOPTOLEMUS: *Desert you? No; what troubles me is that I may be taking you on an unwelcome journey.*

PHILOCTETES: *What do you mean, my son? I do not understand.*

NEOPTOLEMUS: *I will hide nothing. You must sail to Troy, to the Greek army of the Atreidae.*

PHILOCTETES: *Alas! what are you saying?*

NEOPTOLEMUS: *Do not protest until you understand.*

PHILOCTETES: *Understand what? What are you going to do with me?*

NEOPTOLEMUS: *First, to save you from this misery. Then, with your help, to sack Troy.*

PHILOCTETES: *And is this what you really mean to do?*

NEOPTOLEMUS: *It has to be. There is no help for it. Do not be angry with me.*

PHILOCTETES: *Ruin and treachery! Stranger, what have you done to me? Give me back my bow at once!*

NEOPTOLEMUS: *Impossible. Justice and advantage both make me obey my commanders.*

In this passage there are several points to notice. In the first place, the request is made as bleak and uninviting as possible: we note the impersonal expressions δεῖ and ἀνάγκη: 'you must', 'there is no help for it'. Then, there is no talk of glory for Philoctetes; indeed, the impression given is that the glory is mainly for Neoptolemus: 'with your help I shall sack Troy'; 'justice and advantage' implies 'my advantage'. There is no talk of the gods, of any plan they have either for Troy or for Philoctetes. Then, Neoptolemus must needs bring in the Atreidae—and by this time we know what Philoctetes thinks of *them*. Finally, for future reference: we note the vagueness of the phrase 'to save you from this misery', σῶσαι κακοῦ τοῦδε. It is a phrase that may mean much, little, or next to nothing. Certainly it is far from being explicit. In short, the invitation is presented to Philoctetes in such a way that the last thing we expect is that he should accept it. His part has been so built up in the preceding scenes that we take for granted his complete refusal and his passionate denunciation of Neoptolemus' treachery.

This speech nearly breaks Neoptolemus: 'Would to God I had never left Scyros!' It is the abrupt intervention of Odysseus that decides the issue, at least for the moment: but we should observe that this intervention affects Philoctetes, as well as Neoptolemus; for until this moment he had not plumbed to the bottom the infamy of the plot. Moreover, Odysseus is the very man who had caused him to be exposed here, ten years before. In other words, another powerful buttress is added, to make Philoctetes' position the more immovable.

The second attempt at persuasion, if it can be called such, is made now by Odysseus. For the most part it is only a threat of naked force, and we are not surprised when it fails. Nevertheless, Odysseus does advance some reasonable inducement when he says: 'No, we regard you not as a slave, but as the equal of the noblest, with whom you have to capture and destroy the city' (997 f). But he, like Neoptolemus, uses, in the main, impersonal expressions: δεῖ (982), πορευτέα (993), πειστέον (994) —all of which may mean, to Philoctetes, no more than that the Greek commanders have determined that he shall come. Theologians however will observe that Odysseus, unlike Neoptolemus, does mention that it is the will of the gods. Yes—but how does Sophocles make him do it?

> It is Zeus, let me tell you, Zeus, Almighty Zeus, who has decreed this. And I am his servant.

'The devil you are!' we think. We have heard this sort of story before, from villains not unlike Odysseus. If Sophocles wishes us to see in Philoctetes a man who is mistakenly opposing the will of the gods, he is setting about it in a very strange way. Philoctetes' reply is good sense and good theology:

> Loathsome creature! What blasphemies you invent! By pleading the gods you make them cheats.

Odysseus has not tried to be very persuasive. Still, he has in two details advanced beyond what Neoptolemus had said: he has suggested that honour awaits Philoctetes at Troy, and he has stated that it is the will of the gods that Philoctetes should go there. The importance of this is purely structural. As in the matter of Oedipus' banishment, Sophocles is contriving a certain gradation: these two points are mentioned here in order that when the full statement comes from Neoptolemus and Heracles at the end of play we may not be taken completely by surprise. In the same way, when Neoptolemus, in his last long speech, comes out with the news that Philoctetes will be healed at Troy, the audience is not entirely taken aback; it thinks that it has heard something of the kind already. So it has—in Neoptolemus first attempt at persuasion: σῶσαι κακοῦ τοῦδε, 'to save you from this misery', means, at the moment, no more than 'bring you away from Lemnos', but in retrospect it means 'restore you to health'.

But although the two inducements that Odysseus offers do something to prepare the way for the final scene, Sophocles is very careful that they shall be made in such a way that the audience will expect them to have no influence at all on Philoctetes. During these successive attempts at persuasion, which increase in strength, Sophocles is careful that the defence shall always be superior to the attack. The next attempt comes from the chorus; but before dealing with that, we may observe what a good example the Odysseus-scene is of Sophocles' skill in the simultaneous use of three actors.

For a hundred verses (974 to 1073) Neoptolemus is silent, but though silent he is very far from being dramatically inefficient. He stands there with the stolen bow in his hands—and no sensible producer would put him anywhere but in the middle of the stage—and he has to watch this terrible revelation of the callousness of the Greek commander to whose plausible arguments he reluctantly surrendered. The scheme was an astute move to meet a political necessity—and it has come to this. Not only is it barbarous in its cruelty, but also it is quite futile. The audience realises now, even if Neoptolemus' hexameters had not convinced it, that the scheme is futile, for if the presence of Philoctetes at Troy were not necessary, Odysseus would not have been so swift to prevent him from doing away with himself. Odysseus may, a moment later, try to bluff his way through— 'We have the bow, and we can do without you'—but Neoptolemus knows, and we know, that it is bluff. All that Neoptolemus has done is to help to commit a pointless murder; for Philoctetes will die miserably, and the Greek cause will not be helped—in fact it will be ruined. Moreover, as he stands there with the bow, he hears from Philoctetes the bitter truth, that Odysseus has used him only as a catspaw, 'this lad, whom I did not know, unworthy of you, but worthy of me; whose only thought was to obey orders.' He was in an agony of remorse before; what must he be feeling now? He has to listen to Philoctetes' final appeal:

> Son of Achilles, am I not to hear a single word from you?
> Do you leave me like this?
> 'Make off,' says Odysseus; 'you have a generous heart, but do not give him a glance, or you will throw away our success.'

Finally Philoctetes appeals to the chorus, his last resource. They refer him back to Neoptolemus. He cannot escape—nor can he bring himself to speak directly to Philoctetes. He gives his answer to the chorus. He has touched bottom.

What I am calling the third attempt at persuasion is contained in the lyrical dialogue between Philoctetes and the chorus, left behind for the purpose of persuading him, if it can. Probably most readers of Sophocles would agree that the lyrics here are not among Sophocles' most thrilling compositions. They contain no very memorable passages, nothing that finds its way into anthologies. Sophocles, of course, knew this. The whole point of the scene is that he has not called up an impressive battery of philosophic and religious argument, expressed in illuminating poetry, to convince Philoctetes that he should go to Troy. He does not want to make this chorus soar. It would ruin the play if they did.

It would not be to the point to reply that this is a chorus of simple sailors, not of philosophers. That would be to argue that Sophocles was at the mercy of his own creation. But in fact there is no reason why this chorus should not have used weighty religious arguments had Sophocles wanted such. You do not need to be a sage in order to point out that the will of the gods must come to pass, that man should comfort himself with humility in the face of Heaven; still less, in order to suggest that the deliverance of a whole nation from a long war is more important than the satisfaction of a private resentment. A chorus like this could say things like that—but Sophocles does not allow them to.

What does the chorus say here? In the first strophe it says: 'You have brought this calamity upon yourself; it is not a doom imposed on you by a superior power.' This is not an argument likely to impress Philoctetes, in his present mood and situation. In the antistrophe it says 'It is Fate which has brought you to this; it is no guile of ours that has put you into our power. Keep your curses for others; my desire is that you should not reject my friendship.' To call this Fate is nonsense; to disclaim guile is useless; to offer friendship is mockery. In the second strophe it says: 'Certainly a man should speak his mind honestly,[1] but having done so he should not break into the language of hatred. Neoptolemus was only obeying orders to help his friends.' Philoctetes knows this perfectly well: he knows too what those friends are, and what they have done to him. Finally, in the second antistrophe, the chorus says: 'Come with us! It is in your power to escape from this harsh fate.'

Not until this moment does Philoctetes take any notice of what the chorus is saying. We have had what is virtually a long solo lament from Philoctetes, punctuated by these not very impressive remarks from the chorus. It is surely obvious what Sophocles is doing; the very proportions of the lyrics indicate it: the chorus is being kept down in order that our attention may be concentrated on Philoctetes' passionate refusal to help his persecutors. The tepidity of the chorus is explained by the fact that it is acting under orders—Sophocles' orders. It must say nothing to suggest that Philoctetes' refusal, in the circumstances,

---

[1] It seems impossible to make sense of the MSS. reading ἀνδρός τοι τὸ μὲν εὖ δίκαιον εἰπεῖν. I have translated above Arndt's τὰ μὲν ἔνδικ' αἰὲν εἰπεῖν.

is anything but natural. Once more, if at the end of the play we are to see in Philoctetes one who is wrongfully trying to oppose the will of the gods, Sophocles is not being very clever. What he shows us here is a man almost demented by brutal and unnecessary and long-sustained ill-usage. By building him up as he has done, Sophocles has in effect put him beyond the reach of our criticism and censure. This scene leaves us with one thought, that if Philoctetes would rather die than help his enemies, we cannot blame him, and they deserve no better.

Neoptolemus returns, with Odysseus; he can stand it no longer, and has determined to give back the bow. Odysseus is both horrified and incredulous. The conversation turns—as in the first scene—on the difference between cleverness and honesty, τὸ σοφόν and τὸ δίκαιον. Neoptolemus has seen where Odysseus' cleverness has led him, and he will have no more to do with it. Odysseus threatens him with the vengeance of the whole Greek army, but the son of Achilles is unmoved: 'With justice on my side I am not afraid of your threats.' The scene is, so to speak, antistrophic to the scene with which the play opens: there Odysseus, with talk of political cleverness and Neoptolemus' own glory, led the young man by the nose; now the cleverness has proved a sham, the glory unattainable, and disgrace the only outcome; and it is Neoptolemus who is master of the situation. Surely this striking reversal of situation must have been in Sophocles' mind from the moment when he began to design the play—and it has nothing whatever to do with theology, everything to do with political morality; though we must indeed believe that the gods are not indifferent to this. We have not yet heard much about them. Odysseus, not very convincingly perhaps, has claimed to be the servant of Zeus (990), and Neoptolemus, much earlier, hazarded the opinion that Philoctetes' sufferings were caused by the gods for mysterious reasons of their own. Against this we must set the evident implication of the present scene, that Neoptolemus is now acting honestly, which raises the presumption that he is doing what the gods would have him do; and we must set alongside this a passage which we have not yet noticed (1035-1039): 'Ruin seize all of you!' Philoctetes cries; 'And it will, for your unjust treatment of me, if the gods have any regard for justice. And I know they have, because you would never have come here for a miserable man like me unless some goad from heaven were driving you to it.' The play is indeed not yet finished, but so far it has presented us with a consistent design: an act of wanton cruelty has recoiled on its authors, and their astute plan for extricating themselves from their difficulty—one of their own making—is on the point of failing. Odysseus apparently proved to Neoptolemus that public and private interest alike demanded an act of dishonour; now the moral dilemma looks a little less cogent.

In spite of all that Odysseus can say, Neoptolemus gives back the bow, but before he gives it back he makes another attempt to persuade Philoctetes, the fourth attempt in our series, the second which is made by Neoptolemus. It is quite formal, and it fails because, quite naturally, Philoctetes supposes it to be only another trick. But when Neoptolemus has given back the bow and Odysseus has been driven out with contempt, the situation is entirely different. Now Neoptolemus tries again, and this is the occasion on which he says things, both about the future and about the past, which he cannot possibly know. Why does Sophocles arrange things in this illogical fashion, and why does his play not break down in consequence?

We need not separately consider the detail, now mentioned for the first time in the play, that Philoctetes received his wound because he was trespassing on holy ground. This detail is auxiliary to the more important point of the speech, that if Philoctetes goes to Troy he will be cured, but not if he refuses. As the origin of the malady was supernatural, so must its cure be; it is hopeless to expect a natural remedy. This is the reason why the explanation of the whole thing is given here. The reason why it was not given earlier is just as clear. Up to this point Sophocles wants his audience to see Philoctetes as the victim of Greek cruelty, nothing else; he wished to keep the agency of gods out of sight. The situation was to be a purely political one, in the Greek sense of the word. Only now, when the question of healing is for the first time mentioned, is the origin of the malady stated.

But why does Sophocles, quite illogically, give it to Neoptolemus to raise this question and to make such definite statements about it? If Neoptolemus can produce all this information now, in his third attempt to persuade Philoctetes, why could he not have produced it in his first? The need was there; apparently only the knowledge was lacking. And where has the knowledge now come from?

We can go further. There are two characters in the play who could quite logically produce the information which Neoptolemus here produces illogically: Odysseus, because he was present when Helenus made his prophecy, and Heracles, because he is a god. Odysseus had his chance when he tried to persuade Philoctetes. He was desperately anxious that Philoctetes should come, and although he relied mainly on bluster he was not above offering some sort of inducement, as we saw; he even stated that it was the will of Zeus—yet he never mentioned that part of the divine plan that might best have served his purpose. But if, for some unexplained reason, it could not be Odysseus, why not Heracles? But no: Sophocles makes Neoptolemus do it, not only illogically, but also at the cost of depriving Heracles of most of his thunder. While Verrallian realists are exercising their wits on this problem, we will consider it from the truly logical point of view, remembering that a dramatist is a constructive artist.

Robust readers of Greek tragedy, who believe in No Nonsense, may feel like saying: 'The case is very simple. Sophocles was a dramatist; he had therefore to be dramatic, and to hold the attention of his heterogeneous audience. He held back this information about the healing and the imminent fall of Troy simply to make a dramatic climax, and a strong scene between Philoctetes and Neoptolemus.'

It is indeed a dramatic climax, but we may observe that a dramatic climax may be either the true conclusion of a logical development (in which case we want to know what the logic is), or it may be only a theatrical working-up of excitement, like for example the end of the *Iphigenia in Tauris*. Which is this? And in any case Neoptolemus is being dramatic at Heracles' expense.

It is a major dramatic fact, which we must observe and be able to account for, that there is no difficulty whatever in finishing the play quite dramatically without bringing in a *deus ex machina* at all. Odysseus knows what Helenus had said; he is also very anxious to persuade Philoctetes to come with him. Let him therefore do in the play exactly what he would do in reality: let him tell Philoctetes everything, and use what powers of persuasion he can find. Let Philoctetes refuse passionately—

even blasphemously, if the dramatist chooses. Then Neoptolemus, breaking at last with Odysseus, can come back, restore
the bow and put himself unreservedly at Philoctetes' service.
Now there can be a great struggle in the mind of Philoctetes
between his resentment towards the Greek commanders and his
gratitude to Neoptolemus; and the important consideration can
be added that in his hands lies the deliverance from the war of
so many innocent Greek soldiers. At last he decides that he
cannot allow his just rancour to stand in the way of Neoptolemus' own glory and the release of the Greek army. They all
set sail for Troy without the need of a god or of any of the illogicalities, and without any flagging of the dramatic interest. If
we want the parallel between Philoctetes and Heracles, we can
have it; anybody—Neoptolemus or the chorus—can tell us all we
need know about the apotheosis; it does not need the god in
person. Moreover, the play, so designed, would have a serious
import and one not unworthy of Sophocles: we should be left
with the reflection that simple honesty and humanity have
succeeded where fraud and violence had failed, and that in this
way the will of the gods is done.

Having enjoyed the unexpected pleasure of beating Sophocles
at his own game, and finishing the play quite dramatically without using Sophocles' improbabilities, we may ask why we have
been able to do it. The only modest answer is that our ending
makes the play mean one thing, and that Sophocles meant
something else. If, as in our version, the full revelation is made
early, whether by Neoptolemus or by Odysseus, the effect must
be to split our attention between the conspirators and Philoctetes: we shall watch the struggle in Philoctetes' mind between
his own true interest and his long-standing resentment, or, if
the divine plan is emphasised, we shall be frightened on his
behalf that he puts himself into opposition to the will of the
gods. By postponing the revelation, and, in consequence, by
making the attacks on Philoctetes so much weaker than his
natural defences, Sophocles has kept our attention fixed on
Neoptolemus and those whom he is trying to serve. The situation to which he leads us is the complete frustration of Odysseus,
and we watch that with undivided minds. It is perfectly natural,
so we think, that Philoctetes, treated like this, should behave as
he does, and utterly refuse to do anything to help his enemies.

In other words, the play is 'political' rather than theological.

Now we must try to answer the other question, why Sophocles could not wait for Heracles, but committed the improbability of choosing Neoptolemus to announce what was to happen. It is reassuring to find that the only logical answer to this question is the same as the answer to the other question: it is obviously a matter of timing—that is, of dramatic design. The design demanded that Odysseus should first be utterly defeated, and that when this has been accomplished, all possible pressure should be applied to Philoctetes, and that he should still refuse. His refusal in face of everything was obviously a capital point with Sophocles, because it was this that involved the illogicality and the *deus ex machina*.

The point seems quite clear. Philoctetes could not say No to a god; it would be foolish as well as blasphemous. What reason could Sophocles possibly have for making Neoptolemus anticipate Heracles in this illogical and dramatically inconvenient way except that he did want Philoctetes to say No to somebody, in spite of all possible inducements that could be offered him? He will *not* go to Troy, not even to be healed; if the capture of Troy depends on his consent, then Troy will *not* be captured. He cannot refuse these things to Heracles; he can refuse them to Neoptolemus; therefore Sophocles makes Neoptolemus say the things that he ought not to know—things which in any case Heracles too is going to say in five minutes' time. The full pressure must be applied by Neoptolemus; there seems to be no other explanation of what Sophocles does. Now we have to ask why Sophocles wanted this so urgently. What is the design of which this is a necessary part?

The answer to this question seems to be the same as the answer to all the others. In order to find out what it is, we must examine carefully what is said, both by Neoptolemus and by Philoctetes. A moment ago we said that Neoptolemus is made to apply to Philoctetes all possible pressure, In fact, that is not true: the most compelling arguments are carefully avoided, and the whole scene is designed in such a way that, once more, the weight falls on the villainy, and on the frustration, of the Atreidae; and, once more, we are made to feel that Philoctetes' refusal, in the circumstances, is perfectly natural—Neoptolemus actually says so himself.

Neoptolemus' most 'illogical' speech is to this effect:

> I am glad to hear you praise my father. Now, listen to what I
> would have you do. Men have to bear what cannot be avoided,
> but there is no sense in undergoing unnecessary suffering, as you
> threaten to do. But you have become savage: when a friend gives
> you good advice, you treat him as if he were an enemy. But this
> is the truth, and be Zeus my witness: This malady of yours comes
> from your trespassing on Chrysê's domain, and so long as the sun
> rises in the east and sets in the west, it cannot be cured, unless you
> come to Troy, of your own accord, and capture it with this bow
> and with my help[1]. Helenus disclosed this to us, and staked his life
> on the truth of it. He said too that Troy is to fall this very summer.
> Come to Troy, then, where healing and great glory await you.

Philoctetes says in reply that he wishes he were dead. How can
he refuse such a request?—referring to Neoptolemus in the
third person. Yet how can he possibly consent? His own sense
of honour forbids him to help Odysseus and the Atreidae, who
have been his ruin; they are treacherous, and it would be folly
to put himself again in their power. He is surprised that
Neoptolemus himself should have anything to do with them,
after they have robbed him of his father's armour. 'No,' he says,
'take me home as you promised; remain yourself in Scyros, and
leave these villains to perish as they deserve.'

Neoptolemus' reply to this outburst could hardly be milder:
'What you say is reasonable'; λέγεις μὲν εἰκότα. 'Still,' he continues, 'I wish you would trust the gods, and my friendly advice,
and sail with me to Troy.'

'What? To Troy? To that hateful Agamemnon? With this
foot of mine? . . . How can you say such things and not feel
shame before the gods? . . . Are you thinking of my interests
—or of theirs? . . . How can you wish me to surrender myself
to my enemies? . . . Don't you know that they cast me ashore?
. . . No. I will never set eyes on Troy . . . Take me home, and
do not mention Troy again.' This Neoptolemus agrees to do—
wondering however how he will escape the vengeance of the
Atreidae. But Philoctetes has the answer to that question too:
if they venture to attack Neoptolemus, he will come to his
defence with the unerring bow. This is the last turn of the plot

---

[1] In his first attempt at persuasion Philoctetes had said (more uninviting-
ly): 'I am to capture Troy with your help.'

proper; with evident relief Neoptolemus prepares to assist Philoctetes to his ship. The Atreidae are left to face ruin; they cannot even take revenge on Neoptolemus.

In contemplating this scene, we observe once more that Sophocles carefully avoids the argument that by going to Troy Philoctetes would be setting free the Greek army. This would be an argument which Philoctetes could not easily withstand; therefore the army is not mentioned; only the Atreidae. We observe too that the theological argument is not used. Neoptolemus states the fact that Troy is fated to fall that very summer, but he refrains from basing any argument on that fact—though it would not need much theological acumen to say 'What the gods have decreed must come to pass. Opposition is idle, and can only anger the gods. I am afraid to sail home with you, lest a bolt from Zeus should destroy us both.' But no: nothing of the kind is even hinted at. The pressure put upon Philoctetes is most carefully restricted; the arguments used are prudential only—and prudential arguments Philoctetes is entitled to reject, if he wants to. He does reject them, and Neoptolemus entirely accepts the rejection.

To be sure, he does begin by using quite outspoken language about Philoctetes' obstinacy—but what does it amount to? 'You will not listen to friendly advice; you have become savage.' No doubt he has; but who has caused him to become savage? This censure is no more than a dramatic apology for Philoctetes' continued resistance: the man has been made savage—by what? By the sustained ill-treatment that he has suffered.

The effect therefore of this timing, especially when we take it in strict connexion with the arguments used, is to show us that what the Atreidae and Odysseus have done to Philoctetes has so bitten into his soul that he will himself willingly endure his malady to the end rather than rescue his tormenters from the disaster which they so justly merit; and whatever we may choose to think of his attitude, it is notable, and important, that neither Neoptolemus nor Heracles blames him. Neoptolemus may think him ill-advised, and Heracles may magically dissolve his refusal, but neither of them suggests that he is morally wrong. We have here a real climax, and it is one which could not have been reached in any other way but by the illogicality.

As we have seen, the illogical detail about the origin of the malady is part and parcel of the major one, the prophecy of the healing. There is another detail in this passage, mentioned already, which now finds its explanation: Neoptolemus, who had apparently never heard of Helenus until the pseudo-merchant arrived, can now inform us that he offered the Greeks his head if he were not proved to be speaking the truth. The explanation is simple: it is another παραλογισμός, like Neoptolemus' hexameters. The vivid detail convinces us for the moment—and the moment is all that matters in something quite accessory—that Neoptolemus knows what he is talking about: his report is true. If the artist is using distortion he must use it boldly; there is no sense in being half-hearted about it.

There is yet another point. The fact that Troy is to fall this very summer is stated by Neoptolemus, but (as we have seen) not used by him in the subsequent argument; on the contrary it is entirely disregarded, since Neoptolemus agrees to take Philoctetes home, and to have no more to do with the Atreidae —as if this were a possible course. This detail at least might have been reserved for Heracles, who so badly needs something exciting to say. Why did Sophocles give it to Neoptolemus? Pure oversight? That is not very likely, in the middle of a scene which in any case had demanded so much contrivance and calculation. May the explanation be that Sophocles thought it best to make a complete job of the prophecy while he was about it? Or is there something further? The point bears a strong family resemblance to an earlier one—the way in which the merchant, like a man dropping a stone into a pond, told us that Philoctetes was to be persuaded. Though nothing more was said about it for a long time, the idea was there, at the bottom of our minds, making us suspect that Neoptolemus was sacrificing his honour for nothing; and at last the idea was certified. So here: the statement is made, and then disregarded by all concerned.[1] Sophocles turns our attention to other things—but he has told us, virtually, that Philoctetes will in fact go to Troy. As the argument continues, we realise that it will need a miracle to get him there. We are therefore the less surprised when the miracle occurs. I am inclined, therefore, to see in this detail, an illogicality within an illogicality, another 'distortion' in the interest of the whole design. It helps to make the end of the play smooth,

[1] Like Creon's condemnation of Ismene. (See below, pp. 143 f.)

and therefore convincing. The only alternative is to suppose that Sophocles was, for the moment, asleep. Rationalism, of the market-place kind, has certainly nothing to say here.

Anyone who finds the Heracles scene an inevitable and impressive culmination to the whole argument of the play will necessarily disagree with what is being said here. Those on the other hand who find it conventional, or at least contrived, and less exciting than most of Sophocles' poetry and drama, will at once see that there is good reason why it should be so. They will not be unduly impressed with external explanations of the scene—that it was added by Iophon; that Sophocles, for once, could not extricate himself from his plot without divine help; that he wanted to imitate Euripides. It is true, though not in the rudimentary sense, that Heracles 'cuts the knot', but it is one which Sophocles himself has deliberately and skilfully tied, and for an ascertainable purpose.

We have been shown how a σόφισμα, a clever stratagem, was propounded to an inexperienced but honourable young man; admittedly an immoral trick, but still the only solution of a grave political difficulty—in fact, a means of achieving victory and personal glory. We have seen how the 'stratagem' proved to be so repulsive as to be unendurable to Neoptolemus, and at the same time quite useless. It has been made quite clear that what Philoctetes has been suffering was decreed not by the gods but by the Atreidae and Odysseus; also, that what they have done to him has so embittered him that he refuses—recklessly it may be, but quite naturally—to help them now, in spite of the carefully selected inducements held out to him.

But there is something else in the play which we have not yet noticed, and it points in the same direction. So far we have said nothing, except negatively, about the gods. Sophocles himself does not say very much; the 'exciting personal issues' claim most of our attention. Yet what he does say is of great importance, and is very Sophoclean.

If the Greek commanders are to extricate themselves from the long struggle at Troy, the help of two named men is necessary, and it is a coincidence that one of these should be the very man whom they have so conspicuously ill-used. But coincidences, in Sophocles, are not as a rule simply a dramatic convenience; they are rather the revelation and affirmation of a world-order, as for example the Messengers in the *Electra* and the *Oedipus* arrive just when they do. Sometimes this Order is manifestly Justice, or at least Dikê. Sometimes its meaning is hardly to be apprehended, as in the *Oedipus*, or the *Trachiniae*, where the poison that destroys Heracles comes immediately from Nessus. whom he slew, and ultimately from the Hydra, whom also he had slain—both of them justly. Even when we cannot see Justice, we can at least see Order. In the *Philoctetes* we can see both. The crime which the Atreidae committed recoils on them, years later, when they find that they cannot take Troy without their victim's willing help—which he, naturally, will not give them. In this we can see the mysterious principle of Dikê. Philoctetes was right, and eminently Sophoclean, when he said: 'You will perish for what you have done to me, if the gods have any concern for Dikê—as I know they have, or you would not have been compelled to come for me.' Their own sin, after ten years, recoils on their own heads. Further, Sophocles does here just what he does in the *Electra*, and (as I hope to show) in the *Antigone* too: he not only shows that Dikê fulfils itself; he also shows the way in which it fulfils itself: it works in a way which is entirely natural. This is the whole purport of the penultimate scene: to show that Philoctetes, having been wronged in this way by the Atreidae, both in the past and now, will naturally act as he now does.

The theology of the play is therefore almost the opposite of what is suggested by Bowra. The idea that Philoctetes is opposing the Will of the Gods creates in any case severe inconveniences. One is that Philoctetes is a character so entirely sympathetic that we do not easily see him in the guise of an obstructor of the gods who needs a lesson in modesty. Another is that it makes the role of Neoptolemus incomprehensible: when he is lending himself to the villainy of Odysseus, he is helping to oppose the divine will in one way; but behold! when he becomes wholly admirable, recovering his moral poise, and renouncing glory in order to fulfil his promise to Philoctetes, then he is helping to oppose the will of the gods in another way. This may be theology, of a kind, but one misses the Hellenic clarity. The source of the trouble is the assumption that the Will of the Gods, in this play, is represented by their decree that Troy shall fall at a certain time in a certain way. Throughout the greater part of the play the oracle is presented in a conditional form: You shall not take Troy unless you persuade Philoctetes to come of his own accord. Of this, we can make good sense, as I hope we have done. Only in the penultimate scene is the oracle stated as a specific prophecy, that Troy shall fall at a certain time— and then, as we have noticed, Sophocles allows the dialogue to continue on the assumption that this may not happen after all, and he does not make us feel that Neoptolemus is attempting the impossible and the blasphemous in consenting to take Philoctetes home. Surely the immediate dramatic effect of this is to give the specific prophecy only a conventional value: the serious, the really theological end of the play is the idea that the Atreidae and Odysseus are frustrated by what they themselves have done, with the further idea that men like Odysseus, with their apparently clever arguments and schemes, are morally repulsive and politically disastrous; and that they are this because what they do, or attempt to do, runs counter to the will of the gods, or the whole order of things, which is Dikê. Odysseus may worship Athena Victory and Hermes the Deceiver, but victory eludes him, and if anybody is deceived it is Odysseus.

When Neoptolemus makes ready to take Philoctetes to his ship, the logical design of the play is complete. But for two reasons Sophocles cannot leave it here. In the first place, this is an occasion in which history is not so philosophic as poetry: Troy did fall, and the Atreidae were not ruined—or not at Troy. In the second place, the ending would have been philosophically and aesthetically uncomfortable; we should have to contemplate the hero passing the rest of his life in helpless misery because of a single accident for which he was not to blame. This in itself is not necessarily untragic; indeed, the subject of the *Oedipus* is not far removed from this. But the unmerited suffering that comes to Oedipus is bearable—to us—because it is significant of something; it is integrated with the conception of a world-order. The *Philoctetes* too is based on such a conception, but in a different aspect. Here too a pattern of life is disclosed, but it is complete when Philoctetes the victim of the Greek commanders, and Neoptolemus their dupe, decide to leave them to their fate. If now a lifetime of suffering awaited Philoctetes, that would open up another religious problem, to resolve which would need another play. This play would end on a discord. Sophocles therefore, unwilling to leave the problem unresolved, simply removes it from our minds by introducing Heracles to make all well for Philoctetes, and we gladly acquiesce; Philoctetes' wound has in any case been only a datum for the play, not part of its essence.

In composing the speech for Heracles, the poet is careful not to make him say anything that touches on the real philosophic structure of the play, which now stands complete. Nothing is said about the Atreidae, or Odysseus, or Dikê, or the meaning of Philoctetes' long agony. All that has gone before is left intact; Philoctetes' refusal to go to Troy is dissolved in such a way that his reasons for not going remain valid. But his acceptance of glory and health, like the reference to the death of Paris, and the second capture of Troy by the bow of Heracles, all contribute to a sense of finality; and they do this not in any mechanical way, but by suggesting that there is a world-order, and in this case a beneficent one. The play is a Comedy in the sense that wickedness is punished and virtue triumphs. The two aspects of this double termination are in fact incompatible; Philoctetes and Neoptolemus cannot in fact triumph without also giving victory to the Atreidae. But what is impossible in fact is sometimes possible in drama. Here, one might say, Sophocles superimposes an ideal ending on the real one, in such a way that the one does not annul or even obscure the other, but each retains its own validity.

CHAPTER FIVE

Antigone

THE plot of the Antigone is well worth study: it tells us so much about the play, and the play is one which has received diverse interpretations. There is no dispute about its power, or the splendour and subtlety of the character-drawing, or the force with which the central conflict is presented; and if little is said on these matters in this chapter, the only reason is that it has been very well said already. But there is dispute what the central issue is, or perhaps we should rather say, in what terms we should express it, where we should lay the emphasis. Is the play essentially political: the State *versus* the conscience of the individual? Is it about the concept of the Unwritten Laws, and so a contribution to contemporary political theory? Is it on the other hand conceived in the heroic tradition, being a study of an ideal heroine? Is it an Aristotelian tragedy of character; and if so, what is the ἁμαρτία, the 'tragic flaw', in Antigone? Or is the central figure not Antigone but Creon?

Not all these views are incompatible; it may be simply a question where we should lay the chief emphasis. But that is worth finding out, and surely Sophocles himself put it *somewhere*. What we want is not simply an interesting, a partial or a defensible interpretation; we would like to know, as nearly as we can, what Sophocles 'meant'. If he was a competent artist, he has told us.

We may begin with a fifty-year old article by Drachmann,[1] which, I imagine, no one has taken seriously for a long time. This may savour of an exhumation, but nevertheless the proceedings may prove instructive.

The plot of the *Antigone* contains at least as many illogicalities as that of the *Philoctetes*. Drachmann examined and explained them—some of them—quite logically, and it is interesting to

[1] *Hermes* XLIII; republished the following year (in English) in the *Classical Review* (1909).

see where his logic took him, and why. He noticed the following absurdities:

(1) Vv. 249-252 have no meaning. (This is the passage in which the Watchman reports that there was no sign of spade, pickaxe or waggon.) 'That this is nonsense hardly needs saying.'

(2) Vv. 256-258 imply that a light covering of dust protected the body from animals: 'Fine dust lay on it, as if someone were avoiding a curse, and there was no sign that any dog or animal had come and mauled it.' Moreover, what is merely implied here is explicitly stated by Haemon at 696 ff ' . . . who, when her own brother lay slaughtered and unburied, prevented (οὐκ εἴασε, the aorist tense) wild beasts and birds from destroying him.' Further, we learn from Teiresias that when the dust was removed, animals and birds did come and devour the body. But, said Drachmann, it is impossible that a light covering of dust should ward off animals from a dead body—and who can deny that?

These are good points, and I think that they have never been fairly met. To them, Drachmann added weaker ones:

(3) Elsewhere in the play Sophocles uses language that implies actual entombment, as for example at 503: ἐν τάφῳ τιθεῖσα.

(4) Creon's outburst of rage against the Watchman is quite unreasonable, and is left without any explanation.

To account for all this, Drachmann evolved a theory which it is unnecessary to state and refute in detail, but in outline it was this. Sophocles began his play having in mind a version of the story in which Antigone, obviously with help, actually removed the body, and interred it in a convenient tholos-tomb somewhere in the neighbourhood; then, having got as far as the Teiresias-scene, he realised that it would be much more effective if the body were still lying unburied, polluting Heaven and Earth. Therefore he went back and modified the earlier part of the play, substituting the symbolic for the real burial. Now everything can be explained (or nearly everything), including one detail which does not need explanation and is none the better for it, namely Creon's rage. Antigone really had protected the body; she had put it in a tomb. The spade-and-cart passage becomes intelligible: the body had completely disappeared. Antigone's return to the body is also explained. The custom was to offer libations to the dead on the third day, and, naturally, only at a regular grave. This is what Antigone did—except that Sophocles felt justified in disregarding the usual two-day interval.

This is one way of being logical. All is explained—except two things. One of these is Sophocles; for we have to believe that this experienced dramatist wrote about half of his play before he saw that the plot was not quite good enough; then continued with a different plot, and revised the first part accordingly, but in such a slipshod way that he left standing several important details which make manifest nonsense. The other thing which is not explained is the human race, which has unsuspectingly accepted this ill-contrived structure as one of its greatest achievements, without realising that it does not really make sense.

It is easy to laugh at Drachmann's theory, and to diagnose the cause of his error: a naïvely realistic theory of art; but we shall laugh with a better conscience if we can give better answers to the questions which he raised.

Three years after Drachmann's article appeared, another logician, the always-enterprising Rouse, took up the challenge of the famous double-burial.[1] One of the earliest scholars to be troubled by this had been Jebb, who wrote (in 1888): 'The essence of the symbolic act was the sprinkling of the dust. Antigone had done that (v. 245). Was it not then done once for all? . . . I have never seen this question put or answered. The only answer which I can suggest is that on her first visit she had not brought the libations.'

The next question is obvious: Then why not? Jebb had put the question to himself the wrong way round. We should not ask 'Why did Antigone go back?', as if it were a real event into which we are enquiring; we should ask 'Why did Sophocles make Antigone go back, without giving a clear reason for it?' Rouse's explanation is worth considering for a moment, not only because it still has adherents (as I happen to know), but also because it illustrates, in a way different from Drachmann's, how disastrous logic can be when it is the wrong logic. The first burial, said Rouse, was performed not by Antigone at all, but by Ismene. Does she not say so herself?

By taking Ismene's confession seriously, Rouse not only solved the difficulty of the second burial, but also turned Ismene into a much more interesting character than most of us had taken

her to be. First she recoiled from Antigone's proposal; but she
has second thoughts, and in the hope of saving her sister she
goes out quickly and does it herself. But the Guards remove
Ismene's dust, so that Antigone, not knowing that the rite has
been performed, does it again, and is caught. When the sisters
meet again, before Creon, Ismene realises that she has after all
failed to save Antigone, and Antigone has no idea that Ismene
has done anything.

A brilliant plot—though more like Hardy than Sophocles
perhaps—but it has its inconveniences. One is that Ismene
comes to her heroic decision when she is in the changing-room,
and then says nothing about it. This makes things difficult for
the audience, especially as it is being completely absorbed meanwhile in Antigone and Creon, and has no thought for Ismene.
Still worse is the fact that this reading of the situation turns the
part of Creon into an enigma. First he jumps to the conclusion
that political treachery is at work, and threatens the guards with
instant death. In this he is both mistaken and monstrously
unjust. Next, he observes that Ismene, in the palace, is almost
out of her mind with anxiety. The ordinary spectator, in the
audience, might take the reason to be that she was worried
about Antigone; not so the clear-sighted Creon. He jumps to a
different conclusion—and this time he is right: Ismene confesses:

> *I did the deed, if she allows my claim;*
> *I take and bear my portion of the charge.*

This confession Antigone at once rejects:

> *No; Justice will not suffer this, because*
> *You stood aloof, and I refused your aid.*

Ismene naturally replies:

> Ἀλλ' οὐ γὰρ οἶσθα χειρὸς ἐξ ἐμῆς ὅτι
> ἤδη ταφὰς ἐδέξατ' ἄθλιος κάσις;
>
> *What? know you not that our unhappy brother*
> *Had been already sepultured—by me?*

Unfortunately this beautiful and intelligent couplet is not the
poet's, but my own. All that Sophocles allows her to say is: 'I
wish to stand by you in your trouble.' However, Creon is not
deceived: Ismene was directly implicated, and in a moment he
reaffirms the sentence of death which he passed on her before

ever she spoke. He may be cruel, but this time at least he is not mistaken.

But there is a surprise in store for us. Some two hundred verses later (vv. 769 ff) the following dialogue takes place:

CREON: *These girls at least shall not escape their doom.*
CHORUS: *Is it your purpose then to kill them both?*
CREON: *Not her who had no part in it.—I thank you.*

But no fresh evidence has come to light. Yet Creon, quite casually, acquits Ismene as being obviously innocent. And this time he is wrong.

This, surely, is a very expensive explanation of the double burial. It would involve Sophocles in an elaborate though obscure development of a character who immediately disappears from the play without having contributed to it anything worthy of so much attention. It would make the audience look for some significance in the fact that the one 'guilty' sister escapes while the other is condemned; also in the fact that Creon first condemns her on at least some evidence, and then acquits her when she has actually made something like a confession. But the audience would look in vain. Total confusion of this kind is a heavy price to pay for an explanation of the double burial, which even so does nothing to explain the other illogicalities which troubled Drachmann—the spade-and-waggon passage and the supernatural efficacy of the dust. There is indeed much to account for—even more than these two critics realised—but this kind of logic will not help us to do it.

For let us observe what Sophocles does hereabouts. Antigone has appealed to the unwritten Laws. In the middle of his furious reply, Creon condemns Ismene to death, and orders her to be brought before him. And what does Antigone say to this? Does she protest against this monstrous injustice? No. Do we then feel that she ought to; that she is being strangely self-centred in allowing a sister, whom she knows to be innocent, to be condemned without protest? Again, no. But why not? For the same cause which prevents our being surprised when the chorus in the *Agamemnon* says nothing about the destruction of the fleet[1]: the play is not conceived on this personal level at all. What is filling our minds here is the clash between Creon

[1] See below, p. 200.

and Antigone, and although this is a clash of persons, it is still
more a clash of principles. In fact, however vividly we see and
feel the persons, we are shown only those aspects of them that
belong most necessarily to the clash of principles. Instead of
protesting about Ismene Antigone continues her own high
argument, and the whole texture and style of the play are such
that it never occurs to us that she should do anything else. But
we cannot have it both ways. If we are taking that catholic
degree of personal interest in the individual characters which
Rouse assumed, perhaps unconsciously, when he created his
interesting but irrelevant Ismene, then we should now be
wondering from what obscure motives Antigone fails to defend
her sister; and of course in trying to divine these we should miss
the significance of what she is in fact saying. We should be
trying to understand on one level a scene which was conceived
on a different one—a thing which, in the theatre, our uncorrupted commonsense saves us from attempting.

But there are stranger things to come. Ismene arrives, and
confesses—tentatively. Her avowal is instantly disclaimed by
Antigone—rather harshly perhaps, which is a point we will
return to later. Presently Ismene is saying:

> But scorn me not; do not refuse that I
> May share your death and piety towards the dead.

Antigone answers:

> You shall not die with me, nor claim as yours
> What is not yours. My death shall be enough.
> —Parted from you, what life can give me joy?
> —Ask Creon! All your care has been for him.

Soon Ismene is asking:

> Can I do nothing, even at this late hour?
> —Preserve your life; I grudge not your escape.
> —Ah, woe is me! Can I not share your doom?
> —No; you did choose to live, and I to die.

And presently from Antigone:

> Be comforted; you have your life, but mine
> Died long ago, that I might serve the dead.

'You have your life': σὺ μὲν ζῇς. But she hasn't! Ismene too is
under sentence of death. Could anything be more illogical than

this whole dialogue, which simply disregards what we have just been told (and are soon told again), that both sisters are to die? It is exactly parallel with the treatment of Helenus' prophecy at the end of the *Philoctetes*.[1] Yet it is so logical, in the true sense of the word, that I myself, though long familiar with the play, never noticed it until I was writing the second draft for the present chapter. This suggests either that it is a very effective case of artistic 'distortion', or (if Sophocles was unconscious of what he was doing) that it was, to him, the natural and direct means of saying what he wanted to say. In either case it would be part of a design; and if it is, we may hope to find the design into which it fits.

Here then, in the double burial, the spade-and-waggon passage, the miraculous dust, and the whole treatment of Ismene's condemnation, are illogicalities to which we may hope to find a sensible and coherent explanation. If there is one, it will be found by methods unlike those of Drachmann and Rouse; it will not rest on the assumption that Sophocles is directly reporting what might have been a real event. Sophocles was not a photographer. Moreover, it will do what explanations like these do not do: it will explain all the illogicalities, not only a selected few. The play does in fact make perfectly good artistic sense as it stands, so that we will not accept an explanation which requires us to reconstruct it, to drag out of the background something that Sophocles either left there, or did not put there at all. Further, it will explain a host of other dramatic facts, of which these illogicalities are only a special type. As we have spent some time in considering these only, it would be well to redress the balance by looking now at some of the others.

To begin with, there are two points of structure which have been called dramatic blemishes.

When Creon is finally beaten down by Teiresias, and asks the chorus what he is to do, they reply: 'Go and release Antigone, then bury the body.' This, then, is what we expect him to do. In the event, he does the two things in the reverse order, so that he arrives at the tomb too late. On this, Jebb makes two comments. One is that Greek drama shows 'an occasional lack of clearness, and even consistency, in regard to matters which either precede the action of the play, or, though belonging to the

[1] See above, p. 133.

play itself, occur off-stage.' This is certainly true—except that it is an understatement: we have just noticed a 'lack of clearness' in a matter which is certainly not off-stage, for is Ismene under sentence of death, or not? The second comment is that Sophocles was concerned for the rhetorical effectiveness of his messenger-speech: it would have fallen flat had it begun with the scene at the tomb, and ended with the obsequies of Polyneices. That means that Sophocles, for the moment, was not being an artist, but only a rhetorician, if he put effectiveness before meaning and significant structure. Possible, no doubt, but he would also be a not very clever one, for he could easily have avoided the 'blemish' by making the chorus tell Creon to do the two things in the order in which in fact he does them.

A second 'fault' is that by not bringing back the body of Antigone, Sophocles does not give the play the complete unity that it might have had. If this is a fault, it is a rudimentary one —and very thoroughgoing, since he does not even mention Antigone in the last hundred verses. Fault or not, it is a dramatic fact, and obviously one of some importance.

Here are two more details, one of structure, one of style; both are in themselves quite small, but neither in literary criticism nor in experimental science is the significance of a detail necessarily proportionate to its size. At 772, when Creon has acquitted Ismene but reaffirmed his sentence on Antigone, the chorus enquires what form of punishment he will inflict. Creon tells them: imprisonment, and death by starvation. But Creon had already proclaimed what the punishment was to be: death by stoning (v. 36). Why the discrepancy? Why does the dramatist change his mind in public like this? Or is it Creon who changes his mind? The answer may be quite simple, but at least the question exists. If it is not a stupid little oversight, then Sophocles had some reason for telling us that Creon has changed his mind, since there was no commanding necessity for Antigone, in the earlier passage, to specify the method of punishment.

The stylistic detail is that Teiresias, before he delivers his warning to Creon, describes at length the omens on which it is based; he takes more than a dozen verses over it: there was strange clamour among the birds, who were tearing themselves with their talons; frightened by this he tried burnt-offering, but the fatty parts which he laid on the blazing altar would not burn

—another baffling event. Now, one of the older critics made an interesting observation on this passage. He compared it with the similar situation in the *Tyrannus*, where also Teiresias comes with a prophetic message; and he pointed out that in the later play there is no such elaborate description of the technical side of the seer's art. The comparison, he said, shows how Sophocles' own art had matured in the interval; it had become more reticent, and thereby more impressive.

An interesting judgment; but it is made, so to speak, in a vacuum, with no reference to the dramatic context. It could be the case, and I think is the case, that each method is right, for its own purpose. At all events, it is another fact to consider.

From these two specimen details we may turn to matters of at least more apparent importance. What happens to Creon during the extensive lyrical parts of the play?

A modern producer might naturally say: 'During an ode, Creon has nothing to do; therefore he must make an exit at the end of one scene and come back for the next—unless perhaps the ode is a short one. A little awkward perhaps, but not so awkward as to have him standing about quite idle.' On the proscenium-stage, this might be the best thing to do, but what was done in the Athenian theatre? Sophocles, unlike Aeschylus, appears usually to indicate entrances and exits. Thus we read, immediately after the second ode:

WATCHMAN: *We caught this girl in the act.—But where's Creon?*
CHORUS: *Here he comes, opportunely, from the palace.*

It is clear, then, that Creon is not on-stage during the second ode. What of the third? At 581, Jebb, who was usually careful in these matters, prints as a stage-direction: *Exeunt Attendants, guarding Antigone and Ismene. Creon remains*; and this seems to be correct, for when, after the ode, Haemon is seen coming, Creon is already there to receive him.

At the end of this scene Jebb gives: *Exit Creon*—and then forgets to bring him back for his harsh and sudden interruption at 883. A mere slip, of course—or is it a real mistake? *Does* Creon go off at the end of the Haemon-scene? There is no indication in the text of the exit that Jebb prescribes, nor of the entrance that he forgot to prescribe; though this does not prove that Creon remains. If he remains, it is through the fourth ode, which is short, and the Commos, which is long: over a hundred verses, in all, of singing and dancing. We may well think this awkward, as Jebb seems to have done. However, we consider the fact that when this scene comes to an end, with Antigone's last speech and her exit, again there is no indication that Creon leaves the stage as the fifth ode begins: and when it ends, and Teiresias quite unexpectedly arrives, Creon is there to greet him. It looks therefore as if we have to choose between two things equally awkward (unless we make a purely artificial compromise between them): either Creon is on the stage during the third ode, the fourth and the commos, and the fifth, with nothing to do; or during this part of the play he comes and goes twice, with supernatural punctuality, and without any indication in the text.

But is not all this only making a mountain out of a molehill? Possibly. It may be said that it was a pure convention, of which the Greek audience took no notice, that an actor should remain on the stage, stock-still, during an ode, or even a commos.[1] But I am not sure if this disposes of the matter. For instance, eighteenth-century music, and Romantic music, use certain turns of phrase that we may call conventional formulae; we hear such a one in the music of some contemporary of Mozart, or of Beethoven, and we say to ourselves: 'Yes, Mozart (or Beethoven) does that too—but how different it sounds when *he* does it!' The great artist can make purposeful use of a convention which, to another, is merely a convenience. Therefore I think we should be wise to keep in mind the possibility that the presence on the stage, during the lyrical parts, of Creon was a part of Sophocles' design, and means something.

The preceding hardly amounts to a dramatic fact; we will turn to something that undeniably does. It concerns the importance of burial-rites.

Those who write about the *Antigone* tend to be rather apologetic on this matter. It was believed by the Greeks that unless a body was buried, literally or symbolically, the soul of the dead man could not find rest in Hades; this explains why such importance is given, in this play, to the burial of Polyneices. It is remarkable how many commentators have told us this; re-

---

[1] Though I cannot think of another play in which a silent actor seems to be present during a commos.

markable, because one has only to read the play to see that it contains not a single word about the peace of Polyneices' soul. But that would be taken for granted; matters of common knowledge or belief are tacitly assumed between dramatist and audience.

This doctrine of 'tacit assumption' is extremely dangerous to criticism.[1] Up to a certain point it is obviously true: if a dramatist tells us that his hero has lost a leg, he will not add that he has only one left, however important that fact may be to his plot. But it is certainly not true that matters of common knowledge necessarily *are* assumed. In the theatre we look after ourselves; the critic has to use his judgment, and be careful. As to the present matter, we can produce a dozen or more passages from up and down Greek literature to prove that this belief existed—but what of that? If we say that Sophocles believed it, we are saying what we do not know; and if we bring it into our interpretation of the play, we are adding to the play something which demonstrably is not there, with the usual result: we are making it more difficult to notice what *is* there. The demonstration is simple. Negatively, not a single word is said about Polyneices' soul.[2] Positively, there are several moments in the play when Antigone, passionately, even desperately, tells us why she had to bury him, whatever the cost. Are we then to suppose that the most compelling reason of all, the eternal peace of her brother's soul, was 'tacitly assumed'? This would be sheer stultification; the audience could only wonder why on earth she wasn't saying it.

The intrusive idea pushes something else out. What Sophocles emphasises, time after time, is the mangling of Polyneices' body. Antigone says to Ismene (26 ff): 'But Polyneices' body must lie, unlamented and unburied, a rich store of meat for hungry birds.' Creon says (198 ff): 'None shall give him burial. No; he shall lie unburied, his body devoured by birds and dogs, a foul sight to see.' The next reference comes in Haemon's speech. He reports the common people as saying: 'Has she not

---

[1] This topic crops up again with regard to *Hamlet*; p. 259.

[2] Antigone does indeed say of herself (850 ff) 'I have no place either among the living or among the dead'; but since in her next stanza she says 'I am going, unwedded and accursed, to dwell with my father and my mother'— who presumably *had* been buried—she obviously means no more than 'I am going to my living grave'.

done a most glorious thing? When her own brother was slain and lay unburied, did not she save him from being destroyed by hungry birds and dogs?' Finally, we may note the grim detail in the messenger-speech: 'We buried what little was left.'

This is a dramatic fact, and I suggest that it is an important one. It is clearly one which we must take into account when we are considering Antigone's motives. It is perhaps even more important, that it makes it quite unnecessary for us, when we are introducing the *Antigone* to new readers, to remark by way of preface: 'You must understand, and take for granted, that the Greeks had certain religious ideas, foreign to us, about the burial of the dead.' So perhaps they did, but the fact is irrelevant and misleading. What Sophocles relies on and presents again and again is the sheer physical horror, the sense of indecent outrage, that we all feel, modern English as well as ancient Greek, at the idea that a human body, the body of someone we have known and maybe loved, should be treated like this. Let us keep our learned *scholia* for occasions on which they are necessary and useful.

As for Antigone's motives, one would say perhaps, so far as the first scene is concerned, that they are overwhelmingly personal and instinctive. It is one of these scenes in which the reader may profitably remind himself of the literal meaning of the Greek word *theatre*: a place where one looks. The visual effect here may have been important. In the theatre for which Sophocles was writing, the orchestra was a large space—something like eighty feet in diameter. In ten minutes or so the audience will see the chorus moving all over this area in its joyful and confident dance of victory. After that, Creon and his bodyguard will be added. These will dominate the space. In the first scene it will be empty, but for the two girls—and we may be sure that they were brought well out into the middle; the surrounding space will dominate them, two lonely figures; one of whom, out of love, loyalty, humanity, religion, proposes to defy all the strength of the King. There is one reference in the scene to religious duty: the passage (77 f) in which Antigone says to Ismene 'You, if you think fit, may hold in scorn τὰ τῶν θεῶν ἔντιμα, things on which the gods lay great store.' But for this one reference to religious duty, everything is instinctive—her bitter anger, her scorn of Creon, 'the ex-

cellent Creon' (31), her horror that her brother should become meat[1] for animals, her cry: 'It is *my* brother—and yours;
I will not desert him!' and 'He has no title to keep me from my
own!' (45-48). We shall hear rather different language from
her when she confronts Creon and speaks so majestically of the
Divine Law, but it may be that we shall not fully understand
that unless we have first understood this. Here, surely, Sophocles makes us feel that it is her whole being that rises in revolt
against a monstrous decree.

The contrast between the sisters is drawn with a brilliance
and a suddenness which need no comment; but as the scene
ends, we may once more recall the size of the theatre: the
sisters go their separate ways, and each of them has some thirty
yards to walk before she disappears from our sight—thirty yards
in which we have time to think many thoughts.

All this is swept aside, for the moment, by the triumphant
entry of the chorus—citizens of Thebes, who exult to find themselves alive, saved from the direst peril. The traitor who came
to destroy them is himself destroyed; his terrible army is in
headlong flight; their most arrogant champion was cast down
from the battlements, 'in the midst of his cry of Triumph!' by
Zeus; for Zeus hates above everything the loud boaster. At
every gate the Theban champion has been victorious—except
where the two brothers divided their inheritance with the
sword. But Victory has come; thoughts of war can give place to
joyful dances, led by the Theban god, Dionysus.[2]

The typical Aeschylean chorus stands at some distance from
the action, brooding over it, illuminating it for us. This one is
placed in the middle of it, a 'fellow-actor', as Aristotle said.
Being such, it is often made to share the limitations of the other
actors; it sees the fundamental issue no more clearly than Creon
himself. Therefore Sophocles regularly uses it as a vehicle for
his dramatic irony. So in the last stanza of this first ode: the
chorus appeals joyfully to Dionysus, that he will lead the dance;
but the next time it appeals to Dionysus, in the sixth ode, it is
that he will come and save them from threatening pestilence.
In the later odes the chorus often comments on the current

---

[1] 'Meat' is, I think, a reasonable word to use in rendering v. 30.
[2] I fancy that a little can be said about the visual effect of the dances here.
I have tried to say it in the article referred to above (*J.H.S.* 1955).

action, and its comments are the more revealing for being directed to the wrong person. Here however all—or nearly all—is simple: the danger which the city has survived is put before us with all the vividness of song and dance and poetry; we need have no illusions about Polyneices. What is not quite so simple is the reference to the destruction of Capaneus; we are likely to remember this passage when we hear arrogant words from another man's tongue.[1]

Creon, when he arrives, is majestic and authoritative. His first speech is as good an example as we find anywhere of Sophocles' ability to draw a man's character not only in what he says, but also in the way he says it: the long rolling sentences, the weighty rhythms, the grandiloquent use of plurals, brilliantly paint the man himself. Here, we feel, is Power, conscious of itself.

In his general sentiments there is nothing to which we need take exception: complete loyalty to the Polis is his theme. But his particular application of the principle is another matter. The colours in which he paints the traitor's crime are indeed no darker than the crime itself—no darker in fact than the colours just used by the chorus; but when he repeats in all its inhumanity the decree against which Antigone has revolted in indignation and horror, we know the manner of man we are dealing with. He has well said:

> *There is no art wherewith to read*
> *The soul and spirit and sense of any man*
> *Till that by lawgiving and government*
> *He stand revealed and proven.*

Hearing the decree the chorus makes a significant response The chorus is certainly not being ironical, but the irony is there. I translate literally: 'It is your good pleasure, Creon, son of Menoeceus, so to treat him who was loyal to our city and him who was disloyal. It is in your power to impose what law you will, towards either the living or the dead.'

But is it? Ordinary Greek sentiment would certainly reject this as a political theory; it was indeed the reason why tyranny was hated, that the tyrant claimed to impose what law he willed,

---

[1] μεγάλοι δὲ λόγοι μεγάλας πληγάς, in the concluding lines of the play, recall the μεγάλης γλώσσης κόμπους of Capaneus.

without regard for traditional rights and traditional restraints. But it is not enough to think of political law only—and Sophocles takes care that we shall not. During the play we hear a great deal about νόμος, 'law', notably at the end of the Teiresias-scene, where Creon says:

> I fear it may be better to observe
> The laws established, even to life's end.[1]

'You may impose what law you like' is a doctrine which Creon learns is not true; and we may doubt if a Greek audience, in the theatre, could hear it without thinking of the two maxims Γνῶθι σεαυτόν and Μηδὲν ἄγαν: Remember what you are, and Nothing in excess.

Now, with the first entrance of the Watchman, begins that part of the play which is most full of difficulties. Of the difficulties, some we create for ourselves by our own cleverness, others are created for us by the fact that our ideas of religion, and to some extent of drama, are not the same as those of the fifth-century Greeks.

It would be well to begin with the major difficulty, the double burial. To the ordinary audience there is no difficulty at all; the point passes quite unnoticed. That, of course, is what we should expect; Sophocles knew perfectly well what he was doing. For the critic, the difficulty arises when he asks the wrong question: Why did Antigone go back to the body, when she had already done all that was necessary? The correct question is: Why did Sophocles want her to go twice? The answer, naturally, is to be found in the effect which it produces. By ordering things as he has done, he has created an interval of partial knowledge: the audience knows who has done it, but those on the stage do not. The reasons why he wanted this interval will become clear as we proceed. The reason why an audience is not worried by the mechanics of the plot is that Sophocles engages all their attention on matters vastly more important and interesting.

The Watchman enters with the news. It is customary for us, and indeed quite natural, to call this man a comic, or at least a sub-comic character.[2] He seems to us to provide something like

---

[1] The verse translations of the dialogue-sections, in this chapter, are Harrower's. The isometric translations of lyrical parts are my own.

[2] As I did, in my *Greek Tragedy*.

Shakespearean comic relief; indeed, his dialogue with his own soul reminds us very strongly of Gobbo's dialogue with the Fiend. Now, to assert that he is not comic at all might needlessly provoke dissent, but we have to be extremely careful. He is certainly a 'natural', vividly drawn from life; but Sophocles' reason for so drawing him is not a Shakespearean delight that such characters exist, and a willingness to relieve the tragic tension for a moment by putting such a delightful person into his play. If we sit back in our seats enjoying this man, relishing his garrulity, taking the scene as a charming naturalistic thumb-nail sketch, we run the risk of missing the whole point. For example, the detail about the dust is the very reverse of naturalism.

It is quite impossible, said Drachmann, that a light covering of dust should have the effect which is repeatedly attributed to it in this play. In itself, it is not a very important point, but there it is; Sophocles put it there, and we would like to know why. Since the habits of animals and birds of prey are not matters of specialised knowledge, Sophocles is inviting his audience to accept something that they would all recognise to be contrary to ordinary experience. In naturalistic drama, a contrivance of this kind would be no more than a confession that the dramatist had got himself into a difficulty, and could not escape except by a miracle. Drachmann's error was that he thought he was dealing with a Pinero.

In order to put ourselves on the right track, all we have to do is to look at the chorus-leader's next remark, and take it seriously:

> ἄναξ, ἐμοί τοι μή τι καὶ θεήλατον
> τοὔργον τόδ᾽ ἡ ξύννοια βουλεύει πάλαι.

> *My lord, my heart has long been whispering:*
> *Do we not see in this the hand of God?*

After all, we are on quite familiar ground. In the *Electra* Sophocles shows us 'the hand of God' working with, or in, the human actors, as when the Paedagogus enters, instructed by Orestes, but also sent by Apollo. We know too what it means there: what Electra and Orestes are doing is an example of the working of Dikê. In Aeschylus too we have seen the hand of god, as when 'those ancient enemies, fire and water, made a compact'. Nearer perhaps to the present instance is the 'unseasonable frost' which lured the Persian army to its doom when 'the god' scattered his rays and melted the ice. We all say that Greek drama is essentially religious; are we not too prone to treat it as if it were essentially human, or secular, with religious interludes, and to ignore, or to explain away, these light indications of divine participation? One explanation which has been given of the divine action on the Strymon river is that Aeschylus did not know enough geography; shall we then say that Sophocles did not know enough about hungry dogs?

If all this is true, it is obviously important. It means that a purely humanistic interpretation of the play leaves out of account one of its essential features; for the gods, when they are real gods, and not eighteenth-century decoration, are not in the habit of taking a back seat in the theatre. It means that however vivid the character-drawing is, and the personal conflicts, and the particular ethical or political issues, they are all incorporated by the poet into a drama in which the gods are active; they are treated as constituent parts of a 'religious' drama—whatever the word 'religious' may prove to mean in this context. It does not follow that we should try to play down those aspects of the drama which I have called 'humanistic'; Sophocles has made them extremely vivid, and as such they remain. It means rather that we have to find out how they are related to the religious element—for this too we must not try to play down. But it does follow that some of the things that are said about the play are misconceived. The purely naturalistic assumptions of critics like Drachmann and Rouse will no longer be valid. Again, if Sophocles is suggesting, and expecting his audience to understand, that Antigone and the god are working on parallel paths, $\mu\epsilon\tau\alpha\iota\tau\iota\iota$, then we shall obviously be on the wrong track if we begin to look for a Tragic Flaw in Antigone, or imagine that at any moment in the play the audience was beset with the well-known Greek ideas about the behaviour proper to a well-bred Athenian girl. Nor shall we agree with Bowra, when he says[1]: 'Creon begins by seeming to be an ordinary, decent man, and is slowly revealed to be a tyrant'; for on the contrary he is suddenly revealed to be trying to do something that the gods will not put up with.

[1] *Sophoclean Tragedy*, p. 78.

If, on the other hand, all this is not true, are we to believe Drachmann? Or are we to suppose that in this detail about the dust Sophocles is doing something which is beyond explanation?

It may be thought that this is a heavy superstructure to erect on a very small foundation. The answer to this is that what we have so far seen is not the foundation; only one detail which indicates what the foundation may prove to be. Either the complete structure will confirm our present surmise, that Antigone is working together with the god—perhaps unconsciously, like Agamemnon—or it will not, in which case this particular difficulty will still lack an explanation.

In fact, two of the major points that we have already noticed are at least consistent with our present surmise. The first scene represented Antigone as one whose whole being was rising in revolt against Creon's decree; and the decree itself, throughout the play, is represented as an affront to our common humanity. It is an idea that we meet over and over again in Greek tragedy that when someone acts out of one of the fundamental necessities of human life, or in response to what even we can call our deepest and most sacred instincts, he is working with the gods, and the gods with him. Of the three tragic poets, each has his own way of using and presenting this conception, but, basically, it is common to all of them, and is the explanation of their use of the dual plane. It is the Greek way of showing that a universal principle is involved in the particular action.

Now we must go back to our Watchman. He enters, twisting and turning. Why? Not, I think, to divert the audience, but because he is afraid for his life; he has little confidence that his story will be accepted by Creon, or that he will meet with common justice at Creon's hands. Further, it is a story that he himself cannot understand, one which Sophocles wants to invest with an air of mystery. The man's first concern is to show that there was nothing to attract attention: When they came to their post it was of course night-time, and there was nothing whatever to arouse their suspicions—no cart-tracks, no up-cast of earth. All seemed as it should be. Then dawn came, and the watch saw that all was not as it should be: the body was covered with light dust.

If I had been writing the play, I should have stopped there, without adding the detail about the animals. Sophocles does add it, and we have seen, it may be, why he did so: Antigone has succeeded; she was determined that this physical horror should not be inflicted on her brother's body, and it has not been.

He goes on with his tale. When he has done, the chorus-leader makes his remark about 'the hand of god'. It is my own experience that so long as I enjoyed the Watchman as a discreet approach to the comic policeman of our own stage, the Leader's comment passed over my head, as being only conventional piety—the sort of thing that a Chorus *would* say at such a moment. But Creon takes it seriously, and so must we. Throughout the scene we must keep our mirth within bounds, or we shall miss its point. The man is drawn sharply enough; he can say, with clumsy wit, 'Is it your mind or your ears that are hurt? . . . I only hurt your ears; it is the one who did it hurts your mind.' But this is not 'comic relief'. We must remember that the Greek gods operate not in a dim religious light, but in broad daylight.

The Leader's comment makes Creon furious: 'What? Do you imagine that the gods have any care for a traitor like Polyneices?' The clear answer is Yes; they have shown their hand in working with Antigone. The chorus may be abashed by Creon's outburst; for a long time to come they believe Antigone is in the wrong. Nevertheless, they have shown us where the truth lies: the gods are working with Antigone, and Creon is revealed as one who is setting himself in opposition to them. If the body had been buried deep in the earth, that would have shown only the hand of man; the illogicality shows much more.

None of this would have been possible but for the interval of partial knowledge which Sophocles has contrived by the double burial. We need not therefore toy with the idea that Antigone did not bring the libations the first time because the wine was kept locked up at night.

The interval does something else: it makes Creon contemplate the deed in general terms. Not knowing who has done it, he flies to suspicions of political rebellion. If the Watchman had come in with Antigone under arrest, and if then Creon had condemned her out of hand, we should think him a monster. His part would be foreshortened too much. As it is, suspecting bribery (like Oedipus in the other play), he so commits himself that it is difficult for him to draw back when he learns the truth. When he does know who has defied him, and for what reasons, he has the opportunity of relenting, of seeing that circumstances alter cases, that what a king may not forgive in a political enemy should be forgiven in a girl whose only motives were love, loyalty and humanity. But we see that none of this means anything to him; it is all the same. His tyrannical rage and his lack of understanding sweep him on to disaster.

In the third place, it is only because of this interval that the most famous of Sophocles' odes has any reason for existing. The chorus can reflect on the act of disobedience without knowing whose it is; and the fact that we ourselves do know enables Sophocles to invest the ode with a grave and revealing irony. Man, says Sophocles, recalling to our minds the *Prometheus*, has triumphantly raised himself from impotence to dazzling heights, learning to master the elements and brute creation; he has learned speech, and thought, and all the usages of civil life; he has overcome all but Death itself. But his enterprise and skill can lead him to disaster as easily as to success; he will prosper on one condition: that he respects the law of the land and the Dikê of the gods.

The obvious implication is that these two—the law of the land and the Dikê of the gods—are, if not identical, then at least in harmony; *we* know that in the present case they are not. The chorus has in mind the unknown lawbreaker who has buried the body; *we* know that the words fit Creon, and no one else in the play. We therefore interpret this last stanza in a deeper sense: if Man would reap the fruits of his daring and skill, and avoid its perils, he must observe the laws of the gods—and the play, as it develops, will show us what they are, in the present case.

An audience which is following this high argument will not be unduly concerned with realistic detail, provided that the dramatist does nothing, either positively or negatively, to make it think realistically. The Watchman returns, bringing Antigone; we are of course expecting her to be caught. The mention of the libations gives a reason, quite sufficient for the moment, why she returns to the body. If it also makes us feel (as it does) how entirely dedicated she was to her task, no harm is done; we know from the first scene (86 f) that she had no wish for it to be a hole-and-corner affair. But it would be a mistake to say that the second visit was contrived in order to illuminate her character further; this is only incidental. Our deep thoughts are concerned not with Antigone's character, but with the clash between the two conceptions of Law.

She makes her sublime and uncompromising defence—which indeed is as much an attack on Creon as a defence of herself, and does not give Creon much inducement to be merciful. Even so, his complete lack of comprehension is shocking. Her appeal is to what we should call the overriding demand of natural love and common humanity; to him, this is nothing but disobedience, lawlessness and folly, with shamelessness added. It is not enough to say of his behaviour here that it reveals him as the typical tyrant. It does this, of course; but what we should emphasise is that it shows his lack of φρόνησις, 'understanding',[1] his narrowness, and his reckless hybris, of which his blind condemnation of Ismene is a new and gratuitous instance.

We are approaching a veritable constellation of illogicalities; we must be careful to see how, and on what level, they are contrived. In the full tide of his blind rage, Creon suddenly condemns Ismene, unheard. When he does it (we may notice) he is talking of hybris:

> *This woman here*
> *Was conversant with outrage when she broke*
> *The appointed law: now comes a new offence,*
> *To glory in the deed and boast of it.* (480-483)

This wanton condemnation of Ismene is still worse than his whole bearing towards the Watchman. It shows even more clearly the manner of man that we are dealing with—and there, for the moment, the matter rests. Having shown us this, it is, so to speak, put into cold storage until Ismene appears. Creon storms on, in his uncomprehending way, and ends by saying:

> *But this I hate, when one is caught in crime,*
> *Then glorifies it with the name of virtue.*

So we are brought back from the condemnation of Ismene to the moral insensitiveness of Creon, his complete lack of ordinary human sympathy and understanding. We return to the impassable gulf that lies between him and Antigone, and the fact that she says nothing in defence of her sister passes unnoticed,

[1] See v. 1347.

because our minds are engaged on a level that transcends purely
individual relations.

But clearly Sophocles, when he made Creon condemn Ismene,
had more in mind than the illumination of Creon's character.
This would have been a dramatic extravagance, for he could
have done this without bringing her back on to the stage. It is
clear that he wanted her back. Why? And when she has come
back, he writes dialogue which quite illogically assumes that the
sentence will not be carried out. Yet we do not notice how
illogical the dialogue is. Why not? Because our minds are
entirely on something else, on Ismene's unexpected confession,
and the strong contrast of character that is put before us. But
we must be careful.

The confession is certainly dramatic enough:

> *I did the deed—if she allows my plea;*
> *I take my share and burden of the blame.*

The words 'if she allows my plea'[1] make it quite clear that the
confession is a false one. In the first scene Ismene recognised
where her duty lay, but would not stake her life on what she
thought a mad venture. We call her 'weak', as indeed we may,
if we do it in all humility. But now, in a rush of emotion, she
wishes she had done it.

The contrast between the sisters is arresting, as it was in the
first scene; so much so that we do not notice that by all the laws
of commonsense their conversation ought to be quite different
from what it is. We say that the character-drawing here, as
everywhere else in the play, is strong and subtle, and exquisitely
balanced: Ismene is the perfect foil to Antigone. We are a little
disconcerted, perhaps, by the streak of hardness that Antigone
shows here, particularly if we suppose that Sophocles was setting
out to draw a portrait of ideal heroic womanhood; but in general all this is perfectly true. Yet is it enough?

Why does Sophocles repeat this general situation so closely
in the *Electra*? The resemblance is very close indeed—in
situation, character, even in language. An unsympathetic reader
of Sophocles might say that in the creation of characters the
poet's range was oddly limited; that one does not find Shakespeare repeating himself like this. He might support this by

---

[1] εἴπερ ἥδ᾽ ὁμορροθεῖ.

pointing out how slavishly Sophocles repeats himself elsewhere: the central scene of the *Electra*—the Queen's sacrifice, followed immediately by the arrival of a messenger with misleading news, and presently by the death of the Queen—is an exact copy of the central scene of the *Oedipus*.

To such a criticism there might be several replies, but so far as the two central themes are concerned there is one reply which makes others unnecessary: Sophocles was not repeating a mere dramatic effect, but a fundamental idea. The reason why the two central scenes are built to the same pattern is that the same law, the same god, is operating in each case. The reason for the other resemblance is, I suggest, the same. We have scratched the surface, not much more, when we call Ismene a nicely calculated foil to Antigone, Chrysothemis to Electra. Sophocles was indeed interested in contrasts of character, but not simply on this aesthetic or technical level.

When Electra believes Orestes to be dead, she invites Chrysothemis to join her in what she conceives to be her duty. Chrysothemis answers in the same terms as Ismene, and leaves her, despairing of her folly. Thereupon the chorus sings an ode to this effect: 'Why do we not show the same understanding (φρόνησις) as the birds, who are devoted to their parents? Those who are not do not long escape retribution. The loyal Electra, deserted by her sister, is willing to give her life to avenge her father. The noble of heart will not accept disgrace as the price of life. Electra has spurned dishonour, and has chosen wisdom and virtue.'

There is more here than a mere contrast of persons, designed to bring out more fully the character of the heroine. In effect, Sophocles is answering the question: how does Dikê fulfil itself? and the answer is: sometimes through the clear-sighted heroism of people like Electra. A similar idea underlies the present scene in the *Antigone*, and gives, I think, much more force to the 'confession', and explains, rather more satisfactorily, why Sophocles can ignore for the moment Creon's sentence upon Ismene. She had known what her duty was:

> Beseeching pardon from the dead below
> For what is done on sore compulsion,
> I bow my head to them that stand in power.[1]

[1] Vv. 65-67.

Now, as she contemplates the empty life that stretches before her, she wishes that she had done her duty. But, as Antigone tells her, she made her choice, and she must abide by it. We translate this reply: 'But Justice will not suffer this', and the word 'Justice' gives the impression that Antigone means 'It is not fair to *me* that you should now wish to share in my deed.' But the Greek, while not excluding this, lays the emphasis rather differently: Antigone says 'Diké will not suffer this.' Things done have their necessary consequences. Antigone did her duty and must die, conscious however that she has done it; Ismene must live, conscious that she has not. She has chosen to be one of the insignificant majority. She cannot join Antigone now, but is condemned to the life which she preferred to her duty. It involves Sophocles in a kind of dramatic anticipation, for we have to assume, without any explanation, that Creon's sentence will not be carried out. In fact, we do assume it, without the slightest difficulty. All that Sophocles will do, by way of tidying up the illogicality, is to have Ismene acquitted, quite casually, two hundred verses later, when we have entirely lost interest in her.

There is indeed character-drawing here, and it is quick and lifelike; but there is a firm structure of bone beneath it, and if, like the sculptor, we are aware of the underlying structure, the beauty of the whole will be enhanced for us.

But, being on the stage, Ismene is put to yet another use by this master of dramatic form. The action is reaching a natural pause, with Antigone, and for the moment, Ismene too, awaiting execution. The next development of the action, and for that matter of the basic theme of the play too, is to be Creon's uncomprehending and brutal treatment of his son's love. This new theme is announced before the pause, in order to be taken up smoothly after it; and Ismene is the most suitable character to announce it:

> *Antigone is Haemon's plighted bride,*
> *And will you kill her?*

This piece of information could have been given us by anybody, at any moment of the play; but Sophocles does not wish to give it until this moment (for a reason which will become apparent), and Ismene is the best person to present it as he wishes it to be presented.

It has often been remarked that Sophocles does not write a scene for Antigone and Haemon. Why not? The fifth-century Greeks, we are assured, had no interest in romantic love—at least in their art. This is a fact which we have little reason either to deny or to deplore. But I, at least, am not persuaded that Sophocles could not have found anything worthy of his austere attention in the spectacle of two young people in love, and both so near death. In fact, he does give a vivid picture of the desperate courses into which love drives Haemon. If we understand what Sophocles does do with the love-interest here, we shall find a more satisfactory explanation of what he does not do.

Not a word is said about it until we are half-way through; Haemon, like Eurydice, is not mentioned until he is needed. It is not until Creon has repudiated and scorned all of Antigone's motives, and has pitilessly condemned her, and her sister, to death, that, suddenly, we are apprised that she and his son are betrothed: 'And will you kill her?' Let us follow the dialogue, precisely, even though it will involve us in a textual matter. Creon's reply is brutal:

CREON: *There are other women he can bed with.*
ISMENE: *None so closely knit by love as he and she are.*
CREON: *I hate it, when sons have bad wives.*
ANTIGONE: *Dear Haemon! how your father scorns you.*
CREON: *You and your marriage have given me too much trouble already.*
CHORUS: *Will you really take her from your son?*
CREON: *It is the Death-god who will be preventing this marriage.*
CHORUS: *It is fixed then, it seems, that she must die?*
CREON: *Yes, fixed for you and for me.*

In all the manuscripts, the verse given above to Antigone is ascribed to Ismene, but practically all modern editors give it to Antigone. Since however Mr Letters, in his recent book,[1] has strongly argued for the MSS, attribution, it would be proper to give reasons for not following him. One argument is that if Antigone has the verse, the regular alternation of speakers, customary in stichomythia, is disturbed. The critic who is persuaded on other grounds that the verse does belong to Antigone will reply that regularity in stichomythia was the servant, not

[1] F. J. H. Letters, *Sophocles.*

the master, of the poet, and that it was precisely this normal regularity that induced the wrong attribution of the verse in the MSS. Mr Letters urges that nothing but a romantic bias has prompted the alteration. This may be true; but it is possible to do the right thing for the wrong reason. Also that Antigone's love for Haemon is already attested by Ismene's previous remark and that she needs the verse much more than Antigone does. But the question is not what this or that character needs; rather, what the play needs; and here, it seems, there are two points. One is that it is important for us to know that these two young people really are in love with each other, for the love-theme is going to be given very great significance in the tragedy, not merely in the plot. Ismene has indeed told us that they are in love, but this implied affirmation from Antigone herself is wanted. The other point is that if Antigone has the verse—and the superlative φίλτατε, which in my rendering above I reduced to the positive 'dear', would sound not quite natural coming from Ismene—then Creon is assailed by protests, direct or veiled, by everyone present: Ismene, Antigone, and the Chorus; in the face of which he remains unmoved. No plea of ordinary humanity has any effect on him. I think therefore that one can disown romanticism and yet support the change.

We shall see in a moment to what end Sophocles uses the love-interest: that it is, on one level, the means whereby Creon's original decree recoils upon him to crush him; and, on a deeper level, a second offence against the gods, parallel with the first. Not until the first is fully deployed will Sophocles introduce the second; and Ismene is the obvious character to do it. The essence of it is that it is a purely human, even emotional appeal to Creon as a man and a father. Obviously Antigone herself may not make it; she is now beyond such things. Nor would it come so naturally from this political chorus. Haemon's mother might have made it, but Sophocles has good reasons for not yet allowing us to be aware even of her existence. Ismene is the obvious choice.

The two girls are removed, to await death. The third ode, which follows at once, is one of the most beautiful ones that Sophocles ever composed. It re-echoes with two words: ἕρπει, 'it comes', and ἄτα, 'disaster'. The dance-rhythms are extremely vivid; and the ode as a whole rises from a sombre opening, the

disasters that have beset the House of Labdacus, to a dazzling
climax, and then suddenly withdraws again into darkness.

> *Thrice happy is he who has never known disaster.*
> *Once a house is shaken of Heaven, disaster*
> *Never leaves it, from generation to generation.*
> > *'Tis even as the swelling sea*
> > *When the roaring wind from Thrace*
> *Drives blustering over the water and makes it black;*
> > *It heaves up from below*
> > *A thick, dark cloud of mud,*
> *And groaning cliffs repel the smack of wind and angry breakers.*

> *I see, in the house of our Kings, how ancient sorrows*
> *Rise again; disaster is linked with disaster:*
> *Woe in turn must each generation inherit. Some god*
> > *Besets them, nor will give release.*
> > *On the last of royal blood*
> *There gleamed a shimmering light in the house of Oedipus:*
> > *But Death comes once again*
> > *With blood-stained axe, and hews*
> *The sapling down; and Frenzy lends her aid, and vengeful*
> > *Madness.*

> > *Thy power, Zeus, is almighty! No*
> > *Mortal insolence can oppose Thee!*
> *Sleep, which conquers all else, cannot overcome Thee,*
> > *Nor can the never-wearied*
> > *Years, but throughout*
> *Time Thou art strong and ageless,*
> > *In thy own Olympus*
> *Ruling in radiant splendour.—*
> > *For today, and in all past time,*
> > *And through all time to come,*
> *This is the law: that in Man's*
> *Life every success brings with it some disaster.*

> > *Hope springs high, and to many a man*
> > *Hope brings comfort and consolation.*
> *Yet she is to some nothing but fond illusion.*
> > *Swiftly they come to ruin,*
> > *As when a man*
> *Tread unawares on hot fire.*

For it was a wise man
First made that ancient saying:
To the man whom God will ruin
One day shall evil seem
Good, in his twisted judgment:
He comes in a short time to fell disaster.

A short time ago, when we were discussing entrances and
exits, we saw reason to accept Jebb's stage-direction here:
Exeunt Attendants, guarding Antigone and Ismene: Creon re-
mains. Now we can see reasons other than technical ones for
accepting it. The chorus, trying to explain why disaster has
come to Antigone, speaks of Frenzy and Madness; it speaks of
mortal insolence which vainly tries to oppose Zeus; of ἐλπίς—of
which Hope is one possible rendering, but Temptation, perhaps
even Presumption, another; of the man who mistakes Evil for
Good. The chorus, throughout, is thinking of Antigone; but
we can divine, as in the second ode, that it is not Antigone but
Creon whom the words really fit—and somewhere behind the
dance we can see Creon, 'the man whom god will ruin', standing
motionless. The irony is to be seen as well as felt.

In this way the third ode is a significant prelude to the scene
which follows, as the fourth is a significant comment on it.
Haemon tries to reason with his father. He might seem to be
cold, but for the short dialogue at the end of the previous scene;
thanks to that, we know there is indeed love between him and
Antigone, and we can feel what is going on below the surface.
As in Creon's first scene, Sophocles is careful to give him arguments which, up to a point, carry weight; he has the chorus with
him throughout, except for two moments of doubt which do not
last long (211 ff and 278-9). Creon's fault is that he does not
recognise the point beyond which his arguments have no weight.
What he says to Haemon is much the same as what he said to
Ismene, though not so brutally expressed: one woman is as good
as another, provided that she is not a criminal.

Through Haemon, Sophocles tells us what the ordinary citizen
thinks of Antigone: she deserves not punishment but a crown
of gold, for preventing her brother's body from being eaten by
savage dogs and birds. But nothing moves Creon; neither Antigone's appeal to the laws of Zeus and the nether gods, nor
Haemon's implied appeal to his own love for Antigone, and his

explicit appeal to moderation and to the common judgment of Thebes. Creon, although he is fundamentally honest, is so stupid that to the one appeal he retorts (525) 'While I am alive no woman shall rule', and to the other (726 f) 'Am I to be taught by a mere boy?' In one of Sophocles' suggestive similes, he is the branch that tries to resist the torrent, and is snapped off. So he reduces his son to hopeless rage and despair.

When Haemon has fled from his father's presence, several interesting things happen. The first is the casual acquittal of Ismene, a dreadful confession—not that Creon would see the point—of the monstrous injustice of her condemnation. So is this loose end tied up, effective to the last. After this, the chorus is made to ask what form of death Creon has in mind for Antigone.

Now, Sophocles has already told us what penalty has been prescribed: death by public stoning (36). There was no dramatic necessity to mention the precise form of punishment there, except that the alteration gives additional emphasis to what is said here. Public stoning was reserved for public enemies—the only form of execution in which the whole community could actively take part. The alteration serves half a dozen dramatic ends. We are at liberty to reflect, after what Haemon has told us, that the people would refuse to stone one whom they thought worthy of a crown. Then, death by slow starvation makes possible the catastrophe which Sophocles has in mind; also a revealing bit of patterning which we shall notice in the speech of Teiresias. Further, Creon's failure to understand anything is emphasised horribly by the pedantry, or cynicism, of his bread and water, which he says will avert pollution from the city. It is indeed a good example of Sophocles' craftsmanship.

The short fourth ode is, or should be, the beginning of a long musical movement which continues, with an intermission for Creon's speech and Antigone's (883-928), until the end of the fifth ode and the entrance of Teiresias. If Antigone's lament is spoken, and not sung, the play is perceptibly thrown out of balance: for the time being, we have finished with speech and argument, and move into a different region.

The ode speaks of the power of Love: Eros, Aphrodite. Creon thinks that he has disposed of this; Haemon's love for Antigone is something that can be set aside to order—his order. He has no conception of the hidden forces with which he is playing. On the conventional view, which is the one taken by the chorus, Haemon has done something unfilial—though no doubt under great provocation—in addressing his father as he has done, and making obscure threats against him. Love, says the chorus, is invincible, a power that moves through the whole universe, working its will. It twists aside the mind even of the righteous man, so that he acts wrongly; it has stirred up this quarrel of a son with his father. But

> *Love sits on his throne, one of the great Powers;*
> *Naught else can prevail against invincible Aphrodite.*

Love is one of the θεσμοί, the Ordinances; one of the Powers that hold sway in the lives not only of men, but also of animals and the gods. Love, in fact, is a Theos.

What the chorus may itself be thinking is one matter; what its words convey to the audience may be another. We cannot fail to suspect that it is Creon who has set himself in hopeless opposition to this god, and the sequel will confirm this suspicion. Perhaps we shall notice something else: this is what Creon has been doing all the time. The instinctive respect that humanity feels towards a dead body is, in Antigone's words, 'a law that the god prizes' (519), 'something on which the gods lay great store' (77). Creon does not understand this, any more than he understands the power, the 'sacredness' of Love—or for that matter Antigone's love for her brother and her loyalty to her kin; all of which, to him, are only impudent excuses, and in any case things which he can disregard if they conflict with the interests of the state and of its ruler. The love-interest, then, is not merely the pivot on which the catastrophe turns; it is part of the whole foundation of the play: the order which Creon gives to Haemon is exactly parallel to the order which he made in respect of the body: both attempt to override something that is fundamental in human life; both are 'irreligious'.

Once more, we have to consider the technical problem what to do with Creon: is he on the stage, quite idle, from the beginning of this ode, through the long commos, until at last he has something to say and do, at v. 863? As we have seen, there is no indication that he leaves the stage; we shall now see, I think, that there is very good reason why he should not leave it. He may have nothing to do during these hundred verses of lyrics, but he is far from dramatically ineffective.

Antigone enters, under guard, on her way to death. The chorus sings, in a steady 4-4 time (which contrasts with Antigone's more flexible and sensitive rhythms):

> *I too, when I see this sight, cannot stay*
> *Within bounds; I cannot keep back my tears*
> *Which rise like a flood. For behold, they bring*
> *Antigone here, on the journey that all*
> *Must make, to the silence of Hades.*

Antigone calls them to witness:

> *Behold me, O lords of my native city!*
>   *Now do I make my last*
> *Journey; now do I see the last*
>   *Sun that ever I shall behold.*
>   *Never another! Death, that lulls*
>   *All to sleep takes me while I live*
>   *Down to the dark shore of Acheron . . .*

The chorus offers some cold comfort, but Antigone is not listening:

> *They tell of how cruelly she did perish,*
> *Niobe, Queen in Thebes.*
>   *For, as ivy grows on a tree,*
>   *Strangling it, so she slowly turned to*
>   *Stone on a Phrygian mountain-top.*
>   *Now the rain-storms wear her away—*
>   *So does the story run—and*
>   *Snow clings to her always;*
>   *Tears fall from her weeping eyes, for*
>   *Ever and ever. Like to hers, the*
> *Cruel death that now awaits me.*

Again the chorus says what it can. This time Antigone does hear, and is stung to passionate protest:

> *Alas, they laugh! O, by the gods of Thebes, my native city,*
> *Mock me, if you must, when I am gone, not to my face!*
> *O Thebes my city, O you lordly men of Thebes,*
> *O water of Dirke's stream, holy soil where our chariots run,*
> *You, you do I call upon; you, you shall testify*
> *How all unwept of friends, by what harsh decree*
> *They take me to a cavern that shall be my everlasting grave.*

> *O cruel doom! to be banished from earth, nor welcomed*
> *Among the dead, set apart, for ever.*

The common people of Thebes, we have heard, are indignant at Antigone's condemnation; not so this chorus:

> *Too bold, too reckless, you offended*
> *Justice; now that awful power*
> *Takes terrible vengeance, O my child:*
> *For some old sin you make atonement.*

It is certainly not 'just' that Antigone should be so cruelly used; Sophocles has made that plain enough. Yet the suggestion that she is being crushed by Dikê is not one that she repudiates:

> *My father's sin! Here is the source of all my anguish.*
> *Harsh fate that befell my father! Harsh fate that has held*
> *Fast in its grip the whole renowned race of Labdacus!*
> *Ah, the blind madness of my mother's and my father's marriage!*
> *Ah, cruel union of a son with his own mother!*
> *From such as those I drew my own unhappy life;*
> *And now I go to dwell with them, unwedded and accursed.*
> *O brother! through an evil marriage you were slain; and I*
> *Live; but your dead hand destroys me.*

That the sins of the fathers are visited on the children is Greek as well as Hebrew doctrine. Antigone recognises here what Oedipus recognises at the end of the *Tyrannus* (1486 ff), that she is inevitably caught up in the consequences of her father's unconscious sin, though herself innocent. The chorus denies the innocence:

> *Such loyalty is holiness;*
> *Yet none that holds authority*
> *Can brook disobedience, O my child:*
> *Your self-willed pride has been your ruin.*

Antigone gives up in despair:

> *Unwept, unwedded, and unbefriended,*
> *Alone, pitilessly used,*
> *Now they drag me to death.*
> *Never again, O thou Sun in the heavens,*
> *May I look on thy holy radiance!*
> *Such my doom, and no one laments it.*
> *No friend is here to mourn me.*

Few will deny that this is one of the most moving passages in lyric poetry. But it was written for the theatre—and what does the theatre show us here? Antigone, singing her young life away like this; the chorus, sympathetic, but gently condemning her—and then there is Creon, standing somewhere at the back, utterly unmoved. For him, it counts for nothing. He interrupts harshly:

> *Do you not know that there is none would cease*
> *From dirges and laments, if they would serve*
> *To ward off death? Away with her, away . . .*

We saw that his presence during the third ode was not lacking in point; still less here. In the fourth ode, when the chorus said that Love is enthroned among the great Ordinances, we could look at the man who had just threatened to kill Haemon's lover before his very eyes; there follows Antigone's lament, a poignant cry of simple humanity—and Creon cannot hear it.

So we come to Antigone's last speech. Now she has nothing left, except the thought that her father, her mother, and both her brothers will be there to welcome her in Hades. Since she is left without a friend, since no one has a word of understanding for her, since her piety is called impiety by all, her faith in the gods wavers: 'Why should I look to Heaven any more? . . . If all this finds favour in the sight of Heaven, when I have paid for my sin I will confess my fault.' But we soon learn, from Teiresias, that this does not find favour with Heaven. Yet Antigone's question remains. One answer to it is the one given by Socrates in the *Gorgias*: a bad man can kill a good one. In no adult religion do the gods intervene to stop him from doing it; it remains only for the bad man to take what consequences there may be.

It is in this context that the impugned passage 904-920 should be considered. 'The general validity of the divine law, as asserted in 450-460, cannot be intelligibly reconciled with the limitation in 905-907. A still further limitation is involved in 911 ff.' This is part of Jebb's argument against the genuineness of the passage, but it is quite beside the point. In the first place, the limitation expressed in 912 ff (which nobody thinks is spurious) is no less inconsistent with 450-460; and in the second place, Antigone is neither a philosopher nor a *dévote*, but a passionate impulsive girl, and we need not expect consistency from one such, when for doing what to her was her manifest duty she is about to be buried alive, without a gleam of understanding from anybody. She thought she was obeying a divine law—as of course she was; now the gods seem to have deserted her—as they have, for they do not work miracles. Therefore nothing is left to her but her deep instinct that she had to do it, and it is neither surprising nor undramatic that she should now find what reason she can for asserting that in this special case she had no choice.

Creon remains as cold and as hard as iron:

> *I have nothing to say, no comfort to give.*
> *The sentence is passed, and the end is here.*

Antigone sings her last strain:

> *O city of Thebes, where my fathers dwelt,*
> *O land of our race,*
> *Now at last their hands are upon me.*
> *You princes of Thebes, O look upon me,*
> *The last that remain of a line of kings:*
> *How savagely impious men use me*
> *For keeping a law that is holy.*

So Antigone goes to her death, and without a break the music continues into the fifth ode:

> *Such doom did she endure, who was imprisoned*
> *In a chamber like a grave, within a tower,*
> *Fair Danaë, who in darkness was held,*
> *And never saw the pure sunlight . . .*

The ode is not easy to understand. The chorus sings, in succession, of Danaë, Lycurgus, and the two sons of Phineus and Cleopatra. If we consider the ode in a purely intellectual way we might reasonably think that there is something rather elaborate, even frigid, in this parade of mythological parallels to the immuring of Antigone. Is this the best that Sophocles can do, at such a moment? And where does the unity of the ode lie? Three persons are imprisoned: Danaë was innocent, Lycurgus guilty, Cleopatra innocent—but the odd thing is that when Sophocles comes to the imprisonment of Cleopatra, he leaves it out, and makes the chorus sing instead of the blinding of her sons. There is indeed the statement that not even the high-born can escape the power of destiny; but is this trite reflection all that Sophocles can offer as a climax to his heroine's last agony?

So long as we think of a Greek tragic ode as poetry, we are likely to be baffled by this one. But it is not poetry; it is poetry, dancing and music fused into one—and this makes a big difference. Suppose we tried to set this ode to music: how should we begin thinking about the task? Perhaps, if we were wise, by taking Sophocles' own rhythms as our basis; they are so dramatic, and we are not likely to invent better. Particularly in the second half of the second pair of stanzas do the broken iambics lend themselves, if need be, to a mood of savagery. Then we should have to consider the question of mood, of colour. At this point it would strike us that the colouring must be dark throughout; and then we notice that the idea of darkness is emphasised in the language: Danaë had to leave the οὐράνιον φῶς, the 'light of day'; she was hidden in a chamber like a grave. Lycurgus was 'shut up in a rocky dungeon'. Although Cleopatra too was imprisoned, Sophocles passes over that, but not over the idea of darkness. For Ares, the Thracian god of violence, saw

> *A blinding wound, dealt by a cruel rival:*
> *With shuttle in hand she smote the open*
> *Eyes with sharp and blood-stained*
> *Point, and brought to Phineus'*
> *Two sons a darkness that cried for vengeance.*

> *In bitter grief and despair they bewailed their unhappy lot,*
> *Children born to a mother whose marriage proved accursed ...*

Antigone is being walled up, to die. Danaë, though innocent, was shut up away from the light, because of a strange prophecy; Lycurgus, because of reckless impiety; Cleopatra, by a savage supplanter—but instead of making this point, Sophocles makes another and a more pitiful one: the children, wantonly blinded, with 'the sightless orbs of their eyes crying for vengeance'.

This is the way in which Sophocles invites us to take our farewell of Antigone. Is she innocent, like Danaë, or guilty, like Lycurgus, or, like the children, the victim of almost inconceivable cruelty? The chorus does not ask the question, but we know what it thinks: Antigone has defied authority, and authority may not be defied. Therefore this chorus cannot give

direct expression to the pity and horror that we feel as Antigone
is led to her doom; but during the ode, as to the idea of darkness
is added that of sheer cruelty, with vengeance to come, the
audience will find the necessary release and enlargement of its
present emotions. And once more, how dramatic it is that Creon
is there to be looked at, behind the dance. Sophocles is not
going to bring back Antigone's body; only Haemon's and Eurydice's will make the consummation that he has in mind: the
ruin of Creon's own life. It is here that we take farewell of
Antigone, the victim of uncomprehending cruelty. Nowhere is
the Greek Chorus more imaginatively used as a purely lyrical
instrument.

At once Teiresias arrives, and his scene gives us two structural
or stylistic details to consider. One was mentioned above: the
elaborate parade of omens. It will be convenient to take the
other one first. He says to Creon:

> *You shall not live*
> *Through many courses of the racing sun*
> *Ere you have given the fruits of your own loins*
> *To make amends for murder, death for death,*
> *Because you have thrust a child of earth below*
> *And lodged dishonourably a living soul*
> *Within the tomb; but keep upon the earth,*
> *Unburied and unhallowed, one long due*
> *To them that rule in Hades, wherein you*
> *Nor powers above have portion. By your deeds*
> *You have done outrage both to Heaven and Hell.*

The double antithesis might well commend itself to us as an
effective touch of rhetoric, but there is more in it than that.
What we have here is something that we are continually meeting in Sophocles[1]—the idea of a pattern, an ordained rhythm,
that runs through human affairs, and indeed through the whole
universe, which, like Dikê itself, may be intimately concerned
with morality and conduct, as it is here, or be apparently unconnected with them. In the present instance, Creon is told
that he has tried to cut across this pattern; he has infringed
Dikê. Therefore, says Teiresias, the Erinys, the agent of Dikê,
lies in wait for him, and will infallibly punish him.

[1] See above, p. 104.

A few verses later we meet another and a similar point:

> *All your foes,*
> *Tumultuous with wrath, burn to avenge*
> *Their mangled sons who have found sepulture*
> *In maw of hungry dog or beast of prey*
> *Or vulture, bearing an unhallowed stench*
> *Home to their cities' hearth to taint the air.*

If Creon will not freely bury the bodies—for we now understand that not only Polyneices was denied burial—the neighbouring cities, in self-defence, will compel him. Dikê, justice, is not merely a moral quality; it is a natural law. It *will* operate, in one way or another. The rest of the play shows how it operates here. Again we have the dual plane. The Erinys is waiting for Creon—but there is no supernatural intervention. Events take their natural course; but then, the Erinys is the agent of Dikê, and Dikê is the law of Nature.

The connexion between Law and Prophecy has been discussed already.[1] The immediate dramatic purpose of Teiresias' prophecy is of course to break the obstinacy of Creon, but it has also a deeper purpose. Since prophecy implies law, it has the effect of universalising all that follows. The ruin of Creon is not a particular event—'what happened to Alcibiades', in Aristotle's phrase—but the working of a universal law. It is 'what would happen'.

Now, turning back to our stylistic point, we can see the significance of the behaviour of the birds. What Creon has done, in refusing the burial, is an offence against Nature herself, against the laws of the gods, against the constitution of the universe— they are the same thing. As the double offence of Oedipus issued in a physical plague, so Creon's offence issues in the unnatural fighting of the birds, and the unnatural refusal of the fat to burn on the fire. That is the reason why Sophocles elaborately describes the mechanics of Teiresias' art; not the fact that he had not yet mastered the method of reticence and economy.

Creon goes out—so we are given to understand—first to release Antigone, then to bury the body. In fact, as Jebb observed, he does these things in the reverse order. Had Sophocles been concerned with nothing more important than the effective-

---

[1] See above, p. 76.

ness of his messenger-speech, I find it hard to believe that so careful a craftsman would not have gone back and removed the discrepancy. It is a slight one (like the alteration in the method of Antigone's punishment), but it makes its effect, if anyone in the audience should notice it. On his way to the cavern Creon happens to pass the body—what is left of it; and before doing what we were expecting him to do first, he puts himself right with the offended gods by paying it all possible honour. Why indeed should he not? Antigone has the bread and water which he so horribly gave her; she will not die in a hurry. But Antigone is Antigone, impetuous to the last; and Creon learns a truth which is proclaimed by the chorus in the *Agamemnon*[1]: 'Neither by burnt offering nor fruit offering nor libation will you soften the hard will of the gods.'

When the Messenger comes back from the tomb, with his terrible story of a son who tried to kill his father and then killed himself, he ascribes the ruin of Creon's happiness to Fortune:

> *For Chance exalts, and Chance again lays low.* (1158)

We have the advantage of this man: he comes into the play late; we have been in it from the beginning. What he sees only as Chance we know to be Law; Sophocles has corrected him in advance, by making Teiresias speak of the Erinys which is lying in wait for Creon. What Creon has done will have its natural consequences. He has defied some of the elemental forces in human life; they recoil on him and crush him. Antigone was not one to allow herself to be slowly starved to death; nor was Haemon the man to bear calmly the killing of his lover. Aphrodite is indeed not a power to be played with.

Eurydice, as we remarked earlier, is not mentioned until she comes out to hear the story of her son's death. Why does Sophocles keep her in reserve like this? The effect of his contrivance is plain enough: she is a second Haemon, one whom Creon's inhumanity has tortured to a point beyond what humanity can endure, and her death is the climax of Creon's own ruin. She dies, we may recall, 'lamenting Megareus, who had been killed before',[2] and calling down a curse on Creon, τῷ παιδοκτόνῳ

---

[1] *Agamemnon* 69-71.
[2] The earliest version of this story known to us is the rather sophisticated one in Euripides' *Phoenissae*, in which, against his father's will, he sacrificed

'slayer of his sons'. So Creon is left among the ruin that he has brought upon his house; and the last words of the chorus are:

> Of Happiness, far the greatest part
> Is Wisdom, and Reverence towards the gods.
> Proud words of the arrogant man, in the end,
> Meet punishment, great as his pride was great,
> Till at last he is schooled in Wisdom.

To recapitulate then, briefly. What we have seen is a passionate story of conflict and suffering, presented as directly and as vividly as any such story ever has been. But it is set within a religious framework, and is thereby universalised. The centrepiece is unmistakeably Creon. We may prefer to make it Antigone, but if we do, Sophocles' design becomes in some degree unintelligible; in particular, it becomes hard to understand why Antigone's body is not brought back. There is a whole series of conflicts: Antigone with Ismene, Creon with the Watchman, Creon with Antigone, Creon with Haemon, Creon with Teiresias. The immediate cause of these conflicts is the question of burying the body. But we saw that the motives attributed to Antigone are not exclusively what we, in any modern language, should call 'religious'; to a great extent they are what we should call 'instinctive'; she will not have her own brother's body eaten by animals; and when the common people of Thebes praise her, it is not because she has obeyed a law of Zeus, but precisely because she has prevented her brother's body from being eaten by animals. The religious and the human or instinctive motives are not sharply distinguished by Sophocles; indeed, they are fused—and for a very good reason: he saw no distinction between them; the fundamental laws of humanity and the Dikê of the gods are the same thing.

Therefore, behind these personal conflicts lies a greater one: Creon is in conflict with the gods, both the upper and the nether gods; and then his lack of φρόνησις, 'understanding', and of humanity, brings him into conflict with another great Power, Eros-Aphrodite. The connexion between these two conflicts, as we can now see, is direct and illuminating: here is another of the great forces of the cosmos which he thinks his sole decree

himself in order to save the city. This certainly does not seem to be the version that *Sophocles* has in mind.

can override. In fact, the disasters that overwhelm him come directly from this, that his son is in love with Antigone, and has been driven desperate by Creon's treatment of her and of himself. The two planes are as clear, and as closely interlocked in this play as in the others that we have been studying. 'The god' *was* working in what Antigone did, when she protected her brother's body from outrage; 'the goddess' is at work too when Haemon tries to kill his father: equally, the Erinys discharges her function when Creon is caught in the natural consequences of his own folly.

Ancient historians, some of them, are anxious to find in this play, as in the others, Sophocles' own judgments on contemporary Athenian politics: is Creon, in some sense, a portrait of Pericles or of some other political leader of the time? If we want to know what Sophocles thought about contemporary events—and undoubtedly he did think about them—we have to dig very deep; and when we have done that, we find, not particular judgments, but a universal philosophy; for Sophocles, although he was a General, and a public figure, was also a poet, and a profound one; and he conceived his plays as a poet, not as a journalist, however distinguished. His political experiences and judgments passed through his mind; and when they came out, they were transmuted into something else—into that highest form of art which has contemplated, and then can illuminate, human experience.

In this play he does say a great deal indeed about the state and statecraft: a statecraft which will try to pursue a traitor beyond the grave—and will also threaten to kill a young man's lover before his eyes; for these two things Sophocles has joined together, and a historian is ill-advised if he attempts to put them asunder. What Sophocles is saying here is very like what we shall find him saying in the *Ajax*: there are certain ultimates in human life which must be respected, and *will* be respected, because they are 'divine'. From short-sighted calculation (which in this case is Creon's honest but narrow statecraft) we may offend against them. If we do, they will recoil upon us; not by the operation of any supernatural power (for the tragic poets' gods are not supernatural), but through the natural reactions of people who are big enough, or desperate enough, to follow their own instincts and ideals. Life has its own unbreakable laws, and in it, only half-hidden, are terrible forces. These we must always respect. The saving virtue is 'understanding', with reverence towards the gods, which implies reverence towards the ultimate claims of humanity. When the chorus thought they saw the hand of god in the burial, Creon asked indignantly:

> How can you think the gods have any care
> For this vile corpse? Was it for his high honour,
> As one who served them, that they graced him thus?
> The dastard! him that came with fire and sword
> To blast their columned shrines and treasuries,
> And to make havoc of their land and laws?
> What? do you think the gods honour the vile?

The answer is: Yes; for at least he was a man.

CHAPTER SIX

Ajax

THE *Ajax*, as much as any play, demands that we should employ the critical principles which are appropriate to it. Waldock, in his interesting and lively book *Sophocles the Dramatist*, writes about it to this effect: Students of modern literature, when they turn to the study of Greek drama, will be prepared to find that the nature of the Greek theatre and dramatic conventions created special problems for the Greek dramatists,[1] but they will be surprised to find that the most consistent problem was the problem of unity itself. Look at the *Agamemnon*: the Aegisthus-scene is something outside the design of the play, so much so that Mr Kitto, instinctively, ignores it. It is the 'diptych' form beginning to emerge. Look at the *Hippolytus*, the *Antigone*, the *Ajax*. The Greek dramatist (p. 58) uses up his material very fast; the initial charge is too soon spent.[2] Therefore he has to inject a new one; to turn his play into a diptych. Apologists do not succeed, who say, 'Take the right point of view, and unity appears.'

But why stop at the Greek dramatists? We could equally well say of Pindar: Sometimes a single myth gives Pindar all the material he needs; but sometimes he uses it up too quickly, and has to bring in a second one, which may be quite independent of the first. We could well say that Pindar was forced into the diptych-form before ever Aeschylus gave way to it.

With Pindar the case is perfectly clear. Either we read him in a literal fashion, and enjoy his flashing brilliance but find in an ode little unity, structure, or commonsense; or we realise

---

[1] This I believe to be a mistake. See the chapter on Greek and Elizabethan Dramatic Form. Waldock's criticism of my own criticism, on the other hand, is perfectly sound, but 'I hope we have reformed that indifferently.'

[2] Similarly, in the slow movement of the Pianoforte Sonata in A flat, opus 110, Beethoven used up his material so fast that the movement is only seven bars long.—A pity; it was so beautiful while it lasted.

that we have to contribute a good deal ourselves—to bring to his poetry a lively moral and imaginative awareness; in which case the ode ceases to be an assemblage of scattered brilliancies, and becomes a powerful and significant unity. 'The true drama of the *Hippolytus*', says Waldock, 'is bound up with Phaedra. No "inner meaning", no "thesis" that we may care to extract, changes that.' But Euripides 'bound up' the play with Aphrodite and Artemis. If this fact does not interest us, naturally, for us, the play falls to pieces—or, to put it more politely, becomes a diptych. We may call it that; but if a medieval diptych should portray, in one half, the felicity of Heaven, and in the other half the terrors of Hell, we should hardly say that the painter had failed to achieve a unity because he ran short of ideas about Heaven. In fact, if we treat the play simply as a study of a Tragic Hero, we cannot explain its form—only find excuses for it.

There is a late-ancient, or medieval, criticism of the *Ajax* which, although it is written in Greek, is laughable: ἐκτεῖναι θελήσας τὸ δρᾶμα ἐψυχρεύσατο καὶ ἔλυσεν τὸ τραγικὸν πάθος. It is the comment of a Scholiast, and it may be rendered: Because he wanted to prolong the play beyond the suicide of Ajax, Sophocles loses the tragic tension and becomes a bore. This is very like a judgment on *Hamlet* written in 1736 by Sir Thomas Hanmer: 'There appears to be no reason at all in nature why this young Prince did not put the usurper to death as soon as possible . . . The case indeed is this: had Hamlet gone naturally to work, there would have been an end to the play. The poet therefore was obliged to delay the hero's revenge; but then he should have contrived some good reason for it.'[1] According to Waldock, this is the first appearance in critical writing of any sign of uneasiness about Hamlet's delay.

The resemblance between the two criticisms is close, and admits, I think, of a simple explanation: both plays were written in a 'religious' age, and both criticisms were written by men who had lost touch with the spirit of 'religious' art. Rationalism, with its increasing individualism, had formed a barrier between Hanmer and Shakespeare; what divided the Scholiast, or his source, from Sophocles was, ultimately, the radical intellectualist revolution of the late fifth and early fourth centuries B.C., Aristotle's theory, and the Aristotelian tradition,

[1] I owe this to Waldock's essay on *Hamlet*.

were incapable of making real sense of the *Ajax*; Aristotle did not even try to frame a workable theory for the Aeschylean drama; nor is it easy to imagine that his acute and 'secular' mind would have had any great success with the 'religious' poetry of Pindar.

In the *Ajax*, the Scholiast tells us, Sophocles becomes a bore because his material ran out. If he had written the play at the age of fifteen or so, we might be disposed to believe it with no more ado. In fact, he was about fifty—and he was Sophocles. It is perhaps more likely that the Scholiast, and those modern critics who follow him,[1] have for some reason taken hold of the wrong end of the stick.

Of the dramatic facts which we have to assimilate before we can offer an interpretation of the *Ajax*, the premature death of the hero is the most important, but there are many others. However, before we state and discuss these, it will be convenient to say something about the two standard explanations of the form of the play: the importance, to the Greek mind, of burial, and the existence in Athens of the hero-cult of Ajax.

That refusal to bury a dead body was a thing shocking to normal Greek sentiment is a fact that needs no argument. That the soul of a dead man could find no peace in Hades until his body was buried is an idea frequently met with in antiquity—though nowhere in the extant works of Sophocles. We have seen already[2] that Sophocles does not use this belief in the *Antigone*, but concentrates all our thoughts there on the sheer horror of treating a human body like offal. The same, precisely, is true of the *Ajax*, except that Odysseus is made to say to Agamemnon something which implicitly excludes the eschatological doctrine:

οὐ γάρ τι τοῦτον ἀλλὰ τοὺς θεῶν νόμους
φθείροις ἄν

You would not be hurting Ajax at all; you would be infringing the laws of the Gods.

It is not for us to introduce into the play ideas which are left out by Sophocles, in order to help ourselves over a difficulty. Mr Letters, for example, writes impressively about the fate from which the great Ajax is to be saved, the fate of the wandering,

---

[1] Masqueray, for instance, in his introduction to the play (Budé series).
[2] See above, p. 148.

sleepless ghost.[1] But Sophocles refuses to mention this. More pertinent is a remark which Mr Letters makes a little earlier, that the problem is not to show that the play maintains its interest, but that it remains organically one.

Whether the body shall be buried is certainly the question at issue in the last third of the play, but without rewriting these scenes, we cannot maintain that they are concerned with the after-life of Ajax. What then?

We are reminded that Ajax was a revered Attic Hero, and that a Hero must have his tomb, since that was the centre of the cult. Therefore his proper burial was of importance to everyone to whom his cult was of importance, that is, to every Athenian citizen. But, in the first place, the Ajax of this play is very much a man, and not at all a cult-hero. We shall be told: 'Never mind; Ajax was in fact a cult-hero, and what he was in fact, that also he must be in the play.' But the assumption is illegitimate. In Comedy, the Athenians could make great fun not only of cult-heroes but also of gods, and the reason is not simply that Comedy gave the Athenians delicious license to be naughty; it is that they were intelligent people, not bound fast by the formulas of their religion. Cult was one thing, epic poetry, tragedy and comedy were other things, and they did not obstruct each other. Surely we are not to imagine that thoughts of a cult interposed themselves between an Athenian audience and a public recitation from the *Iliad*. In the cult, Ajax was a living Hero; when one was listening to Homer, he was a great warrior fighting before Troy. There is no difficulty in this. In a comedy, he might perhaps be a rumbustious and stupid soldier; in a tragedy, a magnificent tragic hero; a Cult-Hero, certainly, if the dramatist chose so to treat him, but not otherwise. The pious observances and traditions of religion did not rule in the theatre unless the dramatist invoked them; Greek Tragedy was religious, but in a deeper sense than this. It is precisely this confusion between cult-religion and religious drama that made the *Prometheus* unintelligible to Farnell: why, he asked, was Aeschylus not prosecuted for such a presentation of the High God?[2] In the *Oedipus Coloneus* heroisation is specifically made part of the play; in the *Ajax* it is not. The critic may find the play easier

---

[1] F. J. H. Letters, *Sophocles*, p. 154.
[2] *Journal of Hellenistic Studies*, LIII (1933).

to understand if he sees the tomb of Ajax the cult-hero some-where in the background, but he should be quite clear that it is not Sophocles who has put it there, but he himself.

As for the idea that the second half of the play is devoted to the 'rehabilitation' of Ajax, we must be careful. It is true that it sets the character of Ajax in a wider perspective. Odysseus asserts what nobody in the play denies, that in the past Ajax has done glorious things for Greece. He makes us contemplate the life of Ajax as a whole; and as we contemplate it, especially with meaner men present against whom we can measure him, we feel that Ajax is incomparably the most magnificent figure of them all. But no one in the play suggests for a moment that he was not guilty of a monstrous and indefensible crime. His murderous treachery remains; and certainly Sophocles was under no compulsion to suggest, as he does, that even in death the resentful spirit of Ajax is incapable of responding to the gener-osity of Odysseus. In the final scenes we are certainly shown the essential greatness of Ajax, but something more important is afoot than the rehabilitation of Ajax.

The greatness of Ajax is certainly one of the arguments used by Odysseus in urging that he shall be buried, but his ultimate argument is simply that death is the common lot: 'I too shall come to this.' The burial is in no sense the ultimate triumph of Ajax, nor has it anything to do with his cult. It means just what the burial means in the *Antigone*. In each play the dead man has committed a crime which nobody tries to condone; each play represents the tribute of burial as something demanded both by the deepest human instincts and by the laws of Heaven, and its refusal as an outrage upon our common humanity. Let us not forget the background that Sophocles designed for the final scenes: the body of Ajax, and the two suppliants, Tecmessa and the child. It is the ultimate human situation. The burial is the assertion that the claims of humanity override every-thing.

This brings us to another dramatic fact: the tone of the final debate. One scholar after another has found it deplorable— which of course it is. But why? Masqueray says: Teucer, Menelaus, Agamemnon and Odysseus do not realise that their speeches, clever ('heureux') though they may be, are an anti-climax after the entreaties of Tecmessa and the farewell-speech

G

of Ajax. That is to say, Sophocles made a bad miscalculation. That is no doubt possible; it is also possible that the dramatist calculated better than the scholar. 'But,' Masqueray continues, 'we must remember how the Greeks loved speeches, provided that they were adroit.' To which we may reply: where else in Sophocles do we find clever speeches which spoil the play?

Jebb too was uneasy. The tone of the debate, he says, is shocking to modern taste, and becomes understandable only when we remember how freely Demosthenes, for instance, allowed himself vulgar abuse of his opponents. But again, where else do we have to invoke Demosthenes in order to explain Sophocles? To judge from the rest of Sophocles, not to mention Aeschylus, the Greek audience had much the same taste as ourselves, except perhaps that theirs was rather more intellectual and austere. The vulgarity of the Atreidae, and to a smaller extent of Teucer, is a fact; but it is one that we should try to explain, not explain away. Since after all we know a good deal about Sophocles' dramatic style, we should first assume that he made these men vulgar for a dramatic reason, and not because he thought that his audience would expect and enjoy it.

There are other facts that we have to contemplate, hoping that they will arrange themselves into a significant pattern or structure, since Sophocles, presumably, invented and disposed them for this purpose. There are—to set them down in the order of their presentation—the agency of Athena; the character and behaviour of Odysseus; Tecmessa, what she is, what she says, how she says it; the celebrated speech of Ajax, whether deceptive and ironical, or sincere; and the typically Sophoclean idea, used no less than three times, that the sword of Hector kills Ajax, as the belt of Ajax killed Hector. Finally, the greatest fact of all: the splendour of Ajax, his crime and madness, and his suicide. In contemplating these things we may remind ourselves, as we have done before, that a combination which is deep and clever is probably wrong, since a play must make its effect at once, even though more intimate knowledge of it may reveal further subtleties. But an interpretation which is deep and simple may well be correct, for this is Religious Drama.

That the play begins and ends with Odysseus is a fact which has been published before; once by me.[1] Friendly critics—Mr

----

[1] *Greek Tragedy.* p. 121.

Letters, for example—have said that I made too much of this.
Perhaps so, but it was a mistake made in the right direction.
Needless to say, the appearance of Odysseus at the beginning
and at the end is no formal device, designed to give the play a
mere external symmetry. Sophocles did not deal in such second-
rate contrivances. Without exaggerating the importance of
Odysseus in the play, we may legitimately observe what is
obvious: he and Ajax are presented as opposites as well as enemies. Odysseus calls Athena 'dearest of gods to me' (v. 14),
Ajax is under her severe displeasure; in the trial for the arms,
Odysseus is victorious, Ajax defeated; above all, Odysseus shows
that large-minded intelligence, that spiritual, mental and moral
poise, which the Greeks called Sophrosyne and we, in desperation, translate Wisdom; Ajax is brave, sagacious and effective in
action (vv. 119 f), in every way impressive—except that he is
conspicuously lacking in this 'wisdom'. It is perhaps nothing
extraordinary, especially in this most Homeric play, that a hero
should feel resentment when the judgment of his peers prefers
another to himself; but to try to murder the judges is another
matter. This is the most outrageous, and critical, instance of
his lack of 'wisdom', but Sophocles makes it plain that it does
not stand alone. The Messenger informs us that Ajax has spoken
arrogantly of the gods, twice; he, in his pride, said he could
stand firm without aid from the gods. Further, the messenger-
speech uses twice, of Ajax, the phrase κατ' ἄνθρωπον φρονεῖν, to
behave with the modesty that becomes mortal man. This is
what Ajax cannot do. 'Already, when he was leaving home, his
father found him, and truly called him, foolish; for his father
had said, "My son, resolve to win victory with your spear, but
always with the aid of the gods"; and he made an arrogant and
senseless answer: "Father, with the gods' aid the most puny
man may win victory; I am sure I can seize this glory without
them." That was the boast he made.'[1] Whereupon Calchas
added that it is men of great strength but little wisdom that the
gods bring low in disaster.

In the Athena whom we see in the prologue there is little
that is kindly or gracious; like the Artemis of whom we have a
glimpse in the *Electra*,[2] she is as hard and stern as life itself.

[1] Literal translation of vv. 762-770.
[2] In Electra's account of the sacrifice of Iphigenia, vv. 565 ff.

'You see, Odysseus, how great is the strength of the gods. Who was more sagacious or decisive in action than Ajax?'—'I know of none. Still, I am sorry for him, that he is in the grip of disaster. And I say this, thinking of myself as much as of him, because I can see that no man that lives is more than a phantom or an insubstantial shade.' 'Therefore,' replies Athena, 'never use boastful language towards the gods, or indulge in pride, if you exceed another in the strength of your arm or in wealth. A single day can overthrow or restore anything human, and it is the wise that the gods cherish, but they hate the bad.' Athena is reminding us what a changeful and uncertain thing life is. Odysseus illustrates, now and later, how it must be confronted: with Sophrosyne. This implies intelligence and suppleness, but also modesty and pity; a willingness to forgive, to forget injuries and to remember benefits.

As for Ajax, it is true that we have given ourselves the advantage of looking first at the messenger-speech, but even without this it would be clear that he is very different. He is one who must have things his own way; but this is a thing that Life does not permit for long. When he was not judged first, he—being then in his right mind—turned to murder. The madness sent by Athena saved him from that, and saved the Greek captains from him; but Athena, in no kindly way, urged him on in his torturing of the sheep, so that his intention was made both manifest and hideously ridiculous. This is the ἄτη, the infatuate ruin, into which his pride has led him. It will surely be strange if this contrast between the wisdom which the gods cherish and the pride which they punish does not prove to be fundamental to the play.

Now let us consider Tecmessa. She, like the chorus, is loyal to Ajax, utterly dependent on him, and thrown into dire peril by what he has done. Nothing is easier than to write sympathetically about Tecmessa, the only woman in this fierce play, to say that her feminine tenderness and weakness are the perfect foil to the rugged strength of Ajax. Of course they are—but there is more than this. Here is a bald summary of her most moving speech:

Ajax my lord, nothing in life is harder to bear than the blind strokes of fortune. Here am I, free-born, daughter of the wealthiest man in Phrygia, now a slave; so it pleased the gods and your mighty arm. So, since I have become yours, I am loyal to you. By the love that has united us, do not leave me and your son unprotected. Have compassion (αἴδεσαι) for your father, have compassion for your mother, take pity on your son, on me, for the miseries that will be ours. You are all I have; my country you ruined, my parents are dead. If I have brought you any joy, you owe me something in return; ingratitude brings disgrace to a man.

Sophocles has given to his Tecmessa both dignity and intelligence—and something more. Life has been much harder to her than to Ajax; but she has known how to accommodate herself to it. Unlike him, she has known by instinct how the blows of fortune are to be faced, and Sophocles hints a moment later that she has saved something from the wreck: she has her son, in whom she can take delight (v. 559). She has something of that larger wisdom which Odysseus too has; it is in this respect that she is most notably a foil to Ajax.

But her speech brings before us too other elements of the Sophrosyne in which Ajax is lacking: αἰδώς and χάρις, a consideration for others, and gratitude. But as she appeals to Ajax in the name of all those who will be left in misery or jeopardy by his death, we can hardly help asking ourselves a question to which Sophocles gives no answer: What can Ajax now do? However much consideration and gratitude he may feel, is it not too late? In fact, he shows very little of either quality. He makes that grand speech to his infant son, with its famous and tragic couplet:

> ὦ παῖ, γένοιο πατρὸς εὐτυχέστερος,
> τὰ δ' ἄλλ' ὁμοῖος· καὶ γένοι' ἂν οὐ κακός —

My son, be you more fortunate than your father, in all else the same.
So, you would be good enough.

The couplet is tragic, because he lacks so much more than good fortune. Of pity or consideration for Tecmessa there is at the moment no sign whatsoever. He brusquely tells her to be silent, and shuts himself in his tent to die. We are left with this: Ajax is sure that Teucer will protect the child, but Tecmessa and the Chorus look forward only to death or slavery.

But Ajax does not kill himself; he comes out again, to make that speech which has caused so much discussion. Is it sheer, cruel deception? Or is it that Ajax is now genuinely determined

to live, but somehow suffers a change of mind when he reaches
the sea-shore? Or, being still determined to die, does he wish, as
Jebb suggested, to die reconciled to the gods?

It is at once apparent that *something* has happened to Ajax:
he was going to kill himself in the tent, and he has not done it.
There is another point not to be overlooked: the style and tone
of the speech. It is great poetry; it is language of a high intensity, and it would carry conviction. Could we perhaps try to
imagine ourselves in the audience?

The last words we have heard from Ajax were his harsh
words to Tecmessa: 'If you think you can alter my ways at this
late hour, you are thinking like a fool.' When we see him
again, after the mournful ode, not only are we surprised at
seeing him, instead of hearing of his death; we are also surprised,
surely, at his language:

> Ἅπανθ' ὁ μακρὸς κἀναρίθμητος χρόνος
> φύει τ' ἄδηλα καὶ φανέντα κρύπτεται —
>
> *All things doth long, innumerable time,*
> *Bring forth to light, and hide again in darkness . . .*

This is something much more gravely philosophic than anything
we have yet heard, or would have expected, from Ajax.

> *Nothing is firm; the strongest oath is broken,*
> *The stubborn purpose fails. For I was hard*
> *As tempered steel; but now Tecmessa's words*
> *Have softened me, and I have lost my edge.*
> *I pity her, to leave her as a widow*
> *Among my foes, to leave my son an orphan.*

The poetry, of which I attempt a rendering, is more weighty,
more spacious, than anything we have yet heard; it has an
authority which, I think, convinces us at once that Ajax feels
and means what he says. But perhaps an earlier question recurs
to our minds: what can Ajax do, now?

> *Therefore I seek the meadows by the shore;*
> *In holy water I will wash away*
> *My stains, and from Athena's heavy wrath*
> *I will release myself. Then I will go*
> *And find a spot far from the ways of men;*
> *There will I dig the earth, and hide my sword,*
> *My hateful sword, where never mortal eye*

> *Shall look on it again; but Night and Hades*
> *Shall keep it in their darkness evermore.*

Indeed his mood has changed. It is no long time since he was
calling on Darkness to cover him; and then he shut himself up
to die, like an animal, among the animals he had slaughtered.
Here he has a new dignity; gone are the self-pity and the self-
contempt that he has been feeling until now. But what will he
do? The pity for Tecmessa is real—the poetry certifies that; but
his words are ominous. Is it that he thinks with compassion of
those around him only when it is too late for him to act on it?
That all his life he has thought only of himself and of his own
glory, and now, for the first time, sees what he has done for
others? At least, the ode to which we have just been listening
has made our thoughts dwell on the danger into which Ajax
has brought his men, and on the misery which is coming to his
mother and father.

> *For since I had this sword at Hector's hand,*
> *Hector, most hated of my enemies,*
> *Nothing but evil has befallen me*
> *From the Achaeans. No, the proverb's true:*
> Beware the gifts of foes; they bring no good.
> *Wherefore henceforward I shall know that I*
> *Must yield to Heaven's will, and I shall learn*
> *Reverence for the Atreidae: they are Kings;*
> *We must obey them.*

Is there not something a little surprising here? What is the
point of the word τοίγαρ, 'wherefore'? What is the connexion
between Hector's sword and what follows? For Sophocles' audience, no doubt, the connexion was plain; they shared in his
habit of thought. For us it is not plain, and we shall have to
argue it out, if we can. And why does he use the strong word
σέβειν, 'reverence', of the Atreidae? It would be more natural
had the verbs been reversed: To reverence the gods and yield
to the Atreidae. But the latter is just what he cannot do, in any
real sense—and if he does the former, it will be something which
at least he has not conspicuously been doing heretofore. The
choice of the verbs, then, seems to be significant: Wisdom, he
says, demands that he yield to the gods—and that he can do, for
indeed there is no alternative; but wise conduct towards the

Atreidae he has made very difficult by his own acts, and in any
case it is quite beyond his nature; therefore he expresses it in a
word of deliberate exaggeration. What he says next makes this
clearer to us:

> For the greatest powers
> That be, the most invincible, give way
> To privilege: see how the snowy winter
> Makes room for fruitful summer; how the dread
> Circle of night gives place to blazing day;
> The groaning sea is given peace at last
> By raging winds; and sleep that masters all
> Binds fast, yet not for ever, but releases.
> Then how should I not find this wisdom too?

This is magnificent, but it does not sound like humility; and
humility—'to think mortal thoughts', to 'know oneself'—is part
of Wisdom. Has Ajax, in his newly-learned Wisdom, come to
see what Odysseus knows, that Man is but 'a phantom and an
insubstantial shade'? Has he learned to accept the disasters that
life brings, like Tecmessa? The very splendour of the imagery
speaks of his unbroken pride; and we may again note his language, for it is ominous: those mighty opposites Winter and
Summer, Night and Day, when the time comes, $\dot{\epsilon}\kappa\chi\omega\rho o\hat{v}\sigma\iota\nu$,
$\dot{\epsilon}\xi\dot{\iota}\sigma\tau\alpha\tau\alpha\iota$: they 'make room', 'get out of the way'. This is what
Ajax will do; he will 'yield to the gods' because he must, but his
pride will not allow him to humble himself before the Atreidae.
All he can do is to imitate Night and Winter, and 'make room'.
His pity for Tecmessa and his son is genuine, but he can do
nothing for them now. He continues:

> For I have learned today to hate a foe
> So far, that he may yet become a friend,
> And so far I resolve to serve a friend
> Remembering he may yet become a foe.
> Friendship's a haven where we ride at anchor,
> But not in safety.
> > With regard to this,
> All shall be well.

So that Ajax, henceforth, will not push hatred to the utmost
limit. He has learned Wisdom—and we have divined how
barren the lesson is to him.

Tecmessa, go within;
Pray to the gods, and pray again, that I
May win from them all that my heart desires.
And you, my friends, pay me this tribute too.
Tell Teucer, when he comes, to care for me
And to be kind to you, for I must make
A certain journey. Do this that I ask,
And though my fortunes now are very low,
Soon you may hear that I am come to safety.

All this the chorus receives with joy. We may think it simple-minded of them, but we should observe how Sophocles has drawn them: they are, if not simple-minded, at least single-minded; to them, Ajax is of the faction that is wronged; to them, all is well, now that Ajax is recovered from his frenzy:

Ἔλυσεν αἰνὸν ἄχος ἀπ᾽ ὀμμάτων Ἄρης —
The god of Frenzy has lifted the dark cloud from his eyes.

The Atreidae had been ungrateful and cruel to him (v. 616); now his wrath has left him (716 f); all is well. This chorus at least is no 'ideal spectator'.

We are not so confident, and our forebodings are at once confirmed by the Messenger: Athena's wrath still rests on Ajax, and since he has gone out alone it cannot be for anything good. Why Athena is angry we are told most explicitly: the cause is the irreligious arrogance which Ajax has habitually shown. The attack on his commanders and colleagues was only a crowning instance of it. The frenzy, as Athena clearly said, was a special visitation sent by her when Ajax was already seeking the lives of his fellow-captains. That has passed, but—for one day— Athena's anger remains. And what does this mean?

What would happen, if Ajax were for this one day under Teucer's control, is a question which Sophocles perhaps suggests, but does not exactly raise. If it is legitimate to ask it, the answer would be, I suppose, that he might be brought to see what true Wisdom is, in his present case: to make his submission, and to accept what the Greek commanders would do to him. As it is, he has followed his own bent, and gone, broken but still proud, to his death. Tecmessa's appeal did move him; the irony in his speech—a very bitter irony—is that without Wisdom his pity could only be barren. His pride has put it beyond his power to respond to Tecmessa's cry, even when he would.

In Ajax's last speech Sophocles is again at his most magnificent. First, a theme is announced that we have heard before, and shall hear again:

Here stands the slayer, ready for its sharp work; the gift of Hector, my bitterest enemy, whom I hated above any other Trojan; and it is firmly planted in the enemy soil of Troy, newly whetted, well disposed to give me a swift death.

What this means, what part it has in the structure of the play, is a question which we will try to answer when Teucer has given ampler expression to the idea.

Then Ajax prays: first that it may be Teucer who shall find his body, and save it from being 'flung out, a prey for dogs and birds'. This prayer is answered, though it is not the strength of Teucer that preserves the body from outrage, but the humanity of Odysseus. When we are able to set side by side this prayer and its fulfilment, we may well ask ourselves the question which the chorus asked when Polyneices' body was buried: 'Do we not see in this the hand of God?' Surely we do; and it operates, here, in the Wisdom of Odysseus.

His second prayer is not answered, that the Erinyes may destroy the Atreidae and the whole army for destroying him. (The Erinyes did destroy Agamemnon, but that has nothing to do with this play. All that Agamemnon has done here is to participate in a quite reasonable decision about the arms of Achilles.) From this we see how very far Ajax is from having learned Wisdom. Finally, he shows the same frustrated compassion for his parents that he has already shown for Tecmessa and his son. He is certainly not unfeeling; merely helpless:

ἀλλ' οὐδὲν ἔργον ταῦτα θρηνεῖσθαι μάτην —
It is no use to shed idle tears over this.

Ajax has tried to mould life to his own pattern, and he has failed. 'Seek victory', his father had said, 'but always σὺν θεῷ, subject to the guidance of Heaven.' Since he could not accept life on its own terms he has now only one thing to do—to fall on his sword.

Now we must consider Teucer. In his long speech he says two things of especial significance. The first is that by the death of Ajax he himself is ruined; Telamon, fierce father of a fierce son, will drive him into exile. This, it may be, helps us to understand Ajax, but this is not the main point. We have been told already how Teucer barely escaped being stoned to death by the infuriated army, merely because he was Ajax's brother; now he faces the vengeance of Telamon. We may add to this—in fact, we should—the misery which Tecmessa fears for herself and for Eurysaces, and the terror of the chorus (vv. 251 ff) that they too will be stoned to death. All these things would be monstrously unjust. If Sophocles had any reason for bringing them in, what was it, except that they show what happens when the behaviour of men is not governed by Wisdom?

The second point is the full development of the theme of Hector's sword:

How can I part your body from the deadly sword that has killed you? Now you see how Hector, even from his grave, was to slay you. Think on the fate of these two men! By the belt that Ajax gave to him, Hector was bound to the chariot and dragged behind it until he died. Ajax, who had this sword as a gift from Hector, has fallen upon it and is killed—by Hector. Was it not the Erinys who forged this sword, and the grim artificer Death who made the belt? I say that the gods contrived this, as everything else that befalls men.

One thing is evident: Sophocles meant something serious by this, or he would not have said it three times. Another thing is evident: it is yet one more instance of his conception of a pattern or a rhythm that runs through human affairs.[1] In this particular form, the dead reaching out to kill the living, it is to be found in no less than five of the seven plays. In the *Electra* (vv. 1419 ff) 'The dead live; those slain of old drain the blood from their slayers'; and the blood is 'refluent', 'flowing in the reverse direction' (παλίρρυτον). It is the dead hand of Polyneices that is destroying Antigone (*Antigone* v. 871). Oedipus begs Creon (*O.T.* 1451 ff) that he may be driven out upon Cithaeron 'which my parents while they lived designed to be my tomb, that I may die at their hands who sought to kill me'. In the *Trachiniae* Heracles is destroyed through the agency of Nessus, whom he had killed, by the venom of the Hydra, whom also he had killed. As we have seen before, it is one aspect of Diké; that is made unmistakeable here by the mention of the Erinys, the servant of Diké. What Diké is we know: not necessarily our moral

[1] See above, p. 175.

conception Justice, but in any case the eternal law of the Universe, physical and human.

It is critical sin to import into a play something that its author has not put there, but we shall not be doing that, I think, if at this point we remember the great scene in *Iliad VII*, since Sophocles virtually tells us to do it: the single combat between Hector and Ajax which was terminated by the fall of night and ended in the exchange of these gifts. Twice in the play we are told how much Ajax hated Hector. They fought their duel; neither could prevail. Now each has killed the other; the interrupted pattern is complete.

But what does it mean, here? We may go back to a little puzzle noticed above but not resolved. 'The proverb is true,' Ajax said; 'the gifts of an enemy never bring good. Therefore, τοίγαρ, I shall know that I must yield to the gods and reverence the Atreidae.' Why, we asked, does he say 'therefore'? Because he sees what we have called the pattern; he sees that it is Dikê that is wielding Hector's sword, which will kill him. One minor aspect of Dikê is commemorated in the proverb; in a moment Ajax is contemplating more majestic aspects, Night yielding to day and Winter to Summer. From these, superbly, he returns to himself:

> *Then how should I not find this wisdom too?*

What he says next has not been universally admired, at least so far as half of it is concerned. That one should not hate an enemy without remembering that some day he may become a friend, that is admirable. The obverse is not so good; it is a cold and calculating way to think of friendship. Perhaps it is, but let us consider it in its context, and let us reflect on the particular application of it that we find in the play. What Sophocles is saying is that the circumstances of life are baffling and unpredictable, so that it behoves us to be wary and well poised, ready to meet what comes. This is a part, perhaps a minor one, of Wisdom. Yet not a very minor part; for see how Odysseus bears himself towards Ajax at the end: 'I hated him when it was decent (καλόν) to hate him.' But now he is dead. 'He was my worst enemy, but still, I would not scorn him so far as to deny that he was the bravest of us all, after Achilles.' 'But men like him', says Agamemnon, 'are frantic (ἔμπληκτοι).' 'Yes,' replies

Odysseus, 'but many a man is an enemy one day and a friend the next. It is not good to be too rigid in one's judgment.' Presently he says: 'Teucer, I have been your enemy; from now on I offer you my friendship in like measure.'

This illustrates the other half of Ajax's maxim, and it is not cold or ignoble—and it is this half that Sophocles chooses to present. Here is poise and wisdom, in the face of life's uncertainties—the readiness to take the good with the bad, to forget and to forgive. No man is perfect; we should not resent the bad too fiercely when there is good to set in the balance against it.

Now, all this was implicit in what Athena said to Odysseus in the first scene, and in his reply: 'You see how great is the power of the gods? A single day can overturn or restore anything human.'—'I do see it; therefore I pity him, enemy though he is. Man is nothing but a phantom, an insubstantial shade'— 'Therefore avoid pride, if you are stronger or richer than another. It is the wise whom the gods cherish.' In this is announced, if not the theme of the play, at least its general scope; and that is not very different from the Socratic question πῶς δεῖ ζῆν;—how are we to live our lives? The demands that life makes of us are imperious; the strength of the gods is great. The way in which the gods order the universe—their Dikê—is something that we can understand, but only partially. We can see, if we will, the moral laws which are part of Dikê; we can see the majestic alternation of Night and Day, Summer and Winter. Sometimes, in a flash, more is revealed to us, as when we see that the belt of Ajax and Hector's sword fulfilled at last the enmity which was left unslaked on the field of battle. What is the meaning of such things as these? Sophocles does not pretend to answer this question; but he does say that it was an Erinys that forged the sword, and that the gods contrived it. At least it is not meaningless, for it is a manifestation of Dikê.

Since we are so weak and vulnerable, in comparison with the gods, we must have Wisdom. It may save us, or it may not. It could not save Tecmessa from the overwhelming disaster, the ἀναγκαία τύχη, which came upon her: yet this is not quite true, because Tecmessa, having Wisdom, was *not* overwhelmed. It could have saved Ajax. It is, in any case, the only guide through the uncertainties of life.

This, I think, is the connexion—and it is a very intimate one

—between Ajax's reflections about the sword and the proverb, about Night, Winter and Sleep, about the necessity of yielding to the gods and to the Atreidae, and about Friendship and Enmity. As was said above, it is a connexion that we have to argue about, for it is based on a religion which is not our own. This process of arguing out brings with it one grave inconvenience: it gives the impression that the play, to this critic at least, is something of a philosophical treatise. It is of course nothing of the kind, and something had better be said to restore the balance. Let us then, before we go on with the play, contemplate for a moment what Sophocles is putting before us: this magnificent Ajax, surely as splendid a tragic hero as any poet ever created, brought to shame and death by his own blazing pride and his lack of Wisdom. Moreover, when at last his pity is aroused, and he sees what his death will mean to others, he can do nothing for them; only disengage himself from them with words which seem to say one thing but mean another. And again—perhaps the most tragic thing of all—when, on the edge of death, he says that at last he has learned the lesson of Wisdom, we find that he is as far from it as ever: all that he has learned is that it is time for him to go; and he goes, calling down imprecations on his leaders, his old friends, and the army.

Now he lies dead. He has attempted the impossible: to impose his own pattern on life. But the play continues, and we have to discover why, and whether it is a bore to us, as it was to the Scholiast.

The scenes of wrangling that follow are, as Jebb said, 'repugnant to modern taste'; what Jebb did not see is that they are repugnant to Greek taste too. That is the whole point. And they are certainly not a loose addition; they develop naturally out of the conception of Wisdom which we have been considering, and they lead to a climax which is something more profound than a vindication of Ajax.

First Menelaus and then Agamemnon show that they too lack this same Wisdom. They have some excuse indeed for their behaviour; like Creon in the *Antigone* they can adduce respectable principles of statecraft to support their case—but what does it mean? It means what it means in the other play too, that the body of a fellow human being would be eaten by dogs and birds—a degradation of our common humanity and an outrage to the laws of the gods. What is common to this play and the *Antigone* is the passionate assertion that humanity comes first; it must prevail over all our political and even moral calculations.

Menelaus, a small and narrow man, argues thus. Ajax was always insubordinate; but for Athena, we should all have been murdered by him. Insubordination is ruinous to any society. There must be δέος, the fear inspired by authority; where this prevails there is security. Hybris is ruinous; even a strong man may fall from a slight cause. Things go by turns: ἕρπει παραλλάξ ταῦτα. So they do; it is a thought which the play has already impressed on us. But what conclusion are we to draw? Menelaus draws this one: 'Ajax was a man of intolerable insolence. Now it is my turn to be disdainful (μέγα φρονεῖν); he shall not be buried.' In fairness to Menelaus we must not forget the provocation; but as we look at the body of a great man, reckless and criminal though he was, with his wife and child sitting by it as suppliants, we feel that humanity, to say nothing of heroism, deserves more than this; and as we contemplate, as we have been made to do, the insecurity of everything human, we see that Menelaus has not argued far enough. 'These things go by turns,' and (as the chorus remarks at the end of the play) you never know what will happen next. The time might come when a Menelaus would need mercy and forgiveness.

Agamemnon is little better than his brother. He has one good argument: it is intolerable if men like Ajax will not accept the verdict of a court, but resort to violence. This is true—just as it is true that the crime of Polyneices was intolerable; but the claims of humanity are absolute. For the rest, Agamemnon is nothing but foolish arrogance—except when he is so insensate as to ask Teucer: 'Why be so insolently arrogant over something which is a man no longer, only a shadow?' This question has been answered in advance by Odysseus: 'We are all insubstantial shadows.' Things go by turns.

The vulgarity of their manner is the counterpart of the meanness of their thought. Ajax had little Wisdom in the handling of his life, and his lack of Wisdom destroyed him; but nevertheless Ajax was magnificent. In the lack of Wisdom that these men show there is something that dishonours humanity. The question at issue is the burial of Ajax, but behind it looms a bigger one which gives urgency and amplitude to this one: πῶς δεῖ ζῆν; How are we to live? The answer to both is brought by Odysseus. He knows that life is uncertain, that today's foe is tomorrow's friend, that no man is great or good all the time, that we should remember good deeds rather than bad, that we must respect the laws of the gods—and if for this we substitute the modern phrase 'the laws of humanity' we do no violence to the sense. No excuse is offered for what Ajax had done; there is on the other hand generous remembrance of his past services, a recognition that both in his greatness and in his crime he was human; and above all there is respect for the fact of death, to which we all come.

The last scenes, then, are not 'a bore'. The play has a splendid unity; it is both very moving and very profound. It has been called 'a picture-gallery', and the description may pass, provided that we realise that the pictures are so disposed as to call forth emotions and thoughts of very great depth. In creating Ajax, Sophocles has given a picture, seldom equalled, of Man in his splendour and in his folly; and, 'wishing to extend his drama', he made it a profound study of the conditions of human life, and of the spirit in which we should confront them.

CHAPTER SEVEN

Greek and Elizabethan Tragedy

Scene: A Street in Thebes. *Enter* two mechanicals.

FIRST M.: *Godden, Sir. 'Tis a fair day.*

SECOND M.: *A fair day and a foul day, and a fair day for the fowl.*

FIRST M.: *How so, Sir?*

SECOND M.: *'Tis a day when the fowl may go a-fairing. Ergo, 'tis a fair day and a foul.*

FIRST M.: *Foul enough with thee, for it hath befouled thy wits.*

SECOND M.: *Wits, Sirrah? Hark 'ee: if a hungry crow peck a man's eye out, is not that a fair thing for the crow? And is not the crow a fowl?*

FIRST M.: *Truly, 'tis a foul thing that a fowl should eat such fare as a man's eye.*

SECOND M.: *But if that man be a double-dyed traitor? Doth not that make the foul fair?*

Why is it inconceivable that Sophocles should have begun the *Antigone* in this eminently early-Shakespearian manner? That is one question which it seems reasonable to ask and to try to answer. Why do the Greek and the Elizabethan drama differ so widely in form, style and texture?

Another question concerns the illogicalities, or distortions, which we have been examining. We have seen what they are, and why they were contrived; but the question remains why Sophocles *could* contrive them, without irritating or baffling his audience. Unless the explanations given above are quite mistaken, it is plain that he counted on receiving from his audience a response very different from the one which he has received from some of his modern admirers; for these, time after time, ask and try to answer questions which, from Sophocles' point of view, do not exist at all.

The essence of the distortions is that there are certain inconvenient questions which Sophocles does not expect his audience to ask. Why does Neoptolemus know all these things?

Why did Antigone not take the libations with her the first time? When we put the problem in this way, we see at once that there are other questions of the same kind that we may ask. Why, in the *Tyrannus*, does Sophocles pretend that never until this moment has Oedipus told Iocasta the story of his life, and why does this not spoil the play? Further, Sophocles begins this play with two vivid descriptions of the plague that is ravaging the city; it seems to be a capital point. Yet it is never again mentioned. We can of course say, if we like, that at the end, when the offending person is punished, we know that the plague will cease; but if we do this we are adding to the play something that Sophocles did not put there, and in fact the thought does not occur to our minds at all. It is difficult to imagine a Shakespearian play beginning with such an event, so emphatically stated, and ending without any further reference to it. But it is exactly parallel to what we have noticed in the *Antigone*. A pupil of mine, a member of a Drama class unaccustomed to the ways of Greek tragedy, once put the point concisely, and in some surprise: 'In this play, Sophocles forgets Ismene, and we don't mind. Then he forgets Antigone too—and we don't mind.' In a Shakespearian play we should mind. What is the difference?

Nor is this peculiar to Sophocles. Let us consider the following dramatic situation. On the stage is a group of noblemen or counsellors. To them comes a messenger with the news that the fleet has been wrecked, and so far as he knows only the flagship, with the King on board, has escaped. *Exit the Messenger*. How would any Elizabethan dramatist continue? The King is safe, but the flower of English manhood has been devoured by the hungry sea: it is inconceivable that nobody on the stage should say a word about it. But that is exactly what happens in the *Agamemnon*; the chorus begins to sing about Helen, and the storm is never again mentioned. And not only do we 'not mind', but lamentations about the disaster would strike us as irrelevant. Some realist like Verrall or Rouse or Drachmann ought to have come to our rescue with an explanation, but in fact nobody seems to have noticed it. The reason for the failure to mention the disaster is not that these Elders are a Greek chorus, and cannot therefore be expected to behave reasonably; it is that the whole design of the play makes us see that the disaster is yet another instance of the law that punishment follows sin; therefore when the chorus proceeds to speak of Helen and her sin, and the destruction which that brought upon Troy, the continuation is logical—so logical that we never pause to reflect that by the logic of the market-place they ought to be singing of the sorrows not of Troy but of Argos.

It would be easy to extend this list. There is for example the second ode in the *Agamemnon*. When the chorus, having learned that Troy has been captured, begins: Paris has been struck down, it is natural for us to see in this a cry of exultation. In Shakespeare, even in Sophocles, this would be the inevitable interpretation; in Aeschylus it is the wrong one.[1] The reaction which seems so natural does not exist.

We may go further, and observe that Aeschylus does much the same thing in his drawing of individual characters. Often this is very sharp, but the extent of the character-drawing is much narrower than in Shakespeare, and we often succumb to the temptation of trying to make it ampler than it is. For example, there is Headlam's treatment of the scene in the *Agamemnon* between Clytemnestra and the Herald, with which I ventured to disagree in reviewing Thomson's *Oresteia*.[2] Clytemnestra comes out of the Palace, gives no greeting of any kind to the Herald, delivers herself of eleven verses, and then says: 'What need for you to tell me more? Tell him from me that I am waiting, his faithful wife . . . ' Headlam's comment was 'When she has finished, she retires, giving the Herald not the expected reward; only a curt dismissal. The Herald is taken aback, and turns in dismay to the Elders.' His surprise at the Queen's discourtesy the Herald expresses in the couplet 613-614, which Headlam, following the MSS, unlike most editors, gives to the Herald. My criticism was that this is a misconception; that there is no rudeness, and no disappointment; that Clytemnestra has simply no attitude at all to the Herald. Professor Thomson said in reply[3]: 'Instead of greeting him she tells him flatly that she is not going to listen to his message, and disappears before he has had time to say a word. Is this not an attitude?'

No. It would be one in Sophocles, much more so in Shakespeare, but not in the *Agamemnon*, as we shall see in a moment. A later passage illustrates the same point, that the modern

[1] See above, pp. 10-12.   [2] *Journal of Hellenic Studies*, 1940.
[3] *J.H.S.*, 1941

critic is tempted to see personal relations and therefore character-drawing which in fact are not there. In the scene between Agamemnon and Clytemnestra, Headlam and Thomson assume that Clytemnestra is on from the beginning of the scene (as of course they are entitled to do, so far as the text is concerned), and then comment to this effect: Agamemnon makes his first speech without addressing or referring to her; she retorts by doing the same. They ignore each other; there never has been any love lost between these two.

This would be the inevitable interpretation if such a passage occurred in Sophocles or in any modern dramatist, but it is not the correct one here. The proof is simple: it is that nearly all characters in Aeschylus behave like this, and usually rudeness cannot be in question at all.

Thus, when Clytemnestra makes her first entrance, the chorus does indeed greet her, but she does not return the greeting, and at the end of the scene she retires without a word. Then, the Herald behaves to the chorus exactly as Clytemnestra does to him. He comes on, takes the centre of the stage, and begins his speech as if the chorus were not there. But the chorus is not indignant; when the Herald has finished they say 'All hail' as if he had that moment come on, and he replies 'All hail'. And he too, at the end of his scene, simply disappears, like Clytemnestra.

Agamemnon enters, greeted at some length by the loyal chorus. Does he answer them? No, he addresses the gods. This is perhaps right and proper; but when he has finished with the gods and at last speaks to the chorus, is it with some courteous Sophoclean phrase like

$$\pi\acute{o}\lambda\epsilon\omega\varsigma\ \ddot{a}\nu\alpha\kappa\tau\epsilon\varsigma\ \tau\hat{\eta}\sigma\delta\epsilon,\ \kappa o\acute{\iota}\rho\alpha\nu o\iota\ \chi\theta o\nu\acute{o}\varsigma;$$

No, not even a simple ἄνδρες. His manner to them is as remote as Clytemnestra's to the Herald; he says:

$$\tau\grave{o}\ \delta'\ \dot{\epsilon}\varsigma\ \tau\grave{o}\ \sigma\grave{o}\nu\ \phi\rho\acute{o}\nu\eta\mu\alpha\ \ldots$$
As for what you say . . .

Is this rudeness? What conceivable reason could Aeschylus have for making Agamemnon rude to the chorus? But he has reason enough, as we shall see, for making his characters keep their distance from each other.

When Clytemnestra comes out after the murder she does not

greet the chorus; and—the most interesting case of all—when Aegisthus enters, he does not explain where he has come from (though Verrall did), nor does he address either the chorus or Clytemnestra. He begins abruptly:

ὦ φέγγος εὖφρον ἡμέρας δικηφόρου
Welcome! light of the day that brings Justice—

and he goes on for quite a long time, speaking about Atreus and Thyestes. Then the chorus engages him in dialogue—but Clytemnestra does not; she might as well not be there. She neither speaks nor is spoken to, until she intervenes to stop the rising quarrel.

And how do we interpret this? On Headlam's principles we ought to say: 'Clytemnestra is piqued by his pointed ignoring of her'; or, 'These two conceal their guilty love in public, and therefore do not speak to each other.' But no such thought crosses our minds. We are completely occupied with Aeschylus' high argument; and it was in order that we might be free to follow it undisturbed that he avoids these personal matters and keeps his characters remote from each other. The past relations between Agamemnon and his wife, that aspect of Agamemnon's character which would make him courteous or not to the chorus, that aspect of Clytemnestra's which would make her courteous or not to the Herald, the purely personal side of her relations with Aegisthus—all these things, which would be an inevitable, and interesting, part of a modern drama, are quite irrelevant to Aeschylus' theme and would only obscure it. That is the reason why he uses this spacious dramatic texture, in which unwanted personal relationships disappear. The Athenian audience, though intelligent, was not supernaturally so. Aeschylus demands of it considerable power of concentration, that it may follow his thought, his imagery, his closely woven language; it could not possibly do this if at the same time it were being invited to attend to matters of collateral dramatic interest. When Aegisthus enters, acclaiming the 'day that brings Dikê', using the same adjective that the Herald applied to Zeus when the Greeks, using his crowbar, overthrew the walls and temples of Troy, how could the audience possibly take the point if they were looking back and forth from Aegisthus to Clytemnestra, wondering how they would comport themselves in public?

A similar instance can be cited from another play, where also a distinguished scholar went wrong by thinking in terms of naturalism. The chorus of the *Prometheus* consists of Ocean Nymphs who have come into the savage mountains, so far from their own home, to sympathise with Prometheus, 'winning our father's slow consent'. Oceanus himself enters presently, the River that surrounds the inhabited world. No greeting passes between him and his daughters; observing which, Wilamowitz explained that Oceanus was displeased at the unmaidenly desire of his daughters to go on so long a journey.

Surely one can be prosaic without going as far as this? The theme of the play is that a young and victorious god, wishing to destroy the human race and begin again, has been thwarted by Prometheus, who has given to man the means of survival and civilisation. The minds of the audience can move on this level, or they can descend and move on the more personal, almost domestic, level indicated by Wilamowitz. They cannot do both, except by exercising an agility which will be as difficult as it will be barren. Here too the remoteness of Oceanus is deliberate and necessary.

By way of confirmation, we may notice that there is one scene in the *Agamemnon*, and one only, in which one character greets another in what we feel to be a normal way: Clytemnestra comes out of the palace in order to get Cassandra into it, and therefore addresses her directly:

> Εἴσω κομίζου καὶ σύ, Κάσσανδραν λέγω.
> *You too, Cassandra: get you within.*

Moreover, at the end of this scene, and nowhere else, Clytemnestra gives her reason for leaving the stage: I am not going to stand here to be insulted. The direct personal contact here is important; Cassandra is to be seen as Apollo's victim, not Clytemnestra's, therefore Clytemnestra is made to approach her directly, in order to be baffled. But of the other personal relationships, and the facets of individual character which they would bring into existence, it is hardly too much to say that they do not exist. What does it matter, whether Agamemnon and Clytemnestra had always lived a cat-and-dog life, or had lived very amicably until Agamemnon made his disastrous mistake? whether Clytemnestra and Aegisthus are really in love or not?

whether or not, and for what reasons, Agamemnon prefers Cassandra to his wife? We are to see Clytemnestra coming out of the palace, or going in, as the Wrath incarnate called into being by Artemis. We cannot do this, and at the same time watch a Herald fingering his cap and wondering if he is going to get his reward or not, and then expressing resentment when the Avenger withdraws without saying: 'Thank you, my man; here is a purse for you.' While she is speaking, the Herald must be quite motionless. While the Herald is making his first speech, the chorus must be quite motionless. These characters have indeed some relation to each other, but their relation to the developing theme of the play, to the gods, is vastly more significant, and the unimportant must not obscure the essential. Naturalistic treatment of these matters is possible only when one has under-estimated the amplitude and the intellectual concentration of the play—in fact, when we are trying to see it in the wrong focus.

It was of course to prevent our taking this irrelevant personal interest in the characters that Aeschylus evolved his spacious texture, and his dramatic style. The actors keep their distance from each other; they do not, in general, explain their comings and goings, like characters who are seen against a more natural-istic background. The real background that Aeschylus created for this play is not the actual palace, with its retainers and its daily routine, a palace which the temple-haunting martlet might approve; it is the two laws of Hybris and Dikê, the acti-vity of the gods; and the physical palace, by a fine stroke of imagination, becomes part of this real background as the home of the Erinyes.—Or it might be wiser to say, not that Aeschylus evolved this spacious texture in order to prevent his audience from doing something which may never have occurred to him even as a possibility, but rather that his sure instinct made his dramatic style exactly consonant with his dramatic idea. Shakes-peare could not and would not have made his Counsellors appear indifferent to the wreck of an English fleet; Aeschylus not only can: he must.

There is one more point to notice here: how completely in-different this kind of drama is to what we may call the off-stage action. How long does it take a fleet to sail, through a storm, from the Hellespont to Nauplia? Does the Herald actually deliver Clytemnestra's message to Agamemnon? Where does

Aegisthus come from? Questions of this kind, which must receive some slight attention in other forms of drama, do not exist in this one. The reason seems to be that the play does not imply a continuous stream of events on its outskirts, or behind it, with which the stage-events must more or less correspond. The absence of naturalism is quite thorough; even the diction is not much modified to suit the character or mood of the speaker.

It might seem that the style and texture of Sophocles are so different from those of Aeschylus that there is little sense in taking them together as parts of the same problem. The background in Sophocles is much more naturalistic; personal relations are much closer; verisimilitude is studied much more. There is no need to illustrate this at length; a few direct contrasts will serve.

In Sophocles, the interlock of characters is dramatically more significant; therefore the texture is such that they are brought closer together, and closer to us. They normally greet each other; they are conscious of each other's presence; they commonly suggest some reason for their coming or going. This is not an advance in dramatic technique; it is simply a different style, adopted for a rather different sort of tragic idea.

Therefore when Clytemnestra comes out, in the *Electra*, finds her daughter with the chorus, and begins abruptly:

> ἀνειμένη μὲν ὡς ἔοικας αὖ στρέφει
> *Roaming abroad again, it seems?*—

we infer immediately that she is angry. The whole dramatic texture is such that this sounds rude; when Clytemnestra does the same kind of thing in Aeschylus, we infer nothing; in Aeschylus it is common form. Again, when Teiresias, in the *Tyrannus*, enters, being sent for, and addresses neither Oedipus nor the chorus, but begins:

> φεῦ φεῦ· φρονεῖν ὡς δεινὸν ἔνθα μὴ τέλη
> λύῃ φρονοῦντι.

Ah me! what a burden knowledge is, where knowledge cannot avail.

we feel at once that something unusual is afoot.

In Sophocles, entrances and exits are more consciously contrived. Aegisthus simply arrives; Eurydice is careful to explain why she comes out of the palace. The difference is directly connected with the fact that the background in these plays is more naturalistic—perceptibly so, though perhaps not very much. In the *Electra*, for instance, the palace is not a blood-stained haunt of the Erinyes, but a home—one in which Electra is outraged and humiliated by daily association with the murderers. There is little need to continue; it is as if perspective had now been introduced. The characters stand in a much more definite, and delicate, relation to each other, and naturally every other feature of the dramatic style is modified accordingly. Diction becomes far more supple, with much more differentiation for character and mood; the chorus is more plastic, caught up much more closely in the successive situations, and reacting more personally—for which reason the dance-rhythms within a single ode are more varied than in Aeschylus; plot is more elaborate, with more frequent contrasts of situation and mood.

The differences are so great that they may seem to betoken quite a different conception of drama. Watching the suppleness of some of Sophocles' triangular scenes we may well think that we are already half-way to Shakespeare. But we have to be careful.

There is a historical way of explaining these differences, thus: An art naturally grows from the simpler form to the more complex, as more and more possibilities are discovered. Aeschylus, the earlier dramatist, was austere, even stiff in his technique; Sophocles, enjoying the advantage of his pioneering work, made considerable advances in the form and style of drama. As to this, no harm is done—and perhaps not much good either—by the use of the historical method in matters of art, so long as it is recognised for what it is: a superior kind of reporting, an objective record of what happened within the abstraction called Greek Tragic Drama. The harm is done when the abstraction is used in order to explain the realities; and the realities are the individual plays. We may be tolerably certain that Aeschylus and Sophocles did not do this and that in order to develop Greek Drama, still less because the form of Greek Drama was developing. They did this and that because that was what they 'meant'; that was the best way of saying it. Using the historical method unintelligently we may say, for example: 'The introduction of the third actor, which was the next major development, brought with it a higher degree of naturalism, more detailed character-drawing, and a more skilful use of dialogue.' This is certainly one way of reporting facts, but it impresses us more than it should; and the result is that when we try to interpret Sophocles we do not think of these 'improvements' as being themselves a direct expression of the dramatist's thought; on the contrary, we think of them as a historical development already explained by some vague quasi-biological process in the Art of Drama, and therefore exhausted, as far as the business of interpretation is concerned, because they have been already explained and are fully accounted for. So, making the illegitimate separation of matter and form, we look for Sophocles' 'thought' elsewhere, find only part of it, and get that part wrong.

But our concern, as critics, is with individual works of art, each a unique creation; and if the work is first-rate, all its parts and details will have been designed to embody one unique conception. The details of structure, style and treatment are not things already explained on historical grounds; on the contrary, they are the evidence which must guide us to our interpretation of the play. If we find Aeschylus 'stiff' in comparison with Sophocles, the reason is not that he was an earlier dramatist and had not quite mastered all the niceties of dramatic form; but that he, being at least as consummate a master of dramatic form as ever Sophocles was, had different things to say—which he would have said less well had he been silly enough to make use of the Sophoclean 'improvements'.

The differences between Aeschylus and Sophocles are great, but not so fundamental as the resemblances between them. The resemblance is that both are constructive rather than representational, a distinction which will perhaps become clearer as we proceed. It is easy for us to think of Sophocles as a dramatist who took a decisive step forward towards the true end and perfection of drama: complete naturalism; which in fact is not the perfection, but the death of drama. He was, we say, interested in human character above all things, and he used all the subtle resources of his art for the purpose of representing human character in action, though a nobly idealised type of human character. Aeschylus was a 'religious' dramatist; Sophocles represented human life at its best and most heroic.

Perhaps he did, but all this is subordinate. It is indeed this belief that he is essentially a representational artist which makes his distortions so hard to understand. Everything he does appears so 'life-like' that we are taken aback, and perhaps a little resentful, when we find that quite important details in several of his plots are either impossible or improbable. In fact, Sophocles is very close to Aeschylus, and, unless I am gravely mistaken, very different from Shakespeare and other English dramatists. The real basis of a classical Greek tragedy is not the story; Wilamowitz was almost as wrong as a man can be when he said that Greek Tragedy was essentially Saga. Nor is it the people who figure in the story; Sophocles was not a Dickens who had the additional advantage of the classical sense of form. The formative and controlling idea in a Greek play—always excluding those which are not really tragic—is some religious or philosophical conception, and the interest which the dramatist takes in the story, or in the persons is always—I will not say *subordinated* to this, but strictly correlated with it. It is in this respect that Greek drama differs from Elizabethan; not of course that the Greek was philosophical with no interest in individuals, and the Elizabethan interested only in individuals, with no philosophical foundations: the difference lies in the balance which each strikes between the two.

The Greek dramatists seem to have obeyed the same instinct as the early Greek philosophers. These contemplated the innumerable phenomena of the Universe, and assumed instinctively that they were only 'phenomena', appearances; the ultimate reality must be simple, not complex. The poets had the same habit of mind. They looked out on their Universe of human action and suffering, and saw unending variety—and they saw it with that quickness and sharpness in which the Greek was seldom wanting. But it was not his habit to represent this directly. He sought rather to apprehend the unifying simplicity, the fundamental laws; and these, once apprehended, became the framework of his drama. The immediate objects of his observation—the characters, actions, experiences of men— became, so to speak, his raw material, and out of it, discarding and rearranging, he built his new completely intelligible structure. From the material he selected only what was immediately relevant to his purpose, and the purpose was, not to represent a typical human situation, but to recreate the inner reality. Such, after all, is the very meaning of the Greek word ποίησις poiêsis, which has become our word 'poetry'; quite literally it means 'construction'. Let it be said again that of course the English dramatic poets also did this, as any artist must, but the balance between the constructive and the representational activities in the Greek and the Elizabethan respectively is considerable, and explains, to a very great extent, the differences in form and style.

For example, we can imagine, perhaps with some effort, what a series of plays Shakespeare might have made out of the raw material which is used, or implied, in the *Agamemnon*: Atreus and Thyestes, Paris and Helen, Aulis and the sacrifice, the war —with Thersites as a quite unavoidable character, Cassandra (though not Apollo), the storm, Agamemnon's return, and its sequel, and of course Clytemnestra with Aegisthus. It would have become a vast panorama of action and suffering, full of contrasts and conflicts, as full and wide and rich as life itself. But Aeschylus had no interest at all in panoramas. Instead of ranging widely and creating a unity by an inspired process of aggregation, he works inwards. He passes right through this mass of material until he reaches his inner and unifying reality, the conflict between the two laws of Dikê and Hybris; he is not enthralled by the persons he creates. Having reached this conception he recreates it in dramatic form with the material that he has left lying about on the surface, choosing from it only what he needs, using it in what order suits him best (so that Atreus and Thyestes come last), and throwing away the rest. So it comes about that the finished structure has the clarity and force of a single statement, the firmness and the cohesion which we find in a mathematical demonstration, together with that peculiar power which is generated by a work of art in which every detail contributes directly to the same end.

Sophocles does precisely the same. It is no exaggeration to say that every detail in his plays is seen, upon reflection, to arise out of, and contribute to, one single conception. Nothing is there simply because Sophocles got interested in a character or a situation. The reason why the texture of his plays is different from the texture characteristic of Aeschylus is quite simple: his conception of Dikê was different, and he was interested in a different aspect of life. In the *Oresteia* and the *Prometheia* Aeschylus deals, in some sense, with the evolution of civilisation;

in the Danaid-trilogy (if my interpretation is near the truth[1])
with the revelation, through offence and counter-offence, of
what the Law of Zeus really means. In the much simpler *Persae*
he deals with a single but impressive instance of Hybris. In the
three trilogies there is what we may call a forward movement,
from conflict to further conflict and so to an ultimate reconciliation, and in two of them this forward movement is expressed as
a change in Zeus himself. A further point is that in all the plays,
whether there is a single situation, as in the *Persae*, or a series
of situations, each one is simple: one person, or one at a time,
acts with violence. But Sophocles' thought takes quite a different
course. It is not evolutionary; the idea of a progressive deity is
utterly foreign to it. He is indeed not uninterested in the up-
ward path of mankind from barbarism to civilisation, as the
famous ode in the *Antigone* shows, but the establishment of
moral and social order out of chaos is not, as it is in Aeschylus,
an essential part of his religious thinking. He contemplates
rather the human situation at large, as one which is fixed and
governed by laws that do not and cannot change; in his conception of Diké, the World Order, there is no place for anything
progressive; it is something inherent in the nature of the Universe and of Man, something eternal. It includes the known
laws of prudence and morality, but is not identical with these,
since it includes also (as the *Tyrannus* shows) that further and
mysterious region of human experience in which innocent
actions can have terrible results. This World Order he will show
as revealing itself in the complex characters and actions of a
whole group of persons, related to each other whether closely
or quite casually. His chief personages therefore will not simply
clash with each other, as they do in Aeschylus; they will engage
with each other in close and prolonged conflict, bringing into
play their whole personality. Such a spectacle we find more
'life-like' than anything in Aeschylus, as indeed it is; but we
should beware of thinking that the art of drama, in his hands,
is becoming more naturalistic. So it may seem to us, who are
accustomed to more directly representational art, but his art is
essentially just as austere as the art of Aeschylus; it is different
in texture only as his thought is different from the thought of
Aeschylus.

[1] *Greek Tragedy*, pp. 18-22.

The point is of some importance. There is the Corinthian in the *Tyrannus*, a character drawn in so lifelike a way that the Watchman of the *Agamemnon* seems archaic by comparison. He is very like a Shakespearian minor character, a marginal sketch drawn from life, for the fun of the thing. No doubt he was drawn from life, and no doubt Sophocles enjoyed drawing him, but we must be cautious. Headlam quoted this man, in his note on the Herald's encounter with Clytemnestra: messengers in Greek tragedy, Headlam said, regularly expect a reward, and will ask for one, 'in accordance with oriental custom'. That is to say, what is familiar in daily life we expect too on the stage. We have seen that this is an impossible way of interpreting the passage in the *Agamemnon*; it is nearly as disabling here. The details are of course lifelike; if they were not, they would not have served Sophocles' purpose; but if we suppose that Sophocles was *only* being lifelike, we shall not see what that purpose was.

Let us observe how restricted the 'naturalism' is, and to what it is restricted. The man is represented as being completely at his ease, full of confidence, anxious to be helpful. He tells us why he has come in such a hurry: he hopes for a reward now, and presently he hints that he hopes for even more, when Oedipus becomes his King, and learns his secret. But he does not talk about his poor tired legs (like the Old Man in Euripides' *Ion*), or about the wife and family. The character-drawing is strictly organic. One reason why he is made to be frank about his prospective tip we saw above[1] when discussing the double perspective: his arrival at this moment, which is so natural, is also the act of the god (which is just what Hippocrates said about 'the sacred disease'). But there is another point, a very profoundly ironical one—and the irony is repeated when the slave of Laius joins him (vv. 1178-1179): a decent action, which promised to bring him so much good, brings in fact nothing but misery.

Sophocles is really just as austere as Aeschylus, in his methods. He never draws character where character is not necessary. The Messengers in the *Ajax* and the *Antigone* are hardly drawn at all, while the Second Messenger in the *Antigone* is such a blank that we cannot even tell whether a man or a woman is intended; it may be the same person as the First Messenger, or it may not. What does it matter? The person who is speaking

[1] See above, p. 75.

is of no importance; all our attention is to be concentrated on what is said. Comparable to this is the treatment of Antigone and Haemon, which in its turn is directly comparable to the treatment of Cassandra, Agamemnon and Clytemnestra in the scene in which they are on the stage together. In each case there is a situation which is brim full of dramatic possibilities, but neither dramatist will touch any of them except the one which immediately concerns his theme. It would no doubt be an exaggeration to say that there is no 'free' characterisation whatever, but its range is narrow. When a real person, not a mere walking message, is called for, Sophocles always draws him vividly—as for example the Watchman in the *Antigone*; but we have only to compare this man with the Guards whom Anouilh so amply draws in his *Antigone* to appreciate how essentially 'constructive' Sophocles' method is. But the important thing, for the modern reader, is to understand this, as it were, in reverse. Naturalism is a relatively lazy thing; Sophocles is always working hard, and we have to work hard too. Thus, the Watchman is not 'relief', whether comic or otherwise; he is there to illustrate another aspect of Creon's 'injustice' and inhumanity, and it is for us to co-ordinate this one with the others. The second part of the *Ajax*, showing Teucer successively with Menelaus, Agamemnon and Odysseus, is not simply a picture-gallery. The *Electra* is not simply a Portrait of a Lady.

This limitation of character-drawing is to be found in Euripides' tragedies too. There are those who speak of the profound psychological study of Medea; who would make of Hippolytus a man whose mind has been twisted by his illegitimate birth; who see in Hecuba a woman warped by suffering, so that she herself gives way to the lust for vengeance. But all this turns Euripides into a modern, and not a very successful one. It would indeed be possible for a dramatist to treat Medea as a passionate woman who fell violently in love with Jason, helped him by killing her own brother, found her love for Jason turning into contempt and hatred, and finally, after a desperate struggle with herself, brought herself to murder her own children in order to encompass her revenge on him. It might be such a play as Webster wrote—but not Euripides. If we try to do this with his play, we are puzzled, or offended, by his violent foreshortening of the events, by his stiff and rhetorical treatment of Medea's 'psychological struggle', and by his oversimplification of Jason. It is the same with Hecuba, a prostrate victim who suddenly turns oppressor. We cannot follow this as a logical and necessary process in Hecuba's mind and character, because we hardly know what they are; and it is worth noticing that exactly the same thing happens in the *Heracleidae* to Alcmena, whose mind and character are equally vague. In fact, if we try to make these plays in any important degree studies of individual characters, and consequently compare them directly, as we should, with Shakespeare's plays, we can hardly help admitting either that Euripides was a child in these matters, or that the conventions of his theatre almost disabled him. The real power of these plays is revealed only when we see that he was making drama not about individuals but about humanity—humanity torn by contrary passions, or by the conflict between its passions and its reason. We have to look at these characters, as it were, from a considerable distance, as the Athenian audience did literally in the Theatre of Dionysus; the distance being great enough to ensure that we see in due proportion what is significant, and do not try to see in detail what is not there, and would not help Euripides' theme if it were. Bastardy working like a slow poison in the mind of Hippolytus is of no particular interest to Euripides—though it is an idea that Shakespeare found drama- tic. There might be a play conceived on this personal scale which would suggest the tragic predicament into which Human- ity may fall, torn between contrary passions or forces, but this was not the Greek way of doing it. It would be out of scale in a form of drama which presents humanity faced with the gods. If one or two references to the circumstances of his birth help to explain why Hippolytus is exclusively a votary of Artemis, well and good, but it is not for us to exaggerate the importance of these, and to try to turn the play into a psychological study of an individual. He, for whatever reason, is one-sided; Phaedra too is one who loves passionately against her judgment. This is all that matters, and this is all that Euripides gives us.

In the plays which are not tragic, Euripides gives much more, and much less; much less, inasmuch as there is now no profound illumination of human life; much more, however, of detail and variety, both in character and incident. These plays too we should call constructive rather than representational, though in

a different sense, for what is being constructed now is nothing
more than an elegant work of art.[1] But in those plays which are
tragedies the dramatists confine themselves, with great singleness of mind, to the material which the construction of their
themes demanded, and in none of them is there any concession
to naturalism for its own sake.

It has not escaped our notice that Sophocles writes no Romeo-
and-Juliet scene for Haemon and Antigone. That we may not
be unduly depressed by his indifference to the anguish of young
lovers we may notice that there are other obvious scenes which
he omits. We do not see Antigone in the process of coming to
her decision, nor Creon to his. Shakespeare would have set
Creon among his advisers—a grave bishop, it may be, expressing
doubts, cold statesmen approving, the Queen, perhaps, protesting. Again, in Sophocles' play Haemon tells us, very briefly,
how the ordinary Thebans regard Antigone's action; Shakespeare would have taken us into the streets, to hear for ourselves
what they were saying. Creon tells us that Ismene, in the
palace, is behaving like one demented; Shakespeare would not
have been content with merely telling us.

Now, we all know why the Greek dramatists did not make the
lively and expansive drama which the Elizabethans made: the
conditions of their theatre prevented it. They had at the most
three actors, so that the well-populated Elizabethan stage was
beyond their reach. They had no curtain, so that division of the
play into acts, with intermission of time, was impossible; though
if we remember that the Globe theatre had no curtain either,
we amend this, and say instead that the Greek dramatist had on
his hands throughout the play the Chorus which tradition imposed on him, and that this chorus, except in rare circumstances,

---

[1] I have dealt with this at length in my *Greek Tragedy* (chapters XI and
XII), and have nothing to add, except one point which has nothing to do with
Tragedy. In New Comedy, exposure of infants is a regular incident; therefore, it is argued, it must have been a common practice at the time. Perhaps
it was, but New Comedy does not prove it, simply because New Comedy is
not representational but (in the sense just indicated) constructive. It is in
fact artificial; it is elegant comedy, not a photograph of contemporary life;
and the presence of 'realistic' figures like Polemo does not alter the fact.
All that New Comedy proves is that the exposure of infants was known. In
French comedy, the mistress is, or was, a constant feature; this proves only
that the keeping of a mistress was an intelligible stage-convention, not that
it was a regular feature of French life.

H

could not leave the scene of the action and reappear in another, so that the action had to be continuous and on one spot. We say too that the drama grew out of a religious rite in which the chorus was the centre, and that it always remained in close association with religion—in regard to which mankind is always conservative; therefore, in spite of its inconvenience, the Chorus could not be discarded. We cite the masks, also of religious origin.[1] And so we continue, explaining the structure and style of Greek plays by reference to the external conditions of performance, finding reasons which no doubt are good enough to set down in examination papers, but do not survive serious enquiry for ten minutes. They are, quite literally, preposterous.

For let us consider the matter of the three actors. We are told by Aristotle that 'Aeschylus introduced the second actor, and Sophocles the third, with scene-painting'—whatever that was. There it stopped; the actors remained three. Why? Why does Aristotle's account not run as follows?—

> The second actor was introduced by Aeschylus, the third, with scene-painting, by Sophocles. Soon after that, Sophocles introduced a fourth, and Euripides a fifth. Then the restriction on the number of actors was abolished, though the contest between the protagonists remained. At the same time the part of the chorus was gradually diminished, and for the same reason: to make drama more lifelike; for drama is a *mimesis* of men acting, not of men remaining on one spot, making or listening to speeches. Therefore little by little the chorus became withdrawn from the action (as happened also in Comedy, though later), until the chorus did nothing but perform one ode at the beginning of the play and another at the end. Thus it became possible to bring within a single play many people acting in several places, not at random or as it happened, but all composing one single myth. When the scene of action changed, as from Argos to Lycia, it was indicated by a man who went on with a board.

[1] Which may be true, but has nothing to do with the tragic mask. There were no masks in the dithyramb, from which Tragedy is said to have developed; and what Suidas records about Thespis and his experiments suggests —what in any case one ought to have expected—that the masks were due not to religious survival but to commonsense. For Thespis, so Suidas says, first smeared his face with white-lead, then he 'overshadowed' his face with a sprig of purslane, then he devised a mask of linen. Obviously he was doing the opposite to what was contrived by that less skilful primitive actor, Bottom, who will, 'for the more better assurance, tell them that I, Pyramus, am not Pyramus but Bottom the weaver.'

This short history is not in the least unreasonable. It is merely
untrue. Why did these interesting things never happen? We
can talk of the religious conservatism of the Athenians, but since
the Athenians, in little more than a century, took their tragic
drama from its Thespian stage to highly sophisticated comedy
like the *Helen*, one may perhaps be forgiven if one does not
think very highly of their conservatism. The reason why these
things did not happen can only be that the Athenians saw no
reason why they should. They were not afraid of radical change:
they changed the number of actors twice within a generation.
Why only twice? For that matter, why have a rule at all
governing the number of actors?

The answer to the second question is plain enough: the dramatic festival was an ἀγών, a contest, and contests must have
rules, in order that all contestants may start fair. But in what
circumstances was the rule changed? What actually happened
when 'Aeschylus introduced the second actor'?

We have no information at all, but we have analogies close
enough to make possible an intelligent guess. As it happens,
we ourselves have an ἀγών, cricket, in which the number of
actors, over several generations, has varied considerably; but
cricket, πολλὰς μεταβολὰς μεταβαλοῦσα, has settled down with
eleven. As it is a contest the number must be fixed; and if we
ask Why eleven? the only answer is that experience has shown
that eleven is the number which best suits the nature of the
game. On occasion, the restriction may of course be irksome;
many a captain must have wished he had fifteen men in the
field instead of a miserable eleven. Similarly, Sophocles would
obviously have been more comfortable with four actors in the
Coloneus. But in general eleven proved to be the right number
for cricket, and three for the Greek tragic drama.

Moreover, we know in what circumstances the rules of our
contests are altered. Circumstances change; new techniques are
discovered, the implements of the game are improved, and the
balance of the contest is upset. The laws are amended by the
governing body, in consultation with the leading exponents of
the game, when it is the general opinion that a change would
be for the good of the game. It is reasonable to suppose that the
number of actors in Greek tragedy was changed in similar circumstances; that Aeschylus, one of the most successful of the

younger dramatists, found himself increasingly hampered by the one-actor rule, having things to say that were impossible in the existing framework. We may suppose that he was not alone in this; that the majority of the dramatists and amateurs of the theatre were of the same opinion, and that between them they were able to get the second actor. A generation later Sophocles began to find two actors insufficient; he saw dramatic possibilities which could not be developed without a third actor. He too, we must surmise, found enough support—including that of Aeschylus[1]—to have the rule altered again. But if Sophocles, or any other dramatist, ever tried to introduce a fourth, he failed. Taking it broad and long, it was agreed that three was the right number. Indeed, it is interesting to observe that Euripides, at least in his tragedies, was so far from wanting a fourth that he rarely used even the third to its fullest extent. His typical tragic scene is a straight passage between two, as Medea and Jason, with the third actor in the dressing-room taking off one mask and putting on another.

This reconstruction is of course entirely conjectural, but not, I think, unreasonable. In any case there is evidence enough to make us reject, as altogether superficial, the idea that it was external conditions that controlled the form and style of the drama. It was not scarcity of actors that prevented Aeschylus from making Cassandra, Agamemnon and Clytemnestra discuss their prospects of having a comfortable domestic life together. It was not this, nor the compulsory presence of the chorus, which prevented Sophocles from writing a scene for Antigone and Haemon. It was not lack of supers that prevented him from bringing back Antigone's body with Haemon's. The chorus was sometimes an embarrassment to Euripides, but it was retained not because it was a sacred institution—Comedy got rid of it. The reason was that in general it was an instrument which exactly suited the sort of drama which the poets wanted to write. Masks may have magical or ritual associations; that is of no interest to us. They were clearly invented by Thespis (if we are to believe Suidas) for purely theatrical reasons, and remained in vogue because they were wanted. They suited both the theatre

---

[1] One authority, disagreeing with Aristotle, ascribes the change to Aeschylus. It might indeed have been hard to say precisely *who* was really responsible for it.

and the drama: the theatre because it was so large that the natural human face would be only a brown blob to most of the spectators[1]; the drama—at least the 'classical' drama—because in any case the drama avoided purely individual traits and transient moods or emotions. It is arguable, even probable, that these external forms did harden into fixed conventions which cramped rather than liberated the dramatists. For example, it is not obvious to us that the swift and elegant dialogue of plays like the *Ion* and the *Helen* demanded the vast Athenian theatre, the chorus, the masks and all the rest; but this is only to say what we knew already, that by this time Tragedy was approaching its end. While it was still vigorous, still 'religious drama', the external form was the natural expression of its inner spirit, and only the spirit will, in any fruitful way, explain the form.

The idea, then, that it was a traditional dramatic apparatus which, by restricting the dramatist, dictated the form of the tragic drama, is one that cannot be entertained. On the contrary, the dramatists invented and moulded this form because it enabled them to do exactly what they wanted to do: not to represent life in all its dynamic variety, but to present their conception of the principles or forces that operate in life. About this Greek approach to drama, a little has been said already, in the comparison between the dramatists and the philosophers; perhaps another comparison will take us further. But before we proceed, there is one incidental point that claims attention.

Eyebrows will perhaps be raised at the statement made above that the tragic poets 'invented' the tragic form, but it was made deliberately. I can see no sign, in the surviving plays, that the form was at all influenced by any Dionysiac 'ritual sequence', nor that such an assumption in any way contributes to the understanding either of the content or the form of the plays—

---

[1] Dr Wickham has pointed out to me that from perhaps half of the seats not even the lines of the mask would be recognisable (unless the mask were preposterously big), as in Covent Garden or Drury Lane the 'gods', unless they have field-glasses, cannot see any detail of the actors' faces, in spite of bold make-up. What the mask did, for those close enough to see it, was to hide the actor's face—like our make-up—which would be a necessary precaution when one actor was playing several parts. As for the idea that the mask contained some resonating device, I am advised that it is at least not clear how such a thing could be contrived; and anyone who has had the stimulating experience of speaking in a Greek theatre will certify that no such contraption is necessary.

rather the contrary. It certainly helps the critic, to have at his back an impressive general theory of this kind; but it helps him only by relieving him of the necessity of really grappling with his material. The plays do of course contain 'ritual' elements like struggle, suffering, death and triumph—but so does all serious literature; and why such natural expressions of universal human experience must have been derived from a Dionysiac expression of the same thing, I cannot understand. I agree with Pickard-Cambridge (in his *Dithyramb, Tragedy and Comedy*) that it is far from certain that Tragedy 'originated' in a Diony-siac Dithyramb, and that Aristotle's statement to this effect was only Aristotle's theory—and one which it is difficult to accept. The old battle, whether the origin of Tragedy was rites in honour of Dionysus or hero-cults, was a battle about unrealities, based on a misleading biological metaphor. 'Tragedy' does not exist, except as a abstraction. Only *plays* exist, and the origin of these is the minds that make them. The one thing that was never considered in this battle was the one thing that counts: the artists who created the stuff about which the battle raged. That Thespis and the other pioneers in drama borrowed many ideas and much inspiration from Dionysiac sources is highly probable; that they got ideas also from quite different performances, such as the dances in honour of Adrastus, which Herodotus mentions, is just as likely. As soon as we think of men, real men, trying to do new things, we see how nearly meaningless it is to say that the Origin of Tragedy was this and not that.

The fact that Peisistratus made this new art an important feature of his revived and glorified Festival of Dionysus certainly does not prove that it was directly descended from Dionysiac rites, and if we think that it does, then we create for ourselves a difficult question: Why has this Dionysiac offspring so little to say about Dionysus? For if we take into account lost plays of which the titles are known, the proportion of Dionysiac subjects in these plays is certainly not greater than one would in any case expect, seeing how full of dramatic stuff the Dionysus-cycle was. What Peisistratus did is quite easy to understand. As a tyrant leaning on popular support, interested in the arts, anxious to make his regime and his city more splendid, he had at least one good reason to pay particular attention to the old festivals of Dionysus: Dionysus was a god of universal appeal, a god of humanity as such. Other gods might have particular cults which were exclusively the concern of certain families or clans; Dionysus cut right across all such divisions. Having then this good political motive—and possibly others—to enhance the importance of Dionysus; and observing with interest that new conditions and new ideas were bringing into existence a new kind of art, to what festival could Peisistratus more suitably attach this new and exciting thing than to the festivals held in honour of the eminently dynamic god Dionysus? That the connexion between tragic drama and the worship of Dionysus was any closer than this, I find it hard to believe. I think therefore it is true to say that the tragic poets invented the form of drama, and it would remain true even if many features of that form could be shown to have been directly borrowed from Dionysiac performances of which we know next to nothing; for, as Aristotle wisely says, when discussing plots (1451 b 29 ff), even if a poet finds a plot ready-made, in history, he is none the less to be called its 'inventor'. Rightly; for he has seen the significance of it, and has used it for his own purposes.

We were arguing, before this digression began, that the Greek dramatists were not subject to a dictatorship of a traditional form; we have argued since that the control exercised by ritual-sequences and the like is invisible to the naked eye. We may now carry a little further our consideration of what, I think, really does explain the form of the drama, namely the spirit in which the dramatists worked.

The contrasts between Greek and Gothic architecture are a well-worn topic, but there is excellent Greek authority for not shunning the commonplace. This commonplace may be useful; for the spirit of the Greek dramatic poets has much in common, naturally, with the spirit of the Greek builders, and Elizabethan drama, however much it may have owed to the Renaissance, was an heir to the Middle Ages. The obvious points of contrast between the Greek temple and the Gothic cathedral are the simplicity and concentration of the one, the complexity and expansiveness of the other. The ground-plan of the typical cathedral is complex, and may be irregular; in comparison, the plan of the temple is nearly as simple as the plan of a kitchen-table, and normally is strictly symmetrical. It is natural to think of the temple in geometrical terms; the architects seem to have been striving for an almost abstract unity. As for the ornaments, those that were not purely formal were commonly inspired with a single definite idea, such as the triumph of order over disorder. The medieval builders, on the other hand, were impulsive and dynamic; they reached upwards and outwards, delighting in multiplicity of parts, and in richness and variety of decoration; not of course idly, nor without an inner discipline. The unity of the cathedral is such that it could include, besides formal decorations, representations in stone, wood or glass of prophets, saints, martyrs, kings; and these it could combine harmoniously with carved foliage, animals, birds, fishes, and with grotesques, portrait-heads or caricatures. The underlying conception was that all things are the creation of God; all things therefore have their own unique value, and all things combine to proclaim the glory of God. St. Francis could speak of 'my brother the ass', since God created both. This was no anthropocentric universe. The ultimate reality was not some inner principle; it lay beyond, in God, who creates and comprehends all things. The cathedral, the earthly House of God, was a temporal image of eternal Heaven.

Theologically therefore, no created thing can be out of place in the cathedral; all Creation, in its endless diversity, unites in the glory of God. Creation has indeed its ranks and stations, with Man at the head of temporal creatures, but all things have their place. The Whole is infinite, and therefore inexpressible, except symbolically; it is for the artist so to select and to order his material as to suggest this infinity. Hence the philosophical justification, if one were needed, of the many vistas, in every plane, which the cathedral affords; of the complete absorption, the loving care, with which the medieval mason will carve a flower, or a dog. Each separate thing has a double value: it is part of the whole, and it is itself—a unique creation, existing in its own right. Therefore the number of focal points is unlimited; the unity of the whole comes out of the integration of many particulars, and the artistic problem is to relate the subordinate focal points to the dominant one.

Both the spirit and the methods of Elizabethan drama seem to have much in common with this. The ground-plan is much more complex than it is in Greek drama. As the medieval architect could add a Lady Chapel or rebuild a choir without ruining the unity of the building—a thing quite impossible with a Greek temple—so a scene or two can be cut from an Elizabethan play without making complete nonsense of the rest, which would be impossible with any classical Greek play. More important, from our present point of view, is the fact that the minor characters and subordinate incidents in the Elizabethan drama have their independent reality. Launcelot Gobbo is not as important in the play as are Antonio and Shylock, but he is just as 'real'; we appreciate him for his own sake.

It is an important part of the Shakespearian drama—as indeed of the medieval drama too, and of the English novel—that it conveys something of the texture, the 'feel', of ordinary life as we know it. The chief characters and the central action are embedded in a rich context of minor characters and subsidiary actions, some of which are perhaps not very closely related to the main action. The conception is like that of a tapestry or large landscape-painting, in which the minor characters lead the eye gradually from the central figures to the distant horizon; or like many of Dürer's drawings, in which the central figure seems to be jostled and hemmed in on every side by the abounding life of nature and humanity, not lightly sketched in, as a mere background, but drawn vividly and with complete conviction, as if to suggest the totality of things, of which the central incident is a part, and from which it derives its truth and its significance.

So it is in Shakespeare. When a minor character, like Gobbo, is before us, we contemplate him for his own sake, as in a church we may contemplate for their own sakes a shepherd with his dog carved on a bench-end. If a minor character has no very direct connexion with the central theme of the play, 'we don't mind', provided that he is alive; for the implied horizon in Shakespeare is nothing less than the whole of life. We are very willing to shift our focus, from time to time, to other parts of the vast reality which, by implication, surrounds the central action and gives it its significance. In fact, these minor characters *must* be seen in the round. Only if they are real and vivid will they fulfil their true function, which is to suggest that the central tragic action is part of the great stream of human life.

Comparison of a Greek and a Shakespearian historical play

will illustrate the differences most clearly. Shakespeare begins *Henry V* by regretting that he cannot worthily present within his 'wooden O' the glorious deeds that belong to his story; but he does his best. He takes us through the whole stirring tale, from the first deliberations to the marriage with the French princess. But—to ask a vulgar question—what is the play about? There is the development of Prince Hal into King Henry—but we cannot pretend that his is the controlling element in a play. There is the fact that Henry begins by demanding the French throne, and ends by marrying the princess—but if this is important, what has it to do with those cheerful cowards Bardolph, Pistol and Nym, with whom we are very glad to renew our acquaintance—at a safe distance? They have their connexion with the theme of Henry's character, but Shakespeare's reason for bringing them in was not this, but that he liked them. There are too Jamie the Scot, Fluellen the Welshman, and Macmurray the Irishman. They have no unbreakable connexion with the rest, but they do illustrate the diversity of the British nations. The play makes its rich representation of a great and varied people, of a heroic young King, and of a high achievement, and one cannot be much more precise than that. It is not the best of the historical plays perhaps, nor the most tautly constructed, but it is not untypical, and it is far from being a failure. It simply has more focal points than usual.

The contrast with the *Persae* is absolute. Aeschylus is not in the least embarrassed by the confines of his 'wooden O', and does not want

> *A kingdom for a stage, princes to act,*
> *And monarchs to behold the swelling scene.*

His reality is different from Shakespeare's: it is not the events themselves, nor the actors in them, from the highest to the lowest, that engage his interest, but the significance of the events; and that significance, to Aeschylus, is the law that the gods punish hybris. There is nothing in the play that is not directly explained by this one idea. If Aeschylus had had twenty actors at his disposal, and liberty to change his scene from Susa to the Hellespont, and from there to Thermopyle and Artemisium, and from there to Salamis and then to Plataea, it would have been nothing but a nuisance to him. Thermopyle and Artemisium he does not even mention; he refers to no individual Greek except Themistocles—and even he is not named, but appears as 'some Avenging Spirit'. And all this he does in order to make us understand that Xerxes' real antagonist is 'the god', the god, θεὸς μεταίτιος, who works not only in and through the Greeks, but also through the very soil and climate of Greece.

Thus the essential difference between the Greek and the Elizabethan drama may be expressed in the formula Concentration, not Extension. Life is represented not by an inspired aggregation of particulars, so chosen and so disposed that they suggest the inexpressible Whole, but by a rigorous selection followed by a significant disposition which illuminates, as in a living diagram, the very structure of human life. The exciting thing in Shakespeare, apart from his poetry, is the delight—or it may be the revulsion—with which he seizes one character or one situation after another and puts its essence before us. The exciting quality in Aeschylus and Sophocles, apart from their poetry, is the imaginative and intellectual control with which they make every detail a significant part of one illuminating design.

In the theatre, we are instinctively aware of this, and this is the reason why the illogicalities do not strike us until we get into our studies. As we have said, the Greek dramatist uses only one focus. The action is played out within a strictly defined area of brilliant illumination; not on the flat, because there is perspective; but the perspective works only in depth, and reveals the gods. Shakespeare is continually changing his focus, to illuminate, more or less brightly, every part of his more extensive action. The central action, brilliantly lit, is surrounded by areas of milder illumination. The spectator's eye is continually on the move; for Shakespeare's mind is like a revolving light, which may at any moment send out a beam in some unexpected direction, to illuminate something for us. The mind of the Greek dramatist is a fixed light: there is the one area of illumination, and, outside that, a darkness which nothing tempts us to explore, for we know that it conceals nothing which concerns us; and if the critic insists on going out of the play—ἔξω τοῦ δράματος—into this darkness, he finds himself in a region in which anything may happen. Jebb commented on the occasional lack of consistency in regard to matters which occur outside the play, or off-stage. That this comes not from indifference, but from calculation, has perhaps been demonstrated. It does not trouble an audience at all; it troubles the critic only when he looks at Sophocles with Shakespearian eyes, trying to bring into focus what the dramatist has left in the darkness. But this lack of clearness and consistency is just as common with regard to matters within the play and on the stage. The silence of the Elders about the fleet, the prophecy which Neoptolemus impossibly makes, the way in which the condemnation of Ismene is handled—all these things would be impossible in Shakespeare, because they would have complete, solid reality; they would be in focus against the more realistic background, and therefore would appear to be out of drawing, and wrong. In Greek drama the details do not have this kind of reality; our eyes are focussed not on them, but on something behind them —on the gods, the Laws, the universal principles. In other words, the strength of the design makes us quite indifferent to the distortions which are logical and necessary parts of that design.

The differences which we have been considering have some bearing on a problem which deserves more attention than it has received. Plato points out in the *Republic* (395 a) that although Tragedy and Comedy seem to be closely related to each other, the same poets do not excel in both. On the other hand, at the end of the *Symposium*, when most of the guests are under the table, the invincible Socrates is 'compelling Agathon and Aristophanes to admit that the tragic poet who knows his business— τὸν τέχνῃ τραγῳδοποιὸν ὄντα—must also be a comic poet.' Between the two passages there is of course no contradiction. The plain statement in the *Republic* is made in support of Plato's argument that specialisation is necessary for efficiency: 'One man, one job. Look at the dramatic poets.' The point of the other passage is the implication that the poets have no τέχνη: they do not *know* their business, in the Platonic sense of the word, but (as Plato says in the *Ion*) write out of some θεία δύναμις or inspiration. What is common to the two passages is that the Greek poets did not attempt, or were not good at, both forms. Shakespeare excelled in both. Why not the Greeks?

We can go further: Shakespearian tragedy readily admits

comic passages; Greek Tragedy does not.[1] Why the difference?

Let us take up the first of these problems. If we put it in this form: why did the Greek tragic poets never write comic drama? —the answer is that they did, always. A regular part of the tragic tetralogy was the satyric drama, and what we know of this suggests that the nearest modern equivalent is broad farce. We must therefore put the question in Greek, and ask, why did the writers of τραγῳδία, 'tragedy', never write κωμῳδία, or Old Comedy?

The answer to this question is that Tragedy, τραγῳδία, and Comedy, κωμῳδία, are produced by different minds. Old Comedy took as its function the satirical criticism of contemporary Athenian life; its background, whether directly, as in the *Acharnians*, or by inversion, as in the *Birds*, was the streets and meeting-places of Athens. It was essentially local and topical. Neither among the Greeks nor among ourselves is it inevitable that the same man should have the gift of satirising contemporary fashions, follies and persons, and of writing that sort of universal comedy which is independent of time and place; but it is nothing unusual if the same man writes this kind of universal comedy, and tragedy too. For example, the tragic novelist Hardy could also write comedy like *Under the Greenwood Tree*; what could be more natural? But it would indeed have been surprising if he had also written sophisticated satirical comedy like *Antic Hay*; even more surprising if the talented

---

[1] The contrary is often stated, but the facts do not allow us to say more than that naturalistic touches were not avoided. The nearest approach to a comic character, or a comic passage, is the Watchman in the *Antigone*; on whom see above (pp. 155 f). The Nurse in the *Choephori* is usually cited; for what reason, I cannot imagine. She speaks of Clytemnestra secretly rejoicing at the calamity that has befallen the house; she says that this is the most unhappy hour that she has ever known (v. 747). 'That other thing,' she says, 'was cruel enough; but that my own Orestes, to whom I gave myself utterly —τῆς ἐμῆς ψυχῆς τριβήν—to be told that he is dead!'—Are we really to grin, because this broken-hearted creature goes on to speak of the napkins she washed for her baby? The Watchman of the *Agamemnon* is cited. He does speak of 'the ox on my tongue' and of 'the triple-six' which has been thrown him; vigorous expressions both, but who laughs? Finally, there is the concluding scene of the *Persae*, which some critics have found comic. But since little of it is left to us (for obviously the dance and the music took precedence over the words), it is at least rash to suppose that Aeschylus made nonsense of his own play by laughing at those whom the god had brought to ruin.—I maintain, therefore, that Greek Tragedy, while it remained tragic, did not mix tragedy and comedy.

author of this topical skit had also written tragedy like *The Return of the Native*. It is equally difficult to imagine Aristophanes writing tragedy.

But the Satyric drama was utterly different from Old Comedy —which is of course the reason why it maintained its separate existence—and it was the kind of comic drama natural to a tragic poet. As the Greek tragic poet wrote tragic drama against a background of universal law, a tragedy independent of time and place, so he wrote comic drama against the same background —turned upside-down. In the satyric drama, moral law was suspended, or inverted; cowardice, drunkenness and lechery became normal, heroism a thing to laugh at. The satyric drama and tragedy resembled each other, and were unlike Old Comedy, in finding their material in myth, that is to say, in something universal; and the local background of the satyric drama was not the streets of Athens, but the sea-shore or mountain-side. To write this universal comedy all that Aeschylus had to do was to stand on his head, which he seems to have done with enthusiasm and success.

So that the answer to our first question is quite simple. But why were the tragic and the comic elements kept apart like this, instead of being combined in one play? Why do we find, first three tragedies, with no trace of comedy, or virtually none, and then a roaring farce? We can of course talk of the Greek instinct for purity of style, but this is little more than a phrase describing what we would like to explain; and in any case, why should it be in purer style to include a broad farce in the tragic tetralogy than to mingle the tragic and comic in the one play?

It is not in fact merely a matter of the tragic and the comic, but also of the high and the low, the dignified and the humble. Medieval drama and the Elizabethans combined these without any hesitation, incurring thereby the severe displeasure of Milton; for he, like the other great puritan artist, Plato, reprobates 'the Poets' error of intermixing Comic stuff with Tragic sadness and gravity, or introducing trivial and vulgar persons, which by all judicious hath bin counted absurd, and brought in without discretion, corruptly to gratify the people.'[1]

It is of course true that Greek tragedy also included humble characters, and had no objection to treating them with some

[1] Preface to *Samson Agonistes*.

degree of realism, but for all that the difference is a clear one. These slaves and watchmen are brought into the same context as the Kings and Queens, and they speak much the same language. No Greek Puritan could have said that they were 'brought in without discretion, corruptly to gratify the people'. Indeed, they are not 'brought in', as if from another and a baser world; they are simply other human beings, though of smaller stature, who happen to be involved. We do not step out of the world of tragic dignity in order to pass a few minutes in the world of comedy or low life.

Why the difference? It is not that the Greek tragic poets were too high-minded 'corruptly to gratify the people'; the satyric play did nothing else than to serve this reprehensible purpose. But if we go back to the fundamental difference between the Greek and the Elizabethan drama we find a very natural explanation. We argued that a background of ordinary life is an essential part of the Elizabethan drama; that it is one of the means by which the central action is given solidity and reality. (It has this artistic function, even if we regard it also as the natural expression of the Englishman's unending delight in particular things, especially if they are odd or incongruous.) Since life does contain the comic as well as the tragic, the judicious introduction of the comic and the low—Eastcheap, gravediggers, jesters—helps us to feel that the play is 'true to life', for here is the tragic action, surrounded by life.

But since Greek tragedy is not, in this sense, representational, but constructive, its method must be entirely different. When Aeschylus is constructing drama to embody the conception that wrong must be punished, but that blind vengeance leads inevitably to further wrong, and ultimately to chaos, it is quite irrelevant that life comprises the comic as well as the tragic, the small and simple as well as the great. Argos no doubt had its natural 'comics' and its picturesque rascals, but the fact has nothing to do with the theme of the *Oresteia*. Yet the Greek tragic poets were not one-sided solemnities who never laughed, never saw that life is funny as well as serious, that man, besides being moral, spiritual and intellectual, is also an animal. They knew this perfectly well, and they did justice to the other side of life, within the tetralogy, in the satyric play, thereby representing the whole of life, in the Greek 'analytical' fashion, as thoroughly as the Elizabethans did in theirs. The anthropologists may tell us, truly, that the satyric drama was religious in origin; Greek religion was indeed co-terminous with life. But the reason why it survived was not religious conservatism; the Greeks were not the people to keep what they did not need and could not use. It survived because it had an important part to play in the whole.

CHAPTER EIGHT

Religious Drama
and its Interpretation

WE have examined in detail the structure and style of certain classical Greek plays. We assumed that Aeschylus and Sophocles were in complete command of their own art, and had very good reasons for shaping their plays as they did; and we have, I think, found nothing to disturb that assumption. From this examination there has emerged the conception of 'religious' drama, a form of drama in which the real focus is not the Tragic Hero but the divine background. This conception, if it is a sound one, gives rise to several considerations which it may be worth while to discuss briefly.

We may notice, in the first place, that the distinction between religious and secular drama is not a mechanical one. There is religious drama in which gods do not appear, and secular drama in which they do. There are no gods in the *Medea* or *Hecuba* for example, yet these plays must be regarded as religious drama: treated as tragic character-studies they fail, more or less disastrously; they make good sense only when we see that the real Tragic Hero is humanity itself.[1] On the other hand, the *Electra* and *Orestes* of Euripides are quite self-contained tragedies of character, even though gods do appear in them. The essential question is whether the play exists on one level or on two, whether the real focus lies in one or more of the characters, or somewhere behind them; in fact, what the field of reference is.

The next point is that the distinction is independent of the distinction which we were trying to establish in the previous chapter between constructive and representational drama. Religious drama is not peculiarly Greek, though the Greeks had their own way of presenting it. In fact, it will be argued in the next chapter that *Hamlet* must be read as religious drama, in

[1] See my *Greek Tragedy*, pp. 198-200, 219-221, 262, and above, p. 214.

the sense in which we are using the term; and that much criticism of *Hamlet* fails, either wholly or in part, because this fact is not realised. Leaving this point for the moment, we may pass to a nearly related matter.

It may seem bold, even reckless, to suggest that good scholars and sensitive critics have missed a point of the first importance both in Greek drama and in at least one classical English play; nevertheless I think that this is the case, and there may be a very good explanation. Neither today nor for some centuries past have we been in immediate and imaginative contact with a religious culture—with its habits of mind, its natural means of expression.

We may reflect on what has happened to us since the Elizabethan Age. This was one which had by no means lost contact with the late Middle Age; and the drama of this age was played, literally, not on two levels but on three: Heaven, Earth and Hell, side by side. It was a drama with the very widest reference. But the succeeding Age of Reason was entirely out of touch with this; and, as we can see very clearly, it was out of touch with Shakespeare too, in certain important particulars. We know, for example, how Nahum Tate refashioned some of the Tragedies, and how Johnson approved:

> Shakespeare has suffered the virtue of Cordelia to perish in a just cause, contrary to the natural ideas of justice, to the hope of the reader, and, what is yet more strange, to the faith of the chronicles . . . A play in which the wicked prosper, and the virtuous miscarry, may doubtless be good, because it is a just representation of the common events of human life: but since all reasonable beings naturally love justice, I cannot easily be persuaded, that the observation of justice makes a play worse; or, that if other excellencies are equal, the audience will not always rise better pleased from the final triumph of persecuted virtue. In the present case the publick has decided. Cordelia, from the time of Tate, has always retired with victory and felicity.[1]

One is reminded of Aristotle's remark, that in his own day those plays were preferred in which vice was punished and virtue rewarded—and the reason which he gives is τὴν τῶν θεάτρων ἀσθενείαν, 'the debility of the audience'. Debility is something with which one does not easily credit Johnson; but it seems clear

---

[1] *General Observations on Shakespeare's Plays: Lear.*

that there was something in the lucid, orderly and essentially prosaic eighteenth-century mind which made it incapable not only of creating tragedy, but even of understanding it in some of its forms.

Nor did the Romantic movement bring any great amendment. True, it deposed the Rules of Art and exalted Imagination; but by now individualism was rampant. The Hero, with his attendant personages, became the whole play; and it was only natural that in the actual theatre both the hero and the play should become confused with the transcendent genius of the Actor-manager. These excesses have gone, but our own age, though it has recreated a poetic drama, is hardly one which is instinctively attuned to religious modes of thought, so that it is not surprising if the wide outlook of an earlier age is one which we do not understand without some effort.

So far as the interpretation of Greek religious drama was concerned, the Aristotelian tradition reinforced rather than corrected contemporary secularism. It is necessary to examine the connexion between Aristotle's theory and the classical Greek tragedy, and to point out how very tenuous it is.

Aristotle places firmly in the centre of his ideal play the Tragic Hero, with his ἁμαρτία, the flaw in a character otherwise better than the average. In the best form of tragedy, the Hero will make his transit, his μετάβασις, from happiness to unhappiness by the logical working of the flaw, in the given circumstances; and the end is Pity and Fear—emotions which we feel because the hero is ὅμοιος, not unlike ourselves. To Aristotle (though not to the dramatists) the spectacle of a good man ruined by no fault of his own is μιαρόν, shocking, and not tragic. As for the gods, and their function in drama, Aristotle mentions them only once (1454 b 5), and then only to say: 'We assume that the gods can see everything.' That is, they are a dramatic convenience. These points we may consider one by one.

Our analysis of religious drama, if it is correct, shows that the centre of a play is not necessarily a Tragic Hero. It is meaningless to ask whether Agamemnon or Clytemnestra is the tragic hero of Aeschylus' play, and if we think of Ajax as an Aristotelian tragic hero, the structure of Sophocles' play becomes unintelligible. Aristotle's theory, as one would expect, is a perfectly consistent whole, so that what he says about the tragic hero cannot be separated from what he says about the tragic flaw. To how many of the heroes whom we have considered does this doctrine really apply? Agamemnon has indeed ἁμαρτία enough, but it is not presented as a flaw in a character otherwise admirable. What we are shown is practically nothing but his ἁμαρτία. It is true that the Watchman calls him 'my well-loved master', and it may be that diligence might disclose one or two other scraps of information about other aspects of his character, but it is surely obvious that Aeschylus is not at all concerned to present him as a rounded character, better than the average in most respects, but ruined by one fault, so that at the end our cry is: 'O the pity on't!' Effectively, he and Clytemnestra and Medea and perhaps Creon are nothing but ἁμαρτία. Prometheus may be said to show ἁμαρτία in his self-will, but if we try to make this the central feature of the play, we shall not get very far. Sophocles' Electra, like his Antigone, can be said to have a ἁμαρτία; but if Electra has one, it does not ruin her, and Antigone is destroyed because of her virtues, not her faults, if she has any. If we apply the doctrine to Philoctetes or to Neoptolemus, either the doctrine or the play breaks down. In any case, neither this play nor the Electra ends unhappily, nor is it a worse play in consequence.

Of how many of these characters is it possible or profitable to say that they are ὅμοιοι, 'like us', though tending to the better rather than to the worse? Of some, undoubtedly. But when we read or witness the Medea or the Ajax or the Electra, to say nothing of the Oresteia or Prometheus, how much of the total impression that we receive comes from a feeling that we ourselves, in our modest way, resemble these heroes? That our mothers, wives and daughters think this when they contemplate Clytemnestra or Medea is doubtful; nor probably do the rest of us, when we tremble for Xerxes or Agamemnon or Orestes, fear περὶ τὸν ὅμοιον, 'for one like ourselves'.[1] It is arguable that every one of the plays which we have considered creates Pity and Fear, but it is certainly not the case that we always feel Pity and Fear for the tragic hero, nor that these are the most important of the thoughts or emotions aroused by the plays. Do we pity Sophocles' Electra and Orestes? Perhaps we do, but this is not the response that Sophocles is most anxious to stimulate

[1] Poetics 1453 a 6.

in us; and any fear that we may experience on their behalf is discounted by the fact that Apollo stands over them; and it would be no convincing defence of Aristotle's doctrine to transfer our Pity and Fear, in this play, to the two murderers whom Electra and Orestes will destroy.

In fact, what this religious drama gives us is rather Awe and Understanding. Its true Catharsis arises from this, that when we have seen terrible things happening in the play, we understand, as we cannot always do in life, *why* they have happened; or, if not so much as that, at least we see that they have not happened by chance, without any significance. We are given the feeling that the Universe is coherent, even though we may not understand it completely. In this lies the true greatness of the *Tyrannus*. This is a play which Aristotle treats as tragedy of character, and as such it is splendid enough; but how much more splendid is it when we see what Sophocles really meant: that although Life has been so cruel to Oedipus, nevertheless it is not a chaos; and that in his story there is no warrant for our abandoning allegiance to moral law and such prudent foresight as we may have. Pity and Fear are present in abundance, but even so they are overtopped by Awe and Understanding; they are in themselves emotions too personal to be the ultimate explanation of this religious drama.

Another part of Aristotle's theory is that 'one must not represent good characters (τοὺς ἐπιεικεῖς) moving from prosperity to disaster, for this excites neither pity nor fear, but revulsion'. The theory perhaps appears reasonable, but from dramatic theory we may turn to dramatic facts. We may contemplate what Aeschylus does with Orestes. To be sure, Orestes does not pass from happiness to unhappiness; he never was 'happy', and as to what happens to him after his acquittal, whether 'happiness' or not, Aeschylus is silent; the question is utterly irrelevant. But what we do see, in the play, is a man whose character, so far as it is revealed to us, is without blemish; yet he is in a cleft stick, and suffers anguish. Or we may think of Io, without fault, yet tortured. I will not mention Prometheus, because there are those who, although they belong to the human race, believe that Prometheus was at fault in preventing Zeus from destroying it; but what of King Pelasgus in the Supplices? At one moment he is, presumably, 'happy'; at the next he is in the agonising position of having to choose between a dangerous war from which he and his city can gain nothing, and the afflictions that may descend on them all from the offended gods. It is possible, though I think not likely, that all came right for him in the end, but this does not alter the fact that we see this innocent man held fast in a cruel dilemma, and do not find the spectacle 'revolting'.

This matter is discussed by Macneile Dixon.[1] His argument is that the philosophers, from Plato to Schopenhauer, have been uneasy with Tragedy: the philosopher wants a fully rational or explicable universe, but the tragic poets know that the Universe is not such, since it will suddenly knock a man down for no just reason. Sometimes, says Dixon, the 'tragic flaw' is in the Universe, and this is a possibility which the philosopher is reluctant to admit.

This may be true of some philosophers, and of some forms of tragedy, but it does not seem to be sufficient explanation of the discrepancy between the theory of Aristotle and the practice of Aeschylus and Sophocles. In the first place, both these poets were philosophers enough to believe in a world-order—even though Sophocles at least knew that it is not given to man to understand it fully. Both poets 'believed in the gods'; and though this does not mean—though it certainly does not exclude —that they were endowed with a personal piety, it does mean that they believed in a Universe which is ultimately rational. When Aeschylus depicts a conflict between one god and another, which clearly is a sign of a disordered Universe, the reason is plain enough: he is depicting a world-order in the process of evolution. In the end, Zeus reigns without opposition. When Sophocles represents Oedipus as being destroyed though essentially innocent, he is not presuming a flaw in the Universe, but recognising that its majestic order may cut the thread of a single life and requite venial unwisdom with utterly disproportionate penalties, just as he recognises that when the insensibility of a Creon disturbs the path of Dikê, then an Antigone and a Haemon and an Eurydice may be destroyed. In these plays the innocent do suffer, and their suffering is not 'revolting'; and the reason for this is that their suffering is seen to be part of a world-order, which though not always beneficent, is at least intelligible.

[1] W. Macneile Dixon *Tragedy* (London, 1924).

But Aristotle's theory, for whatever reason, takes no account of this religious drama. In this fact lies the explanation of our difficulty, that he, like Johnson, finds unmerited suffering 'revolting'. In the kind of tragedy which he is analysing it would be revolting—in a Tragedy of Character, in which our attention is focussed upon the hero, why and how he acts; and on the 'inevitable or probable' way in which one error brings all to ruin. If in watching such a man, having our attention directed to nothing but his character, his situation, his actions, and their consequences; being made aware of no all-embracing world-order, but on the contrary finding a microcosm in the hero himself—if in a drama of this kind we were shown that the hero, guilty of no sin, no error of judgment, so acted that in the natural or inevitable course of events he worked his own damnation, we should certainly feel that the play was 'revolting'; and we should feel this because it would imply that the Universe was unintelligible, even if not positively malignant.

Evidently, so far as religious drama is concerned, where Aristotle is right he is right by accident, and if his theory is drawn from dramatic practice and not evolved from philosophic prepossessions, it is from the practice of a contemporary kind of drama—unless indeed it is from a single play, the *Tyrannus*. Certainly it does not in the least fit any other extent play by Sophocles, to say nothing of Aeschylus. If it is based on a different drama—which perhaps we ought to assume, since Aristotle was something of a scientist, accustomed to the observation of facts—that drama would be one which we might call humanistic, or secular; if on the *Tyrannus*, then on the *Tyrannus* interpreted in a purely humanistic way, as the tragedy of a great man, with the divine background omitted. If we would frame a general theory of the classical Greek drama, it must be on lines already indicated, to this effect.

The tragic poet so constructs his play that the actions of the characters, being likely ones, combine to produce a result which is seen to be inevitable, either in prospect, as in the *Agamemnon*, or in retrospect, as in the *Antigone*, or both. This result may be said to display the validity of divine law in human affairs. The chief character or characters—for there may well be no single 'tragic hero'—may themselves commit grave error which leads them to disaster, or they may, like Sophocles' Electra, Antigone,

Philoctetes, be persons who are affected by, and resist, the wrongful actions of others, in which case the play may end, for them, 'happily'. These are all matters of indifference—whether there is one chief character or more, whether he is good or bad, and whether, in consequence, the play ends happily or unhappily. One thing is constant: the assertion of a world-order, symbolised by the presence or activity of the gods. Sometimes, as in the *Oresteia* and *Prometheia*, the poet shows this order in evolution. Sophocles shows it in operation. In Euripides it is often presented by implication rather than directly: it consists of a due balance of forces, such as for example of Aphrodite and Artemis, or Reason and Ecstasy, or the Rational and the Irrational, a balance which he will often call σωφροσύνη or 'wisdom'. Euripides is 'the most tragic of the poets' because in his drama this balance, or order, seems the most unattainable.

That is to say, religious drama is a distinct kind, with principles of its own, different from those of tragedy of character, the form of tragedy that Aristotle analysed. These principles we have tried to find inductively, by observing the facts. We have seen that it is a form of drama which can use naturalism, but can and frequently does set it at defiance; that it can draw character sharply, but does not exist in order to study and display character; it can indeed almost entirely dispense with character-drawing. The individual, however vividly he may be drawn, however complex and delicate may be the relations between him and the other individuals in the play, never absorbs all our attention; he never, so to speak, grows in his creator's hand. Religious drama contains gods as well as men, and where gods are present they must take precedence. Only when the human drama in the foreground is seen against the background of divine action is the structure and significance of the play truly seen.

If we ask why Aristotle should have evolved a theory which so notably does not agree with the facts of the classical Greek drama, our answer can only be speculative; and perhaps it is well to remember that when we say 'Aristotle' we mean, necessarily, Aristotle as revealed to us in the *Poetics*. Aristotle the man may have had a great love for Aeschylus; about this we can know nothing.

Wilamowitz suggested that Aristotle, as a foreigner from

Stageira, did not understand 'the pure Attic spirit'. But perhaps the interval of time that separated him from Sophocles and Aeschylus was more potent than the interval of space that separated Stageira from Athens.

We may reflect on the extent and the swiftness of the change which came over the intellectual temper of Greece between say 450 B.C. and 400. It is roughly true to say that up to the time of Socrates and the Sophists, the poets had been among the profoundest and most active of the Greek thinkers. In the earlier part of the fifth century, poetry, religion, history, myth, philosophy, had not yet finally parted company, though the separation was becoming imminent. Herodotus, like any epic poet, says that one of his motives in composing his History was to preserve great deeds from oblivion. The word 'history' means 'enquiries', and with a splendid indifference Herodotus prosecuted and wrote into his book enquiries which we should distinguish as historical or geographical or archaeological or anthropological or biological[1] or something else—all this in a work designed 'to preserve great deeds from oblivion', and suffused with a religious feeling. Specialism had not yet won the day. In a similar way, Aeschylus and Sophocles were considerable philosophers, but philosophers who gave out the results, not the processes, of thought, and expressed them in their art. But within the space of one generation the Greeks, always intelligent, became intellectualist. Problems of religion, conduct, philosophy, politics, became the subject of systematic and specialised enquiry, and so gradually ceased to be the material for art. The old intuitive approach to the truth no longer served; Socrates dismissed the poets because they could not answer his questions, which undoubtedly would not have been technical or aesthetic questions, but moral ones. As soon as matters of morality and conduct and the rest become the province of scientific philosophy, they cease to be the material for the poets. The sophist's radio-call, 'it all depends what you mean by . . . ', is the poet's warning; authority is being transferred from him to the systematic enquirer. Those wide regions which had been his natural home began to contract; the significant, constructive use of myth could not for long hold out against the new analytical spirit. A century after the death of Sophocles another con-

[1] 'Now I will describe the nature of the camel' (III, 103).

siderable poet was making his appearance in the Greek world—Theocritus; but how much less intrinsically important were the themes which he handled! When Theocritus uses myth, in his Epyllia, it is only to make attractive poetry. He takes a theme which Euripides also had used—a woman in love: the second Idyll is a strong and beautiful poem, and a complete contrast to Euripides' treatment of Medea and Phaedra in this, that it has no wider reference. It is in fact the source of the poem's strength that it concentrates our attention on Simaetha—on her situation, not the human situation; on the particular moods and emotions which successively assail her. It is not, essentially, a question of better poetry or worse, but of a different attitude to poetry.

Signs of the change, as we have said before, appear in tragedy itself, in the later fifth century—in 'romantic' drama like the *Iphigeneia in Tauris* or the *Ion*, and in high comedy like the *Helen*. What is the reason? War-weariness is often cited; the Athenian audience no longer had the stomach for profound and strenuous drama. Weariness no doubt played its part, but in all the arts, not in drama only, the current was setting strongly away from the old seriousness towards elegance or prettiness, and individualism or even sensationalism. One might refer to the individualism of early fourth-century sculpture, or the collapse of vase-painting into mere fussiness. The war does not seem to be a sufficient explanation. It was not the war that caused the sudden flowering of prose-literature which accompanied the decline of serious poetry. The old Greek world had known no real division between art, religion and philosophy; but that world was rapidly transforming itself into a new one, in which art and philosophy were each becoming autonomous, to the advantage, no doubt, of philosophy, but not of art.

As far as Tragedy is concerned, we have the testimony of Aristophanes, as well as the silent judgment of the Alexandrine critics who made the Canon, that Sophocles and Euripides left no worthy successors. In the circumstances, that is what might have been expected; the serious things were now being said in prose. Sometimes we hear it asserted that every age, as a matter of course, has its great artists, and if we do not see them the reason is that the great artist has to wait a generation for recognition; comforting doctrine, but as a general theory quite untrue. The greatness of Aeschylus and Sophocles, rather less so, perhaps, of Euripides, was fully recognised in their own time, and the succeeding centuries produced nothing to compare with them—though they did produce Plato and Aristotle and Zeno and Epicurus and a long line of mathematicians and scientists. We also hear today, from music critics, of 'the tyranny of the Classics'; the indications are that fourth-century Athens similarly turned back to the fifth-century Classics—perhaps for a similar reason: these had had more important things to say.

Unhappily, we cannot have any more than a very general idea about the tragedy that was contemporary with Aristotle. We have one pointer in certain of the late plays of Euripides. There is perhaps another in the brief reference that Aristotle makes to the *Antheus*, by Euripides' younger contemporary Agathon: he says simply that the entire plot was invented by the dramatist. From this it is a likely inference that the play was of a romantic or melodramatic kind; a dramatist who had something of importance to say would hardly be tempted to abandon the weight and authority which established myth could confer on him.

We hear of rhetoricians, like Theodectes, who turned themselves into tragic poets. We know, from Aristotle, that the cycle of myths used by the poets was now smaller; also that historical subjects began to reappear: Theodectes wrote a play about Maussolus, recently dead (unless it was an earlier Maussolus[1]), and Moschion one about Themistocles, and possibly another, the *Pheraeans*, about the murder of Alexander of Pherae. These sound very like a species of Heroic Drama, reminding one of Dryden rather than of Aeschylus.[2] Finally, there is great force in a remark of Professor Fraenkel's, that Aristotle's dry and quite barren analyses of such things as the various ways of managing recognition-scenes faithfully reflect one of the chief interests of the contemporary theatre. It would be no new phenomenon, that in times when the artists have nothing of great importance to say they give great attention to the means by which to say it. Certainly everything points to the conclusion

---

[1] T. B. L. Webster, *Art and Literature in Fourth Century Athens*, p.65

[2] If the recently discovered Gyges-fragment comes from a real play, and not from some 'closet-drama', I should ascribe it without any hesitation to this or an even later period, certainly not to the early fifth century.

that the fourth century was such a time, with the result that Tragedy, being driven in upon itself, became elegant and rhetorical, or sensational; in any case self-conscious, more concerned with its own technique than with anything that matters; a period of *pièces bien faites*.

There are strong resemblances between the *Aufklärung* of the late fifth and early fourth centuries B.C. and of the seventeenth and eighteenth centuries A.D. In each case the human mind seems to have achieved its new clarity by contracting its field of vision; in each case, a classical Tragedy, poetry at its most comprehensive, almost disappeared over the horizon; appreciated for its incidental merits, but not really understood; leaving as its successors Heroic or a rhetorical tragedy, and either witty or sentimental comedy. Aristotle was indeed not so much out of touch with the spirit of his classical tragedy as the run of eighteenth-century critics were with theirs; he would certainly not have approved if a fourth-century Nahum Tate had rewritten the last part of the *Antigone* in order to save Antigone from death and so bring the play into closer accord with poetic justice; and although his preferred type of tragic ending was not one of which the tragic poets themselves had thought very highly, and although his theory was incapable of accounting for plays like the *Trojan Women*, he did at least call Euripides 'the most tragic of the poets', and despise, unlike Johnson, 'the debility of the audiences'. But the fact remains that if we would understand the spirit and the methods of the classical Greek Tragedy, we must study Aeschylus and Sophocles and Euripides in the appropriate way, without allowing ourselves to be deflected by the ideas natural to a 'secular' age, whether that be the fourth century before Christ or the eighteenth or twentieth A.D.

An article in the *Contemporary Review*[1] illustrates the importance of understanding what the Greek dramatic poets meant by their divine background. The writer of this article takes the gods seriously, as one should, and at their face-value—their modern face-value: as a controlling element not only in the design of the plays, but also in the actions and sufferings of the characters. He argues that the human characters can do nothing

[1] F. H. C. Brock: 'Oedipus, Macbeth, and the Christian Tradition.' (*Contemporary Review* CLXXVII, pp. 177 ff.)

but realise and reveal 'the unalterable interweaving threads in the web of Fate', and that 'any attempt to explain human fortunes in terms of human behaviour, or to establish any relationship between guilt and misfortune is entirely absent'—a remark which is indeed made specifically of the *Tyrannus*, but by implication of Greek Tragedy in general. Believing this, he quotes with approval something said by Mr Ivor Brown, the dramatic critic, that it is difficult for the modern audience to maintain interest in 'these fate-driven men'; and he draws the sharpest distinction between Greek tragedy, 'ridden by the theological doctrine of Nemesis, and by the unscientific theory of determinism which that entails', and the Shakespearean tragedy, 'in which human fortunes are not determined beforehand by a divine decree, in which the punishment of wrongdoing is not something immediate and particular, but in which the world means good, and will by its nature and the laws of its operation vindicate that principle against those who offend'.

It is indeed difficult to imagine a presentation of Greek Tragedy which could be more exactly the opposite of the truth, or a description of the Shakespearean Tragedy which would more clearly bring out its resemblances to the Greek. 'It [Greek Tragedy] was not content, as modern science is content, to regard the world as a framework of inexorable law within which mind, with free activities, could operate, playing upon these laws and bringing them into action, even manipulating them to its own ends'—because Fate, or the gods, have determined everything beforehand, and will intervene arbitrarily. To operate and exploit natural laws is of course no part of drama or of any other art; but in so far as scientific thought and Greek drama have a common element, it is well expressed in the foregoing sentence, if only we delete the negative. It is indeed disastrous to misconceive the function of the gods in this drama.

Divine activity, as I have tried to show, is a controlling element in this Religious Tragedy precisely because it represents 'the framework of inexorable law', or, it may be, of inherent natural forces. Our business is to see that the divine activity neither controls human activity and suffering nor renders them merely pathetic, but is rather a generalised statement about them. The divine background holds up to us, so to speak, the system of co-ordinates against which we are to read the significance of what the human actors do and suffer. The gods are a controlling element in the plays, but not in what the actors do and suffer: that is entirely their own affair. The reason for saying that the divine element controls the play is this: the dramatist does not allow the human actors to do or suffer anything which does not have significance when it is read against the co-ordinates. The previous domestic history of Agamemnon and Clytemnestra is something that Aeschylus keeps out.

Hence comes, in the plays, the combination of lifelike vividness with that 'constructiveness' which can be very far from 'lifelike' or naturalistic: the persons and their actions must be real, true to life, not generalised into flabbiness, or they will not convince us of anything; they will naturally be vivid and sharp because (despite my mathematical metaphor) the dramatist was an artist, not a demonstrator; what he was seeking to communicate was communicated by sheer impact. But the vividness, the 'truth to life', was restricted (for good artistic reasons) to what made immediate sense when the audience correlated it, as it instinctively would, with the universal co-ordinates in the background.

In this connexion we might quote a good passage by Thibaudet which Professor Gomme quotes in another context[1]: 'L'histoire, telle que la propose Thucydide, unit et fait servir l'un à l'autre deux caractères qui, semble-t-il, s'excluent: la plus grande exactitude matérielle et la plus grand généralité. D'ailleurs, quand on croit qu'elles s'excluent, c'est qu'on ne pense pas à l'art, qui les implique au contraire toutes deux et emploie l'une à la perfection de l'autre.' If, in place of 'la plus grande exactitude matérielle', we substitute what perhaps is its artistic analogue, vividness in the presentation of particulars, we can say that the tragic poets also combine two characteristics which may appear to be contraries but in fact serve and reinforce each other: sharpness of detail, and the greatest possible generality. The way in which Thucydides combined his two elements is not our present affair; of the means which the tragic poets used, the most important was the religious framework of their plays.

In the next chapter the structure of *Hamlet* will be examined, and the suggestion will emerge that this too is 'religious drama';

[1] A. W. Gomme, *The Greek Attitude to Poetry and History*, p. 139: A. Thibaudet, *La Campagne avec Thucydide*, p. 49.

that if we try to make the Tragic Hero the focus, the form of the play is not an artistic unity. Those who read this chapter will not need to be told that my knowledge of *Hamlet* criticism is much less than it should be. If therefore they think that it is an impertinence, I will add to the impertinence by blaming Professor Dover Wilson. It was his brilliant book on *Hamlet*, so stimulating, so very nearly persuasive, so entirely 'secular', that impelled me for my own satisfaction to study *Hamlet* closely in order to see what would happen if the same critical methods were used on it as have been used here on Aeschylus and Sophocles. I have been encouraged to think that the results are worth putting into print.

CHAPTER NINE

Hamlet

(1) THE PROBLEM OF HAMLET

SURELY the real problem of *Hamlet* lies in certain facts briefly reported by Waldock,[1] that up to the year 1736 no critic seems to have found any great difficulty in the play, but since that date one interpretation after another has been proposed and rejected. In 1736 Sir Thomas Hanmer, enquiring why Hamlet does not kill Claudius at once, explained that if he had done, the play would have ended somewhere in Act II; and that Shakespeare, anxious to avoid this disaster, did not manage to make Hamlet's delay dramatically convincing. As we have seen, there is a strong family likeness between this reasoning and what the Scholiast said about the *Ajax*, that Sophocles, wishing to prolong the play, made a mess of it. But let us not laugh too soon at Hanmer: our own day has produced critics willing to make his necessary assumption, namely that *Hamlet* is incompetently constructed. There are critics of the 'historical' school who have persuaded themselves—or at least have sought to persuade others—that the play contains chunks of earlier material which Shakespeare could not or did not assimilate, like some ostrich with tin-cans inside him. Critics of a psychological turn have woven fantasies around the play so tightly that it has become quite unable to move, with the natural result that Mr Eliot has written it off as a failure, since 'nothing that Shakespeare can do with the plot can express Hamlet for him'. Hamlet has been professionally psycho-analysed. What the Baker Street Irregulars do for fun certain Stratford Irregulars have tried to do in earnest: to treat Hamlet as a real person, having an existence outside the play. The irreverent outsider is tempted to say that the great triumph of Mr Michael Innes' *The Mysterious Affair at Elsinore* is that it

[1] *Hamlet*: A Study in Critical Method, p. 3.

246

succeeds in being even funnier than some of the serious books about the play.

In this confusion of criticism there is not much that is entirely unfamiliar to the student of Greek Tragedy. What is new to him is the *mystique* which has grown up about *Hamlet*: the suggestion that there is in it something unique and ineffable which sets it apart not only from other plays but also from all other works of art, except perhaps the Mona Lisa. Perhaps this is well founded, but it is a little bewildering—and, if Waldock is right, it did not begin until a century after Shakespeare's death. A thing is commonly said about the role of Hamlet which would scarcely be said of any other role; it is accepted and expanded by Professor Dover Wilson as follows:

> There are as many Hamlets as there are actors who play him; and Bernhardt has proved that even a woman can score a success. Of a role so indeterminate almost any version is possible; with a character so fascinating and so tremendous in outline hardly any impersonator can fail.[1]

As for Bernhardt's exploit, and what it proves, we may reflect that in 441 B.C., or thereabouts, a man played the role of Antigone. Whether or not he scored a success in it is not recorded; if he did, it is certainly not because the role is indeterminate in composition. Since a play, like a piece of music, must be interpreted, something must necessarily be left to the interpreter; but so elementary a point as this is not in question if we say 'There are as many Hamlets as there are actors capable of playing the part.' What is implied, to put it bluntly, is that in creating this part, as in creating no other, Shakespeare signed a blank cheque, and left it to the actor to draw what sum he can. Did he? About Goethe's idea of Hamlet Dover Wilson says that its 'condescending sentimentalism' almost makes one angry. He has not much more patience—nor have I—with the paralysed intellectual that Coleridge imagined, nor with the ruthless Renaissance Prince that Dr de Madariaga has recently devised. Here then, for a start, are three Hamlets whom Dover Wilson is willing not only to boo off the stage but also to argue out of existence. And rightly, for they have no existence; to give them existence we should have to remake the play.

[1] *What happened in Hamlet*, p. 238.

I

The cheque, then, is not a blank one. It may be that in creating this role Shakespeare left more than usual to the player of it, but this is far from saying that 'almost any version is possible'. Perhaps almost any version can be made effective on the stage—but only to an audience which does not very much mind whether the play as a whole makes sense or not. We ought not to quarrel with the producer or actor whose first concern is to 'put the play across'—which he will do, naturally, by rendering the play according to the intellectual and emotional idiom of his own time; if he does not to some extent do this, he is not likely to act or produce Shakespeare very often. But as the scholar and critic does not live by selling theatre seats, his duty is a different one: it is to disregard contemporary habits of thought entirely, so far as he can, in order to understand Shakespeare's, so that he may see the play without distortion. Today the amateur critic of *Hamlet* can profit greatly by the information which modern scholarship has made available about Elizabethan and Jacobean thought. We should however reflect that no such study can do more than tell us what Shakespeare *might* have thought; if we would know what he did think, there is nothing to do but to study the play, and to be very careful neither to bring anything into it which its creator did not put there, nor to leave out anything that he did.

It seems that criticism of the play has been concerned, in the main, with the character of Hamlet; the play is something draped around him, something designed to present his character. For example, the recent film version carried as a subtitle: The tragedy of a man who could not make up his mind. Since this film was as far as possible from being a travesty made by barbarians for illiterates, but was a distinguished piece of work, we may assume that this is a representative modern view; but how far it is from the truth, how little it explains the form of the play, becomes apparent as soon as we begin to consider that form constructively. What if *Hamlet* is a play which it would be reasonable to call 'religious drama', as we are using the term here? What if the ingrained individualism of the last two centuries—to say nothing of romanticism—has blinded us to one aspect of the play without which it cannot possibly appear as a firm and coherent structure? To put it provocatively: suppose that *Hamlet* is just as much a play about Hamlet as the *Ajax* is a play about Ajax, and no more?

That a modern audience can be baffled by a classical English play, precisely because it is now unfamiliar with the wide perspective of 'religious' drama, I happened to have demonstrated to me while struggling with this chapter. It befell me to see, four times within a week, an admirable production, on an Elizabethan stage, of *The Duchess of Malfi*. The interesting point was the behaviour of the audiences. They laughed consumedly in the right places, but they also laughed in wrong places, notably in the last scene, where corpse is piled on corpse; but in these places the laughter would begin—and then fall stone-dead; the audiences were obviously puzzled.

In comparison with Shakespeare, Webster is perhaps not more than a poster-artist of genius. Still, the play has a perfectly clear moral structure: the French Court has been purged, and is at peace with itself; the Italian Courts have not, and the play works out the 'inevitable or probable' ruin caused by the various forms of wickedness rampant in Ferdinand's Court. There is room perhaps for civilised amusement at Webster's violence, but the puzzled laughter indicated an audience confronted— and who can wonder?—by something which was outside its experience, but quite intelligible, and familiar, to another layman who happened to be familiar with Greek religious drama. Talk about 'the Elizabethan taste for horrors' should not blind us to the fact that all those who die in this last act have caused their own death, directly or indirectly, by their own sins. To Webster, sin was horrible; to us it is merely out of fashion.

In *Hamlet*, eight people are killed, not counting Hamlet's father; of the two families concerned in the play, those of King Hamlet and Polonius, both are wiped out. Eight deaths are enough to attract attention, and to make us wonder if the essential thing has been said when the play is called 'the tragedy of a man who could not make up his mind'. And the manner of these deaths is no less significant than their number. Claudius murders King Hamlet by poison; thereafter, a metaphorical poison seeps through the play: rottenness, cankers, 'things rank and gross in nature' meet us at every turn. Then at the end it once more becomes literal poison: Gertrude, Claudius, Laertes, Hamlet are all poisoned; and on Claudius, already dead or dying from the poisoned rapier, Hamlet forces the poisoned cup. The Ghost had said:

> *Nor let thy soul contrive*
> *Against thy mother aught; leave her to Heaven.*

So too Horatio observed:

> *Heaven will direct it.*

And what does Heaven do with Gertrude? Of her own accord, and in spite of a warning, she drinks poison. These are plain and striking dramatic facts; how far does 'Hamlet's fatal indecision' explain them? Are they an organic part of a tragedy of character? Or did Shakespeare kill so many people merely from force of habit?

Before examining the structure in detail we may orientate ourselves a little more exactly by examining another dramatic fact: the way in which Shakespeare presents the death of Polonius. Polonius seems often to be interpreted as something of a Dickens character. Thus Granville Barker, writing about the Reynaldo scene, and its 'verbiage', speaks of 'a tedious old wiseacre meddling his way to his doom'; and explains that in this scene Shakespeare, having changed his mind about Polonius, is making a transition from 'the not unimpressive figure' of the earlier scenes 'who has talked sound sense to Laertes and Ophelia' to the more comic figure that he later becomes.[1] The facts of the play, as it seems to me, directly contradict such an estimate. Polonius, like everything else in Denmark, is rotten. The proof of this may wait; we are concerned at present with the manner of his death.

In Act III Scene 1—a magnificent scene, provided we do not try to be clever with it—Claudius and Polonius arrange to spy on Ophelia and Hamlet. There will be occasion later to consider the scene in detail; for the moment we will consider only this, that Shakespeare is concerned to emphasise the indecency of it. Hamlet is—or was—in love with Ophelia and she with him. (The other view, that she is a hussy and he a trifler, brings to mind an unamiable phrase of Housman's: 'This suggestion does dishonour to the human intellect.') It will do us no harm to remember what Love so often is in Shakespeare: not merely a romantic emotion, but a symbol of goodness, even a redemptive

[1] *Introduction to Hamlet*, p. 61.

power. We have been told often enough in the play what Claudius and Gertrude have made of Love; we ought to have noticed how Polonius thinks of it. In this scene the pure love of Ophelia is being used by two evil men who besmirch everything they touch. This would need argument—and plenty is available —except that in this very scene Shakespeare makes further argument unnecessary: Polonius gives Ophelia a book, evidently a holy book. Lying, spying, double-dealing, are second nature to this wise old counsellor; even so, the formal indecency of what he is doing now makes him uneasy:

> *Read on this book,*
> *That show of such an exercise may colour*
> *Your loneliness.—We are oft to blame in this,*
> *'Tis too much proved, that with devotion's visage*
> *And pious action we do sugar o'er*
> *The Devil himself.*

So, Polonius, there you are—and there too is Claudius, who also confesses at this moment the rottenness of his soul.

These two, then, for their own purposes exploit a young love and the exercise of devotion, sugaring o'er the Devil himself. At the end of the scene Polonius proposes to do the same thing again. He hides behind a second arras, and finds that to be too busy is some danger.

Evidently, the character of Hamlet and the death of Polonius are not unconnected, but it is not the case that Shakespeare contrived the latter merely to illustrate the former. The perspective is wider than this. If we will not see the 'divine background', whatever that may prove to be in this play, what shall we make of what Hamlet now says?—

> *For this same lord*
> *I do repent: but Heaven hath pleased it so,*
> *To punish me with this, and this with me,*
> *That I must be their scourge and minister.*

A shuffling-off of responsibility? No; this has the authentic ring of Greek, that is to say of 'religious', tragedy. The deed is Hamlet's, and Hamlet must answer for it. But at the same time it is the work of Heaven; it is, so to speak, what *would* happen, what ought to happen, to a man who has been sugaring o'er the

Devil himself. Denmark is rotten, Polonius is rotten; his death, and the death of seven others, are the natural outcome.

The case is similar with Rosencrantz and Guildenstern. What kind of a man, we may ask, was this Hamlet, that without turning a hair he should so alter the commission that

> He should the bearers put to sudden death,
> Not shriving-time allowed?

It is a legitimate question, but not the first one to ask. The first question is: what is the significance of the whole incident in the total design of the play? Where does Shakespeare himself lay the emphasis? For after all, it is his play. When Hamlet tells the story to Horatio, Shakespeare might have made Horatio say:

> Why, man, this was a rash and bloody deed!

What Horatio does say is very different:

> So Guildenstern and Rosencrantz go to 't.

Before we tell Shakespeare what we think of Hamlet's behaviour we should listen to what Shakespeare tells us. These two young men are friends to Hamlet:

> Good gentlemen, he hath much talked of you;
> And sure I am two men there are not living
> To whom he more adheres.

Hamlet himself corroborates:

> My excellent good friends! How dost thou, Guildenstern? Ah, Rosencrantz! Good lads, how do you both?

The casual, undergraduate-like obscenity that follows establishes the unaffected ease that subsists between them at this moment. Hamlet has no closer friends, unless perhaps it is Laertes, whom also he kills and by whom he is killed, or Horatio, whom he just prevents from killing himself.

But something has just happened to these two young men: they have been suborned by Claudius and Gertrude:

> GUILDENSTERN: But we both obey,
> And here give up ourselves in the full bent
> To lay our service freely at your feet
> To be commanded.

'We here give up ourselves'—to a murderer and to his guilty

wife. Nor is this all that Shakespeare has to tell us about them:

> The cease of majesty
> Dies not alone, but like a gulf doth draw
> What's near it with it; it's a massy wheel
> Fixed on the summit of the highest mount,
> To whose huge spokes ten thousand lesser things
> Are mortis'd and adjoined; which when it falls,
> Each small annexment, petty consequence,
> Attends the boisterous ruin. Never alone
> Did the king sigh, but with a general groan.

Sophocles was not the only tragic poet to understand tragic irony. For these words, spoken of King Claudius, have a much more vigorous reference to the death of King Hamlet; he is the 'massy wheel' which in its fall brings down sundry small annexments—one of whom is the wise speaker of these verses; for they are spoken by Rosencrantz. If then our first question is, What kind of man is Hamlet, that he sends these two to their death? the fault is not Shakespeare's but our own, for lowering our sights contrary to his instructions.

Much of what has just been said needs further justification. We have also many other dramatic facts to note and to use. Perhaps we can kill two birds with one stone by surveying the first six scenes of the play, in which are laid down the foundations of the whole structure, and by prefixing to this a consideration of a matter which has not indeed escaped notice, that there is a resemblance between *Hamlet* and the *Oedipus*.

(2) HAMLET AND THE OEDIPUS

The *Oedipus Tyrannus* begins by describing twice, once in dialogue and once in lyrics, the plague which is afflicting Thebes. The cause of the plague is the presence in the city of a man who has done two things foul and unnatural above all others: he has killed his own father, and he is living incestuously with his own mother. The details of the plague are so described that we can see how its nature is strictly proportioned to its cause: to death is added sterility; the soil of Thebes, the animals, and the human kind are all barren. The meaning is obvious—unless we make it invisible by reducing the play to the stature of Tragedy of Character: what Oedipus has done is an affront to what we should call Nature, to what Sophocles calls Dikê; and since it is the first law of Nature, or Dikê, that she cannot indefinitely tolerate what is ἄδικον, or contrary to Nature, she rises at last against these unpurged affronts. The plague of sterility is the outcome of the unnatural things which Oedipus has done to his parents.

Hamlet begins in the same way. The two soldiers Marcellus and Bernardo, and Horatio, who is both a soldier and a scholar, are almost terrified out of their wits by something so clean contrary to the natural order that

> *I might not this believe*
> *Without the sensible and true avouch*
> *Of mine own eyes.*

Professor Dover Wilson, learned in sixteenth-century demonology, has explained that the eschatology of Horatio and Hamlet is Protestant, that the Ghost is a Catholic ghost, and that Bernardo and Marcellus are plain untheological Elizabethans. On this it would be impertinent for an ignoramus to express an opinion, but it does seem that if the 'statists' in Shakespeare's audience, and scholars from the Inns of Court, saw and savoured theological *expertise* in this scene, they would be in danger of missing the main point: that the repeated appearances of the Ghost are something quite outside ordinary experience. Horatio the scholar has heard of something similar, in ancient history, 'a little ere the mightiest Julius fell'. So perhaps this present unnatural terror 'bodes some strange eruption to our state'; or —a less disturbing thought—perhaps the ghost is concerned for some uphoarded treasure hidden in the womb of the Earth.

But at this point Shakespeare decides to write some poetry— and he is never so dangerous as when he is writing poetry:

> *It faded on the crowing of the cock.*
> *Some say that ever 'gainst that season comes*
> *Wherein our Saviour's birth is celebrated,*
> *The bird of dawning singeth all night long:*
> *And then, they say, no spirit dare stir abroad,*
> *The nights are wholesome; then no planets strike,*
> *No fairy takes, nor witch hath power to charm,*
> *So hallowed and so gracious is the time.*

Pretty good, for a simple soldier. The intense and solemn beauty of these verses lifts us, and was designed to lift us, high above

the level of Horatio's conjectures. The night 'wherein our
Saviour's birth is celebrated' is holy and pure beyond all others;
therefore these nights which the Ghost makes hideous by rising
so incredibly from the grave, are impure beyond most. Unless
Greek Tragedy has bemused me, this passage does more than
'give a religious background to the supernatural happenings' of
the scene[1]; they give the 'background', that is, the logical and
dynamic centre, of the whole play. We are in the presence of
evil. Hamlet's own prophetic soul recognises this as soon as he
hears of the Ghost:

> Foul deeds will rise,
> Though all the earth o'erwhelm them, to men's eyes.

If we may assume that Shakespeare had not read Sophocles—
and that Hamlet had not read him, at Wittenberg, behind
Shakespeare's back—the parallel with the *Oedipus* becomes the
more interesting; for when Oedipus has at last discovered the
truth the Chorus observes:

> ἐφηῦρέ σ' ἄκονθ' ὁ πάνθ' ὁρῶν χρόνος,
> δικάζει τὸν ἄγαμον γάμον πάλαι
> τεκνοῦντα καὶ τεκνούμενον.

*Time sees all, and it has found you out, in your own despite. It
exacts Dikê from you for that unnatural marriage that united
mother with son.* (1213-1215)

'Foul deeds will rise': there are evils so great that Nature will
not allow them to lie unpurged. So, returning to the battlements with Hamlet, and enquiring with him

> Why thy canonized bones, hearsed in death,
> Have burst their cerements; why the sepulchre
> Wherein we saw thee quietly inurned
> Hath o'ped his ponderous and marble jaws
> To cast thee up again—

we learn the cause: fratricide, incest, 'Murder most foul, strange
and unnatural'.

Here, most emphatically stated, are the very foundations and
framework of the tragedy. We can, of course, neglect these, and
erect a framework of our own which we find more interesting
or more congenial to us. We can say, with Dr Gregg, that the

---

[1] Dover Wilson, *What Happens in Hamlet*, p. 67.

Ghost is all my eye; or, with Professor Dover Wilson, that the first act, 'a little play of itself', is 'an epitome of the ghost-lore of the age'—in which case it becomes something of a learned Prologue to the real play[1]; or, like Dr de Madariaga, we can neglect this encircling presence of evil, and substitute what we know of sixteenth-century Court manners; or, again without constant reference to the background which Shakespeare himself erected, we can subtly anatomise the soul and mind of Hamlet, on the assumption that Hamlet is the whole play. But if we do these things, let us not then complain that Shakespeare attempted a task too difficult for him, or conclude that the play is an ineffable mystery. Turning it into 'secular' tragedy we shall be using the wrong focus. The correct focus is one which will set the whole action against a background of Nature and Heaven; for this is the background which the dramatist himself has provided.

(3) THE FIRST SIX SCENES

Shakespeare begins on the battlements, then takes us to the Room of State, then to Polonius' house, then again to the battlements, then back to Polonius' house. Why?

The first scene ends with Marcellus' speech, and its suggestion that evil is abroad. Two minutes later we are looking at the King in Council—a scene, incidentally, in which elegant ladies are quite out of place, though they certainly do brighten up the stage. We are listening to the suspicious rhetoric with which Claudius is talking of his marriage, and tendering his thanks to his Lords, whose 'better wisdoms have freely gone with this affair along'. Only Hamlet, in his inky black, holds aloof. It is an arresting spectacle; what did Shakespeare mean by it? Either Hamlet is right, and all the rest wrong, or they are right, and he is being unreasonable.

Prudence and piety alike forbid me lightly to disagree with my colleague Dr Bertram Joseph where Shakespeare is concerned, but our first impression of Claudius is an important matter. Dr Joseph writes:

When the play opens it is by no means certain that Claudius is a

[1] Or, if it is not this, let it be shown what its organic function is. Shakespeare, having a capacious mind, may well have been keenly interested in contemporary ghost-lore, but our first question is: what has he done with it as a creative artist? Or has he done nothing with it?

villain. Even when the Prince swears vengeance there is still a strong possibility that the Ghost's word ought not to be taken. What we have seen of Claudius suggests a clear conscience: we have been present whilst a very gracious and most noble-looking renaissance monarch transacted private and public business with an admiring court around him.[1]

But did Shakespeare really intend his audience to be deceived even for a moment by Claudius? The King tells us, in his first long and twisting sentence, that he has married his brother's wife—which, so we are told, contemporary thought held to be incestuous; and we may observe how Shakespeare makes him say it: he has taken to wife 'our sometime sister', and that does not make it sound any the better. Nor does he allow Claudius to suggest any reason or excuse for the hastiness of the marriage[2]; there is only that elaborate and frigid talk about 'defeated joy' and the rest of it. And surely the physical appearance of Claudius must be such that it makes sense to us when Hamlet, showing Gertrude his picture, calls him a 'mildewed ear', a 'moor'. If what we have seen is a noble-looking Prince, we shall be at a loss when Hamlet compares him to a satyr; satyrs were ugly, as well as lewd.

No; we are meant to see from the start that there is something seriously amiss with Claudius, even though his Court—all but Hamlet—approve of him and of what he has done:

> *Nor have we herein barred*
> *Your better wisdoms, which have freely gone*
> *With this affair along: for all, our thanks.*

Very well; if the Court accepts as king a 'mildewed ear' who has made an unseemly marriage in unseemly haste, so much the worse for the Court. They are wrong, and Hamlet is right—and alone, now as later.

Claudius is a hypocrite, but he is no fool; the Norwegian affair he handles very competently. Next, he has to consider two identical petitions, one from Laertes and one from Hamlet. Laertes is at once given permission to return to France, as a compliment to Polonius:

---

[1] *Conscience and the King*, p. 51.
[2] Of course, we can think up reasons for ourselves—just as we can, if we like, add bits of paint to another man's picture.

The head is not more native to the heart,
The hand more instrumental to the mouth,
Than is the throne of Denmark to thy father.

But Hamlet is refused leave to return to Wittenberg.

Why does Shakespeare contrive this? As far as Laertes is concerned we can say that it is necessary that he should be introduced, and then removed from the scene until he is wanted; though the sharp juxtaposition of the two young men ought to make us suspect that the dramatist is appealing to our imaginations as well as helping his plot along. So far as Hamlet is concerned, it is here, I think, that Professor Wilson steps gallantly and gaily forward on the wrong foot. It is absurd, he says, to suppose that either Shakespeare or his audience knew or cared anything about Danish Constitutional History, so that any learning which the Shakespearian critic may acquire on this subject is irrelevant to *Hamlet*.—Nothing could be better sense. But surely it does not follow, as Wilson says it does, that Shakespeare must have composed the scene with the English constitution in mind; that it is to be understood as being, virtually, a meeting of the English Royal Council. It is surely the common experience that we go to the theatre willing to accept, without prepossessions, what the dramatist offers us; willing to accept anything in reason, and a good deal that is out of reason, provided that the dramatist makes it dramatically significant. After all, this Room of State is in Elsinore, not in London. The advantage of this, to Shakespeare, was that since nobody in the audience knew or cared what the Danish constitution was, in whatever century this is supposed to be, the dramatist could go ahead and assume what suited him best. If 'statists' and other clever men in the audience could not, with Shakespeare, escape from contemporary London, but turned Act I Scene 2 into a meeting of the Privy Council, and thereby found it obvious that Hamlet had been illegally, or by a trick, cheated of the succession, and that therefore he was (though he does not say so) smarting with indignation against the Usurper,[1] and that it was for this reason that Claudius did not want Hamlet to leave Denmark, if the statists did this—which is more or less what Verrall did with Aeschylus and Euripides—it was their own look

[1] We are bidden to consult Johnson on the Usurper—and why not? We have already consulted this robust critic on Cordelia.

out; Shakespeare was not asking them to do it. He was asking them to use indeed all the quickness of mind which they could bring with them, but imaginatively and responsively, not analytically; within the play, not somewhere behind it; to understand, not to add. For although it is true, as Professor Wilson says, that the knowledge and experience which is common to dramatist and audience can be tacitly assumed by both, we have to be very careful how we apply this principle. It so easily slides into another which is not so sensible, namely that matters of common knowledge necessarily are so assumed. And then one is in danger of saying that although the mention of a thing in a play proves its relevance, the fact that it is not mentioned proves its relevance even more conclusively: it was so obviously relevant that there was no need to mention it; it was 'tacitly assumed'.[1]

No; the idea of usurpation and thwarted ambition will appear in due course, and in due subordination, when Shakespeare is ready for it; it has no place in these scenes, which he is doing his best to fill with something different.[2] We know, from the presence of the Ghost and Marcellus' speech about it, that evil is abroad. We can already suspect that the too facile Claudius is at the centre of it, and that perhaps his chief adviser Polonius is not far removed from it. What we are clearly shown is that Hamlet would like to escape from it all, back to Wittenberg and his studies. But he may not.

He says:

> *I have that within which passeth show;*
> *These but the trappings and the suits of woe.*

What it is that he has within we learn from the first soliloquy, the depth and bitterness and despair of which are only diminished if we try to add to what he says conjectures of our own about disappointed ambition. He has sustained two blows that make him reel: that his mother should have committed what to him at least is incest; and that she should have done it contrary

---

[1] See also above, p. 148.

[2] 'I am too much i' the sun' is sometimes taken to mean 'I am cheated out of the succession'. But why should it mean this? In *Much Ado*, II, 1, Beatrice says that she is 'sunburn'd', meaning that she is unmarried, without the natural shelter and comfort of a husband and children; so has Hamlet now lost a father and a mother. The whole context is one of personal grief and desolation.

to all reason, taking a satyr—something lewd and ugly—in the place of a Hyperion. His faith both in goodness and in reason is shattered; now he has nothing to live for; the whole world

> *is an unweeded garden*
> *That grows to seed; things rank and gross in nature*
> *Possess it merely.*

And he cannot escape. His request has been refused that he may be allowed to return to Wittenberg; a more dreadful way of escape is also barred, for the Everlasting has fixed his canon 'gainst self-slaughter. Perhaps Hamlet has built his life too exclusively on reason and religion; nevertheless he has so built it; and that is what this passage is about, not Usurpation. The soliloquy is a direct continuation of Marcellus' speech: Evil is abroad; Hamlet has seen part of it, and is shattered.

Abruptly we are taken to Polonius' house. Here we meet Laertes, whom we have already seen, set over against Hamlet, and Ophelia, of whom we yet know nothing. There is something architectural in the construction of these early scenes; the composition is dramatic, not narrative.

If we are convinced that *Hamlet* is a play about Hamlet, perhaps we shall take little notice of Act I Scene 3; in 'What Happens in *Hamlet*' the scene appears not to happen at all, since it is never mentioned. But are we entitled to decide for ourselves which parts of the play exist and which do not? We must contemplate the whole design, not parts of it only. What Shakespeare is doing here is to tell us that Hamlet and Ophelia are in love, and to show how certain malign influences are beginning to play on that love. On Hamlet's side there is Gertrude: the sudden and complete despair. 'Frailty, thy name is woman' is a phrase which constant quotation has invested with an archness that we have to think away. On Ophelia's side there is, to begin with, the worldly prudence of Laertes:

> *For Hamlet, and the trifling of his favour,*
> *Hold it a fashion and a toy in blood,*
> *A violet in the youth of primy nature,*
> *Forward, not permanent, sweet, not lasting,*
> *The perfume and suppliance of a minute,*
> *No more.*

'Malign' : is that not too strong a word? Perhaps it is; but let

us see what happens next, for this is only preparation. Presently
Laertes is saying, repeating the imagery of flowers and perfume
which always plays around Ophelia:

> *The canker galls the infants of the spring*
> *Too oft before their buttons be disclosed,*
> *And in the morn and liquid dew of youth*
> *Contagious blastments are most imminent.*
> *Be wary then; best safety lies in fear.*

Does it? Laertes may be right, but 'contagious blastments' are
at hand against which not even fear can be a defence. Polonius
enters.

So far we have only seen Polonius, not heard him. We have
seen him standing at the right hand of Claudius and Gertrude
—and that is no great recommendation. He begins by giving
to Laertes that advice which we all learned by heart at school,
being told perhaps that it is the quintessence of human wisdom,
which it certainly is not, though it may be the quintessence of
worldly wisdom—and that is something. Then comes his advice,
or rather his statements and instructions, to Ophelia. What are
we to make of these?

> *In few, Ophelia,*
> *Do not believe his vows, for they are brokers,*
> *Not of that dye which their investments show,*
> *But mere implorators of unholy suits,*
> *Breathing like sanctified and pious bawds*
> *The better to beguile.*

In short, he hears that his daughter is on affectionate terms with
a young man, of whom we know no ill, except perhaps that his
spirit is too fine for this 'unweeded garden'; and these are the
thoughts, and this the language, to which he naturally turns.
Is it not perhaps a little over-generous to speak, as Granville
Barker does, of Polonius' 'meddling'? Would it not be fairer,
both to Polonius and to Shakespeare, to call him a disgusting
and dirty-minded old man?

We have seen Hamlet; we have now seen Ophelia. In these
two successive scenes they are set side by side, each of them
exposed to malign influences. The rest of the play will conform
what this already suggests: these two are colleagues in disaster;
and later we may find reason to regard Laertes, his friend and

her brother, as a third victim. That is to say, we should not try to consider everything in the play as something that reveals or influences the mind and the fate of the one tragic hero, Hamlet; rather should we contemplate the characters as a group of people who are destroyed, and work each other's destruction, because of the evil influences with which they are surrounded. Hamlet is not the centre of the play; he is the epicentre.

We return to the battlements. Almost at once Shakespeare makes a terrific noise: he blows trumpets and lets off a gun or two. Why? When Beethoven makes a sudden *ff* we expect to find some musical significance in it; should we expect less from Shakespeare? A dramatist should not let off guns in the theatre merely for the fun of it. That he meant something is suggested by the fact that he was willing to pay for it—like Sophocles— with an inconsistency, namely the assumption that Horatio is a stranger to Denmark and its customs:

> *What does it mean, my lord?*

What it means is—to put it briefly—that Claudius is boozing, a low Danish habit which Hamlet finds disgusting. Once more, he seems to be alone.

But why the gun-fire? In a later scene we read: *Trumpets sound, and cannon shot off within.* More guns—and now we understand: Claudius is drinking again, and Gertrude drinks, and the drinks are poison. This is what it all comes to.

Next, the Ghost; the foul deeds arise; they are as foul as Hamlet's 'prophetic soul' could possibly have imagined, and they are presented in the foulest of colours. To murder in its most treacherous form was added the corruption of 'my most seeming- virtuous Queen'. The two themes of the first soliloquy are prominent here too—lust and unreason. As virtue

> *never will be moved*
> *Though lewdness court it in a shape of Heaven,*
> *So lust, though to a radiant angel link'd,*
> *Will sate itself in a celestial bed*
> *And prey on garbage.*

There is too the stupifying thought that 'my most seeming- virtuous Queen' should

> *decline*
> *Upon a wretch whose natural gifts were poor*
> *To those of mine.*

'Frailty' indeed! In what now can a man put his trust? 'O most pernicious woman!' 'Smiling, damned villain!'

> *I'll wipe away all trivial fond records,*
> *All saws of books, all forms, all pressures past*
> *That youth and observation copied there,*
> *And thy commandment all alone shall live*
> *Within the book and volume of my brain.*

This sudden revelation of unsuspected depths of evil and treachery, together with the awful insecurity that it brings, are the very essence of Hamlet's tragedy. Whether he can 'make up his mind' or not, his mental and spiritual life lies in ruins.

> *There are more things in Heaven and Earth, Horatio,*
> *Than are dreamt of in your philosophy.*

Commentators must never stop pointing out what 'your' means in this passage: not *tua philosophia* but *ista philosophia*. One student of philosophy is talking to another, and the one has suddenly had his faith in reason, to say nothing of goodness and purity, undermined and shattered.

There is another point to notice hereabouts. As Aeschylus in the *Agamemnon* turned the Palace of Atreus into the very headquarters of the Furies, so Shakespeare makes Denmark a concentration of evil: 'Something is rotten in the state of Denmark'; 'At least, I'm sure it may be so in Denmark'; 'Is it a custom?—Ay, marry is't; but to my mind, though I am native here . . .' Later, when we hear 'Denmark's a prison' we hear these undertones too; it is a prison, full of evil—and Hamlet was denied leave to escape. He is locked up with evil; and more than that: it is for him alone to know, and to grapple with, the worst evil of all. For the Ghost will not speak to any but Hamlet, and that only on 'more removed ground'. And what is the point of the cellarage scene? For reasons that Shakespeare thinks either obvious or irrelevant, since he does not mention them, Hamlet swears his companions to secrecy; the Ghost too will have them swear. As neither Horatio nor Marcellus comments on the unusual circumstance that a Ghost joins in their conversation from below, it seems plain that they are supposed not to hear it—as Gertrude does not, in the bedroom scene. Therefore the cellarage scene presents us with this spectacle: Hamlet alone hears the Ghost; the Ghost, like Hamlet, will have the whole affair kept secret; three times, and in vain, Hamlet tries to get away from the Ghost—causing Horatio to exclaim 'O day and night, but this is wondrous strange'; and finally Hamlet gives way. He is chained to his awful secret, in his prison. This, surely, is the plain effect of one of the most extraordinary pieces of 'theatre' in the whole of Shakespeare.

Now Shakespeare takes another leap, back to the house of Polonius, for the Reynaldo scene. This is one which producers commonly omit; the awkward fact is that Shakespeare put it in. The social habits of our time make it impossible for producers to give us *Hamlet*; all that we get is *Selected Scenes from Hamlet*. But if the critic omits a scene, either he is distorting the play, or Shakespeare made an artistic blunder in writing it. What does the Reynaldo scene do for us?

To Dover Wilson it means one thing only: it shows us that several weeks have elapsed, so that we are the more anxious to learn how Hamlet has been faring.[1] If this is all, it is rather long, and Shakespeare would be a clumsy dramatist—inventing a character, Reynaldo, whom we never see again, and sending him on a mission that contributes nothing to the play (since it does not matter twopence if Reynaldo gets to Paris or not) merely to inform us that several weeks have elapsed. But this is what happens when we neglect the 'religious' background, and make the hero the sole point of reference.

In fact, the scene is a clear and logical part of a very firm structure. All we have to do is to be quite simple-minded about it, and to trust our dramatist.

Perhaps Shakespeare thought we might recollect how Polonius talked to Laertes when last we saw him:

> *To thine own self be true,*
> *And it must follow, as the night the day,*
> *Thou cans't not then be false to any man.*

This time he is talking not to, but about, Laertes. He is saying to a servant: 'Go to Paris with this money for my son; but before you visit him, find out from other Danes in Paris how he is behaving himself.' Polonius is one who chooses his servants well; Reynaldo himself is hardly the soul of honour:

> *My lord, I did intend it.*

[1] *What Happens in Hamlet*, p. 209.

'Use suggestive talk about him', says Polonius.

Ay, very well, my lord.

You may put on him, says Polonius, what forgeries you please; 'marry, none so rank as may dishonour him', but 'drinking, fencing, swearing, quarrelling, drabbing; you may go so far'. At this even Reynaldo is shocked:

My lord, that would dishonour him.

'Faith no;' you must not suggest that he is openly incontinent, but you must worm your way about, drop hints, 'by indirections find directions out'. In short, go to Paris and spy on my son.

Now, this is far too positive a scene to be written off as a mere fill-up, invented in order to whet or satisfy our curiosity about the Hero. During this scene we ought surely to be thinking about Polonius, not about Hamlet. What are we to make of him? Granville Barker speaks of his 'tediousness', 'verbiage', 'hair-splitting'; but what would we naturally think of a man who spoke *to* his son like that, and then *about* his son like this? And why should we suppose that Shakespeare is changing his mind about him as Dr Barker says? The Polonius who gives these revolting instructions to Reynaldo is the same man who, in effect, said to his daughter, in the morn and liquid dew of her youth: Don't be a fool; all the man wants is to seduce you. He is the same Polonius who, in his capacity of wise counsellor, stood at the right hand of Claudius and Gertrude. He is not meant to be an amusing buffoon; nor, I suspect, is his habitual mode of speech meant to be funny. Perhaps we are too ready to think of style as a dramatic ornament and not as a dramatic instrument.

For example, Ophelia is given language like this:

> He took me by the wrist, and held me hard,
> Then goes he to the length of all his arm,
> And, with his other hand thus o'er his brow,
> He falls to such perusal of my face
> As he would draw it . . .

> . . . That done, he lets me go;
> And with his head over his shoulder turn'd
> He seemed to find his way without his eyes;
> For out o' doors he went without their help,
> And to the last bended their light on me.

There are those who, although they have read this speech, can arrive at the conclusion that Ophelia was a fast young hussy whose previous relations with Hamlet are, at best, extremely suspicious. This is an offence against the two arts of poetry and drama at once. It assumes that high intensity in dramatic poetry means nothing in particular, that it can be turned on and off casually, like a tap. That is not true. Poetry is not an ornament to poetic drama; it is an organic part of the whole; one of the many instruments whereby the dramatist communicates his meaning to his audience. When poetry rises to these heights, it is because the inner pressure of thought and emotion forces it up. Conversely, the impact of such poetry on a receptive audience raises it also to a height at which banal and second-rate ideas do not exist. The quality of the poetry in this passage is alone enough to answer questions about Ophelia which should never have been asked.

So it is with the style that Shakespeare consistently gives to Polonius. It amuses us, but it is not meant as a mere decoration of the play, as a casual source of entertainment; it is an exposure of the man himself. As the style is bogus, so is the man. For example, Shakespeare, who had the dramatist's natural instinct for sharp juxtaposition, makes both Hamlet and Polonius talk about the theatre. Hamlet is always shrewd, vigorous, intellectually clean; Polonius, with his 'historical-pastoral-comical', is the exact opposite. A small point, but typical. His very speech, like his mind and soul, is full of those 'indirections' which in the end lead him to his death.

The Reynaldo scene, then, far from making us think about Hamlet, makes us think hard about Polonius, and it confirms our previous estimate, that he is a treacherous and dirty-minded old man. But this only raises another question: for what purpose did Shakespeare want him to be like this? Clearly he thought it of some importance, or he would hardly have written a passage of more than seventy verses about an incident which, 'logically', has no bearing on the plot.

The answer to this question ought to be obvious. It *is* obvious, I think, as soon as we contemplate the play in its true perspective, which is not the perspective of tragedy of character. Shakespeare has been moving about between the Battlements, the Room of State, and Polonius' house; doing this, he has built up a background of treachery, lust, unreason, suspicion, crime. Horatio spoke the truth when he said 'Heaven will direct it'; we know to what consummation Heaven does direct it: to the destruction of both these two houses. The characters who, under Heaven, work out this grim consummation, are complex; so too are their actions. Everything is lifelike, for human life is the field in which the gods work. We shall find problems enough, but we shall not be likely to solve them, and so make clear sense of the play, unless we do our best to see everything within the framework which Shakespeare has so firmly designed in these opening scenes.

(4) HAMLET AND LAERTES

In this first part of the play we have met the six chief characters. They are significantly contrasted and juxtaposed. On the one side are Claudius the arch-criminal, Gertrude whom he has corrupted, 'won to his shameful lust', and Polonius his worthy counsellor. Over against these are the three young people who find themselves surrounded by this atmosphere of evil, and are either corrupted by it or destroyed by it or both at once. By anticipation, we have also taken a glance at two other victims, first entrapped, then destroyed: Rosencrantz and Guildenstern.

Laertes, paired with Hamlet in the second scene, is removed before we gain a clear impression of him, except that he seems to be a dutiful son, an affectionate brother, and not without sense. His part in the tragedy does not properly begin before Act IV. But if we look at it now, it may help us to understand Hamlet, since in several ways Shakespeare clearly treats him as Hamlet's counterpart. Laertes, with a father to avenge, is placed in exactly the same position as Hamlet; his behaviour in this position is utterly different; but they share a common destruction.

Unlike Hamlet, Laertes acts with vigour. He is a headstrong youth; he is grievously hurt. On bare suspicion he forces his way into the King's presence, ready to kill him at once. Where Hamlet had said 'Look you, I'll go pray', Laertes is ready to 'cut his throat i' the church'. Hamlet shrank from 'the dread of something after death', remembered 'God's canon 'gainst self-slaughter', contemplated even the possibility that 'It is a damnèd ghost that we have seen' To kill Claudius is 'such bitter business as the day would quake to look on'. He sees everything in the light of conscience:

> Is't not perfect conscience
> To quit him with this arm?

Laertes on the other hand has no scruples:

> To Hell, allegiance! vows, to the blackest devil!
> Conscience and grace, to the profoundest pit!
> I dare damnation: to this point I stand,
> That both the worlds I give to negligence,
> Let come what comes; only I'll be revenged
> Most throughly for my father.

Nothing could be sharper than this contrast; yet the two men come to the same end. How? Why? With Laertes the case is plain. Since it is so plain, it may help us to understand the case of Hamlet, because we may certainly assume, as a reasonable working hypothesis, that these two personal tragedies are designed to be coherent parts of the complete tragedy.[1] Laertes is drawn into the spreading circle of evil, is corrupted by it, and is destroyed. Laertes, as we have just seen, is resolute, even reckless. He has a high, or at least a lively, sense of honour; with him, the duty of avenging his father overrides everything. At the same time, there is in him something of his father's 'indirection'—enough to make him listen to the King's treacherous plan to make use of an unbated foil; enough even, in his present rage, to make him improve on that, by using poison. Furthermore, as Polonius first gave unctuous advice about Honour to Laertes, and then sent Reynaldo so disgustingly to spy on him, so now Laertes talks pedantically of his honour in the midst of the blackest treachery:

> . . . But in my terms of honour
> I stand aloof, and will no reconcilement
> Till by some elder masters of known honour
> I have a voice and precedent of peace
> To keep my name ungored.

We can note these faults without in the least failing in sympathy

---

[1] This is one of the two reasons why no attempt is made here to discuss the Hamlet-Laertes contrast as a stage in the development of the English Revenge-tragedy.

towards him; uncritical sympathy may be agreeable in life, but it will not help us to understand plays. We can sympathise with him—and, what is more, we can understand Shakespeare—when we remember what he has suffered, what he is by training, and how plausibly—how truly indeed—Claudius accuses Hamlet. Most of all do we sympathise with him and pity him when he sees the truth, too late:

> *The foul practice*
> *Hath turned itself on me: lo, here I lie,*
> *Never to rise again . . .*
> *Exchange forgiveness with me, noble Hamlet.*

We can certainly interpret Laertes as an Aristotelian tragic hero; but Shakespeare's tragedy here is wider than anything that Aristotle describes; it is Aeschylean in its amplitude: the original crime, and the rottenness that prompted it, surrounds it, and flows from it, corrupts this essentially decent youth and leads him to dishonour and death. The point is made explicitly when Laertes cries:

> *The King, the King's to blame.*

He and Hamlet may fittingly 'exchange forgiveness'; they are colleagues in tragedy, just as are Hamlet and Ophelia.

(5) HAMLET AND OPHELIA

Ophelia's tragedy is much more closely intertwined with Hamlet's than her brother's is. To understand it, we shall have to consider what Hamlet was, and what he has become; what a fair prospect there was, and why it ends in madness and death. We shall be led to the same conclusion: The King, the King's to blame; except that in this case two companions in evil, Gertrude and Polonius, contribute much. It is the 'unweeded garden' that does not allow Ophelia to flower. We will attempt to follow, though with necessary digressions, this joint tragedy.

> *Doubt thou the stars are fire;*
> *Doubt that the Sun doth move;*
> *Doubt truth to be a liar;*
> *But never doubt I love.*
> *O dear Ophelia, I am ill at these numbers; I have not art to reckon my groans; but that I love thee best, O most best, believe it.*

We know something of the unclouded Hamlet who wrote this love-letter, Hamlet as he was. Not only have we Ophelia's own heart-broken speech:

> O what a noble mind is here o'erthrown . . .

We also are given, from time to time, glimpses of the real Hamlet—at moments when, so to speak, he forgets; as, for example, when he so gaily welcomes, and jests with, Rosencrantz and Guildenstern, or the Players; or when he talks with such clean, good sense about the theatre. In his portrait of the essential Hamlet, Shakespeare has succeeded, as no one else, in putting before us a man of genius: the courtier, scholar, soldier; 'eye, tongue, sword'; the artist, the philosopher; the gay companion and the resolute man of action. These last two points are emphasised by Shakespeare, almost as if he foresaw a ghostly line of critics to come, who would try to turn his Hamlet into a gloomy, introspective romantic failure, or into an Aristotelian hero cursed with the fatal flaw of indecision. How a tragic flaw must be handled we can learn from Sophocles—and Shakespeare did not need to learn: Sophocles made Oedipus hasty and hot-tempered not only in the fatal encounter at the cross-road, but time after time, as in his dealings with Teiresias and Creon. A point so elementary is not likely to have escaped Shakespeare; yet whenever he can he represents Hamlet as being swift, even reckless in action. Hamlet does not say to Horatio: 'I'll join you on the battlements—only not tonight.' He does say:

> Unhand me, gentlemen:
> By Heaven, I'll make a ghost of him that lets me—

and what is more, we believe it. Indecision, indolence, listlessness, are as far as possible from being native to him.

Such is the real Hamlet who loved Ophelia and whom Ophelia shyly loved, in the morn and liquid dew of her youth, when contagious blastments are most imminent.

Drama, as we have said before, is the art of significant juxtaposition. Over against these glimpses of Hamlet as he is by nature, Shakespeare sets his picture of Hamlet as he has now become, Hamlet 'mad'. Over against this promise of a happy love—

> I hoped thou shoulds't have been my Hamlet's wife—

he sets the twisted, hideous thing that it has become. What twisted it, and what the connexion is between this and the rest of the play, is not hard to see, since Shakespeare was quite a competent dramatist. In order to apprehend his meaning we need only to observe what he does, to assume that he had intelligent reasons for doing it, and to get it all into the right focus.

Our survey of the first six scenes we left unfinished. We took it as far as the Reynaldo-passage, which by the wrong logic is unnecessary, but by the true logic is an integral part of the whole structure. *Exit Reynaldo: enter Ophelia*: that is the whole point. To this entrance we can, if we choose, supply a background other than the one which Shakespeare has supplied: one constructed out of Court manners under the Tudors, for instance, with special reference to young ladies like Anne Boleyn, helped out with parts of the play that we have not yet heard, taken out of their context. But as Shakespeare's background is not unimpressive, and does not make nonsense of the scene before us, we may as well try to use it.

We saw Hamlet, sitting apart in the Room of State, in utter despair contemplating not only incest, but unintelligible incest too, in his own mother. Shakespeare has no Zeus or Apollo to give infinite depth to his perspective, but he does use the Ghost, to suggest that Nature herself is in revolt against deadly sin. To incest, fratricide and the deliberate corrupting of Gertrude are added, so that Hamlet's mind reels under the shock. An overwhelming revelation of evil has made nonsense, for him, of all that he was and thought and knew:

> *I'll wipe away all trivial, fond records,*
> *All saws of books, all forms, all pressures past . . .*

When Ophelia tells Polonius that he looked

> *As if he had been loosed out of Hell*
> *To speak of horrors,*

her description is exact; we have ourselves seen him peering into Hell, and recoiling from it in horror. Shakespeare has interwoven with this the dirtiness of Polonius; and then, for Hamlet, comes Ophelia's inexplicable rejection of him.

What then is passing through Hamlet's mind as he takes her by the wrist and holds her hard? Shakespeare does not tell us; perhaps he thought that we should understand. So we shall, if we attend to his construction and not to our own reconstructions. We have met, so far in the play, only one thing that is not foul with corruption: Hamlet's and Ophelia's love. Gertrude's sin has destroyed Hamlet's trust in purity; the nastiness of Polonius, leading to the 'repulsion', has made his feeling of insecurity complete. Dover Wilson says that Hamlet comes to Ophelia hoping for comfort but finding none. This, I think, is too small for the background; and to think of Ophelia as a 'jilt' is surely to mistake the size of the play. Ophelia's tragedy is that she is innocently obedient to a disastrous father; Hamlet's, in respect of Ophelia, is that Love has become confused with foulness, and that he knows not what he can trust.

> *He falls to such perusal of my face*
> *As he would draw it:*

Hamlet is taking farewell, not of Ophelia, but of love and innocence and goodness.

> *He seemed to find his way without his eyes,*
> *For out o' doors he went without their help.*

'Out o' doors'—into what? Into what Shakespeare is going to show us, time after time: into deliberate and bitter obscenity. *Corruptio optimi pessima*: the rottenness in Denmark has corrupted Love itself. Upon which, Shakespeare turns on Polonius with savage irony. He makes the crass man say: 'This is the very ecstasy of love.' No it isn't; it is indeed ecstasy, as the word is used in this play, but it is the death of love.

Here we may interrupt our consideration of Hamlet and Ophelia and go back to Hamlet's two boyhood friends. If we are on the right track, we shall find that Shakespeare, juxtaposing once more, treats the theme of Friendship exactly as he is treating the theme of Love; in other words, that the structure of the play is strong and clear: a view which will perhaps not seem incredible.

We saw how Hamlet receives them: with open-hearted enthusiasm. But they have been sent for, as he quickly divines, and his friendship for them becomes a ruthless enmity:

> *There's letters sealed; and my two schoolfellows—*
> *Whom I will trust as I will adders fanged—*
> *They bear the mandate; they must sweep my way*
> *And marshall me to knavery. Let it work!*

In this 'foul and pestilent congregation of vapours' Friendship can survive no more than Love. We may blame Hamlet as much as we like; the important thing is to understand how 'my sweet Hamlet' comes to do these things. Laertes does much the same to Hamlet, and Hamlet to him:

> *I have shot mine arrow o'er the house*
> *And hurt my brother.*

'Virtue never will be moved'; but anything less than immoveable virtue is corrupted by this omnipresent evil. The lesser tragedy of Rosencrantz, Guildenstern and Hamlet runs parallel to the greater tragedy of Ophelia and Hamlet; and that one runs parallel to the complete tragedy that involves them all.

From the wreckage of friendship we may return to the developing ruin of love, the next stage in which is the shockingly indecent scene in which Polonius reads Hamlet's letter to Claudius and Gertrude. Such an incident could no doubt be made unobjectionable by careful treatment; Shakespeare's contrivance is to make it as revolting as possible. There is the major indecency, that a love-letter, extorted from Ophelia, should be bandied about between people such as these. Then there is the bogus, insincere style in which Polonius is made to talk—a style that earns him a sharp but ineffective reproof from Gertrude. His daughter's happiness is at stake, and he talks in a way which shows that honesty and simple human feelings mean nothing to him. In addition to this, the man lies:

> *No, I went round to work,*
> *And my young mistress I did thus bespeak:*
> *Lord Hamlet is a prince, out of thy star;*
> *This must not be.*

But we happen to know who said this to Ophelia, and it was not Polonius; what *he* said was nothing so clean. Then, always ready with 'indirections', he propounds a clever scheme of spying, and (as Dover Wilson points out) does it in language more suitable to the farmyard.[1] So does Shakespeare underline Laertes' warning against 'contagious blastments'. The dramatic

---

[1] This is the point at which Professor Wilson suggests the 'double entrance' for Hamlet, in order that Hamlet may overhear the plot. Only on this assumption, says Professor Wilson, is the Nunnery scene intelligible. I shall try to show later that it is more intelligible without it.

power with which our presentiment of disaster is being built up may well remind the Hellenist of the first half of the *Agamemnon*.

Now we are shown what certain contagious blastments have done to Hamlet. Whether 'fishmonger' means fishmonger or whoremonger matters little to the general sense; in any case we have 'maggots in a dead dog' and the pun on 'conception' to show us where Hamlet's thoughts are now. For him, love has been poisoned.

When Hamlet and Polonius meet again, later in the scene, Hamlet cries: 'O Jephthah, judge of Israel, what a treasure had'st thou!' Shakespeare's audience, perhaps, knew its Old Testament better than we do today; if it did not know the story, there was the old ballad, which Hamlet quotes, to remind them:

> And Jephthah vowed a vow unto the Lord, and said, If Thou shalt without fail deliver the children of Ammon into my hands, then shall it be that whatever cometh forth from the doors of my house when I return in peace from the children of Ammon shall surely be the Lord's, and I will offer it up for a burnt offering . . .
>
> And Jephthah came to his house, and behold his daughter came out to meet him with timbrels and with dancing . . .
>
> And she said to her father, Let this thing be done for me: let me alone for two months, that I may go up and down on the mountains, and bewail my virginity, I and my fellows . . .
>
> And it came to pass at the end of two months that she returned unto her father, who did with her according to the vow which he had vowed.[1]

So did Jephthah destroy his daughter: Hamlet says 'Am I not i' the right, old Jephthah?' But if he is, then 'Polonius! Polonius is to blame!'

In order to keep company with Hamlet and Ophelia, we will pass over the long Pyrrhus and Hecuba passage, and come to Act III Scene 1; and here we have to make up our minds, if we can, on matters of great importance to the play: in chief, whether or not Hamlet knows that he is being spied on, and by whom; and what the meaning of the nunnery scene is.

On the first point, Dover Wilson is justifiably severe on 'the traditional stage-business of Polonius exposing himself to the eye of Hamlet and the audience, which has hitherto been the

[1] *Judges*, XII, 30-39.

only way open to stage-managers of putting any meaning at all into the scene'. As Wilson says, the chief counsellor of Denmark is neither stupid nor clumsy; to make him, in any degree, a figure of fun, is to deface the tragedy.[1] Polonius is treacherous, crafty, insincere, disastrously wrong in judgment; but he, like Claudius, is quite capable of playing his own game competently.

This raises a question: Why has a tradition arisen which defaces the tragedy? Something, obviously, has been misunderstood. Dover Wilson thinks that an earlier stage-direction has been lost: one that concerns the 'double entrance'. My view is that what has been lost is the real amplitude of the tragedy, and that this has been lost through an undue, a quasi-romantic, concentration on the character and the personal fortunes of Hamlet; 'religious' tragedy has been treated as if it were 'secular' tragedy.

Dover Wilson 'puts meaning into the scene' by making Hamlet overhear the plot when it is first devised. Our texts make Hamlet 'enter, reading' at Act II Scene 2, 169. Wilson would have him enter the inner stage, unseen by the others, some ten verses earlier, so that he hears how Polonius will 'loose his daughter to him', and will hide behind the arras with Claudius. Therefore, in the present scene, Hamlet enters, having been 'closely' sent for. 'His mind is not on the plot, his uncle, or Ophelia. He speaks of his utter weariness of life—and then he sees Ophelia'; and he 'finds her prepared not only with a speech but with the gifts also'; and 'the unhappy girl sadly overplays her part'. Suddenly Hamlet sees everything: here is the decoy, and the two spies will be behind the arras. Now he thinks the worst of Ophelia, and everything he says from this point is intended for all three of them. 'Where's your father?' is a final test of Ophelia's honesty—and Ophelia tells him a lie.[2]

That such treatment will make the scene play effectively is likely enough—but on what dramatic level? As Professor Wilson indicates later,[3] on the level of 'exciting dramatic intrigue'. But was this Shakespeare's level?

There is a less ingenious way of 'putting meaning into the scene', one which will require us to do no more than to continue to think about the play as we have been doing.

---

[1] *What Happens in Hamlet*, p. 131. On Polonius, see below, pp. 276 f.
[2] *What Happens in Hamlet*, loc. cit.   [3] See below, p. 277.

The whole scene is beautifully constructed, in four parts. It opens with the King, Polonius, Rosencrantz, Guildenstern, Gertrude—and Jephthah's daughter. The two young men are soon dismissed, not without some Shakespearean irony directed against Claudius:

> *It doth much content me*
> *To hear him so inclined.—*
> *Good gentlemen, give him a further edge*
> *And drive his purpose on to these delights.*

These two having withdrawn, we are left with the guilty King and Queen, Polonius their trusty adviser—and with Ophelia, in danger, perhaps, of some contagion. The business in hand is briefly expounded to Gertrude: to discover

> *If 't be the affliction of his love or no*
> *That thus he suffers for.*

Gertrude is one of Shakespeare's most profoundly tragic characters. She desires nothing more than the happy union of her son with Ophelia. But if anyone has done more than Polonius to blast this fair prospect, it is Gertrude herself. She says to Ophelia, in complete sincerity:

> *I do wish*
> *That your good beauty be the happy cause*
> *Of Hamlet's wildness: so shall I hope your virtue*
> *Will bring him to his wonted way again*
> *To both your honours.*

But we know that the cause is not the happy one of Ophelia's good beauty, but the unhappy one—among others—of Gertrude's evil lust; and that as for Ophelia's virtue, the Queen, with help from Polonius, has made it almost incredible to Hamlet.

With this tragic speech, the Queen follows Rosencrantz and Guildenstern off the stage; Ophelia's good beauty and her virtue are left in the hands of the two men. Lest we should fail to observe what the real dramatic situation is, Shakespeare puts it into words for us—not that this is of much help, if we are determined to read the scene as a dramatic intrigue. As Ophelia waits, at least pretending to read on her holy book, Shakespeare makes these two men confess the rottenness that is in their souls:

> *With devotion's visage*
> *And pious action we do sugar o'er*
> *The Devil himself.——*
>
> *O, 'tis too true!*
> *How smart a lash that speech doth give my conscience!*
> *The harlot's cheek, beautied with plastering art,*
> *Is not more ugly to the thing that helps it*
> *Than is my deed to my most painted word.*

So declaring themselves, they hide behind the arras.

This is the end of the first part of the scene, and this is the impressive setting for what is to follow. The second part is the soliloquy. Hamlet's problem, as it is presented here, is not how to kill Claudius; not even whether to kill Claudius. This has been subsumed into something much greater: how to deal with a world which has lost its meaning, from which nevertheless one cannot escape. Not Denmark only, but this whole life is a prison, and the way out is barred. 'No one but Shakespeare', says Dover Wilson, 'could have interrupted an exciting dramatic intrigue with a passage like this.'[1] Certainly it is an interruption, if there is an exciting dramatic intrigue; but if Shakespeare is doing something much more important and tragic, then there is no interruption at all, but a smooth and a very powerful continuation; for Hamlet is giving utterance to his despair in the very presence of the men who chiefly embody the evil which has created it.

The third part of the scene now begins, itself too a logical continuation.

OPHELIA: *My lord, I have remembrances of yours*
　　　　 That I have longed long to redeliver.
　　　　 I pray you now receive them.

HAMLET: 　　　　　　　　　　*No, not I;*
　　　　 I never gave you aught.

OPHELIA: *My honour'd lord, I know right well you did;*
　　　　 And with them, words of so soft breath composed
　　　　 As made the things more rich: their perfume lost,
　　　　 Take these again; for to the noble mind
　　　　 Rich gifts wax poor when lovers prove unkind.——
　　　　 There, my lord.

[1] *What Happens in Hamlet*, p.128.

'Her speech', said Dowden, 'has the air of being prepared.' Certainly she has taken the trouble to put it into verse; rather good verse. Professor Wilson adds: 'She has romantically arranged a little play-scene', which she proceeds to spoil by over-acting. But surely this will not do? Surely the quality of the poetry—once more—is alone enough to knock this idea on the head? Or is one being sentimental in saying that the simplicity of 'There, my lord' is one of the most moving things in the play? 'Their perfume lost' recalls the flower metaphor, which began when Laertes said:

> *The canker galls the infants of the spring*
> *Too oft before their buttons be disclosed.*

We may briefly observe what happens to the metaphor. It recurs in Hamlet's words to Gertrude:

> *Such an act . . . takes off the rose*
> *From the fair forehead of an innocent love*
> *And sets a blister there.*

In the second mad-scene Ophelia's flowers speak much more poignantly of the evil which is destroying her and will destroy others.

> *Hadst thou thy wits, and didst persuade revenge,*
> *It could not move me thus.*

So Laertes, when first he sees his ruined sister; words which threaten that more evil will come of this evil. Then Ophelia gives him his posy:

OPHELIA: *There's rosemary, that's for remembrance; pray you, love, remember: and there is pansies; that's for thoughts.—*

LAERTES: *A document in madness: thoughts and remembrance fitted.*

What Ophelia 'turns to favour and to prettiness', the thoughts and remembrance of Laertes are going to turn into something else—into treachery and a double death. Then fennel and columbine for Claudius turn to prettiness his cajolry and ingratitude; and Gertrude's rue points (apparently) to her ruth, and convey to us a hint of her carnal lust.[1]

---

[1] Cogan's *Haven of Health*: 'The second property is that rue *abateth carnal lust*, which is also confirmed by Galen.' (From a note in Hudson's edition of *Hamlet*.)

The last flowers are those that Gertrude strews on Ophelia's grave:

> *Sweets to the sweet: farewell!*
> *I hoped thou shouldst have been my Hamlet's wife;*
> *I thought thy bride-bed to have decked, sweet maid,*
> *And not have strewed thy grave.*

In all this, Shakespeare is doing what Aeschylus also did: he is making a sustained image express his thought: good is blasted by evil, and beauty turned to bitterness.

'Their perfume lost': these are not the words of an Ophelia romantically play-acting, but the words of Shakespeare developing his tragic conception. Polonius, true to his character, has 'loosed her to him', but she is unaware of this, and is untainted by his coarseness. Instructed to be in the lobby at a certain hour, to see Hamlet, she gives back the memorials of a love that has been killed. By whom? Not by her fault, unless it is a fault in a daughter to be obedient to a wise father. Not even entirely by Polonius. He has indeed put an obstacle in the path of love, one which lovers in romance always surmount: but Gertrude's act has so poisoned Hamlet's mind that, far from having the will to surmount it, he turns from Love itself in disgust. It may not be logical in Ophelia, as Dover Wilson says, to reproach Hamlet with being unkind, but surely it is not in the least unnatural if she, being herself so innocent, should think reproachfully of him, that he should not have persisted in spite of the obstacle. Critics find the tone of 'romance' here, and indeed it is already sounded in Hamlet's pastoral-romantic 'Nymph'; but the explanation is not that Ophelia is romantically play-acting. She is desperately sincere. The effect of the slightly romantic echo, 'nymph' and the 'unkind lover', is to throw the tragedy into darker relief.

> *I humbly thank you; well, well, well.*

To Dowden, the repetition denotes impatience; to Dover Wilson, boredom. Perhaps both, if a man can be bored with Hell, and impatient with horrors.

> *No, not I;*
> *I never gave you aught.*

Hamlet recoils from the very idea of love; and when Ophelia persists, in complete sincerity and innocence—to one who can

K

no longer believe that these qualities exist—he breaks out violently:

> *Ha ha! Are you honest? are you fair?*

To my mind, this becomes more, not less, dramatic when we assume that Hamlet is unaware of the 'lawful espials'. To his now poisoned mind beauty itself is become a thing of evil: 'This was sometime a paradox, but now the time gives it proof.' 'I loved you not', because the old stock is diseased; he is—so he thinks now—incapable of anything so wholesome as love. The perfume is indeed lost; we shall soon see what takes its place.

'Get thee to a nunnery.' We must believe what we are told: that 'nunnery' was a contemporary slang-word for a bawdy-house. Not a bad joke, of its kind; but certain modern instances show that an indecent perversion of a word does not acquire the force of law. The objection to the bad sense here is not that it is coarse, but that it would be inept. In the soliloquy Hamlet showed how desperately he wishes he could get out of this world; he would escape if he could, but the way of the bodkin is barred. But Ophelia can escape from life; no need for her to continue the foul farce, to be a 'breeder of sinners'. 'Get thee to a nunnery': a refuge from evil, not a flight into evil. Nothing else makes sense of the passage. 'We are all arrant knaves, all; believe none of us.'—And, speaking of arrant knaves, 'Where's your father?'

If, by some means or other, Hamlet is made aware that Polonius is listening, there is no difficulty in making the passage dramatic, in a somewhat obvious fashion. The difficulty is to find a reasonable way of making him aware of it, and then to explain why he does not immediately stride across to the arras, disclose the schemer, and discomfit Ophelia. If on the other hand Shakespeare designed what Dover Wilson supposes, and Hamlet knows that both Polonius and Claudius are there, we have to find some explanation why Hamlet should presently be so reckless as to say 'Those that are married already, all but one, shall live.' Perhaps that can be done, even if the explanation is no more than that the reckless remark is reckless. But there is a more general, and therefore more serious, objection to this treatment of the scene. 'Everything he says, I repeat, for the rest of this scene [viz. from 'Ha ha! are you honest?'] is intended for the ears of Claudius and Polonius, whom he knows to be behind the arras.' Then, none of it has any considerable meaning, apart from the threat; and this would have some meaning, but no explanation. Hamlet's talk of Honesty and Beauty and the falseness of women loses all its sap if we are to suppose it to be turned on for the edification of the hidden listeners; but if it is said directly and exclusively and desperately to Ophelia, then it has a meaning, as I hope I have shown, which is not only tragic but also a direct continuation of the soliloquy. In short, the soliloquy is no 'interruption' of an exciting dramatic intrigue', but a perfectly steady development, in complete harmony with all of the play that we have yet examined.

The question remains, why Hamlet suddenly asks 'Where's your father?' How did Shakespeare expect his audience to respond to this? If agility of intellect has not diminished in us our power of imaginative response, there is no difficulty, and much tragic point. There is nothing surprising, in Hamlet, that he should jump from arrant knaves in general to this arrant knave in particular, the father of the girl he is talking to. But the jump is extremely dramatic, as well as natural. Polonius has in any case caused mischief enough by 'playing the fool' in his own house, interfering with Ophelia's affairs; he is at this moment 'playing the fool' in Hamlet's house, and, continuing so to do, will soon meet his death in it. Had it been possible to 'shut the doors on him', things would have fallen out very differently.

All this being revealed, as if by a flash of lightning, Hamlet returns to his former theme, with no more thought of Polonius. The whole world is corrupted; purity is of no avail; few women are pure, and no men. 'God has given you one face, and you make yourselves another . . . you nickname God's creatures.' To us, improving on Nature is no more than intelligent; but a Greek poet could have made it sound ominous to a Greek audience, and so, I suspect, could an English poet to an English audience in whom the medieval tradition was still alive. In this speech, Hamlet's despair and horror, which we first saw in his first soliloquy, reaches its climax: 'It hath made me mad.' It is on this climax that Shakespeare makes him utter, in the most natural way possible, the parenthetic remark which transforms the whole situation: ' . . . all but one, shall live.'

The fourth part of the scene speaks for itself. The two con-spirators emerge. The King is alarmed—though even more certain cause for alarm is in store for him. Polonius is still obstinate and foolish; and, being wedded to indirections and spying, he conceives the brilliant plan which will be his death.

Until they meet in the graveyard, Hamlet and Ophelia meet only once more—at the Gonzago-play. For the understanding of what passes there, all the clues are in our hands. Hamlet affronts her with a stream of obscene jests. The reason is not that he thinks her to be a loose woman; he has little cause to think that, except that his faith in all mankind is shaken. Still less is the reason for such talk the fact that it is normal Court badinage; it is horrifying, and Shakespeare meant it to be horrifying. This it is to which Hamlet came, when 'out of doors he went', having taken leave of all that is good and healthy; he has made himself come to terms with evil; since he cannot escape from it, either by running away to Wittenberg or by death, he must live with it—and it is corrupting him.

Claudius had said: 'Love! his affections do not that way tend.' No, not now; we have travelled a long way from 'O dear Ophelia, I am ill at these numbers'. But the path we have followed is a perfectly clear one. In the last scene Hamlet reached, so far as the expression of it is concerned, the climax of his disillusion and revulsion; which indeed is not against love only, as many another passage proves; so let us not speak overmuch of 'sexual obsession', nor listen with undue attention to certain psycholo-gists. Love happens to be one of Shakespeare's symbols of good-ness; the perversion of love is black sin. In the wild and agonised speeches of the Nunnery scene Hamlet cried out on marriage and honest love; in the play-scene there is little crying out, since he 'must be idle'; but we can see what has taken the place, in his mind, of love and healthfulness: lewdness and a cruel in-decency. Moreover, between the two scenes, to make his mean-ing still more clear, Shakespeare has placed that despairing comparison of Ophelia's between the Hamlet that was and the Hamlet that is; the present Hamlet is torture to her. The 'contagious blastments' have nearly finished their work. She lacks only one more blow to lose her mind and life altogether, and that comes, in the death of the beloved father who had played his part in destroying her love. Again we may notice a significant parallel; she is driven mad, and he goes 'mad'. What has destroyed this sane and healthy love is the whole corrupt situation, working on their characters and actions.

This is made very clear in the graveyard scene, a scene which might have made the climax to a lesser play than *Hamlet*, but here is only the antechamber to the climax.

We have to observe first how Shakespeare uses his Clowns much as the Greek dramatist used his Chorus; for they fill our minds with generalised thoughts about mortality and the vanity of human life, before we are brought, as by a gradual contraction of the focus, to the particular tragedy. Again we may find a close parallel in the *Oedipus Tyrannus*, in the same ode which was quoted earlier; for when Oedipus has at last discovered the truth, the Chorus, beginning remotely, reflects: 'Ah, you generations of men! Even when you are alive what can I call you but a thing of naught?' What has befallen Oedipus is universalised by being treated as a particular example of a general truth. So in this scene, Shakespeare deepens the significance of Ophelia's tragedy by leading us to it *via* Yorick and Imperial Caesar. Death, we are reminded, is the ultimate fact.

Next we may notice what great emphasis Shakespeare lays on the matter of suicide. He loses no opportunity. The scene begins:

> *Is she to be buried in Christian burial that wilfully seeks her own salvation?*

And presently the Second Clown is saying:

> *Will you ha' the truth on 't? If this had not been a gentlewoman, she should have been buried out of Christian burial.*

Then there are the 'maimed rites', which are so much emphasised, not least by Laertes' indignant iteration: 'What ceremony else? . . . What ceremony else?'

> *I tell thee, churlish priest,*
> *A ministering angel shall my sister be*
> *When thou liest howling.*

Why does Shakespeare make so much of Ophelia's 'doubtful death'?

When we are reading about the *Ajax* or the *Antigone* we are commonly told that the Greeks laid great importance on the proper burial of a body; it is interesting therefore to find Shakespeare doing exactly the same thing—possibly for the same reason. It was argued above[1] that Sophocles was not concerned with superstition or ritual; that to him the burial of a body was the recognition of our common humanity and of its transcendent claims. In the present scene Shakespeare sets before us, on the one hand, the purity of Ophelia:

> *Lay her i' the earth,*
> *And from her fair and unpolluted flesh*
> *May violets spring!*

and on the other hand, the eternal dishonour which would have been hers

> *But that great command o'ersways the order.—*

for which Claudius—or Gertrude?—is entitled to what credit he has earned. Except for this,

> *For charitable prayers,*
> *Shards, flints and pebbles should be thrown on her.*

This is the fate to which Ophelia was so nearly brought. Even so,

> *We should profane the service of the dead*
> *To sing a requiem and such rest to her*
> *As to peace-parted souls.*

All this amounts to a very insistent statement, and surely the plain effect of it is to make us feel how utterly this pervasive evil has blasted Ophelia. Even in her death she barely escapes its malign influence. Shakespeare is determined that no peaceful radiance shall play over the consummation of Ophelia's tragedy. Here, where corruption and evil reign, nothing peaceful or radiant is possible.

This impression is deepened by the wild and grim scene that follows. When last we saw Hamlet and Laertes together it was in the Room of State; now they meet again, the brother and the lover, to struggle desperately and incoherently over Ophelia's body. This it is to which love and brotherly affection and friendship have been brought.

We may notice finally how Shakespeare completes the structure and sense of the scene, and of this whole aspect of the tragedy, by the presence of Gertrude.

[1] Page 196.

> *Sweets to the sweet, farewell.*
> *I hoped thou shouldst have been my Hamlet's wife;*
> *I hoped thy bride-bed to have decked, sweet maid,*
> *And not have strewed thy grave.*

As we have remarked before, it is a tragic speech. But we know—and Gertrude seems to suspect—what it is that has blasted these fair hopes:

> *I doubt it is no other but the main,*
> *His father's death, and our o'erhasty marriage.*

That caused Hamlet's 'madness'; that is the ultimate cause of Ophelia's death. It was Gertrude who, yielding to the 'shameful lust' of Claudius, contributed to this manifold ruin more than anyone, except Claudius. It was her act that twisted his mind from love to obscenity:

> *Such an act*
> *That blurs the grace and blush of modesty,*
> *Calls virtue hypocrite, takes off the rose*
> *From the fair forehead of an innocent love*
> *And sets a blister there.*

Now, broken-hearted, she laments the outcome. The scene is very nearly the consummation of Gertrude's tragedy, as well as of Ophelia's. She yielded to the King; it only remains for her to drink the King's poison.

(6) HAMLET AND HIS MADNESS

We have now examined some important parts of the structure: the first six scenes, which lay the foundation of all that follows, and the tragedies of Hamlet and Laertes, of Hamlet and Rosencrantz and Guildenstern, of Hamlet and Ophelia. We saw how the beginning of the play resembles the beginning of the *Oedipus*, suggesting that this play, like that one, should be considered not as a personal, individual tragedy of character, but something much wider in scope, something more like Religious drama. What we have so far seen of the play confirms this suggestion: the three individual tragedies just mentioned at once cohere when we see that in each case Love or Friendship is perverted by the all pervading evil in Denmark. This evil is not indeed confined to Claudius, but what he has done is its most disastrous manifestation. Aeschylean language is appropriate:

the murder of the King and the corruption of his wife are the πρώταρχος ἄτη,[1] the first crime that begins a chain of crime and disaster; and this chain we followed, in part, as far as the harsh and jangling scene in the churchyard. Now we can begin to consider the central part of the whole structure. If it does not reasonably and harmoniously combine with what we have already established, something will be wrong, either in our interpretation or in Shakespeare's design. We have many things to consider: Hamlet's character, the nature of his madness, all his dealings with Claudius and his fatal delay, all that concerns Hamlet and the Players, and one recurrent theme that has not yet been mentioned: Fortinbras, 'Strong-in-the-arm'. On each of these topics, taken in isolation, it would be possible to say many things; but we must try to contemplate them as Shakespeare has presented them, namely as parts of a big design which we are justified in assuming to be clear and complete.

Hamlet says to the Ghost:

> *Haste me to know 't, that I with wings as swift*
> *As meditation or the thoughts of love*
> *May sweep to my revenge.*

Then why doesn't he do it? The question is a reasonable one, and the answer to it ought to be in the play. It is in fact a problem which continually vexes Hamlet himself, as we see in the soliloquy 'O what a rogue and peasant slave am I!', and again in the last soliloquy:

> *I do not know*
> *Why yet I live to say 'This thing's to do'*
> *Sith I have cause and will and strength and means*
> *To do 't.*

Hamlet does not know the reason; if *we* do not, then Shakespeare has miscalculated.

Some tell us that what is paralysing Hamlet is the thought that the Ghost may be an evil spirit sent by the devil to damn him. If this statement is true, the play is one thing; if it is not true, it is quite a different thing. We must therefore be clear about it.

Whether the Ghost is honest or not is a question which is

---

[1] *Agamemnon* 1192.

raised in Act I—and then (as it seems to me) settled, both for Hamlet and the audience, at least for a long time. Then, quite suddenly, it is raised again. These are dramatic facts which we have to assimilate and understand. What contemporary theologians wrote about Spirits is important, but we must not allow it to distract our attention from what Shakespeare actually does.

> *Remember thee!*
> *Ay, thou poor Ghost, while memory holds a seat*
> *In this distracted globe . . .*

If Shakespeare did not want this passionate speech to carry instant and complete conviction, he should never have written it in such terms.[1]

Presently Hamlet says to Horatio:

> *Touching this vision here*
> *It is an honest ghost; that let me tell you.*

We can hardly go behind that.

It is true that in the Cellarage-scene Hamlet uses expressions which (as Dover Wilson has shown) are appropriate to evil spirits: 'old mole', 'worthy pioneer'. But these expressions too have their context: Hamlet is in violent reaction from the strain to which he has been subjected; he is also bent on keeping the whole thing secret (as the Ghost is too), and therefore is trying to throw dust in his companions' eyes. There is nothing here to remove from our minds the solid conviction just established that it is an honest ghost.

In that conviction we remain until the very end of Act II. In all conscience, this act contains enough to occupy our full attention, and nothing to prompt demonological speculation. We do not, nor cannot, think of the Ghost's credentials when Hamlet is holding Ophelia by the wrist, or talking with Rosencrantz and Guildenstern, or with the Players—or even during the early part of the following soliloquy. 'O what a rogue and peasant slave am I! he cries, in an agony of self-reproach; 'I can say

---

[1] 'And shall I couple Hell?' These words could certainly indicate hesitations about the provenance of the Ghost, if such hesitations were already established by the context; but as the context points in the opposite direction we shall much more naturally take them in a different sense. Hamlet invokes to his aid the 'host of Heaven, and Earth'; shall he also invoke Hell, the home of the powers of evil? 'O fie!'—This seems quite straightforward.

nothing . . . Am I a coward?' Surely it makes nonsense of this whole passage if we are murmuring to ourselves, as we listen to it: 'No, Hamlet, you are no coward. You know, and we know, what the trouble is: the Ghost may be a spirit from Hell, come to tempt you to your everlasting damnation.' If that were Hamlet's difficulty, why on earth should he not say so?

Then, quite suddenly, he *does* say so:

> *About, my brain! I have heard*
> *That guilty creatures sitting at a play . . .*
> *. . . If he but blench*
> *I know my course. The spirit that I have seen*
> *May be the Devil . . .*

We know that it is not the Devil, and we cannot now go back on the whole of Act II and reconsider it in the light of this sudden remark. We must assume that Shakespeare placed it here because this is where he wanted it[1]; we must contemplate Hamlet's inaction and his 'madness' on this assumption. Why *did* he delay, if it was not from misgivings about the Ghost? We will return to the Battlements and try to observe what Shakespeare does, not supplying material of our own drawn from extraneous sources.

Perhaps we may take a preliminary hint from the parallel with Laertes which is established later. He too seeks revenge from Claudius. He forces his way into the palace at the head of a mob, ready for instant action. 'Calmly, good Laertes', says Gertrude; and he answers:

> *That drop of blood that's calm proclaims me bastard.*

He is in a high passion, and the subtle Claudius strikes while the passion is hot:

> *Not that I think you did not love your father;*
> *But that I know Love is begun by time,*
> *And that I see, in passages of proof,*
> *Time qualifies the spark and fire of it . . .*
> *. . . That we should do*
> *We should do when we would; for this* would *changes,*
> *And hath abatements and delays as many*
> *As there are tongues, are hands, are accidents.*

[1] See below, p. 302

Hamlet too was in a passion, no less than Laertes, but when he pictured himself 'sweeping to his revenge' he did not know the worst. When he does, he speaks as one who finds that the whole basis of his life has collapsed beneath him: 'all forms, all pressures past.' The difference between him and Laertes is twofold. Laertes, when it is his turn to avenge his father and his sister, can accommodate himself to the task by giving way to strong passion and an elastic conscience; Hamlet has the passion, but he also has a mind and a conscience, and these must go with him in all that he does. But what is even more important is that he is not confronted, like Laertes, with a single and particular task which he may perform, however repugnant it may be, and then return to his normal ways. Besides being a soldier and a prince, he is something of a philosopher; he must have a coherent universe. But what he now hears from the Ghost makes nonsense, for him, of all that he has ever learned and thought. 'I'll sweep to my revenge' now becomes 'Look you, I'll go pray.' Is there anything surprising in this? To run a sword into Claudius might have been a simple matter; he was ready enough to 'make a ghost' of anyone who 'let' him. But his task does not present itself to his mind now in any such circumscribed way; he sees it like this:

> *The time is out of joint; O cursed spite*
> *That ever I was born to set it right!*

Far easier to kill Claudius than to do this; but Hamlet, being Hamlet, can see the particular crisis only in its widest context.

It has been pointed out before[1] that Shakespeare is careful not to emphasise that Hamlet is delaying; he avoids bringing Hamlet and Claudius face to face. We can of course frustrate Shakespeare, as many do, by bringing in what he has left out—'what any intelligent audience would at once perceive'; but if we do this, we must expect not to resolve but to create puzzles. It is a sound observation, that Shakespeare minimises our sense of Hamlet's delay, but it is a negative one; it suggests that he is covering something up. What he does is something much more positive.

---

[1] As by Waldock, *Hamlet*: 'He is generally engaged in doing something that effectively prevents our thinking of his delay' (p. 85).

Preparation for what is to follow is made by Horatio:

> *What if it tempt you toward the flood, my lord . . .*
> *And there assume some other horrible form*
> *Which might deprive your sovereignty of reason*
> *And draw you into madness?*

The Ghost does indeed take him to the edge of an abyss; he is indeed drawn into madness. What he sees, as he peers into this abyss, is what a Laertes would never see: evil so appalling, so unfathomable, that he has no foundations left either for action or for passion. The 'madness' into which he is drawn is one of the spirit, not of the brain; he suddenly finds himself in a world in which 'your philosophy' is no guide.

The clearest distinction is made, in the play, between the genuine 'madness' and the 'antic disposition' which Hamlet assumes at times when he is 'mad' only north-north-west. In the passage of the 'wild and whirling words', the immediate recoil from an intolerable tension, he takes refuge in foolery because he is in no state to talk rationally. A commonplace man might have remained in control of himself; Hamlet cannot, because his all-embracing apprehension has seen so much in what the Ghost has revealed. A man cannot in one moment renounce 'all forms, all pressures past', and remain steady in mind, spirit and purpose.

Out of all this comes, first, the idea of assuming an 'antic disposition' as a protection and disguise; second, a real paralysing despair in the face of a life that has suddenly lost its meaning. Between the two, the distinction is quite clear. When he is assuming the antic disposition, Hamlet's mind is conspicuously clear and quick; there is such 'method in his madness' that his speech is full of double meanings; he talks to the audience, so to speak, over the heads of his interlocutors. But his real 'madness' is something much deeper.

In the second act Shakespeare is doing two things: he is showing us the extent to which despair has overwhelmed Hamlet, and at the same time he is showing us how the general evil, ever taking new forms, increases its pressure on him. The act begins with the Reynaldo-scene and ends with the soliloquy 'O what a rogue and peasant slave am I'. If we consider the scenes in order, we may find that their connexion with each other, and with the preceding Ghost-scene, becomes apparent.

By the lewd imaginations of Polonius, Hamlet is cut off from Ophelia, his chief contact now with health, sanity, goodness. At once we are shown the effect of this, in the scene in which he looked

> *As if he had been loosed out of Hell*
> *To speak of horrors*

He comes to Ophelia, takes his silent farewell of Love, and goes out into obscenity.

Love has been poisoned for him; so too, as we soon begin to suspect, is Friendship. For it is at this point that Shakespeare introduces the two 'good lads', and has them

> *Here give up ourselves, in the full bent,*
> *To lay our service freely at your feet,*
> *To be commanded.*

For the moment it can be no more than a suspicion, as also it is only in retrospect that we can feel the irony in Guildenstern's next remark:

> *Heavens make our presence and our practices*
> *Pleasant and helpful to him!*

But it is not long before we see Hamlet and his two friends together, and see open-hearted welcome swiftly giving place to mistrust.

Before this happens, Shakespeare gives us the scene in which the letter is read, and Polonius will 'loose his daughter to him'; a scene which does not yet affect Hamlet, but does affect our understanding of Shakespeare's design: the indecency of it makes us feel even more strongly what sinister influences are abroad.

Now it is that we have our first direct glimpse of Hamlet since the cellarage-scene. How many weeks have passed is a question of no importance whatever; it is indeed a question that we shall not even ask ourselves unless we have already missed the only thing that matters, namely that Hamlet has gone 'out o' doors'; that he has suffered a terrible revulsion. His language here—'good kissing carrion', 'conception is a blessing . . .'—shows what he has come to, and the dramatist has made it plain enough why he has come to it. Polonius he thinks of as only a 'tedious old fool'; he has not seen so much of Polonius' work as we have. So far, there is no puzzle whatever in his 'delay'; we shall be faced with the question later, in Shakespeare's own good time. Meanwhile, he is providing us with the solution of the puzzle:

> You cannot, sir, take from me any thing that I will more willingly part withal—except my life, except my life, except my life.

Existence has become meaningless to him; how can he, in this spiritual numbness, find the energy and the sense of purpose to kill Claudius? As he says, a moment later, to his two friends, Denmark's a prison, the world's a prison, Denmark is one of the worst. This goodly frame, the Earth, this most excellent canopy, the air—'why, it appears no other thing to me than a foul and pestilent congregation of vapours'. There is nothing good or bad, but thinking makes it so; Hamlet's thinking makes the world bad. Indeed, he has found another reason for thinking so even in the short interval that has elapsed since the 'kissing-carrion' dialogue: the discovery that his two friends have come as spies in the service of his enemy. Nowhere can he find any-thing sound and healthy; he is in truth 'most dreadfully attended'.

There are those who tell us that he is also smarting with resentment that he had been cheated of the succession. Shakes-speare himself does not seem to be one of them. So far not a word has been said on that topic. Something of the sort is suggested by Rosencrantz in his remark about ambition, but Hamlet's reply makes it plain how utterly insignificant this is in comparison with what is really oppressing him:

> O God, I could be bounded in a nut-shell, and count myself a king of infinite space, were it not that I have bad dreams.

It is true that in a later scene he says to the same Rosencrantz: 'Sir, I lack advancement', but this is the scene in which the recorders are brought. It should be evident that this is an answer which Hamlet thinks good enough for Rosencrantz, a bungler who tries to play on Hamlet without knowing the stops. It will not help us to understand the play if we try to bring in what Shakespeare has left out, or to bring something in at our time and not at his. For the idea of usurpation let us wait, as he did, until Act V.

The next thing that happens is that the arrival of the Players is announced; and the whole episode of the Players is long enough, and strange enough, to call for separate treatment. Before we embark on that it will be convenient to anticipate some later scenes in order to finish the consideration of Hamlet's madness.

One of the difficult passages in the play is the speech that Hamlet makes to Laertes just before the duel:

> *What I have done*
> *That might your nature, honour and exception*
> *Roughly awake, I here proclaim was madness.*
> *Was't Hamlet wronged Laertes? Never Hamlet:*
> *If Hamlet from himself be ta'en away*
> *And when he's not himself does wrong Laertes,*
> *Then Hamlet does it not; Hamlet denies it.*
> *Who does it then? His madness. If 't be so,*
> *Hamlet is of the faction that is wronged;*
> *His madness is poor Hamlet's enemy.*
> *Sir, in this audience,*
> *Let my disclaiming from a purposed evil*
> *Free me so far in your most generous thoughts*
> *That I have shot mine arrow o'er this house*
> *And hurt my brother.*

If this speech had come down to us as a fragment, deprived of context, it would be hard not to judge it as insincere, a sophistical attempt to disclaim responsibility; the style could easily be represented as deliberately false. Having the complete context, we can see that such an interpretation would be wrong; it would make nonsense of the whole scene.

> *But I am very sorry, good Horatio,*
> *That to Laertes I forgot myself;*
> *For by the image of my cause I see*
> *The portraiture of his. I'll court his favours ...*

Hamlet cannot be supposed to be insincere to Horatio; therefore his speech to Laertes must be taken as his honest attempt to 'court his favours': that is, to win back his good will. (It might indeed be said, as a logical alternative, that Hamlet, though sincere, is deceiving himself, but this would attribute to him a blindness that nothing else in the play warrants.) Moreover, Hamlet is being presented now in a mood of solemn acceptance;

he has just said: 'The readiness is all'; insincerity and sophistical elaboration would jar disastrously. There is indeed insincerity, and worse, in the scene, but it is on the part of Laertes:

> ... *But, till that time,*
> *I do receive your proffered love like love,*
> *And will not wrong it.*

The dramatic context, then, compels us to interpret differently. Hamlet, in making this emphatic distinction between Hamlet and Hamlet's madness, is saying something of importance, something that Shakespeare wanted to be said at this particular moment. He says, with all possible emphasis, that the cause of what Laertes has suffered is Hamlet's madness; and apparently he expected his audience to make sense of this.

Our previous discussion of the madness led us to associate it, very closely and directly, with the crimes of Claudius and the basely inspired interference of Polonius; it is the outward expression of the fact that a sudden revelation of immeasurable evil has shaken the foundations of Hamlet's mental and spiritual life. Two other references confirm this association. One of them occurs in the nunnery-scene. In a crescendo of spiritual despair Hamlet cries that beauty itself is foul; that he himself, though 'indifferent honest', is tainted and full of offences; that all men are knaves; that the rare woman who is honest will never escape calumny; that women in their wantonness jig, amble, lisp; and it all leads to the cry: 'It hath made me mad'. As before, the madness is nothing but Hamlet's conviction that sin reigns everywhere.

The other passage occurs in the scene with Gertrude. We have to ask ourselves, in this scene, why Shakespeare brings the Ghost back at this particular moment. Obviously, 'to whet thy almost blunted purpose'; though in fact the purpose has just been showing more edge than at any time since the scene on the Battlements; for if Claudius had not been on his knees, but gaming or swearing, or if it had been Claudius, not Polonius, behind the arras, he would now be a dead man. But the Ghost is indifferent to the reasons for Hamlet's delay; the Ghost wants one thing only, and is interested in one thing only: revenge. The cry for revenge cuts across Hamlet's despair and blunderings with the unsympathetic indifference of a Greek deity; this thing is to be done, and the call of Necessity makes no allowances.

But in fact the dialogue here is in the main concerned with something else: madness, 'ecstasy'. 'Alas! he's mad!'

> QUEEN: *This is the very coinage of your brain:*
> *This bodiless creation ecstasy*
> *Is very cunning in.*
>
> HAMLET: *Ecstasy!*
> *My pulse, as yours, doth temperately keep time,*
> *And makes as healthful music: 'tis not madness*
> *That I have uttered; bring me to the test,*
> *And I the matter will reword, which madness*
> *Would gambol from. Mother, for love of grace,*
> *Lay not that flattering unction to your soul*
> *That not your trespass but my madness speaks.*

To such as cannot see ghosts, the visitation is nothing but the 'coinage of your brain'; but the Ghost is real, and the reason why it is there is the 'trespass' of Gertrude and the worse crimes of Claudius. What to others appears to be madness in Hamlet is in fact the dark shadow cast upon him by their own sins.

This is what Shakespeare means by the 'madness', and this, I think, is what he has made abundantly clear. If this is so, then Hamlet's speech to Laertes, far from being sophistical, is very serious and very significant. He is saying what Laertes himself says later: these disasters are the direct outcome of the sins of others.

(7) THE PLAYERS

Between the 'quintessence of dust' passage and Hamlet's meeting with Claudius in the prayer-scene lies a whole tract of the play which, as we ponder on its structure, gives rise to some awkward questions. It begins with a Hamlet paralysed by despair, and ends with one willing to act, though an ironic circumstance renders his willingness abortive. What has happened, to arouse Hamlet from his paralysis?

Something new has entered the circle of the action: the Players have come. Shakespeare does some odd things with these Players; it will be worth our while to see what they are, and to discover, if we can, why he does them. The idea of the 'mouse-trap' is straightforward enough, but Shakespeare gives us so very much more than this requires. First of all, when

Rosencrantz reports that the Players are coming, Shakespeare makes this the occasion for a long, anachronistic and (at first sight) completely irrelevant passage on 'the late inhibition'. This is strange, but stranger still is what follows: the Players arrive, and at once Hamlet calls for a certain passionate speech, 'Aeneas' tale to Dido'; and this continues to an intolerable length—as Shakespeare himself points out; for one of the few sensible things that Polonius says in the whole play is: 'This is too long'. Not only is it too long, but it is third-rate stuff too— 'total gules', 'o'ersized with coagulate gore'; dreadful bombast. It is not until all this is over that Hamlet has the idea of the Gonzago-play, then, the Players being dismissed, we hear the tortured soliloquy: 'O what a rogue and peasant slave am I.' Act III Scene 1 follows; we have already considered it twice. The Gonzago-play is close at hand, but before he is ready for it, Shakespeare devises yet another passage for Hamlet and the Players, in which he gives them instruction in their art—and this too might seem superfluous; and finally he writes for Hamlet a speech to Horatio which goes far beyond the matter in hand. In all this there is a great deal that a producer can leave out; why did the dramatist put it in?

The Gonzago-play, in its general outline, may be said to explain itself; and as for the Pyrrhus-Hecuba passage, we can at least hopefully tell ourselves that it is designed to give the cue for Hamlet's Hecuba-soliloquy. That leaves 'the late inhibition' and Instructions to the Players to be accounted for. But in fact the soliloquy is very far from being a sufficient explanation of the Pyrrhus-episode: a passage half as long and twice as good would have given the cue for Hecuba just as well—and therefore much better.

These are structural and stylistic points that seem to invite contemplation; there is also this, that a remarkable change comes over Hamlet as soon as the Players are mentioned. At one moment, 'it goes so heavily with my disposition' that the nobility of man delights him not, and the majestical roof is only a foul congregation of vapours. Shakespeare makes a deft transition, and at once Hamlet is all eagerness:

> He that plays the King shall be welcome; his Majesty shall have tribute of me; the adventurous knight . . . the lover . . . the humorous man . . . What players are they?

At once his indifference and despair slip from him; he discusses
theatre-politics with enthusiasm and great shrewdness. What
are we to say about this, and the anachronism of 'the late
inhibition'? I suppose there can be no doubt that Shakespeare
inserted the passage in order to make the point that the 'children
are misguided, to 'exclaim against their own succession'; but
when we have said this, we have by no means said everything.
Such topical points can be introduced into a play by a suspension
of dramatic illusion which is either deliberate, as in the Para-
basis of the Aristophanic Comedy, or as the result of sheer incompetence; but if we do not feel that dramatic illusion is in
suspense, if we do not feel that it is the author himself, not the
character, who is making the point, then, however topical and
anachronistic it is, it does become part of the play and of the
character-drawing. No one will say that there is suspension
of dramatic illusion here. No one will say that it was a
matter of indifference to Shakespeare who should make this
point—whether Hamlet or Rosencrantz or Guildenstern or
perhaps Polonius. He chooses Hamlet; and although he may
have had extra-dramatic reasons for choosing this topic, it is
in fact Hamlet who makes this intelligent point, and this
necessarily affects our estimate of him. Further, Shakespeare,
who was not a dolt, must have foreseen and designed this consequence.

Why then did he do it? What is the effect of the passage?
Possible comment would be: How eagerly does Hamlet, the
man of dreams, take refuge from life in the unreal world of the
theatre. But this would be silly. For one thing, Shakespeare is
not the man to think of the Theatre as something less 'real' than
life; to him, always, the theatre is the true image of life.
Indeed, in this particular passage: the boys 'carry it away' over
the men-players, and 'it is not very strange; for my uncle is
King in Denmark, and those who would make mows at him
while my father lived, give twenty, forty, fifty, an hundred
ducats a-piece for his picture in little'. For another thing,
Hamlet is not a man of dreams, nor does he talk about the
theatre as a dreamer, but on the contrary as an acute man of
affairs. If in this passage he is taking refuge, it is from something that is unclean and suffocating into something that is
clean, ordered and intelligible. Here, in the theatre which is

the true image of life, Hamlet finds himself once more on ground where for him there is a firm foothold.

Explanation may sometimes be subtle in a case where the thing itself is simple and bold. What we see, on the stage, is that Hamlet suddenly regains a grip on himself, and more confidence. A sharper contrast can hardly be imagined than the one between 'What is this quintessence of dust?' and the keen way in which, now, and again later, Hamlet talks of the business and the art of the theatre. Now he casually tosses to Guildenstern some information that he was far from giving them five minutes before: 'My uncle-father and my aunt-mother are deceived . . . I am but mad north-north-west.' His talk with Polonius, when he arrives, is very different from the last talk they had; then it was 'kissing carrion'; now it is 'Buz, buz'. Hamlet is in high spirits—until he runs a metaphorical sword through Polonius by calling him 'old Jephthah'. It is no escape from reality; it is simply the essential Hamlet—Hamlet as he was, as he ought to be.

Now we may try to take up a challenge that no critic of the play has the right to decline: the long Pyrrhus-Hecuba episode. What is the point of it all?

We have seen that Hamlet has recovered something of his poise, at least for the moment. As soon as he has welcomed the Players, in so friendly and courteous a manner, he flies straight at it, like a French falconer.—Flies at what? 'Come, a passionate speech!' Not any passionate speech, but a particular one, one which—oddly enough—'I chiefly loved'; taken from a play which, one is not surprised to hear, 'was never acted, or not above once'; 'and thereabouts in it especially where he speaks of Priam's slaughter.'

'A passionate speech'; we have already noticed that the connexion between passion and action receives some emphasis, though not until later scenes; but we may recall here a highly characteristic simile which Hamlet used to the Ghost:

> Haste me to know 't, that I, with wings as swift
> As meditation or the thoughts of love
> May sweep to my revenge.

Anyone might speak of the swift thoughts of love; who but Hamlet would use meditation as an image of speed? Yet meditation, on things so evil, has swept him not to action but into despair.

It is out of this despair that Hamlet calls for 'a passionate speech', 'especially where he speaks of Priam's slaughter'. He gets it—all false and bloody:

> *The rugged Pyrrhus—he whose sable arms,*
> *Black as his purpose, did the night resemble*
> *When he lay couched in the ominous horse . . .*

We are entitled to remember this when we come to:

> *Now 'tis the very witching time of night*
> *When churchyards yawn, and Hell itself breathes out*
> *Contagion to the world.*

In this twofold association of vengeance, slaughter and night there is perhaps nothing accidental.

Hamlet continues quoting, recalling to the Player's memory 'The hellish Pyrrhus,

> *. . . roasted in wrath and fire,*
> *And thus o'ersized with coagulate gore,*
> *With eyes like carbuncles.*

So it goes on, 'horridly tricked with blood'. What did Shakespeare expect his audience to think?

The dismal stuff continues implacably; we are shown the more than life-size picture of the unnerved father falling with the whiff and wind of Pyrrhus' fell sword, and senseless Ilium, punctually falling, takes prisoner Pyrrhus' ear.—What *are* we to think?

> *So, as a painted tyrant, Pyrrhus stood,*
> *And, like a neutral to his will and matter,*
> *Did nothing.*

The versification picks out these last two words; for the first time in the play we are encouraged to take note that Hamlet is doing nothing. He has called for 'a passionate speech', surely, because he is conscious how his own passions have led him nowhere; he has not swept to his revenge. But if passionate vengeance is like this, if he is trying to cast himself for the role of Pyrrhus—we see that Hamlet can never do it. But,

> *after Pyrrhus' pause,*
> *Aroused vengeance sets him new a-work;*
> *And never did the Cyclops' hammers fall*
> *On Mars's armour, forged for proof eterne,*
> *With less remorse than Pyrrhus' bleeding sword*
> *Now falls on Priam.*

What can we think, except that Hamlet's 'aroused vengeance' shall so hammer Claudius? The grim bombast goes on, to the dismay of Polonius: 'This is too long.' 'Say on; come to Hecuba.' Now it is Hamlet who interrupts:

PLAYER: *But who, O who had seen the mobled Queen* . . .
HAMLET: *The mobled Queen?*
POLONIUS: *That's good;* mobled Queen *is good.*

In what tone of voice does Hamlet interrupt? Polonius gives us a clue, if we want one. Deep and lively sympathy with others is not conspicuous in Polonius; he could interrupt his reading of a love-letter to his own daughter with the comment: '*Beautified* is a vile phrase.' So now: 'mobled Queen' is only a pretty phrase that takes his fancy. Therefore to Hamlet it is something very different. He has said to the Player 'Come to Hecuba'; but when the Player does come to Hecuba he says something that takes Hamlet aback; there seems to be something with which he had not reckoned: 'the mobled Queen'. He has been able to bear without comment the outrage on 'the milky head of reverend Priam', but 'the mobled Queen' is another matter; it moves his pity. Her bisson rheum threatens the flames—for Shakespeare's imaginary author has no truck with classic restraint; the Player too, rising to the climax, turns his colour, and has tears in 's eyes. Polonius can stand no more of it; and so ends, for Hamlet and for us, the passionate tale of vengeance—in pity and tears.

As a mere cue for the soliloquy, Aeneas' tale is too long; Polonius is quite right. Admittedly, Hecuba's grief has to be motivated, but the odd thing is that the motivation is three times as long as the grief. It is long enough to claim our attention in its own right, not merely as a prelude to something that is coming. If that were all, then we in the theatre should be puzzled and bored. Unless the dramatist has miscalculated, these forty verses about Pyrrhus were designed to make their own positive effect on our minds. Our first impression is perhaps: Hamlet, aware of his own lapsed passion, is trying to rekindle it; he would take on, if he can, the role of the vengeful Pyrrhus. Our second impression: This verse is shoddy stuff. Exactly; as the high poetry of Marcellus' speech, or of Ophelia's, was no mere dramatic ornament, but itself a dramatic instrument, so is this bad poetry: Pyrrhus' revenge is nothing but maniac bloodthirstiness. To this level Hamlet cannot descend. He asked for the speech; he gets it—and it misses fire. What does strike him is the mobled Queen, pity for the victim of this frenzy.

'Now I am alone'; and being alone he asks himself in anguish the question that Shakespeare has so far kept in the background: Why cannot I do it? The question is one that Hamlet cannot answer; *we* can, if we have been attending to the play, because while Shakespeare has been keeping the question out of sight he has been concerned with supplying the answer, against the time when the question should arise.

'Why', says Hamlet, 'can this Player be so moved by the imagined woes of a remote Hecuba, and I do nothing for my own murdered father?'

> *What would he do*
> *Had he the motive and the cue for passion*
> *That I have?*

Very likely, we may answer, nothing at all, if we are to refer Hamlet's question to real life; but Hamlet refers it to the stage:

> *He would drown the stage with tears,*
> *And cleave the general air with horrid speech . . .*

Of course he would—but if this is all, Hamlet can do it as well as any player; in fact, he is very soon doing it: 'Bloody, bawdy villain . . .' The difference between them is not (as Hamlet suggests) that he is himself lacking in natural passion; still less true is it that he is a coward. He has himself already given us a hint of the difference:

> *Seems, madam! nay, it is; I know not seems . . .*
> *. . . these indeed seem,*
> *For they are actions that a man might play:*
> *But I have that within which passeth show.*
> *These but the trappings and the suits of woe.*

The Player can give rein to his sensibility without let or hindrance; his affair is only with his imagined picture. In Hamlet, passionate action was checked by his awareness of the immense evil that has been revealed: 'Look you, I'll go pray.' This, for Hamlet, was the moment of crisis. Being what he is, he could do no other; but the moment for instinctive, passionate action went by. Through the Pyrrhus-episode he has attempted to recreate in himself the passion which did not sweep him on to his revenge. The attempt fails; such mindless stuff as this is not for Hamlet. What does touch him, in these false heroics, is 'The mobled Queen'—pity for the innocent victim. Since in his mind his passions are conjoined with something greater, namely his moral and intellectual awareness, they do not rule his actions; therefore when they are stimulated by the Player, they find issue only in wild words.

What he says next follows quite logically. The desire for vengeance is there; but his whole mind, not his passions only, must go with him in what he does; therefore,

> *I'll have these players*
> *Play something like the murder of my father*
> *Before mine uncle: I'll observe his looks;*
> *I'll tent him to the quick: if he but blench*
> *I know my course. The spirit that I have seen*
> *May be the Devil . . .*

The 'timing' of this, naturally, is important. The misgiving about the Ghost, standing where it does, sounds almost like an afterthought; certainly we cannot at this late stage make it the explanation of all that Hamlet has said, felt and thought hitherto. We must ask ourselves: what is the plain effect of this new turn of thought? If we accept, as we surely must, that so far the word of the Ghost has enjoyed full authority, both with us and with Hamlet, then we come to something like this: that the task before Hamlet is so daunting that he cannot face it even on the command of a Spirit which he has not hitherto questioned; his own Reason must convince him, beyond any doubt. If this, or something like it, is the impression that we receive, it is strengthened a little later, when again the Ghost comes into question. Hamlet says to Horatio:

> *If his occulted guilt*
> *Do not itself unkennel in one speech,*

> *It is a damned ghost that we have seen;*
> *And my imaginations are as foul*
> *As Vulcan's stithy.*

The plain import of this, surely, is not that Hamlet is racked with theological doubts; rather, the evil is so inconceivably foul that he is driven to question what really admits no questioning, namely that the Ghost was in truth his father's spirit. But if the test which he now devises proves what he does not really doubt, then 'I know my course'; he could not kill in a hot passion, still less in cold; but, his reason once fully convinced, he can constitute himself an executioner. Aroused vengeance has set him new a-work—and dangerous work it is. He does know his course; he follows it, and again he fails; and again we shall see that the reason of his failure is not irresolution or the desire to procrastinate.

The scene that follows, the decoy-scene, we have examined already.[1] Here we may briefly recall the thickening cloud of evil that it puts before us: the two confessions, the prostitution of love and of religion, the spectacle of the two young people visibly 'benetted round with villainies', the great soliloquy, the nunnery-scene. On the soliloquy, it has been well said by Dover Wilson: 'Hamlet has worn his problem to the bone.' We have seen what his problem is: how to make any sort of terms with a life that means nothing to him and offers no escape. This predicament he generalises, in a picture of life which displays only its 'fardels'; the oppressor's wrong, the proud man's contumely, the law's delays, the pangs of despised love. The answer would be suicide; but this may not be: one thinks, in dread, of what may lie beyond death. So, by thinking, by not simply shutting one's eyes and going for it, we become cowards; resolution is blunted, great enterprises abandoned.

This passage looks backwards and forwards. Looking backwards, it puts into a few words what we have been made to feel already. Why did Hamlet not march straight from the battlements and kill Claudius? 'Conscience' and 'thought' are the answer; Hamlet does not wear either moral or intellectual blinkers, like Laertes. 'Am I a coward?' Very far from it. 'Do I lack gall, to make oppression bitter?' No, but he sees that the

[1] Pages 275-282.

'oppression' is a many-headed hydra, and that one sword-thrust will not end it.

It looks forward, to Laertes and to Fortinbras. Laertes does wear blinkers; he goes straight forward, with no thought or conscience, to his goal, kills the wrong man—and himself—and sees the truth too late. Fortinbras is one who has the better fortune of not living in the prison that Denmark is; how he would have fared under the test we cannot say, though we can guess. Fortinbras has ambition in plenty. When it is misguided, he submits to the better reason of Old Norway; when it is 'divine ambition', and 'when honour's at the stake', he risks all for an egg-shell', 'an enterprise of pith and moment' indeed, undertaken without nice calculation, being, to Hamlet's first thinking, absurd. But Honour beckons, Fortinbras follows—and it is, in the end, Fortinbras who sits on the throne that should have been Hamlet's.

Before he is ready for the Gonzago-play, Shakespeare puts two other matters to our consideration: the Instructions to the Players, and Hamlet's speech to Horatio. The first of these we may read as a mere interlude: a foil to the more intense scenes that precede and follow it, and an opportunity taken by the dramatist to say something about his own art. But it may still be true, as in the passage about 'the late inhibition', that Shakespeare, in doing this, is not entirely turning his back on his play. We can at least notice that what Hamlet commends to the Players is a classical balance between passionate excess and tameness. They are to acquire a temperance that gives smoothness; they are not to overstep the modesty of nature, but to do justice to nature. We may observe this or not; but if we do, we shall notice that the advice is closely akin to the peculiar virtue that Hamlet praises in Horatio. For Horatio is not 'passion's slave'; in him, blood and judgment are so well commingled that he is superior to Fortune; he suffers everything, and therefore (in a different sense) he suffers nothing; his balance is perfect, therefore he is not overthrown. Clearly, Hamlet perceives, and values, in Horatio those qualities in which he feels himself to be lacking. His own godlike reason, his grace, his enthusiasm for beauty in all its forms—all these are a 'goodness growing to a plurisy', which make him singularly vulnerable in a desperate situation like the present. He is incomparably finer than Horatio, but we may suspect that Horatio's 'blood' would soon have settled with Claudius, and that his 'judgment' would have withstood the shock of Gertrude's guilt. This passage, reinforced it may be by the other, perhaps gives a hint of the 'solution' which the poet, had he been so ill-advised, might have given to the problem of evil, as it is presented in the play: the 'modesty of nature', *aurea mediocritas*, blood and judgment commingled, are the best defence against that which by its nature is destructive.

All these matters—not to overstep the modesty of nature, not to tear a passion to tatters, to have blood and judgment well commingled—Shakespeare finds reason to insert between the first inception of the Gonzago-play and its enactment. He reminds us too of 'the purpose of playing, whose end, both at the first and now, was and is to hold, as 'twere, the mirror up to nature'. The Play now holds a mirror up to Claudius.

The role assigned to Hamlet in the Play-scene is surely one of the most complex in the whole of drama. Superficially, he must be idle. On a deeper level, he is playing against Claudius a desperate game that must end in death for one of them. On a deeper level still, there is Hamlet 'mad'; the Hamlet whose sweetness has been corrupted into bitter obscenity. Of these levels, each is revealed in the dialogue that passes before the play begins, in what Hamlet says successively to Claudius, Polonius, and Ophelia.

> KING: *How fares our cousin Hamlet?*
> HAMLET: *Excellent, i' faith; of the chameleon's dish. I eat the air, promise-crammed; you cannot feed capons so.*

Hamlet is willing for Claudius to suppose that disappointed ambition is the source of his strange behaviour; it is plausible, and it will throw him off his guard. With Polonius, Hamlet is 'idle'; the second-rate pun, 'It was a brute part of him to kill so capital a calf there', excellently conveys the impression of irresponsible levity; and the words 'I was killed i' the Capitol' are not without their grim irony. Then it is the turn of Ophelia. We must remember what has gone before; then we shall appreciate the bitter tragedy that is half-concealed here. We must remember 'O dear Ophelia, I am ill at these numbers', and all that followed, until Hamlet cried 'Get thee to a nunnery!' The last thing that Ophelia has said is:

> *O woe is me,*
> *T' have seen what I have seen, see what I see!*

Now we are to watch Ophelia, in love with the Hamlet that was, tortured with the Hamlet that is, being assailed by his obscenities, bearing with them, unbesmirched by them.[1] If we remember these things, we shall understand Ophelia's part here. We shall also understand Hamlet—that his lewdness is deliberate, and springs from despair.

About the dumb-show very diverse views have been taken. One general consideration seems to be relevant: that it is a structural detail both in the Gonzago-play and in *Hamlet*, and that, Shakespeare being what he is, one would normally expect it to be a deliberate and efficient detail in both. In fact, a common assumption is that in *Hamlet* it is only a mechanical necessity: Shakespeare had to tell his real audience what the Gonzago-play was about. The dramatist, so it is implied, had landed himself into a contradiction: he had to tell his real audience without telling the stage-audience. On that basis one tries to show how he managed it, or one denies the contradiction. Perhaps one or the other of these can be done, but one reader at least is left uneasy: in a dramatist of Shakespeare's class, should we not expect the dumb-show to be, not a mere necessity, but an integral part of the whole?

The difficulty is that Claudius does not take public offence at what he sees. Therefore we must either explain this fact, or assume that he does not see it—or that, seeing it, he does not understand that it may concern him. This last is surely untenable: if one has committed a murder in this particular way and then sees the representation of such a murder on the stage, one would be likely to take some quiet notice of it, if not public notice.

Assume that he does not see it: what then? On the stage, of course, he can be made to look in some other direction; nothing is easier. But there is something unnatural in the spectacle of an actor on the stage carefully not taking notice of something that is being put before him, especially when that actor has previ-

---

[1] 'You are keen ,my lord, you are keen.'—'Still better, and worse.' I take it that the words 'Still better' are said directly to Hamlet, in the tone of understanding forbearance with one who is 'blasted with ecstasy'; and that the words 'and worse' are an aside, expressing Ophelia's real feelings.

ously announced his interest in the performance. But we must consider the real audience.

Claudius is on the stage, watching Hamlet and Ophelia, perhaps chatting with Gertrude. 'Hautboys play'—and Claudius takes no notice (though it would be difficult *not* to take notice of the raucous sixteenth century 'hautboys'). The dumb-show begins; the loving King and Queen are easy enough to interpret. Still Claudius does not look up. Is he going to? *This*, surely, is what will excite the audience—especially when the Poisoner appears. If Claudius does look, then Hamlet's plan is ruined (for this is our present assumption). The audience will be on tenterhooks. The show goes on; the King continues not to look. The dangerous moment passes, and we all sigh with relief: the cat was visibly half out of the bag, but fortunately Claudius was busy talking.

And what conceivable reason could Shakespeare have for contriving a tense little scene of this kind which leaves no results whatever, except bewilderment that Hamlet should have allowed it? The audience has been informed, but it has also been excited—about a situation that comes to nothing.

Professor Wilson's well known interpretation avoids the naïveté of this. It saves Shakespeare's reputation as a technician, but at a high cost to his reputation as an artist. This theory accepts that Shakespeare had reasons for imparting information to his real audience over the heads of his stage-audience, and with great boldness and ingenuity finds an answer to the question why Hamlet allowed it, by arguing that the whole thing, dumb-show and prologue too, was contrary to Hamlet's instructions to the Players, and nearly disastrous to him. To answer the whole argument in detail would take a long time; let two points only be taken.

One is that Hamlet's own comments during the performance, though they can perhaps fairly be interpreted as conveying rage and vexation, are at least no less compatible with his assumed 'idleness'—a tone of amused disdain for the performance, continually interspersed with indecencies directed at Ophelia. 'Miching mallecho', 'lurking' mischief: if Hamlet were seeing his whole plan ruined, is 'miching' the word he would use? 'The players cannot keep counsel'—as if to say: 'Terrible fellows, these actors. Always talking.' 'Pox! leave thy damnable faces, and begin.' Poor Lucianus, having entered, has been kept hanging about on the stage, unable to get on with his speech, by Hamlet's dialogue with Ophelia; he has had to improvise some business, and Hamlet calls it 'damnable faces'—as if to suggest to the Court that the whole show is really beneath their distinguished notice. There is certainly nothing in the text to compel us to assume that Hamlet is furious with the Players.

But there is a more serious objection to the theory. When the disaster of the dumb-show has been averted (by good stage-management), another disaster threatens: a Presenter arrives on the scene; and he will assuredly tell Claudius what Claudius must not yet guess, and did not notice during the dumb-show. But, 'to Hamlet's joy, and the spectator's delighted amusement, he turns out to be—a Prologue! And his three lines of silly jingle leave the cat still in the bag.'[1] That all this, on the stage, is dramatically effective, is plain enough; the question is, what does it effect? For let us get the whole thing into its context. 'The spirit that I have seen may be the Devil': is it a gross exaggeration to say that on this one throw Hamlet has staked not only his temporal but also his eternal welfare? Are Hamlet's imaginations as foul as Vulcan's stithy, or are they not? This is the issue in which Shakespeare has invited his audience to interest itself: nothing less. When the question is resolved, then Hamlet can fittingly relieve the tension by indulging in wild jocularity with Horatio—as he did on the battlements. When it is being put to the proof, why should Shakespeare direct the minds of his audience away from its importance by contriving a passage of dramatic *bravura*, and moving them to 'delighted amusement'?—a passage that would be admirable in a sophisticated comedy, but not here?

It seems worth while to examine the alternative: that Claudius does see the dumb-show, and that both Hamlet and Shakespeare intended that he should see it. This interpretation, condemned as 'the second tooth theory', does indeed involve its difficulties; indeed, if we are to regard what is afoot as a straight personal attack by Hamlet on a usurper, I would agree that they are insuperable; but so far we have found little in the play to make us think on this quite personal and secular level.

[1] *What happens in Hamlet*, p. 186.

I suggest, with diffidence, that there is something else that is worth examining. *Did* Shakespeare need the dumb-show in order to give information to his real audience? The degree of obtuseness that should be imputed to our Elizabethan ancestors is admittedly more safely estimated by an expert in sixteenth century England than by one who has barely escaped from fifth century Athens; but Shakespeare has already told his audience, twice, that they are going to see 'something like the murder of my father', and since he presumably expected them to have enough intelligence and imagination to follow the rest of *Hamlet*, it is difficult to believe that they were an audience that had to have everything spelt in capital letters before they could read it. Moreover, he has provided a useful running commentary through Hamlet himself. In other words, may the dumb-show be the result not of necessity but of deliberate contrivance?

Looking at the antecedents, we observe that Hamlet has spoken to the Players, in some contempt, of 'inexplicable dumb-shows'; therefore, when his own play begins with a dumb-show, we shall certainly take notice of it, and expect it not to be 'inexplicable'. Also, we have been told, through the mouth of Polonius, that the King and Queen 'will hear this piece of work'; they have expressed interest in it, and we should expect them to behave accordingly. Certainly, it will look odd if Claudius puts an end to it before it has begun. Again, we are hardly going behind Shakespeare's back if we remember that Claudius is quite certain that no living man knows of his awful secret; how should Claudius know that the dead man had revealed it to Hamlet? We know too, especially if we have been reading on the lines and not between them, that the secret is one that oppresses him:

> The harlot's cheek, beautied with plastering art,
> Is not more ugly to the thing that helps it
> Than is my deed to my most painted word.
> O heavy burden!

As we watch Claudius watching the dumb-show, we should not forget that he is one who carries a burden. He has also heard, from Hamlet, something that can be construed as a threat against his own life: ' . . . all but one, shall live.' As for Hamlet, if he is seeking to entrap a usurper, that is one thing; what he has told us is another: that he is testing the Ghost, and his own imaginations, as well as Claudius; that he will 'catch the conscience of the King'. The last we have heard about usurpation is 'O God, I could be bounded in a nut-shell and count myself a king of infinite space. . .' If we read in personal and political terms what Shakespeare has expressed in rather different ones, we must not be surprised if we meet trouble.

In the dumb-show (as Granville Barker has pointed out) the Poisoner is 'a fellow', presumably therefore something like a hired assassin, certainly not the King's brother. (It is not until Hamlet is good enough to explain 'This is Lucianus, Nephew to the King,' that any hint is given that the assassin is of the victim's own family.) Pouring poison into the ear is certainly a startling coincidence, but no living man knows that Claudius has done this. We note further: the murderer kisses the crown, but does not try it on his own head; and though he wins the Queen's love, there is no hint that he becomes king. If Hamlet's plan was to ensure that the royal pair should watch the play with some attention, this is well contrived. Why he, or Shakespeare, should want to ensure this is another matter.

But why does the King not stop the performance at once? Granville Barker's answer to this is reasonable: 'What should he do? If the thing is a mere coincidence, nothing. If it is a trap laid, he is not the man to walk straight into it—as he would do by stopping the play before it is well begun. He must wait and be wary.' He can of course stop the performance by simply rising and leaving the room; Kings do not have to explain their actions to lesser mortals. No; but lesser mortals cannot be prevented from drawing their own conclusions. Open displeasure at the dumb-show could, conceivably, put ideas into Hamlet's head about the manner of his father's death. But beyond all this, there is the point that Claudius has every reason to find out, if he can, what is in Hamlet's mind. The poisoning *must* be coincidence, but the entertainment, and Hamlet's behaviour, had better be watched.

The difficulty, in fact, is not to explain why Claudius tries to see it through; granted the challenge of the dumb-show, his behaviour is quite reasonable, and makes a dramatic scene.

But why challenge him at all, instead of suddenly springing the mouse-trap? Because, although we may prefer to read the whole scene as a personal duel, with the dispossessed heir as challenger, that is not the way in which Shakespeare thought and wrote it. From this 'secular' point of view it is not easy to see why Hamlet should even allow Claudius to know that there is anything in the bag at all, still less that it may be the cat. But neither the scene nor the play as a whole is conceived on this level; on this level other parts of the play too are objectionable or inexplicable—for example, the tedious irrelevance of the Reynaldo scene, or the melodramatic incident of the pirate ship. The challenge of the dumb-show, which on any level becomes dramatic, is part of the whole moral structure of the play. The thought that guilt cannot be hidden is fundamental to it. 'Foul deeds will rise', said Hamlet, at the outset; and soon we shall be hearing Gertrude say something similar: 'Guilt spills itself in fearing to be spilt.' And what is the significance of the Cellarage scene, except that there the Ghost and Hamlet wish those crimes to be kept secret which at the end of the play have to be proclaimed to all? Therefore Shakespeare deliberately contrives the dumb-show, challenging Claudius to conceal his guilty secret if he can. But he cannot; the burden of his guilt is too great for his self-control.

Before we leave the play-scene there is one more point that we should notice. The dialogue between the King and the Queen is slow, and there is perhaps good reason why it should be, but the King has something to say which may occupy our minds a little while we are watching Claudius:

> *What to ourselves in passion we propose,*
> *The passion ending, doth the purpose lose.*
> *The violence of either grief or joy*
> *Their own enactures with themselves destroy.*

Proof enough that when he was writing the Gonzago-play Shakespeare had not forgotten *Hamlet*, for it has an obvious relevance to the passion felt by Hamlet on the battlements, and to his subsequent inaction.

With the climax of the Gonzago-play, so relentlessly stage-managed by Hamlet, the King's guilt breaks through his guard. Hamlet challenged him, and has caught his conscience. But he

L

has also challenged himself, and we are to see how he can respond.

(8) HAMLET AND CLAUDIUS

Since the arrival of the players Hamlet has recovered the will to act. Although he has not swept to his revenge, he has swept to the brink of it. That the Gonzago-play has completely changed the situation, for Hamlet, is plain; he has made open declaration of war on Claudius. But we should take a wider view than this; and the play, if we attend to its design, will see to it that we do. It will not let us overlook the fact that it is the tragedy of two houses, not of Hamlet only. If we consider what Shakespeare now does, after the Gonzago-play, we shall find a very powerful development that logically connects the exposition in the first six scenes with the catastrophe. The first critical scene here is of course the very remarkable one that passes between Hamlet and Claudius.

Before he is ready for this scene, Shakespeare writes some preliminary ones. Throughout the Gonzago-play the strain on Hamlet has been great; as in the first act, he finds immediate release in jocularity with Horatio—jocularity which this time is triumphant, not anguished. After this come the scenes with Rosencranz and Guildenstern and with Polonius; the antic disposition takes charge, and the effect is to show that Hamlet, intellectually, is master of these men and of the situation. Guildenstern cannot play on Hamlet's pipe, and Polonius humours him as one would a madman. These men have come with an urgent and repeated summons from the Queen. She, as we know, was to be 'round with him':

> But if you hold it fit, after the play
> Let his Queen-mother all alone entreat him
> To show his grief: let her be round with him,
> And I'll be placed, so please it, in the ear
> Of all their conference.

So said Polonius, at the end of Act III Scene 1. But when they meet, it is not the Queen who is round with Hamlet, but he with her. With Gertrude, Hamlet does all that he set out to do; he sets her up a glass wherein she sees what she is, and she is conscience-stricken. With Polonius, he does what he never intended, though not more than Polonius deserved. With Claudius, he fails. But all this is introduced by a short and significant soliloquy:

> *'Tis now the very witching time of night,*
> *When churchyards yawn, and Hell itself breathes out*
> *Contagion to this world: now could I drink hot blood,*
> *And do such bitter business as the day*
> *Would quake to look on.*

Hamlet has demonstrated to himself that it will be an act of justice to kill Claudius; it will also be something that he longs to do—

> *to fat the region kites*
> *With this slave's offal.*

Nevertheless, it presents itself to him as something essentially evil; the language of this soliloquy can hardly fail to bring back to our minds what was said on the battlements about nights that are wholesome and nights made hideous because of unnatural sin. It was no 'airs from Heaven' that the Ghost brought, but 'blasts from Hell'; it is to this same night of contagion that Hamlet delivers himself as he resolves at last to do what he must.

From now on we see much more of Claudius than we have done yet. We know of his two great crimes; we know from his own lips that he is oppressed by the evil that he has done. Now, by Hamlet's declaration of war, he is driven further and further into villainy. First, he will, for his own safety, send Hamlet into exile—for exile is all that is mentioned yet. Rosencrantz receives his commission, and in his ignorance answers with the unconscious irony that we have already noted:

> *The cease of majesty*
> *Dies not alone, but like a gulf doth draw*
> *What's near it with it.*

The death of King Hamlet is indeed a 'gulf', a whirlpool; already we have passed its perimeter and are approaching its centre. Polonius indeed is very close to it:

> *Fare you well, my liege;*
> *I'll call upon you ere I go to bed.*

Now it is the turn of Claudius to bare his soul in a soliloquy —his 'limed soul', as he truly says. A frightening speech, if we can remember that once upon a time men believed in the possibility of eternal damnation.

> *Is there not rain enough in the sweet Heavens*
> *To wash it white as snow?*

Doubtless there is, if Claudius will fulfil Heaven's conditions. What they are, he knows; fulfil them, he cannot; he cannot give up his crown, his own ambition, and his Queen. But at least he can bow his stubborn knees, and, like more than one person in the *Agamemnon*, he says: All may be well. But that is not the way of the gods, either there or here.

The imaginative energy of Shakespeare is a thing to wonder at. On top of this profoundly tragic soliloquy comes Hamlet, and a stroke of tragic irony as great as any in Sophocles—and very like some of them. It is the only moment in the play when Hamlet is alone with Claudius; it is a moment in which he is in a black enough mood to kill him. Yet he fails to do it, and thereby, as it happens, he leads to his own death. Clearly it is a moment of great significance, but the real significance has not always been seen.

'Now might I do it pat, now he is praying'; which meant, to Bradley, 'Now I *might* do it—if only I were not irresolute.' But this is ruinous to the play; for if this were the reason, there would be a most inartistic disparity between the amplitude of the play and the individual, personal nature of its theme; tragedy of character, however great the character, ought not to be so indiscriminate as to involve the death of seven others. But Hamlet makes it clear in the rest of his speech what the reason is—and it is one which has given great offence to some of his admirers. It is not religious scruple, as if he were obeying a maxim: never kill a man while he is praying. On the contrary, it is the thought that if he strikes now, Claudius will go to Heaven. About this, let us by all means say that it shows Hamlet to be disconcertingly ruthless and unchristian in his lack of charity. But having said this let us not suppose that we have said the significant thing. The tragic point here is something much more wide-reaching than this. Hamlet is conspicuously a man of intellect, 'in apprehension how like a god'; at this, his one opportunity (as it proves), he brings his intellect to bear, and—like Oedipus—he is betrayed by it. His reason is almost god-like, but not quite; it does not show him that the whole basis of his present calculation is false. He reasons, being ignorant of the material fact; and the material fact is:

> *My words fly up, my thoughts remain below;*
> *Words without thoughts never to Heaven go.*

A Laertes in Hamlet's position would have killed his man and been safe. He would have felt no more religious scruple than Hamlet; on the other hand, he would not have 'scanned' the question. He would have acted on the instant, just as Hamlet himself does ten minutes later, with Polonius.

That Hamlet lacks charity here cannot be denied; what ruins him here however is not that, so much as what a Greek would call πλεονεξία, seeking too much, or even hybris. The mere death of Claudius is not enough for him; he will have him eternally damned as well, arrogating to himself a judgment which should be left to Heaven. He little knows how far Claudius is from being 'fit and seasoned for his passage'; not knowing this, and reaching out too far in his calculations, he misses all.

So, immediately after the Gonzago-play, we see how two of the chief actors in the tragedy move perceptibly nearer the centre of the 'gulf'. In the scene that follows a third is sucked down. Hamlet 'took him for his better', but things are not allowed to fall out so simply for Hamlet, and it was only Polonius. It was a 'rash and bloody deed'; but Shakespeare bespeaks no pity either for Polonius or, later, for Rosencrantz and Guildenstern, who did make love to the same employment. What he does say—or rather, what he makes Hamlet say, though without any hint of correction or dissent—is:

> *For this same lord*
> *I do repent; but Heaven hath pleased it so,*
> *To punish me with this, and this with me,*
> *That I must be their scourge and minister.*

This is the first of a series of events in which we are given to understand—again without any contradiction—that 'Heaven is ordinant'. What does Shakespeare mean by this? For we shall not easily suppose that on each occasion he is using only an empty formula, or simply 'characterising' Hamlet as a religious man. Shakespeare, it may be, means what Sophocles meant when his chorus-leader said:

> *Do we not see in this the hand of God?*[1]

or when he indicates that Apollo presides over the vengeance which Electra and Orestes took on their father's murderers. It is not that the god, or Heaven, *makes* these things happen; rather that there is an overruling Order, a Divine Justice, which makes itself perceptible in affairs like these; and sometimes the dramatist will make use of an apparent miracle, or a strange coincidence, to emphasise the idea that a universal law is operating.

Certainly we are left to suppose that Justice is operating here, and that it operates, on this occasion at least, when Hamlet acts on the spur of the moment. He kills an intruder, imagining, hoping, that it is Claudius. 'As kill a king!' Gertrude, horror-stricken, repeats Hamlet's dreadful accusation. 'Ay, lady, 'twas my word'—and he raises the arras; but he has not killed the king who killed a king. Yet he has hardly killed the wrong man, for the dead man was at least the king's counsellor and supporter, the treacherous father, the spy who was ready to sugar o'er the Devil himself.

In the scene with Gertrude, Shakespeare makes Hamlet cover ground which we have trodden already. There is very good reason why he should; our attention is kept fixed on what is the basis of the whole tragedy. The wickedness of Gertrude's 'incest', the sheer unreason of her preferring a man like Claudius to a paragon like her true husband—these are instances of that evil which 'takes off the rose from the fair forehead of an innocent love', and 'sweet religion makes a rhapsody of words'. Scholars speak of Shakespeare's 'obsession with sex'. In this play at least, when we listen to Hamlet's horrifying language about

> *honeying and making love*
> *Over the nasty sty,*

let us be clear what the poet is really obsessed with: it is with sin and corruption. Gertrude's guilty and unnatural love is merely one form that this has taken, as Claudius's foul and unnatural murder is another. It is from deadly sin that

---

[1] *Antigone* v. 279. See above, p. 153.

Hamlet is trying to recall his mother, to repentance and grace:

> *And when you are desirous to be blest*
> *I'll blessing beg of you.*

He paints her sin in the dirty colours in which he sees it.

The struggle for Gertrude's soul ends with a return to the struggle against Claudius:

> *I must to England; you know that?*

At once Hamlet returns to the mood of the last soliloquy, in which Hell itself was breathing out contagion to the world. The knavery of Claudius he will meet by knavery of his own: 'Let it work!'

'There is an old saying that high prosperity, when it reaches its peak, dies not childless, but has offspring; out of good fortune is born misery without end. But my thought takes a lonely path of its own. It is wickedness that begets a numerous offspring, resembling its parents; but in the house that pursues Justice, prosperity breeds fair fortune. Among the wicked, old sin breeds new sin, and a wicked spirit of recklessness, with black ruin for the family.'[1] *Hamlet* might serve as an illustration of this Aeschylean text. Claudius, the 'limed soul', in struggling to be free, is still more engaged, and in his struggle he smears others with the same deadly concoction in which he himself is held fast.

To begin with, there are the consequences, to Claudius, of the death of Polonius. No fewer than three times does he speak of the danger in which this involves him:

> *O heavy deed!*
> *It had been so with us, had we been there . . .*
> *Alas, how shall this bloody deed be answered?*
> *It will be laid to us, whose providence*
> *Should have kept short, restrain'd, and out of haunt*
> *This mad young man.*

Again:

> *So, haply, slander—*
> *Whose whisper o'er the world's diameter*
> *As level as the cannon to its blank*
> *Transports his poisoned shot—may miss our name*
> *And hit the woundless air.*

---

[1] *Agamemnon* 751-771, paraphrased.

Again:

> *How dangerous is it that this man goes loose!*
> *Yet must not we put the strong law on him:*
> *He's loved of the distracted multitude . . .*

Therefore, as we now learn, the King will add another treacherous crime to his tally: Hamlet is to be murdered in England:

> *Till I know 'tis done,*
> *Howe'er my haps, my joys were ne'er begun.*

This evil intention is frustrated, and the failure of the King's plot is presented by Shakespeare in a way that must be carefully observed. Unlike the Greek dramatists, Shakespeare did not work in a convention that permitted him to use the gods in his theatre; nevertheless, references to Providence now become very frequent, and perhaps we should not dismiss them too lightly. For instance, if we remain with our feet firmly planted on the most prosaic level we can find, secure in the knowledge that at least we can fall no lower, we shall have to say, when the pirate-ship turns up, that the magnificent Shakespeare is condescending to a stale contrivance that would discredit a second-rate melodrama; and having said this we shall for very shame begin to cast about for excuses or explanations, like the prosaic critics who do not understand why Aeschylus freezes the Strymon.

We will go back to the point where Hamlet is being sent to England. He has his suspicions, and the way in which they are conveyed to us is worth noting:

HAMLET: *For England!*
KING: *Aye, Hamlet.*
HAMLET: *Good.*
KING: *So 'tis, if thou knew'st our purposes.*
HAMLET: *I see a cherub that sees them.*

One of the older editors explains: Hamlet means that he divines them, or has an inkling of them. That is indeed what he means, but what he says is: 'I see a cherub that sees them', and the phrase is not idly chosen.

But before he puts Hamlet on board ship, Shakespeare contrives, in a rough and ready way, that he shall meet the Norwegian Captain, and in an even rougher and readier way, he clears the stage for a final soliloquy. At first sight this soliloquy is not easy to understand. But the meaning of the whole passage becomes plain when we see that it is a parallel to the Pyrrhus-Hecuba passage. Superficially, each of them is super-fluous—proof enough that Shakespeare thought them necessary. Each ends with a soliloquy, and each soliloquy with an important declaration. Naturally, to these formal resemblances an inner one corresponds, as is clear from the fact that each soliloquy asks the same torturing question: Why cannot I act? But how far, or how deep, does the resemblance go?

In each case Hamlet is contrasted with someone who *can* act. The earlier passage showed us that Hamlet, by no means defi-cient in passion, cannot give rein to it, like the Player. Now he is set over against Fortinbras, and the theme is Honour.

> *How all occasions do inform against me*
> *And spur my dull revenge! What is a man*
> *If his chief good and market of his time*
> *Be but to sleep and feed? A beast, no more.*
> *Sure, He that made us with such large discourse,*
> *Looking before and after, gave us not*
> *That capability and godlike reason*
> *To fust in us unused . . .*

If any man has 'that capability and godlike reason' it is Hamlet himself; no one could be more of a man, less of a beast that only sleeps and feeds. So that when, a moment later, he again asks himself the baffling question

> *Why yet I live to say* This thing's to do,

we know that the answer is not 'bestial oblivion'. Nor is it cowardice. The answer is hidden from Hamlet, but it would indeed be a strange play if it were also hidden from us. First he was held back by a sense of evil that paralysed him—an evil that he came to think barely credible. The paralysis disappeared; he convinced his reason, and was ready to do it—not out of passion but as a necessary act of justice. Yet it was precisely his reasoning that betrayed him: if only he had known what Claudius knew so well at that moment, Claudius would have been dead. To follow Reason is godlike, but can be perilous to such as are not gods.

Now he is confronted with something which seems to him to deny all reason:

> *Why then, the Polack never will defend it.*

He has before him men who are following a different guide to conduct—twenty thousand men going to their graves like beds, all for so miserable plot of ground,

> *Led by a delicate and tender prince*
> *Whose spirit with divine ambition puffed*
> *Makes mouths at the invisible event*
> *Exposing what is mortal and unsure*
> *To all that fortune, death and danger dare*
> *Even for an eggshell.*

True greatness, he reflects, is to demand indeed great argument before acting, but to find that argument even in a straw, 'when honour's at the stake'. 'How stand I then?'

Inspired by this example, Hamlet decides: he must follow where Honour beckons. But we must observe how the speech ends, for the end illuminates much:

> *O from this time forth*
> *My thoughts be bloody, or be nothing worth.*

To Fortinbras, following Honour is—we must not say easy, but at least simple; to Hamlet, placed as he is, it is not. We must not sentimentalise him. He was ready to 'make a ghost of him that lets me', and he has little compunction in sending Rosencrantz and Guildenstern to their death; nevertheless, he has already told us, twice, what he thinks of this business. Shakespeare makes it quite plain what is happening to him—that he feels himself being inexorably dragged down, as on a 'massy wheel', to actions which, being free, he would condemn. 'Hell itself breathes out contagion to this world', and he is affected by it. The same thought he repeats to Gertrude:

> *They must sweep my way*
> *And marshal me to knavery.*

The path of honour, to Fortinbras, is straightforward; in Denmark, Hamlet's fineness must necessarily suffer corruption.

It has been the burden of all Hamlet's self-questionings hitherto, that he is losing his honour.

> *Who calls me villain? breaks my pate across,*
> *Plucks off my beard, and blows it in my face?*

Now, having surmounted his paralysis, having convinced his reason, having reconciled himself to 'knavery', he becomes resolute. But by now it is dangerously late; Claudius is fully warned and deeply committed. Indeed, the question is whether the villain Claudius will not destroy Hamlet, and triumph. In the event, villainy does triumph, to the extent that it destroys Hamlet; but we can hardly fail to notice how often, in what remains of the play, Shakespeare reminds us that there is an overruling Providence which, though it will not intervene to save Hamlet,[1] does intervene to defeat Claudius, and does guide events to a consummation in which evil frustrates itself, even though it destroys the innocent by the way.

We may not follow Hamlet's fortunes yet without distorting the structure; for Shakespeare now engages our interest in other events, and these are not merely contemporaneous with those but are also complementary to them, cohering with them in the wide design of the play. As in the first six scenes, we must be prepared for significant juxtaposition.

(9) PROVIDENCE

What we are to be concerned with is the madness and then the death of Ophelia, the return of Laertes, the willingness of 'the false Danish dogs' to rebel against Claudius, the failure of his present plot against Hamlet, and the hatching of the new double plot by Claudius and Laertes together. If we try to take, as the essence of the play, the duel between Hamlet and Claudius, or the indecision of Hamlet, or any other theme which is only a part, not the whole, of the play, then much of this act is only peripheral; but everything coheres closely and organically when we see that the central theme is the disastrous growth of evil.

How, for instance, does Shakespeare introduce the madness of Ophelia? In a very arresting way indeed:

> *I will not speak with her.*

These few words reveal much. We last saw Gertrude utterly contrite at the sins which Hamlet had revealed to her. She has received a straight hint that she is living with her husband's murderer; she has seen Polonius killed, and his daughter crazed —all this the direct or indirect consequence of the villainy in which she has been a partner. No wonder that she would avoid

---

[1] Cf. p. 170: the discussion of Antigone's last speech.

being confronted with this latest disaster: 'I will not speak with her.'

But Horatio tells her that she must, lest worse happen:

> 'Twere good she were spoken with, for she may strew
> Dangerous conjectures in ill-breeding minds.

She gives way, hoping to make the best of it:

> Let her come in.—
> To my sick soul, as sin's true nature is,
> Each toy seems prelude to some great amiss.
> So full of artless jealousy is guilt,
> It spills itself in fearing to be spilt.

She is frightened by her knowledge of her own guilt, but against this she sets the thought that too great consciousness of guilt, and too great circumspection in hiding it, may of themselves reveal that guilt to the world. It is one of the themes that run through the play, that sin breaks through every attempt to keep it secret: 'Foul deeds will rise.' The oath of the cellarage-scene was sworn in vain.

After this it is the King's turn to show what offspring his own sins are breeding for him, and what he says does but repeat, more urgently, what he has said before.[1]

> When sorrows come, they come not single spies,
> But in battalias.

Polonius is dead, Hamlet gone, the people mudded—

> and we have done but greenly
> In hugger-mugger to inter him—

and Laertes has come secretly from France, to hear 'pestilent speeches of his father's death'.

> O my dear Gertrude, this,
> Like to a murdering-piece, in many places
> Gives me superfluous death.

Immediately upon this comes Laertes, at the head of an incipient rebellion. The Court may be subservient and complaisant, but among the people Claudius commands little respect:

> Thick and unwholesome in their thoughts and whispers
> For good Polonius' death,

---

[1] In Act III, Scene 5. See above, p. 317.

and bearing 'great love' for the exiled Prince. Claudius has given a handle to any enemy he may have, and the people are willing to take from him the crown which he has done so much to win. But he is equal to the occasion; Hamlet has gone to his death, and Laertes can be talked over.

With Laertes he has little trouble:

LAERTES: *And so have I a noble father lost;*
A sister driven into desperate terms,
Whose worth, if praises may go back again,
Stood challenger on mount of all the age.

KING: *Break not your sleeps for that: you must not think*
That we are made of stuff so flat and dull,
That we can let our beard be shook with danger,
And think it pastime. You shortly shall hear more:
I loved your father, and we love ourself;
And that, I hope, will teach you to imagine—
Enter a Messenger.

Sophocles too used Messengers in this way.[1] Claudius is confronted with news which we have briefly learned already. His plot has failed; Hamlet is back in Denmark. To Claudius it is incredible:

How should it be? how otherwise?

The full story of his escape we are still to learn, but we may suspect that there was indeed a cherub that saw the King's purposes. But for the plot that has failed he substitutes another, since he 'loves himself'. Laertes consents—like two other men, now dead—to serve Claudius:

KING: *Will you be ruled by me?*
LAERTES: *I will, my lord,*
So you will not o'errule me to a peace.
KING: *To thine own peace.*

But hardly so, since it involves Laertes first in treachery, then in death.

Again a Messenger interrupts the King:

KING: *. . . wherein but sipping,*
If he by chance escape your venomed stuck,
Our purpose may hold there.—
Enter the Queen.
How now, sweet Queen?

[1] See above, pp. 74, 75.

QUEEN: *One woe doth tread upon another's heel,*
          So fast they follow.—Your sister's drowned, Laertes.

Death has struck again. It is the fitting climax to this part of the play. Since it began, with the Queen's vain declaration: 'I will not speak with her', our thoughts have not been encouraged to stray very far from the idea of evil breeding evil, and leading to ruin. Each toy *is* prelude to some great amiss. The present one reaches its consummation in the scene that follows; and the horrible spectacle of Hamlet and Laertes struggling with each other beside the grave[1] points the way to the end. Sophocles, in the *Electra*, has a vivid image of the irresistible advance of Vengeance on the criminals:

ἴδεθ' ὅπου προνέμεται
τὸ δυσέριστον αἷμα φυσῶν Ἄρης —

See how Ares (Violence) advances, breathing implacable slaughter

except that the word which I have translated 'advances' really means 'grazes its way forward', as a flock will slowly and deliberately eat its way across a pasture, in a way which nothing but satiety will stop. The same feeling of inevitability prevails here.

At the end of the Churchyard-scene we are told what happened on the North Sea. We last saw Hamlet being sent away, under guard, for 'instant death'. It looked as if Claudius might triumph. But Hamlet is home again. All we know of the manner of his escape is what we have learned from his letter to Horatio; everything turned on the veriest accident—seconded by Hamlet's own impetuous valour. Shakespeare now chooses to amplify the story; and the colour he gives it is surely a definite and significant one, and entirely harmonious with the colours of the whole play.

> *Sir, in my heart there was a kind of fighting*
> *That would not let me sleep.*

This time, as when he killed Polonius, and as always henceforth, Hamlet yields to the prompting of the occasion:

---

[1] Not *in* the grave. To what Granville Barker has to say about this (*Introduction to Hamlet*, 162 f) add that Ophelia's body is not coffined—or how could Laertes say: 'Hold off the earth awhile, Till I have caught her once more in mine arms'?

HAMLET: *Rashly—*
> *And praised be rashness for it: let us know*
> *Our indiscretion sometimes serves us well*
> *When our deep plots do pall; and that should teach us*
> *There's a divinity that shapes our ends*
> *Rough-hew them how we will,—*

HORATIO: *That is most certain.*

HAMLET: *Up from my cabin . . .*

This is a very different Hamlet from the one who sought confirmation—or disproof—of what the Ghost had told him, and who sought more than mere death for Claudius. It is the Hamlet who did the 'rash and bloody deed' on Polonius, where also 'rashness' serves the ends of Providence.

As for what Hamlet did to Rosencrantz and Guildenstern,[1] we must be on our guard against seeing the obvious and missing what is significant. There is no irrelevant reproof in Horatio's brief comment:

> *So Rosencrantz and Guildenstern go to 't.*

Hamlet continues:

> *Why, man, they did make love to this employment;*
> *They are not on my conscience; their defeat*
> *Doth by their own insinuation grow.*
> *'Tis dangerous when the baser nature comes*
> *Between the pass and fell incensèd points*
> *Of mighty opposites.*

This is not Hamlet trying to exculpate himself. Shakespeare is not interested in that kind of thing here. He is saying: 'This is what happens in life, when foolish men allow themselves to be used by such as Claudius, and to get themselves involved in desperate affairs like these.' To prove that this is what he meant, we may once more reflect what Horatio might have said, and then listen to what he does say:

> *Why, what a King is this!*

How could Shakespeare more decisively draw our attention away from a nice and private appraisal of Hamlet's character, as expressed in this affair, and direct it to the philosophic or 'religious' framework in which it is set? Horatio says just what Laertes says later: 'The King! the King's to blame.'

[1] See above, p. 252.

It was a lucky chance, though not an unlikely one, that Hamlet had his father's signet in his purse; but this is how Hamlet puts it:

> *Why, even in this was Heaven ordinant.*

It was also a lucky chance that the pirate ship caught up with them at this time; and our natural response is: Here too Heaven was ordinant. But it was no lucky chance that Hamlet (with his well-known indecision) was the first and only man to board the pirate.[1]

Once more, the English tragic poet recalls the Greek. In the *Agamemnon* 'some god' took the helm of the King's ship, saved it from the storm, and brought it to land, that Agamemnon might suffer what Justice demanded. Hamlet is a hero very different from Agamemnon, but he too is brought safely back from the sea by Providence; it is no part of the universal design that villainy should triumph. And further: it is through the actions of men that the designs of Providence are fulfilled—through the reckless courage of Hamlet, through the valour and intelligence of the Greeks, in the *Persae*, through the resolution of Electra and Orestes in Sophocles' play. The gods and men are 'partners', μεταίτιοι. This is not to say that the religion or philosophy of Shakespeare was the same as that of Aeschylus and Sophocles, nor that his drama was influenced by theirs, either directly or indirectly; only that they were all tragic poets, grappling with the same fundamental realities, and expressing themselves in what is recognisably the same dramatic language.

Once more Hamlet and Claudius confront each other, and Claudius, we know, has another deadly plot ready. Horatio warns Hamlet that the time is short; but Hamlet replies 'The interim is mine'.

But there is no interim at all; the tide has run out, and Hamlet seems to feel it: 'If his fitness speaks, mine is ready.' That Claudius is fit for death is plain enough; but what of Hamlet? 'I will forstall their repair hither,' says Horatio, 'and say you are not fit.' Every word in this dialogue makes us feel that the tragic action is at last poised, ready for the catastrophe.

---

[1] On contemporary ideas about Chance and Providence, Dr Joseph has written a valuable commentary (*Conscience and the King*, pp. 130-151).

Hamlet has his 'gaingiving', but he defies augury: 'Mine is ready.' Even more forcibly we are made to feel that Providence is working in the events; an eternal Law is being exemplified: 'There is a special providence in the fall of a sparrow.' But if Providence is working, what is the catastrophe intended to reveal?

The significant design of the catastrophe is unmistakeable. The action of the play began with poison, and it ends with a double poison, that of Claudius and that of Laertes. Gertrude, left to Heaven as the Ghost had commanded, drinks Claudius's poison literally as she had once done metaphorically. Claudius is killed by both, for Hamlet first runs him through with Laertes' poisoned sword, and then makes him drink his own poisoned cup. Laertes himself confesses: 'I am most justly slain by my own treachery'; and in his dying reconciliation with Hamlet he accepts, in effect, what Hamlet had said to him earlier in his own defence:

> *Hamlet does it not, Hamlet denies it.*
> *Who does it then? His madness. If 't be so,*
> *Hamlet is of the faction that is wronged.*

For Hamlet's 'madness' was but the reflection of the evil with which he found himself surrounded, of which Claudius was the most prolific source. So Laertes declares: 'The King! The King's to blame.' Hamlet's death shall not come on Laertes, nor the death of Polonius on Hamlet, but both on Claudius. Horatio, on the other hand, is forcibly prevented from sharing in this common death. He has stood outside the action; he has not been tainted. What is taking place is something like the working-out of Dikê, and in this there is no place for heroic suicide. Hamlet is destroyed not because evil works mechanically, but because his nature was such that he could not confront it until too late.

> *Fie, 'tis an unweeded garden,*
> *That grows to seed; things rank and gross in nature*
> *Possess it merely.*

Weeds can choke flowers. These weeds have choked Ophelia, and at last they choke Hamlet, because he could not do the coarse work of eradicating them. First, his comprehensive awareness of evil, reversing every habit of his mind, left him prostrate in anguish and apathy; then, the desire for vengeance being aroused, he missed everything by trying to encompass too much; finally, pursuing Honour when it was nearly too late, he found it, but only in his own death. So finely poised, so brittle a nature as Hamlet's, is especially vulnerable to the destructive power of evil.

In the first act, the sinister Claudius drank to Hamlet's health, and guns proclaimed to Heaven and Earth the 'heavy-headed revel'. Now in the last scene the guns roar again: Claudius is drinking to Hamlet's death. The action has completed its circle. The guns remind us of what Hamlet said when first they spoke: some vicious mole of nature, like their birth, wherein they are not guilty; the overgrowth of some complexion that breaks down the pales and forts of reason; some habit that o'erleavens, or works too strongly for, plausive manners—all these bring corruption to a man whose virtues else may be 'pure as grace, as infinite as man may undergo'. All this we see fulfilled in Hamlet. Gertrude's sin, his 'birth', has worked in his mind to spoil it; his philosophic 'complexion', too absolute, was overthrown and turned to 'madness'; his habit of 'godlike reason' betrayed him at the great crisis.

But does Hamlet 'in the general censure take corruption'? This is a question which Shakespeare answers by letting off guns for a third time.

> *Let four captains*
> *Bear Hamlet, like a soldier, to the stage;*
> *For he was likely, had he been put on,*
> *T' have proved most royally: and for his passage*
> *The soldiers' music and the rites of war*
> *Speak loudly for him.*

This time the guns proclaim neither swinish coarseness nor black treachery, but Honour.

(10) CONCLUSION

This examination of *Hamlet* has been based on the same assumptions as our examination of certain Greek plays: that the dramatist said exactly what he meant, through the medium of his art, and means therefore exactly what he has said. We have tried therefore to observe what in fact he has said, considering every scene and every considerable passage (as one would in analysing a picture, for example, or a piece of music), not passing over this or that because it did not happen to interest us, or illustrate our point; nor being too ready to disregard a passage on the grounds that it was put there for some extraneous reason; remembering too that a dramatist can 'say' things by means other than words. I do not so flatter myself as to suppose that anything new has been brought to light. Nevertheless, if this general account of the play is acceptable, if its structure has been made to appear purposeful, in details big and small, such that the interpretation (blunders excepted) carries some measure of authority, then the critical method and the assumptions on which it is based may be held to be sound. It seems to me that this may be true.

As we said at the outset, the first thing that strikes us, or should strike us, when we contemplate the play is that it ends in the complete destruction of the two houses that are concerned. The character of Hamlet and the inner experience that he undergoes are indeed drawn at length and with great subtlety, and we must not overlook the fact; nevertheless, the architectonic pattern just indicated is so vast as to suggest at once that what we are dealing with is no individual tragedy of character, however profound, but somethin: more like religious drama; and this means that unless we are ready, at every step, to relate the dramatic situation to its religious or philosophical background —in other words, to look at the play from a point of view to which more recent drama has not accustomed us—then we may not see either the structure or the meaning of the play as Shakespeare thought them.

Why do Rosencrantz and Guildenstern die, and Ophelia, and Laertes? Are these disasters casual by-products of 'the tragedy of a man who could not make up his mind'? Or are they necessary parts of a firm structure? Each of these disasters we can refer to something that Hamlet has done or failed to do, and we can say that each reveals something more of Hamlet's character; but if we see no more than this we are short-sighted, and are neglecting Shakespeare's plain directions in favour of our own. We are told much more than this when we hear Horatio, and then Laertes, cry 'Why, what a King is this!', 'The King, the King's to blame'; also when Guildenstern says, with a deep and unconscious irony 'We here give up ourselves . . . ', and when Laertes talks of 'contagious blastments'. Shakespeare puts before us a group of young people, friends or lovers, none of them wicked, one of them at least entirely virtuous, all surrounded by the poisonous air of Denmark (which also Shakespeare brings frequently and vividly before our minds), all of them brought to death because of its evil influences. Time after time, either in some significant patterning or with some phrase pregnant with irony, he makes us see that these people are partners in disaster, all of them borne down on the 'massy wheel' to 'boisterous ruin'.

In this, the natural working-out of sin, there is nothing mechanical. That is the philosophic reason why character and situation must be drawn vividly. Neither here nor in Greek drama have we anything to do with characters who are puppets in the hands of Fate. In both, we see something of the power of the gods, or the designs of Providence; but these no more override or reduce to unimportance the natural working of individual character than the existence, in the physical world, of universal laws overrides the natural behaviour of natural bodies. It is indeed precisely in the natural behaviour of men, and its natural results, in given circumstances, that the operation of the divine laws can be discerned. In *Hamlet*, Shakespeare draws a complete character, not for the comparatively barren purpose of 'creating' a Hamlet for our admiration, but in order to show how he, like the others, is inevitably engulfed by the evil that has been set in motion, and how he himself becomes the cause of further ruin. The conception which unites these eight persons in one coherent catastrophe may be said to be this: evil, once started on its course, will so work as to attack and overthrow impartially the good and the bad; and if the dramatist makes us feel, as he does, that a Providence is ordinant in all this, that, as with the Greeks, is his way of universalising the particular event.

Claudius, the arch-villain, driven by crime into further crime, meets at last what is manifestly divine justice. 'If his fitness speaks . . . ' says Hamlet; the 'fitness' of Claudius has been speaking for a long time. At the opposite pole stands Ophelia, exposed to corruption though uncorrupted, but pitifully destroyed as the chain of evil uncoils itself. Then Gertrude, one of Shakespeare's most tragic characters: she is the first, as Laertes

is the last, to be tainted by Claudius; but while he dies in forgiveness and reconciliation, no such gentle influence alleviates her
end. In the bedchamber scene Hamlet had pointed out to her
the hard road to amendment; has she tried to follow it? On this,
Shakespeare is silent; but her last grim experience of life is to
find that 'O my dear Hamlet, the drink, the drink! I am
poisoned'—poisoned, as she must realise, by the cup that her
new husband had prepared for the son whom she loved so
tenderly. After her own sin, and as a direct consequence of it,
everything that she holds dear is blasted. Her part in this
tragedy is indeed a frightening one. She is no Claudius, recklessly given to crime, devoid of any pure or disinterested motive.
Her love for her son shines through every line she speaks; this,
and her affection for Ophelia, show us the Gertrude that might
have been, if a mad passion had not swept her into the arms of
Claudius. By this one sin she condemned herself to endure,
and, still worse, to understand, all its devastating consequences:
her son driven 'mad', killing Polonius, denouncing herself and
her crime in cruel terms that she cannot rebut, Ophelia driven
out of her senses and into her grave—nearly a criminal's grave;
all her hopes irretrievably ruined. One tragic little detail, just
before the end, shows how deeply Shakespeare must have pondered on his Gertrude. We know that she has seen the wild
struggle in the graveyard between Laertes and Hamlet. When
the Lord enters, to invite Hamlet to the fencing-match, he says:
'The Queen desires you to use some gentle entertainment to
Laertes before you fall to play.' 'She well instructs me', says
Hamlet. What can this mean, except that she has vague fears
of Laertes' anger, and a pathetic hope that Hamlet might
appease it, by talk more courteous than he had used in the
graveyard? It recalls her equally pathetic wish that Ophelia's
beauty and virtue might 'bring him to his wonted ways again'.
The mischief is always much greater than her worst fears. We
soon see how Hamlet's gentle entertainment is received by
Laertes; and she, in the blinding flash in which she dies, learns
how great a treachery had been prepared against her Hamlet.

    We cannot think of Gertrude's death, and the manner of it,
without recalling what the Ghost had said: Leave her to
Heaven. But if we are to see the hand of Providence—whatever
that may signify—in her death, can we do other with the death

of Polonius? A 'casual slaughter'? A 'rash and bloody deed'?
Certainly; and let us by all means blame Hamlet for it, as also
for the callousness with which he sends Rosencrantz and
Guildenstern to their doom; but if we suppose that Shakespeare
contrived these things only to show us what Hamlet was like,
we shall be treating as secular drama what Shakespeare designed
as something bigger. In fact, Hamlet was *not* like this, any
more than he was, by nature, hesitant or dilatory; any more
than Ophelia was habitually mad. This is what he has become.
The dramatist does indeed direct us to regard the killing of
Polonius in two aspects at once: it is a sudden, unpremeditated
attack made by Hamlet, 'mad', on one who he hopes will prove
to be Claudius; and at the same time it is the will of Heaven:

> *For this same lord*
> *I do repent; but Heaven hath pleased it so*
> *To punish me with this and this with me,*
> *That I must be their scourge and minister.*

Surely this is exactly the same dramaturgy that we meet in
Sophocles' *Electra*. When Orestes comes out from killing his
mother, Electra asks him how things are. 'In the *palace*',[1] he
says, 'all is well—if Apollo's oracle was well.' Perhaps it was a
'rash and bloody deed'; it seems to bring Orestes little joy. We
may think of it what we like; Sophocles does not invite us to
approve, and if we suppose that he does, we have not understood his play, or his gods. Apollo approves, and Orestes, though
he acts for his own reasons, is the gods' 'scourge and minister'.
Polonius, no unworthy Counsellor of this King, a mean and
crafty man whose soul is mirrored in his language no less than
in his acts, meets a violent death while spying; and that such a
man should so be killed is, in a large sense, right. Hamlet may
'repent'; Orestes may feel remorse at a dreadful act, but in each
case Heaven was ordinant.

The death of Laertes too is a coherent part of this same pattern. To this friend of Hamlet's we can attribute one fault; nor
are we taken by surprise when we meet it, for Shakespeare has
made his preparations. Laertes is a noble and generous youth,
but his sense of honour has no very secure foundations—and

---

[1] I italicise this word in order to represent Sophocles' untranslateable μέν,
which suggests a coming antithesis that in fact is not expressed.

Polonius' farewell speech to him makes the fact easy to understand. His natural and unguarded virtue, assailed at once by
his anger, his incomplete understanding of the facts, and the
evil suggestions of Claudius, gives way; he falls into treachery,
and through it, as he comes to see, he is 'most justly killed'.

Of Rosencrantz and Guildenstern, two agreeable though un-
distinguished young men, flattered and suborned and cruelly
destroyed, there is no more to be said; but there remains
Hamlet, last and greatest of the eight. Why must he be destroyed? It would be true to say that he is destroyed simply
because he has failed to destroy Claudius first; but this is 'truth'
as it is understood between police-inspectors, on duty. The
dramatic truth must be something which, taking this in its
stride, goes much deeper; and we are justified in saying 'must
be' since this catastrophe too is presented as being directed by
Providence, and therefore inevitable and 'right'. If 'there is a
special providence in the fall of a sparrow', there surely is in the
fall of a Hamlet.

Of the eight victims, we have placed Claudius at one pole and
Ophelia at the other; Hamlet, plainly, stands near Ophelia. In
both Hamlet and Ophelia we can no doubt detect faults: she
ought to have been able to see through Polonius, and he should
not have hesitated. But to think like this is to behave like a
judge, one who must stand outside the drama and sum up from
a neutral point of view; the critic who tries to do this would be
better employed in a police-court than in criticism. We must
remain within the play, not try to peer at the characters through
a window of our own constructing. If we do remain within the
play, we observe that what Shakespeare puts before us, all the
time, is not faults that we can attribute to Ophelia and Hamlet,
but their virtues; and when he does make Hamlet do things
deserving of blame, he also makes it evident on whom the blame
should be laid. The impression with which he leaves us is not
the tragedy that one so fine as Hamlet should be ruined by one
fault; it is the tragedy that one so fine should be drawn down
into the gulf; and, beyond this, that the poison let loose in
Denmark should destroy indiscriminately the good, the bad and
the indifferent. Good and bad, Hamlet and Claudius, are
coupled in the one sentence 'If his fitness speaks, mine is ready'.
That Claudius is 'fit and seasoned for his passage' is plain enough

is it not just as plain that Hamlet is equally 'ready'? What has
he been telling us, throughout the play, but that life can henceforth have no meaning or value to him? Confronted by what
he sees in Denmark, he, the man of action, has been reduced to
impotence; the man of reason has gone 'mad'; the man of
religion has been dragged down to 'knavery', and has felt the
contagions of Hell. There is room, though not very much, for
subtle and judicious appraisal of his character and conduct; the
core of his tragedy is not here, but in the fact that such sur-
passing excellence is, like the beauty and virtue of Ophelia,
brought to nothing by evil. Through all the members of these
two doomed houses the evil goes on working, in a concatenation

> *Of carnal, bloody and unnatural acts,*
> *Of accidental judgments, casual slaughters,*
> *Of deaths put on by cunning and forced cause,*

until none are left, and the slate is wiped clean.

The structure of *Hamlet*, then, suggests that we should treat
it as religious drama, and when we do, it certainly does not lose
either in significance or in artistic integrity. As we have seen
more than once, it has fundamental things in common with
Greek religious drama—yet in other respects it is very different,
being so complex in form and texture. It may be worth while
to enquire, briefly, why this should be so.

One naturally compares it with the two Greek revenge-
tragedies, the *Choephori* and Sophocles' *Electra*, but whether
we do this, or extend the comparison to other Greek religious
tragedies like the *Agamemnon* or *Oedipus Tyrannus* or *Antigone*,
we find one difference which is obviously pertinent to our enquiry: in the Greek plays the sin, crime or error which is the
mainspring of the action is specific, while in Hamlet it is something more general, a quality rather than a single act. Thus,
although there are crimes enough in the *Oresteia*, what we are
really concerned with, throughout the trilogy, is the problem
of avenging or punishing crime. The *Agamemnon* is full of
hybris, blind folly, blood-lust, adultery, treachery; but what
humanity is suffering from, in the play, is not these sins in
themselves, but a primitive conception of Justice, one which
uses, and can be made to justify, these crimes, and leads to
chaos; and the trilogy ends not in any form of reconciliation or

forgiveness among those who have injured each other, nor in any purging of sin, or acceptance of punishment, but in the resolution of the dilemma.

Hamlet resembles the *Choephori* in this, that the murder of a King, and adultery, or something like it, are the crimes which have to be avenged; also that these can be avenged only through another crime, though perhaps a sinless one; but the differences are deep and far-reaching. They are not merely that Orestes kills, and Hamlet shrinks from killing. We may say that both in the Greek trilogy and in Shakespeare's play the Tragic Hero, ultimately, is humanity itself; and what humanity is suffering from, in *Hamlet* is not a specific evil, but Evil itself. The murder is only the chief of many manifestations of it, the particular case which is the mainspring of the tragic action.

This seems to be typical. In the *Antigone* a whole house is brought down in ruin, and, again, the cause is quite a specific one. It is nothing like the comprehensive wickedness of Iago, or the devouring ambition of Macbeth, or the consuming and all-excluding love of Antony and Cleopatra. It is, quite precisely, that Creon makes, and repeats, a certain error of judgment, ἁμαρτία; and I use the phrase 'error of judgment' meaning not that it is venial, nor that it is purely intellectual, but that it is specific. It is not a trivial nor a purely intellectual mistake if a man, in certain circumstances, rejects the promptings of humanity, and thinks that the gods will approve; but this is what Creon does, and the tragedy springs from this and from nothing else. He is not a wicked man—not lecherous or envious or ambitious or vindictive. All this is irrelevant. He is simply the man to make and maintain this one specific and disastrous error.

This contrast between the specific and the general obviously has a close connexion with the contrast between the singleness of the normal Greek tragic structure and the complexity of *Hamlet*. In the first place, since Shakespeare's real theme is not the moral or theological or social problem of crime and vengeance, still less its effect on a single mind and soul, but the corroding power of sin, he will present it not as a single 'error of judgment' but as a hydra with many heads. We have shown, let us hope, how this explains, or helps to explain, such features of the play as, so to speak, the simultaneous presentation of three Creons: Claudius, Gertrude and Polonius, each of them, in his own degree, an embodiment of the general evil. Hence too the richer character-drawing. Claudius is a drunkard, and the fact makes its own contribution to the complete structure; if Sophocles had made Creon a drunkard, it would have been an excrescence on the play. Hence too the frequent changes of scene in the first part of the play; also the style of speech invented for Polonius and Osric. The general enemy is the rottenness that pervades Denmark; therefore it is shown in many persons and many guises.

Then, not only are the sources of the corruption diverse, but so are its ramifications too. We are to see how it spreads, whether from Claudius or from Gertrude or from Polonius, and how it involves one after another, destroying as it goes. To be sure, Greek tragedy shows us something similar—but it is not the same. For example, the condemnation of Antigone leads to the death of Haemon, and that to the death of Eurydice; in the *Oresteia* too there is a long succession of crime. In fact, we remarked above that Claudius recalls the *Agamemnon* and its πρώταρχος ἄτη, the crime that sets crime in motion. So he does; but there is a big difference. Both in *Hamlet* and in the Greek plays crime leads to crime, or disaster to disaster, in this linear fashion, but in *Hamlet* it spreads in another way too, one which is not Greek: it spreads from soul to soul, as a contagion, as when Laertes is tempted by Claudius, or, most notably, when, by his mother's example and Polonius' basely inspired interference, Hamlet's love is corrupted into lewdness, or when he turns against his two compromised friends and pitilessly sends them to death.

Extension of evil in this fashion is, I think, foreign to Greek tragedy. Clearly, it involves a dramatic form which is complexive, not linear and single, like the Greek. Of his successive victims, Sophocles does not even mention Haemon until the middle of the play, and Eurydice not until the end; and the effect is most dramatic. In *Hamlet* there are eight victims, all of whom we have to watch, from time to time, as they become more and more deeply involved.

Further, not only are more people involved at the same time in this more generalised Tragic Flaw, but they are involved more intimately, which again makes for a richer dramatic texture. We may compare Hamlet with Orestes. Externally, they are in a similar position. But when Aeschylus has shown us that Orestes is an avenger pure in heart, and that his dilemma is from every point of view an intolerable one, it is not far wrong to say that his interest in Orestes, as a character, is exhausted; anything more would be unnecessary. Hamlet exists in a different kind of tragedy, one which requires that we should see how the contagion gradually spreads over his whole spirit and all his conduct.

The same contrast exists between Hamlet and Sophocles' Orestes and Electra. She, one might say, is drawn much more intimately than the Orestes of Aeschylus. True; but still she is drawn, so to speak, all at once: There is the situation, here is Electra, and this is the way in which it makes her act. It is not Sophocles' conception to show how her mother's continuing crime gradually warps her mind, by a stealthy growth of evil. If she is warped, it has all happened already. His dramatic interest in the characters of the avengers is focussed on this, that they, being what they are, and being affected by Clytemnestra's crime in this way, will naturally act as they do.

It is, in short, a general statement which I think will bear examination, that Greek tragedy presents sudden and complete disaster, or one disaster linked to another in linear fashion, while Shakespearean tragedy presents the complexive, menacing spread of ruin; and that at least one explanation of this is that the Greek poets thought of the tragic error as the breaking of a divine law (or sometimes, in Aeschylus, as the breaking down of a temporary divine law), while Shakespeare saw it as an evil quality which, once it has broken loose, will feed on itself and on anything else that it can find until it reaches its natural end. So, for example in *Macbeth*: in 'noble Macbeth', ambition is stimulated, and is not controlled by reason or religion; it meets with a stronger response from Lady Macbeth, and grows insanely into a monstrous passion that threatens a whole kingdom. It is a tragic conception which is essentially dynamic, and demands the very unhellenic fluidity and expansiveness of expression which the Elizabethan theatre afforded. Whether this is a reflection of some profound difference between Greek and Christian thought is a question which I am not competent to discuss.

Index

Index of passages discussed